HARCOURT HORIZONS

★★★★★★★★★★ HARCOURT HORIZONS

The Pledge of Allegiance

I pledge allegiance to the Flag

of the United States of America,

and to the Republic

for which it stands,

one Nation under God, indivisible,

with liberty and justice for all.

HARCOURT **HORIZONS**

People and Communities

![Harcourt logo] **Harcourt**

Orlando   Austin   Chicago   New York   Toronto   London   San Diego

Visit *The Learning Site!*
www.harcourtschool.com

HARCOURT HORIZONS

PEOPLE AND COMMUNITIES

General Editor

Dr. Michael J. Berson
Associate Professor
Social Science Education
University of South Florida
Tampa, Florida

Contributing Authors

Dr. Sherry Field
Associate Professor
The University of Texas at Austin
Austin, Texas

Dr. Tyrone Howard
Assistant Professor
UCLA Graduate School of
Education & Information
Studies
University of California at
Los Angeles
Los Angeles, California

Dr. Bruce E. Larson
Associate Professor of Teacher
Education and Social Studies
Western Washington University
Bellingham, Washington

Series Consultants

Dr. Robert Bednarz
Professor
Department of Geography
Texas A&M University
College Station, Texas

Linda McMillan Fields
Social Studies Supervisor
Spring Branch Independent
School District
Houston, Texas

Dr. Asa Grant Hilliard III
Fuller E. Callaway Professor
of Urban Education
Georgia State University
Atlanta, Georgia

Dr. Thomas M. McGowan
Professor
Curriculum and Instruction
College of Education
Arizona State University
Tempe, Arizona

Dr. John J. Patrick
Professor of Education
Indiana University
Bloomington, Indiana

Dr. Cinthia Suzel Salinas
Assistant Professor
School of Education
University of Colorado
Boulder, Colorado

Dr. Philip VanFossen
Associate Professor,
Social Studies Education,
and Associate Director,
Purdue Center for
Economic Education
Purdue University
West Lafayette, Indiana

Dr. Hallie Kay Yopp
Professor
Department of Elementary,
Bilingual, and Reading
Education
California State University,
Fullerton
Fullerton, California

Maps
researched and prepared by

Readers
written and designed by

Take a Field Trip
video tour segments provided by

Copyright © 2003 by Harcourt, Inc.

All rights reserved. No part of this
publication may be reproduced or
transmitted in any form or by any means,
electronic or mechanical, including
photocopy, recording, or any information
storage and retrieval system, without
permission in writing from the publisher.

Requests for permission to make copies of
any part of the work should be mailed to:

School Permissions and Copyrights
Harcourt, Inc.
6277 Sea Harbor Drive
Orlando, Florida 32887-6777
Fax: 407-345-2418

HARCOURT and the Harcourt Logo are
trademarks of Harcourt, Inc., registered in
the United States of America and/or other
jurisdictions. TIME FOR KIDS and the red
border are registered trademarks of Time
Inc. Used under license. Copyright © by
Time Inc. All rights reserved.

Acknowledgments appear in the back of
this book.

Printed in the United States of America

ISBN 0-15-320180-0

2 3 4 5 6 7 8 9 10 032 10 09 08 07 06 05 04 03 02

Contents

xiv   **Reading Your Textbook**

A1   **Atlas**

A14   **Geography Terms**

· UNIT ·

1

Learning About Communities

1   **Unit 1 Introduction**

2   **Preview the Vocabulary**

4   **Start with a Photo Story**
Snapshot of a Community: Eagle, Colorado
by Diane Hoyt-Goldsmith
photographs by Lawrence Migdale

11   **Chapter 1 Communities Are People**

12   **Lesson 1 People Live in Communities**

16   **Lesson 2 People Work at Many Jobs**

20   **Chart and Graph Skills**
Read Graphs

22   **Lesson 3 Many People, One Community**

26   **Lesson 4 People Getting Along**

30   **Citizenship Skills**
Solve a Problem

32   Chapter 1 Review and Test Preparation

35   **Chapter 2 Communities Are Places**

36   **Lesson 1 Where on Earth Is Your Community?**

42   **Map and Globe Skills**
Read a Map

44   **Lesson 2 Communities Are Different Sizes**

48   **Lesson 3 Every Community Has a Story**

54   **Chart and Graph Skills**
Read a Time Line

56 Examine Primary Sources
A History Museum

58 Chapter 2 Review and Test Preparation

60 Visit
A Community Project

62 Unit 1 Review and Test Preparation

64 Unit Activities

· UNIT ·

2

Citizenship and Government

65 Unit 2 Introduction

66 Preview the Vocabulary

68 Start with a Story
Peace and Bread: The Story of Jane Addams
by Stephanie Sammartino McPherson

73 Chapter 3 People and Their Local Government

74 Lesson 1 Leaders in the Community

78 Lesson 2 Communities Have Governments

82 Citzenship Skills
Resolve Conflict

84 Lesson 3 Community Governments Provide Services

90 Lesson 4 Branches and Levels of Government

96 Map and Globe Skills
Identify State Capitals and Borders

98 Chapter 3 Review and Test Preparation

101 Chapter 4 Our Nation's Government

102 Lesson 1 The National Government

108 Chart and Graph Skills
Read a Table

110 Lesson 2 Citizens Have Rights and Responsibilities

114 Citizenship Skills
Make a Choice by Voting

116   **Lesson 3 Models of American Citizenship**

122   **Lesson 4 Symbols of National Pride**

128   **Examine Primary Sources**
Patriotic Symbols

130   Chapter 4 Review and Test Preparation

132   Visit
Young Active Citizens

134   **Unit 2 Review and Test Preparation**

136   Unit Activities

· UNIT ·

3

Communities Are Everywhere

137   Unit 3 Introduction

138   Preview the Vocabulary

140   Start with a Story
Robinson Crusoe by Daniel Defoe
adapted by Pleasant DeSpain
illustrated by Rich Nelson

145   **Chapter 5 A Community's Geography**

146   **Lesson 1 Describing a Place**

152   Map and Globe Skills
Read a Landform Map

154   **Lesson 2 What People Add to Places**

159   Reading Skills
Predict a Likely Outcome

160   **Lesson 3 People and Their Environments**

166   Map and Globe Skills
Find Intermediate Directions

168   Chapter 5 Review and Test Preparation

171   **Chapter 6 Thinking Like a Geographer**

172   **Lesson 1 The World in Geographers' Terms**

178   Map and Globe Skills
Use a Map Grid

180   **Lesson 2 Physical Processes**

186   Chart and Graph Skills
Compare Bar Graphs

188 Lesson 3 Human Processes

192 Examine Primary Sources
Many Kinds of Maps

194 Chapter 6 Review and Test Preparation

196 Visit
Niagara Falls

198 Unit 3 Review and Test Preparation

200 Unit Activities

· UNIT ·

4

Many Kinds of People

201 Unit 4 Introduction

202 Preview the Vocabulary

204 Start with a Folktale
John Henry retold and illustrated by Ezra Jack Keats

209 Chapter 7 American Culture

210 Lesson 1 Stories People Tell

218 Reading Skills
Tell Fact from Fiction

220 Lesson 2 Real American Heroes

228 Lesson 3 Our American Heritage

236 Chart and Graph Skills
Read a Cutaway Diagram

238 Chapter 7 Review and Test Preparation

241 Chapter 8 The Many People of a Community

242 Lesson 1 A Nation of Immigrants

248 Lesson 2 The Potato Famine

251 Citizenship Skills
Make a Thoughtful Decision

252 Lesson 3 Cities of Many Cultures

258 Map and Globe Skills
Use a Population Map

260 Lesson 4 People Express Their Culture

266 Reading Skills
Determine Point of View in Pictures

268 **Lesson 5 Holiday Customs and Traditions**

272 **Examine Primary Sources**
Cultural Objects

274 Chapter 8 Review and Test Preparation

276 **Visit**
A Powwow

278 **Unit 4 Review and Test Preparation**

280 Unit Activities

· UNIT ·

5

Communities over Time

281 Unit 5 Introduction

282 Preview the Vocabulary

284 Start with a Journal
**How We Crossed the West: The Adventures
of Lewis and Clark** by Rosalyn Schanzer

291 **Chapter 9 Learning About the Past**

292 **Lesson 1 Continuity and Change**

298 **Reading Skills**
Identify Cause and Effect

300 **Lesson 2 Exploring Your Community's Past**

304 **Examine Primary Sources**
A Time Capsule

306 **Lesson 3 Tracing a Community's History**

312 **Chart and Graph Skills**
Understand Time Periods

314 **Lesson 4   Communities in Ancient Times**

322 Chapter 9   Review and Test Preparation

325 **Chapter 10 Our Nation's History**

326 **Lesson 1 America's Earliest Communities**

332 **Lesson 2 Newcomers Arrive**

336 **Map and Globe Skills**
Follow Routes on a Map

338 **Lesson 3 A New Nation**

344 **Lesson 4 Building the Nation's Capital**

350 **Lesson 5 The Nation Grows**

356 🌐 **Map and Globe Skills**
Compare History Maps

358 **Lesson 6 United States in Modern Times**

362 Chapter 10 Review and Test Preparation

364 Visit
Monuments and Memorials in Washington, D.C.

366 **Unit 5 Review and Test Preparation**

368 Unit Activities

· UNIT ·

6

People Working in a Community

369 Unit 6 Introduction

370 Preview the Vocabulary

372 Start with an Article
"Henry Ford's Dream"
from *A Kid's Guide to the Smithsonian*

377 **Chapter 11 Making and Selling Products**

378 **Lesson 1 Henry Ford Makes a Product**

384 🌐 **Map and Globe Skills**
Read a Product Map

386 **Lesson 2 Inventions Lead to New Products**

392 **Examine Primary Sources**
A Safer Bicycle

394 **Lesson 3 How a Business Works**

400 📰 **Reading Skills**
Tell Fact from Opinion

402 **Lesson 4 Free Enterprise**

406 **Lesson 5 The World Marketplace**

412 🌐 **Map and Globe Skills**
Use Latitude and Longitude

414 Chapter 11 Review and Test Preparation

417 Chapter 12 Being a Thoughtful Consumer

418 Lesson 1 How People Earn and Use Money

422 Chart and Graph Skills
Read a Flow Chart

424 Lesson 2 Saving Money

428 Chart and Graph Skills
Use a Line Graph

430 Lesson 3 Making a Budget

434 Citizenship Skills
Make an Economic Choice

436 Lesson 4 People Who Share

442 Chapter 12 Review and Test Preparation

444 Visit
An Auction

446 Unit 6 Review and Test Preparation

448 Unit Activities

Reference

R2 Biographical Dictionary

R7 Gazetteer

R12 Glossary

R19 Index

Features You Can Use

Skills

CHART AND GRAPH SKILLS

20 Read Graphs

54 Read a Time Line

108 Read a Table

186 Compare Bar Graphs

236 Read a Cutaway Diagram

312 Understand Time Periods

422 Read a Flow Chart

428 Use a Line Graph

CITIZENSHIP SKILLS

30 Solve a Problem

82 Resolve Conflict

114 Make a Choice by Voting

251 Make a Thoughtful Decision

434 Make an Economic Choice

MAP AND GLOBE SKILLS

42 Read a Map

96 Identify State Capitals and Borders

152 Read a Landform Map

166 Find Intermediate Directions

178 Use a Map Grid

258 Use a Population Map

336 Follow Routes on a Map

356 Compare History Maps

384 Read a Product Map

412 Use Latitude and Longitude

READING SKILLS

159 Predict a Likely Outcome

218 Tell Fact from Fiction

266 Determine Point of View
in Pictures

298 Identify Cause and Effect

400 Tell Fact from Opinion

Citizenship

DEMOCRATIC VALUES

80 Justice

441 Common Good

POINTS OF VIEW

340 Declaring Independence

Music and Literature

4 *Snapshot of a Community:
Eagle, Colorado*
by Diane Hoyt-Goldsmith
photographs by Lawrence Migdale

68 *Peace and Bread:
The Story of Jane Addams*
by Stephanie Sammartino McPherson

125 "The Pledge of Allegiance"

140 *Robinson Crusoe*
by Daniel Defoe
adapted by Pleasant DeSpain
illustrated by Rich Nelson

204 *John Henry*
retold and illustrated by Ezra Jack Keats

218 "The Ballad of Davy Crockett"

284 *How We Crossed the West:
The Adventures of Lewis and Clark*
by Rosalyn Schanzer

372 "Henry Ford's Dream"
from *A Kid's Guide to the Smithsonian*

Primary Sources

EXAMINE PRIMARY SOURCES

56 A History Museum
128 Patriotic Symbols
192 Many Kinds of Maps
272 Cultural Objects
304 A Time Capsule
392 A Safer Bicycle

ANALYZE PRIMARY SOURCES

112 Campaign Buttons
309 Land Granted to the London Company and the Plymouth Company
427 1906 Stock Certificate

Biography

15 Walt Disney
39 Matthew Henson
76 Oscar Arias Sanchez
107 Ruth Bader Ginsburg
120 Martin Luther King, Jr.
173 William Doolittle
190 Julia Morgan
229 Elisabet Ney
233 Sarah Josepha Hale
321 Mansa Musa
339 Benjamin Franklin
347 Benjamin Banneker
399 Lance Armstrong
405 Jane Bryant Quinn
437 Andrew Carnegie

Geography

86 Central Park in New York City
183 The Grand Canyon
217 The Cumberland Gap
351 Rivers and Mountains
407 The Silk Road

Heritage

25 Fourth of July
93 Louisiana Parishes
120 Dr. Martin Luther King, Jr., Day
127 The Liberty Bell
253 Olvera Street, Los Angeles
264 Places of Worship
271 New Year's Day Celebrations
333 Columbus Day
439 Clara Barton National Historic Site

Science and Technology

46 Washington's Metro
177 Mapping from Space
383 Industrial Robots

Charts, Graphs, and Diagrams

21 Picture Graph of Books Checked Out in One Week
21 Bar Graph of Books Checked Out in One Week
86 Central Park in New York City
91 The Branches of the United States Government
92 Levels of Government
104 United States Representatives from Six States
108 Model Table
109 Offices in the National Government
148 Landforms and Bodies of Water
159 Island Growth Rate Information
166 Intermediate Directions
178 Grid Pattern
187 Earthquakes in the United States: Magnitude 5
187 Earthquakes in the United States: Magnitude 3
191 Disaster Plan Tips

237 The Statue of Liberty

251 Choices and Consequences

265 Followers of Five Religions in the United States

298 Cause and Effect

299 Community of Stormville

315 Sumerian Cuneiform

318 The Acropolis

349 Washington, D.C.

379 Ford's Assembly Line

403 Supply and Demand

422 Flow Chart A: How Money Flows from People to Industry and Back

423 Flow Chart B: How Goods and Services Flow from Industry Back to People

425 How Interest Can Grow at 10% a Year

428 How to Read a Line Graph

429 Tip-Top Toy Company Stock

Maps

A2 World: Political

A4 World: Physical

A6 Western Hemisphere: Political

A7 Western Hemisphere: Physical

A8 United States: Overview

A10 United States: Political

A12 United States: Physical

2 Location of San Antonio, Texas

38 Dividing the World into Northern and Southern Hemispheres

39 Dividing the World into Eastern and Western Hemispheres

40 The World

41 North America

43 Eagle, Colorado

45 United States Towns Named Washington

63 Asheville, North Carolina

86 Central Park in New York City

97 States and Their Capitals

118 The Underground Railroad

135 Virginia

153 Landform Map of the United States

156 Pan-American Highway

165 The Panama Canal

167 Intermediate Directions

174 Regions of the United States

176 One State, Three Regions

179 Downtown Corpus Christi, Texas

183 The Grand Canyon

199 Landform Map of Idaho

217 The Cumberland Gap

243 Immigrants to the United States, 1820–1950

245 Immigrants to the United States Since 1951

259 Population Map of Mexico

279 Indiana's Population

308 Location of Jamestown

335 The Thirteen Colonies

337 The Age of Exploration

345 Washington, D.C.

351 Rivers and Mountains

352 Civil War States

357 United States in 1776

357 United States in 1821

367 Route of Lewis and Clark

385 Product Map of Indiana

407 The Silk Road and Marco Polo's Routes

410 Some Major Worldwide Exports

412 Latitude

412 Longitude

413 Europe: Latitude and Longitude

447 Product Map of Texas

Time Lines

54 Time Line of Eagle's Early History

122 Time Line of Our Country's Flags

312 Time Line A: Decades and Centuries

313 Time Line B: Millenniums

Reading Your Textbook

Getting Started

Your book has six units.

Look at the first pages of a unit to learn what the unit will be about.

You will see some of the most important vocabulary words in the unit.

You can read a story or a poem about the main topic of the unit.

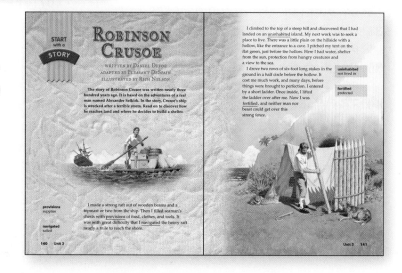

The Parts of a Lesson

Read the Main Idea section to know what to look for as you read the lesson.

Learn the new vocabulary.

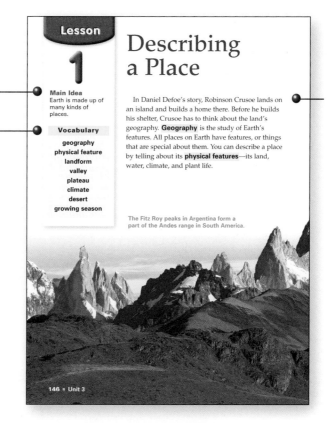

Lesson

1

Main Idea
Earth is made up of many kinds of places.

Vocabulary

geography
physical feature
landform
valley
plateau
climate
desert
growing season

Describing a Place

In Daniel Defoe's story, Robinson Crusoe lands on an island and builds a home there. Before he builds his shelter, Crusoe has to think about the land's geography. **Geography** is the study of Earth's features. All places on Earth have features, or things that are special about them. You can describe a place by telling about its **physical features**—its land, water, climate, and plant life.

The Fitz Roy peaks in Argentina form a part of the Andes range in South America.

146 ■ Unit 3

Read the introduction and each short section of the lesson.

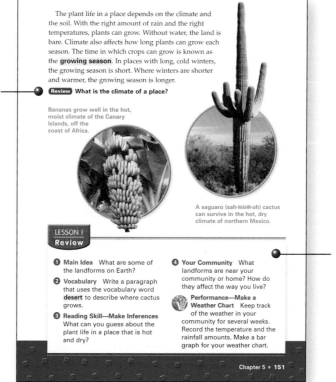

The plant life in a place depends on the climate and the soil. With the right amount of rain and the right temperatures, plants can grow. Without water, the land is bare. Climate also affects how long plants can grow each season. The time in which crops can grow is known as the **growing season**. In places with long, cold winters, the growing season is short. Where winters are shorter and warmer, the growing season is longer.

Review What is the climate of a place?

Bananas grow well in the hot, moist climate of the Canary Islands, off the coast of Africa.

A saguaro (sah-WAHR-oh) cactus can survive in the hot, dry climate of northern Mexico.

Answer the **Review** question at the end of each short section to see if you remember what you read.

LESSON 1
Review

❶ **Main Idea** What are some of the landforms on Earth?

❷ **Vocabulary** Write a paragraph that uses the vocabulary word **desert** to describe where cactus grows.

❸ **Reading Skill—Make Inferences** What can you guess about the plant life in a place that is hot and dry?

❹ **Your Community** What landforms are near your community or home? How do they affect the way you live?

Performance—Make a Weather Chart Keep track of the weather in your community for several weeks. Record the temperature and the rainfall amounts. Make a bar graph for your weather chart.

Chapter 5 ■ 151

At the end of the lesson, answer the questions and do the activity.

Skills

**You will practice all these kinds
of skills as you read this book.**

Map and Globe Skills

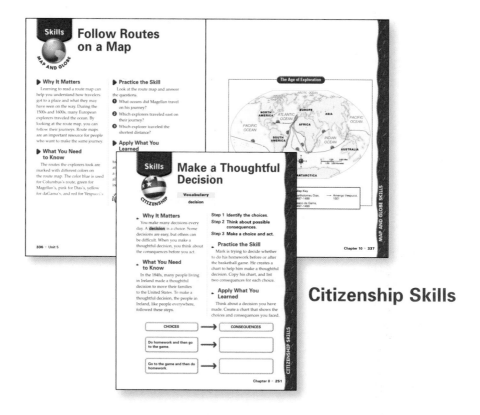

Citizenship Skills

Chart and Graph Skills

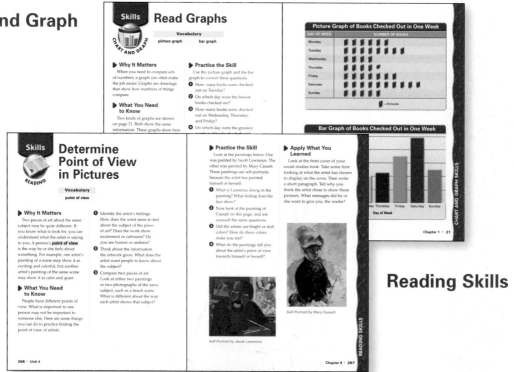

Reading Skills

Special Features

Examine Primary Sources

Learn about documents and objects from the past that are important to the present.

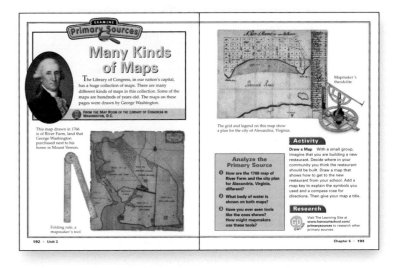

Visit . . .

See and read about places in the United States and around the world.

Atlas

Study maps and learn about kinds of land and bodies of water.

For Your Reference

Biographical Dictionary

Read about the people in your book.

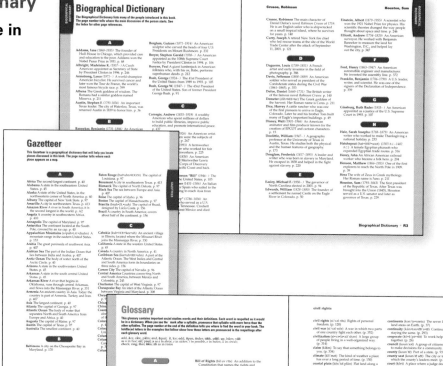

Gazetteer

Find out more about places around the world.

Glossary

Look up definitions, or meanings, of vocabulary words.

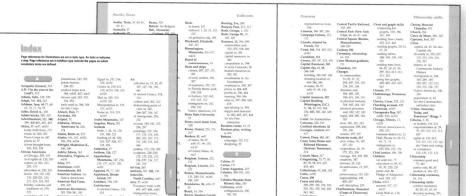

Index

Look up topics you want to read about. The page numbers with the topic names tell you where to find the information in your book.

Atlas

 ## The World

A2 WORLD: POLITICAL

A4 WORLD: PHYSICAL

A6 WESTERN HEMISPHERE: POLITICAL

A7 WESTERN HEMISPHERE: PHYSICAL

United States

A8 OVERVIEW

A10 POLITICAL

A12 PHYSICAL

Geography Terms

A14

The World
POLITICAL

ARCTIC OCEAN

180° 160°W 140°W 120°W 100°W 80°W

80°N

Greenland
(DENMARK)

ALASKA
(U.S.)

60°N

CANADA

NORTH
AMERICA

40°N

UNITED STATES

Azores
(PORTUGAL)

ATLANTIC
OCEAN

Bermuda
(U.K.)

20°N   Tropic of Cancer

Area of inset

Midway
Islands
(U.S.)

MEXICO

CAPE VERDE

HAWAII
(U.S.)

PACIFIC
OCEAN

VENEZUELA   GUYANA
SURINAME
COLOMBIA   FRENCH GUIANA
(FRANCE)

Equator

ECUADOR

Tokelau
(N.Z.)

KIRIBATI

Galápagos
Islands
(ECUADOR)

BRAZIL

SOUTH
AMERICA

PERU

American
Samoa
(U.S.)

French
Polynesia
(FRANCE)

BOLIVIA

SAMOA

Cook
Islands
(N.Z.)

PARAGUAY

20°S   Tropic of Capricorn

CHILE

TONGA

Pitcairn
(U.K.)

Easter Island
(CHILE)

URUGUAY

Niue
(N.Z.)

ARGENTINA

40°S

PACIFIC
OCEAN

Falkland
Islands
(U.K.)

South
Georgia
(U.K.)

60°S   Antarctic Circle

80°S

180° 160°W 140°W 120°W 100°W 80°W

Central America and the Caribbean

100°W

30°N

N
W · E
S

ATLANTIC
OCEAN

Gulf of Mexico

BAHAMAS

Tropic of Cancer

20°N

CUBA

Turks and
Caicos (U.K.)

Puerto
Rico
(U.S.)

Anguilla (U.K.)
St. Martin (FRANCE AND NETH.)

Cayman
Islands
(U.K.)

HAITI   DOMINICAN
REPUBLIC

ANTIGUA AND BARBUDA
Montserrat (U.K.)

BELIZE

JAMAICA

Virgin Islands
(U.S. AND U.K.)

ST. KITTS
AND NEVIS

Guadeloupe (FRANCE)

DOMINICA

Caribbean Sea

GUATEMALA   HONDURAS

Martinique (FRANCE)

ST. LUCIA

EL SALVADOR

NICARAGUA

Aruba
(NETH.)

Netherlands
Antilles
(NETH.)

BARBADOS

ST. VINCENT AND
THE GRENADINES

PACIFIC OCEAN

GRENADA

TRINIDAD AND
TOBAGO

10°N

0   200   400 Miles
0   200   400 Kilometers

Panama
Canal

10°N

Azimuthal Equal-Area Projection

COSTA
RICA

A2

PANAMA

90°W   80°W   70°W   60°W

| National border |

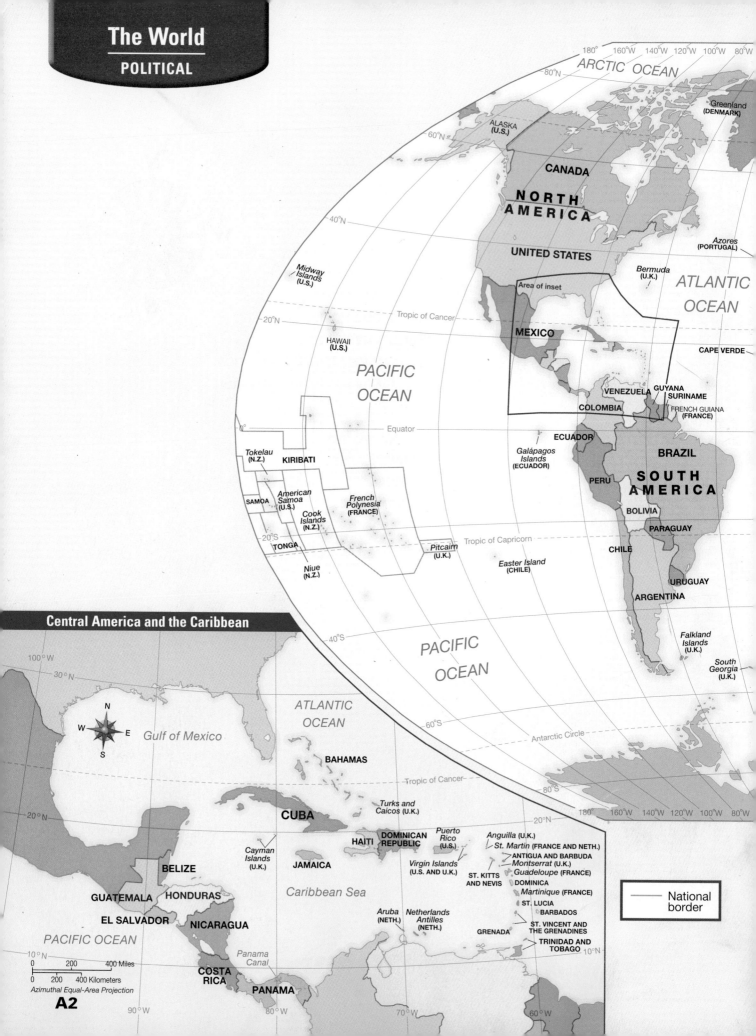

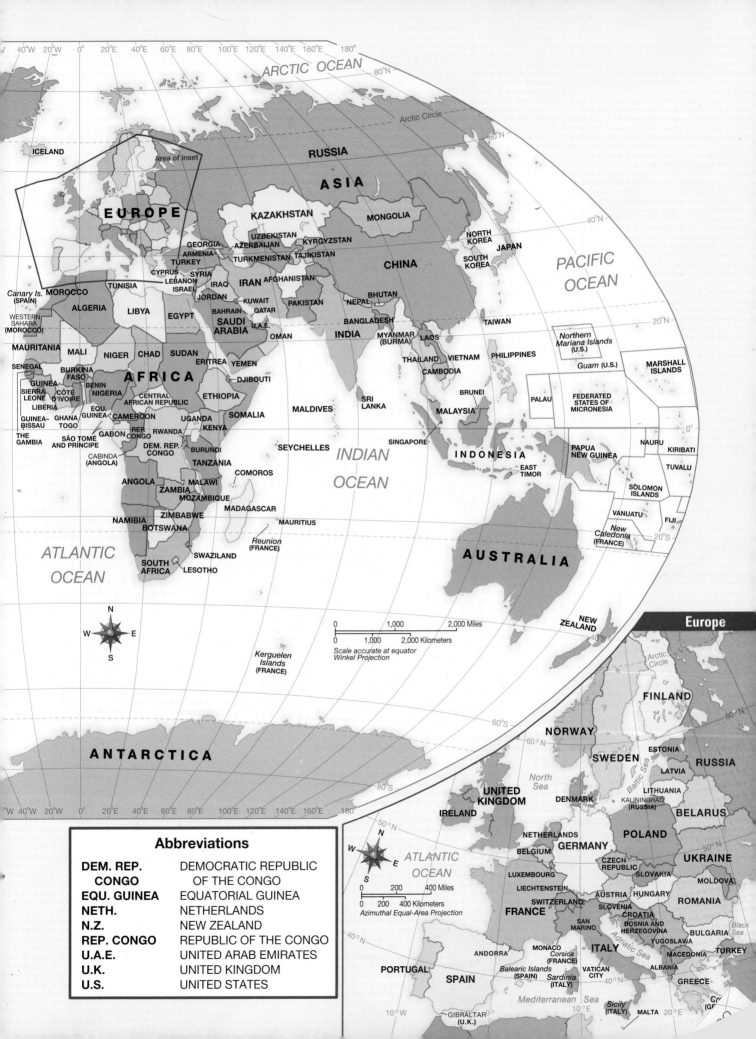

The World
PHYSICAL

Legend:
- Arid
- Evergreen forest
- Grassland
- Mixed forest
- Mountains
- Tundra
- ⎯ National border
- ▲ Mountain peak

ARCTIC OCEAN

180° 160°W 140°W 120°W 100°W

80°N

Beaufort Sea

Queen Elizabeth Islands

Baffin Island

Denali (Mt. McKinley) 20,320 ft. (6,194 m) ▲

Great Bear Lake

Great Slave Lake

Hudson Bay

60°N

Bering Sea

Yukon R.

Mt. Logan 19,550 ft. (5,959 m) ▲

Mackenzie R.

NORTH AMERICA

Aleutian Islands

Gulf of Alaska

Vancouver Island

Columbia R.

ROCKY MOUNTAINS

Missouri R.

Great Lakes

Newfoundland

40°N

Mt. Whitney 14,495 ft. (4,418 m) ▲

Colorado R.

GREAT PLAINS

Mississippi R.

Ohio R.

APPALACHIAN MTS.

Bermuda

ATLANTIC OCEAN

Rio Grande

Gulf of California

Tropic of Cancer

20°N

Hawaiian Islands

Gulf of Mexico

Yucatán Peninsula

Cuba

Bahamas

Hispaniola

Pico de Orizaba 18,855 ft. (5,747 m) ▲

West Indies

Caribbean Sea

PACIFIC OCEAN

Equator

Galápagos Islands

Orinoco River

Guiana Highlands

AMAZON BASIN

Amazon R.

Polynesia

SOUTH AMERICA

ANDES MOUNTAINS

Brazilian Highlands

Tropic of Capricorn

20°S

Atacama Desert

Gran Chaco

Paraná River

Mt. Aconcagua 22,834 ft. (6,960 m) ▲

Pampa

Patagonia

40°S

PACIFIC OCEAN

Falkland Islands

Strait of Magellan

Cape Horn

Tierra del Fuego

60°S

Antarctic Circle

80°S

Antarctic Peninsula

Ross Sea

180° 160°W 140°W 120°W 100°W 80°

Northern Polar Region

Sea of Okhotsk

ASIA

120°E

90°E

60°E

30°E

EUROPE

Kamchatka Peninsula

150°E

Novaya Zemlya

Severnaya Zemlya

Barents Sea

New Siberian Is.

Baltic Sea

North Sea

0   400   800 Miles
0   400   800 Kilometers
Azimuthal Equidistant Projection

ARCTIC OCEAN

North Pole

Svalbard

Norwegian Sea

British Isles

Wrangel Island

180°

Bering Strait

Greenland Sea

Bering Sea

BROOKS RANGE

150°W

Beaufort Sea

North Magnetic Pole

Queen Elizabeth Islands

Baffin Bay

Greenland

70°N

Iceland

ATLANTIC OCEAN

30°W

PACIFIC OCEAN

NORTH AMERICA

Arctic Circle

50°W

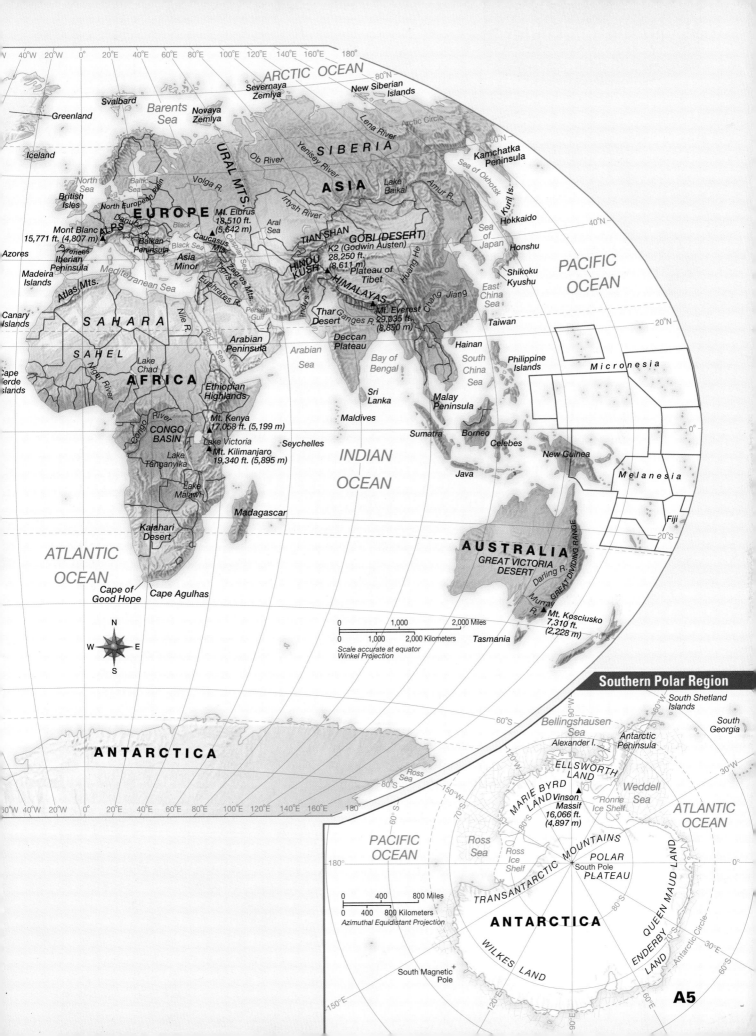

ARCTIC OCEAN

40°W 20°W 0° 20°E 40°E 60°E 80°E 100°E 120°E 140°E 160°E 180°

80°N

Greenland

Svalbard

Severnaya Zemlya

New Siberian Islands

Barents Sea

Novaya Zemlya

Arctic Circle

60°N

Iceland

SIBERIA

Lena River

Kamchatka Peninsula

North Sea

URAL MTS.

Ob River

Yenisey River

ASIA

Sea of Okhotsk

Kuril Is.

British Isles

Baltic Sea

EUROPE

Volga R.

Irtysh River

Lake Baikal

Amur R.

40°N

Hokkaido

North European Plain

Mt. Elbrus 18,510 ft. (5,642 m)

Aral Sea

Sea of Japan

Mont Blanc 15,771 ft. (4,807 m)

Danube R.

ALPS

Caucasus Mts.

TIAN SHAN

GOBI (DESERT)

Honshu

Azores

Balkan Peninsula

Black Sea

Caspian Sea

K2 (Godwin Austen) 28,250 ft. (8,611 m)

Plateau of Tibet

Shikoku Kyushu

East China Sea

Pyrenees

Iberian Peninsula

Asia Minor

Zagros Mts.

HINDU KUSH

Huang He

Chang Jiang

Madeira Islands

Mediterranean Sea

Tigris R.

Euphrates R.

HIMALAYAS

Mt. Everest 29,035 ft. (8,850 m)

PACIFIC OCEAN

Atlas Mts.

Persian Gulf

Indus R.

Taiwan

20°N

Canary Islands

SAHARA

Nile R.

Red Sea

Arabian Peninsula

Thar Desert

Ganges R.

Deccan Plateau

Hainan

Cape Verde Islands

SAHEL

Niger River

Lake Chad

Arabian Sea

Bay of Bengal

South China Sea

Philippine Islands

Micronesia

AFRICA

Ethiopian Highlands

Sri Lanka

Malay Peninsula

0°

Congo River

Mt. Kenya 17,058 ft. (5,199 m)

Maldives

CONGO BASIN

Lake Victoria

Mt. Kilimanjaro 19,340 ft. (5,895 m)

Seychelles

Sumatra

Borneo

Celebes

New Guinea

Lake Tanganyika

INDIAN OCEAN

Java

Melanesia

Lake Malawi

Madagascar

Fiji

20°S

ATLANTIC OCEAN

Kalahari Desert

AUSTRALIA

GREAT VICTORIA DESERT

GREAT DIVIDING RANGE

Darling R.

Cape of Good Hope

Cape Agulhas

Murray R.

Mt. Kosciusko 7,310 ft. (2,228 m)

N
W   E
S

0   1,000   2,000 Miles
0   1,000   2,000 Kilometers
Scale accurate at equator
Winkel Projection

Tasmania

40°S

ANTARCTICA

60°W 40°W 20°W 0° 20°E 40°E 60°E 80°E 100°E 120°E 140°E 160°E 180°

South Shetland Islands

South Georgia

60°S

Bellingshausen Sea

Antarctic Peninsula

Alexander I.

ELLSWORTH LAND

Weddell Sea

ATLANTIC OCEAN

30°W

PACIFIC OCEAN

MARIE BYRD LAND

Vinson Massif 16,066 ft. (4,897 m)

Ronne Ice Shelf

Ross Sea

TRANSANTARCTIC MOUNTAINS

POLAR PLATEAU

South Pole

QUEEN MAUD LAND

180°

Ross Ice Shelf

ANTARCTICA

ENDERBY LAND

WILKES LAND

Antarctic Circle

30°E

0   400   800 Miles
0   400   800 Kilometers
Azimuthal Equidistant Projection

South Magnetic Pole

A5

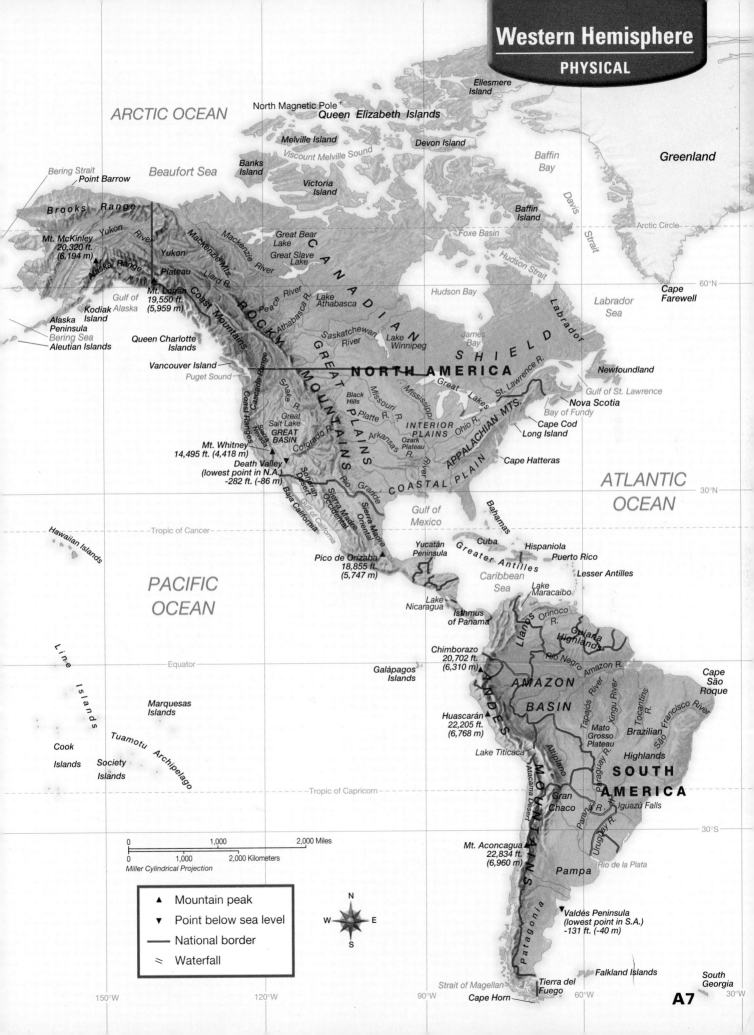

ARCTIC OCEAN

North Magnetic Pole +
Queen Elizabeth Islands

Ellesmere Island

Greenland

Melville Island

Devon Island

Baffin Bay

Viscount Melville Sound

Bering Strait
Point Barrow

Beaufort Sea

Banks Island

Victoria Island

Baffin Island

Davis Strait

Arctic Circle

Brooks Range

Yukon

Mackenzie Mts.

Foxe Basin

Hudson Strait

60°N

Cape Farewell

Mt. McKinley
20,320 ft.
(6,194 m)

Yukon River

Mackenzie River

Great Bear Lake

Great Slave Lake

Hudson Bay

Labrador Sea

Alaska Range

Yukon Plateau

Liard R.

CANADIAN

James Bay

Labrador

Mt. Logan
19,550 ft.
(5,959 m)

Peace River

Lake Athabasca

SHIELD

Gulf of Alaska

Coast Mountains

Athabasca R.

Saskatchewan River

Lake Winnipeg

Newfoundland

Kodiak Island

ROCKY

GREAT

Gulf of St. Lawrence

Alaska Peninsula
Bering Sea
Aleutian Islands

Queen Charlotte Islands

NORTH AMERICA

Nova Scotia

Vancouver Island

Coast Ranges

Cascade Range

MOUNTAINS

Black Hills

Missouri R.

Mississippi

Great Lakes

St. Lawrence R.

APPALACHIAN MTS.

Bay of Fundy
Cape Cod
Long Island

Puget Sound

Snake R.

PLAINS

Platte R.

Ohio R.

Sierra Nevada

Great Salt Lake
GREAT BASIN

Colorado R.

Arkansas

INTERIOR PLAINS

Ozark Plateau

River

COASTAL PLAIN

Cape Hatteras

Mt. Whitney
14,495 ft. (4,418 m)

Death Valley
(lowest point in N.A.)
-282 ft. (-86 m)

Baja California

Sonoran Desert

Rio Grande

Sierra Madre Occidental

Sierra Madre Oriental

Gulf of Mexico

Bahamas

ATLANTIC OCEAN

30°N

Hawaiian Islands

Tropic of Cancer

Gulf of California

Yucatán Peninsula

Cuba

Greater Antilles

Hispaniola

Puerto Rico

Lesser Antilles

Pico de Orizaba
18,855 ft.
(5,747 m)

Caribbean Sea

Lake Maracaibo

PACIFIC OCEAN

Lake Nicaragua

Isthmus of Panama

Llanos

Orinoco R.

Guiana Highlands

Line Islands

Equator

Galápagos Islands

Chimborazo
20,702 ft.
(6,310 m)

ANDES

Rio Negro

Amazon R.

AMAZON BASIN

Cape São Roque

Marquesas Islands

Huascarán
22,205 ft.
(6,768 m)

Tapajós River

Xingu River

Tocantins R.

São Francisco River

Cook Islands

Tuamotu Archipelago

Society Islands

Lake Titicaca

Altiplano

Mato Grosso Plateau

Brazilian Highlands

SOUTH AMERICA

Tropic of Capricorn

Gran Chaco

Paraná R.

Iguazú Falls

30°S

Mt. Aconcagua
22,834 ft.
(6,960 m)

Paraguay R.

Uruguay R.

Atacama Desert

MOUNTAINS

Pampa

Rio de la Plata

0   1,000   2,000 Miles
0   1,000   2,000 Kilometers
Miller Cylindrical Projection

▲ Mountain peak
▼ Point below sea level
— National border
≈ Waterfall

N
W   E
S

Patagonia

Valdés Peninsula
(lowest point in S.A.)
-131 ft. (-40 m)

Falkland Islands

South Georgia

Strait of Magellan

Tierra del Fuego

Cape Horn

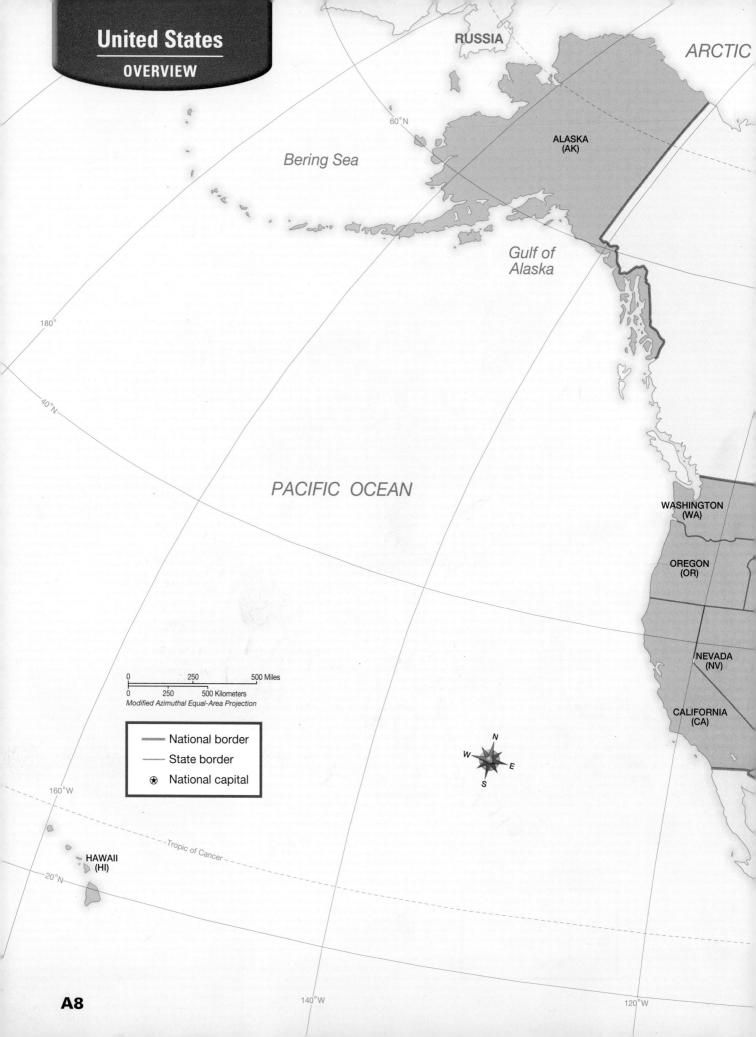

RUSSIA

ARCTIC

60°N

Bering Sea

ALASKA
(AK)

Gulf of
Alaska

180°

40°N

PACIFIC OCEAN

WASHINGTON
(WA)

OREGON
(OR)

NEVADA
(NV)

| 0 | 250 | 500 Miles |
| 0 | 250 | 500 Kilometers |

Modified Azimuthal Equal-Area Projection

CALIFORNIA
(CA)

N
W   E
S

─── National border
─── State border
⊛ National capital

160°W

Tropic of Cancer

HAWAII
(HI)

20°N

140°W

120°W

United States
POLITICAL

RUSSIA

ARCTIC OCEAN

ALASKA

CANADA

Fairbanks•

Bering
Sea

•Anchorage

Yukon River

Yukon River

Juneau★

Gulf of
Alaska

PACIFIC
OCEAN

0	250	500 Miles
0	250	500 Kilometers

CANADA

Seattle•
★Tacoma
Olympia•
Spokane•
WASHINGTON

Portland•   Columbia River

★Salem

•Eugene

OREGON

Great Falls•

Helena★ **MONTANA**

Billings•

Yellowstone R.

IDAHO

★Boise

Snake River

Pocatello•

WYOMING

Casper•

Lake
Tahoe

•Reno

NEVADA

Sacramento•★

San Francisco•
•Oakland
•San Jose

Carson City

Great
Salt
Lake

Ogden•

★Salt Lake City
•Provo

UTAH

Cheyenne

Denver•

Colorad
Spring

COLORADO

Puebl

•Fresno

CALIFORNIA

•Bakersfield

Las
Vegas•

Colorado River

Legend	
Northeast	⊛ National capital
South	★ State capital
Middle West	• Major city
West	National border
	State border

**PACIFIC
OCEAN**

Los Angeles•

•San Bernardino

San Diego•

Flagstaff•

ARIZONA

★Phoenix

Tucson•

Santa Fe★

Albuquerque•

NEW MEXICO

Roswell•

•El Paso

Rio Grande

MEXICO

N
W E
S

PACIFIC
OCEAN

Honolulu★

HAWAII

Hilo•

20°N

0	100	200 Miles
0	100	200 Kilometers

0	250	500 Miles
0	250	500 Kilometers

Albers Equal-Area Projection

100°W   90°W   80°W   70°W

CANADA

NORTH DAKOTA Grand Forks
★ Bismarck   • Fargo

SOUTH DAKOTA
• Rapid City   Pierre ★

NEBRASKA
Lincoln ★

MINNESOTA
• Duluth
St. Paul ★ Minneapolis

WISCONSIN
Madison ★
Milwaukee •

Sioux Falls
Sioux City •

IOWA
Cedar Rapids •
Davenport •
Des Moines ★

Omaha •

KANSAS
Topeka ★
Kansas City •
• Wichita

MISSOURI
Jefferson City ★
St. Louis •
• Springfield

OKLAHOMA
Oklahoma City ★   • Tulsa
Fort Smith

ARKANSAS
Little Rock ★

TEXAS
• Amarillo
• Lubbock
Fort Worth
• Abilene   • Dallas
• Odessa
Austin ★
Houston •
• San Antonio
• Laredo   • Corpus Christi
Beaumont •

Lake of the Woods

Lake Superior

Sault Sainte Marie •

MICHIGAN

Lake Michigan

Green Bay •
Grand Rapids ★
Lansing
Flint •
Detroit •

Lake Huron

Lake St. Clair
Lake Erie

• Rockford
Chicago •
Gary •

ILLINOIS
Peoria •
Decatur •
Springfield ★

INDIANA
South Bend •
Indianapolis ★

OHIO
Toledo •
Akron •
Columbus ★
Cleveland •

Dayton •
Cincinnati •

Wheeling •

KENTUCKY
Louisville •
Frankfort ★
Lexington •
Evansville •

TENNESSEE
★ Nashville
Knoxville •
Chattanooga •

PENNSYLVANIA
Harrisburg ★
Pittsburgh •

WEST VIRGINIA
Charleston ★

VIRGINIA
Richmond ★
• Roanoke
• Newport News
• Norfolk

MAINE
Augusta ★

Lake Champlain
VERMONT
Burlington •
Montpelier ★
NEW HAMPSHIRE
Concord ★
NEW YORK
Manchester •
Syracuse •
Rochester •
Albany ★
Buffalo •

Lake Ontario

• Portland
Boston ★
Worcester •
MASSACHUSETTS
Hartford ★ Providence ★
RHODE ISLAND
CONNECTICUT
• Bridgeport
Newark • • New York City
Trenton ★
NEW JERSEY
Philadelphia •
• Wilmington
Baltimore • • Dover
Annapolis ★ **DELAWARE**
Washington, D.C. ☆ **MARYLAND**

St. Lawrence River

MISSISSIPPI
Meridian •
Jackson ★

ALABAMA
Huntsville •
Birmingham •
Montgomery ★

GEORGIA
Atlanta ★
Macon •
Columbus •

NORTH CAROLINA
Greensboro •
Winston-Salem •
Raleigh ★
Charlotte •

SOUTH CAROLINA
Columbia ★
• Charleston

Savannah •

LOUISIANA
Shreveport •
Baton Rouge ★
New Orleans •

Biloxi •   Mobile •
• Tallahassee ★
Jacksonville •

FLORIDA
Orlando •
Tampa •
St. Petersburg •
Lake Okeechobee
West Palm Beach •
• Miami

Mississippi River
Arkansas River
Red River
Lake Texoma
Missouri River
Platte River
Ohio River
Rio Grande

ATLANTIC OCEAN

BAHAMAS

Gulf of Mexico

CUBA

50°N
40°N
70°W
30°N
80°W

A11

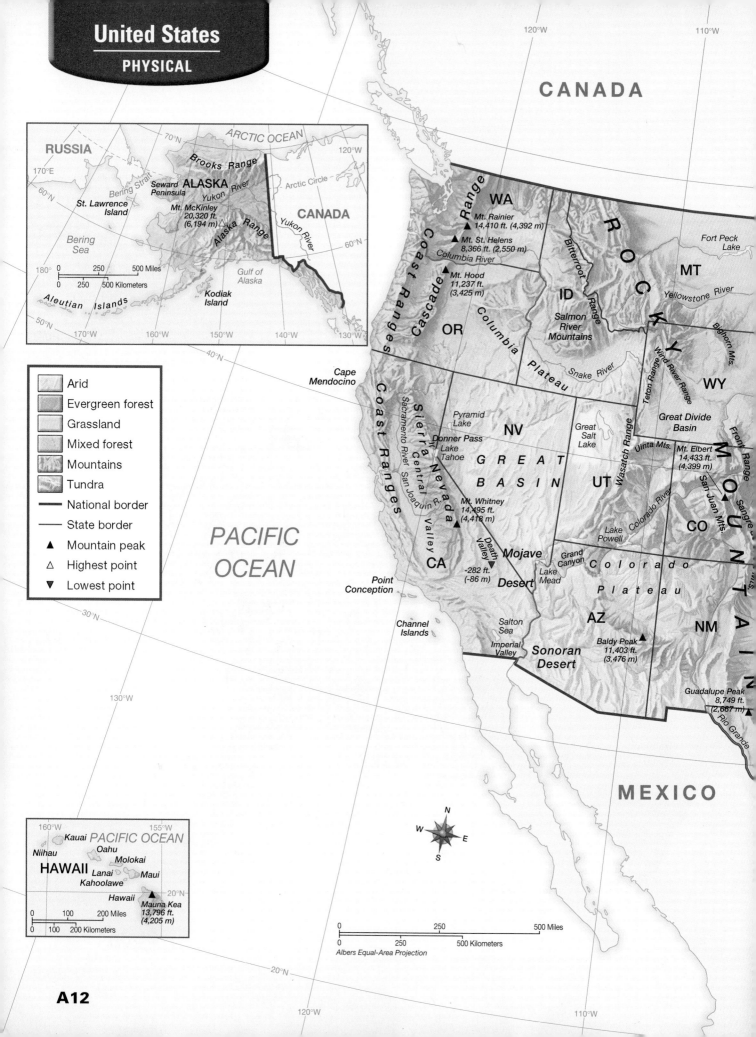

United States
PHYSICAL

CANADA

120°W   110°W

RUSSIA

ARCTIC OCEAN

170°E

Brooks Range

70°N   120°W

60°N

Seward Peninsula   ALASKA   Arctic Circle

St. Lawrence Island   Yukon River   CANADA

Mt. McKinley 20,320 ft. (6,194 m)△   60°N

Bering Sea   Alaska Range   Yukon River

180°   0   250   500 Miles
0   250   500 Kilometers

50°N   Gulf of Alaska

Aleutian Islands   Kodiak Island

170°W   160°W   150°W   140°W   130°W

WA
Mt. Rainier 14,410 ft. (4,392 m) ▲
Coast Range
Cascade
▲ Mt. St. Helens 8,366 ft. (2,550 m)
Columbia River
▲ Mt. Hood 11,237 ft. (3,425 m)
OR
Columbia Plateau
Bitterroot Range
ID
Salmon River Mountains
Snake River
MT
Fort Peck Lake
Yellowstone River
Bighorn Mts.
ROCKY
Teton Range
Wind River Range
WY
Great Divide Basin
Front Range

40°N

Cape Mendocino

Coast Ranges

Sierra Nevada

Sacramento River   San Joaquin R.   Central Valley

Pyramid Lake
Donner Pass
Lake Tahoe
NV
GREAT BASIN
Great Salt Lake
Wasatch Range
Uinta Mts.
Mt. Elbert 14,433 ft. (4,399 m) ▲
UT
Lake Powell
Colorado River
San Juan Mts.
CO
MOUNTAIN
Sangre de

PACIFIC OCEAN

Legend

☐	Arid
☐	Evergreen forest
☐	Grassland
☐	Mixed forest
☐	Mountains
☐	Tundra
—	National border
—	State border
▲	Mountain peak
△	Highest point
▼	Lowest point

Mt. Whitney 14,495 ft. (4,418 m) ▲

Death Valley -282 ft. (-86 m) ▼

Mojave Desert

CA

Grand Canyon
Lake Mead
Colorado Plateau

Point Conception

30°N

Channel Islands

Salton Sea
Imperial Valley
Sonoran Desert

AZ
Baldy Peak 11,403 ft. (3,476 m) ▲

NM

Guadalupe Peak 8,749 ft. (2,667 m) ▲

130°W

Rio Grande

MEXICO

HAWAII inset

160°W   PACIFIC OCEAN   155°W

Kauai
Niihau   Oahu
Molokai
HAWAII   Lanai   Maui
Kahoolawe

20°N
Hawaii
▲ Mauna Kea 13,796 ft. (4,205 m)

0   100   200 Miles
0   100   200 Kilometers

N
W   E
S

0   250   500 Miles
0   250   500 Kilometers
Albers Equal-Area Projection

20°N

120°W   110°W

100°W   90°W   80°W   70°W

50°N

CANADA

ME

Mt. Katahdin
5,269 ft.
(1,606 m)

Moosehead
Lake

St. Lawrence River

VT

Mt. Washington
6,288 ft.
(1,917 m)

Lake of
the Woods

Isle
Royale

Lake Superior

Keweenaw
Peninsula

Upper Peninsula

Lake Huron

NY

Lake
Champlain

White Mts.

Green Mts.

NH

Cape Ann

Upper
Red Lake

Lower
Red Lake

Mesabi
Range

MA

Cape
Cod

Lake Ontario

Adirondack
Mountains

Connecticut R.

ND

Leech
Lake

Mille
Lacs
Lake

CT

RI

Lake Sakakawea

MN

WI

Wisconsin River

Lake
Michigan

Lower Peninsula

Niagara
Falls

Finger
Lakes

Hudson R.

MI

Lake
St. Clair

Lake Erie

Mississippi River

Lake
Winnebago

PA

Long
Island

NJ

SD

Lake
Oahe

Missouri River

IA

OH

Allegheny Mts.

MD

DE

Delaware
Bay

70°W

Black
Hills

Illinois River

Wabash River

Potomac R.

APPALACHIAN MOUNTAINS

North Platte R.

Sand Hills

NE

IL

IN

WV

VA

Cape
Charles

40°N

I N T E R I O R

Platte River

Ohio River

James R.

Chesapeake
Bay

South Platte R.

P L A I N S

Missouri River

MO

CENTRAL PLAINS

KY

Roanoke R.

Albemarle
Sound

Smoky Hills

Lake of
the Ozarks

Cumberland
Gap

Cape Fear River

Cape
Hatteras

KS

Harry S. Truman
Reservoir

Ozark Plateau

Lake
Barkley

Cumberland R.

Mt. Mitchell
6,684 ft.
(2,037 m)

NC

Red Hills

Arkansas

TN

Cape
Fear

OK

Canadian   River

River

Mississippi River

Tennessee R.

SC

G R E A T   P L A I N S

Ouachita Mountains

AR

Clark
Hill Lake

Savannah River

P I E D M O N T

Red River

Lake
Texoma

Stone
Mountain

Oconee R.

**Llano
Estacado**

Sabine River

MS

Tombigbee R.

Alabama R.

GA

Chattahoochee R.

Ocmulgee R.

Altamaha R.

C O A S T A L

P L A I N

ATLANTIC

OCEAN

Toledo
Bend
Reservoir

LA

AL

Okefenokee
Swamp

30°N

TX

Brazos River

Sam
Rayburn
Reservoir

Lake
Maurepas

St. Johns River

Pecos River

**Edwards
Plateau**

Colorado River

Lake
Pontchartrain

Mobile
Bay

Cape
Canaveral

Galveston
Bay

Mississippi
Delta

FL

C O A S T A L   P L A I N

Rio Grande

Gulf of Mexico

Tampa
Bay

Lake
Okeechobee

BAHAMAS

Everglades

Cape
Sable

Florida Keys

Straits of Florida

CUBA

100°W   90°W   80°W

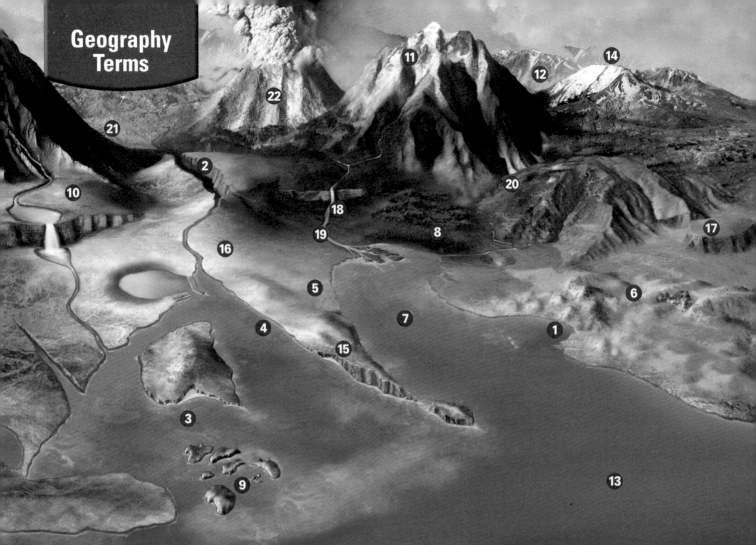

Geography Terms

1 bay an inlet of the sea or some other body of water, usually smaller than a gulf

2 canyon deep, narrow valley with steep sides

3 channel deepest part of a body of water

4 coast land along a sea or ocean

5 coastal plain area of flat land along a sea or ocean

6 desert dry land with few plants

7 gulf part of a sea or ocean extending into the land, usually larger than a bay

8 hill land that rises above the land around it

9 island land that has water on all sides

10 lake body of water with land on all sides

11 mountain highest kind of land

12 mountain range row of mountains

13 ocean body of salt water larger than a sea

14 peak top of a mountain

15 peninsula land that is almost completely surrounded by water

16 plain area of flat or gently rolling low land

17 plateau area of high, mostly flat land

18 river large stream of water that flows across the land

19 riverbank land along a river

20 source of river place where a river begins

21 valley low land between hills or mountains

22 volcano opening in the earth, often raised, through which lava, rock, ashes, and gases are forced out

Learning About Communities

A folk art
wooden eagle

Citizens of Eagle, Colorado

Learning About Communities

❝ **We are a nation of communities . . . like a thousand points of light in a broad and peaceful sky. ❞**

—President George Bush, in a speech on August 18, 1988

Preview the Content

Before you study the unit, write a few sentences telling what you already know about communities. Then organize your sentences in a two-column chart with the headings **People** and **Places**.

People	Places

citizen   A person who lives in and belongs to a community. (page 12)

location   The place where something is found. (page 36)

Location of San Antonio, Texas

RUSSIA

ALASKA

CANADA

0 400 Miles

0 400 Kilometers

PACIFIC OCEAN

CANADA

N

W   E

S

WASHINGTON

MONTANA

NORTH DAKOTA

MINNESOTA

MICHIGAN

NEW HAMPSHIRE

VERMONT

MAINE

OREGON

IDAHO

WYOMING

SOUTH DAKOTA

WISCONSIN

NEW YORK

MASSACHUSETTS

RHODE ISLAND

PACIFIC OCEAN

NEVADA

UTAH

COLORADO

NEBRASKA

IOWA

ILLINOIS

INDIANA

OHIO

PENNSYLVANIA

CONNECTICUT

NEW JERSEY

DELAWARE

CALIFORNIA

KANSAS

MISSOURI

WEST VIRGINIA

KENTUCKY

MARYLAND

VIRGINIA

ARIZONA

NEW MEXICO

OKLAHOMA

ARKANSAS

TENNESSEE

NORTH CAROLINA

SOUTH CAROLINA

ATLANTIC OCEAN

TEXAS

San Antonio

LOUISIANA

ALABAMA

GEORGIA

FLORIDA

PACIFIC OCEAN

HAWAII

0 100 Miles

0 100 Kilometers

MEXICO

MISSISSIPPI

Gulf of Mexico

0 200 400 Miles

0 200 400 Kilometers

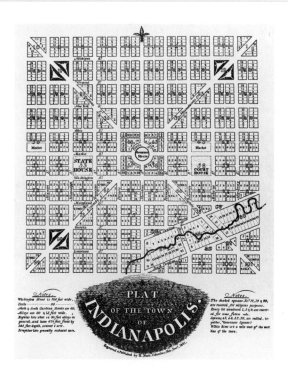

history The story of what has happened in a place. (page 48)

natural resources Materials from nature, such as wood, that people can use to meet their needs. (page 17)

custom A people's way of doing something. (page 22)

Snapshot of a Community: EAGLE, COLORADO

by Diane Hoyt-Goldsmith

photographs by Lawrence Migdale

If you took photos of your community, what would they show? Maybe your first photos would be of your family and friends or your home and school. Perhaps others would show your community's leaders, shops, and celebrations. You might take pictures of the land near your community. Your photos would show ways your community is the same as and different from others. Read to find out what makes Eagle, Colorado, special to those who live there.

Nicole lives in a beautiful place. Her home is in the mountains, in a town that is named for the nearby Eagle River. Eagle, Colorado, is a good place to live.

Nicole and her friend Oscar are in the third grade at Eagle Elementary School. They are studying the history of their town. Eagle, Colorado, is a good place to learn.

On the weekend, Nicole helps her father shop for groceries at the City Market. Every other month she goes to Sandy's Beauty Salon for a haircut. Eagle, Colorado, is a good place to find the things you need.

The leaders of the town help solve the community's problems. Other citizens also help one another in many ways. Working together, the people of Eagle, Colorado, make their town a place where they can feel safe.

EAGLE FOOD DRIVE

Start the Unit Project

A Class Magazine With your classmates, make a magazine about your community. As you read this unit, take notes about the people, places, and events in your community. Your notes will help you decide what to include in your magazine.

When summer comes, it's time for the town's special celebration. People come from miles around to watch roping and riding at the Eagle County Fair and Rodeo. Nicole and her family never miss it. With flags waving, Eagle, Colorado, is a good place to feel proud.

Think About It

1. How did the town get its name?

2. Compare Eagle, Colorado, with your community. How are the two communities alike, and how are they different?

Use Technology

Visit The Learning Site at **www.harcourtschool.com/ socialstudies** for additional activities, primary sources, and other resources to use in this unit.

New York City

This busy street is in Manhattan, a section of New York City. People use many kinds of transportation to get to and from businesses and homes. They may walk or drive or take a bus, a taxi, or the underground subway.

Locate It

NEW YORK

Manhattan

New York City

Communities Are People

66 Ours is a . . . nation . . . where in community we enter into the bond of learning together. **99**

—Virginia Hamilton,
Children's Books and Their Creators, 1995

CHAPTER READING SKILL

Identify Main Idea and Supporting Details

The **main idea** is what the selection you are reading is about. The **supporting details** are the things that show that the main idea is true.

As you read this chapter, list the main ideas and the supporting details for each lesson.

MAIN IDEAS	SUPPORTING DETAILS

People Live in Communities

Main Idea
People live in communities for different reasons.

Vocabulary

community
citizen
business
goods
museum
biography

Like the people of Eagle, Colorado, you live in a community. A **community** is a group of people who live or work together in the same place. It includes all of its citizens. A **citizen** is a person who lives in and belongs to a community.

To Belong

One reason people live in communities is that they like to do things with others. Whether their community is large or small, they enjoy feeling that they belong.

Review Why do people live in communities?

People meet in front of this shop in Eagle, Colorado.

Locate It

Eagle, Colorado

Chicago, Illinois, has a busy business center.

FAST FACT Chicago's downtown business center is called "The Loop." It got this nickname from the city's elevated train system, which circles, or loops, the area.

To Work

Many people live where they do to be near their work. Most towns and cities have a downtown area, or business center. A **business** is an activity in which workers make or sell goods or do work for others. **Goods** are things that can be bought or sold.

Review Why do many people live where they do?

To Have Fun

People like to have fun in their free time. Most communities have parks where citizens can picnic, play games, and enjoy the outdoors.

There may be interesting places to visit, such as zoos and museums. A **museum** is a place where objects from other times and places can be seen. Theaters may offer movies, plays, and concerts.

Review **What are some places in a community where people can enjoy themselves?**

Japan

Czech Republic

People in communities all over the world have fun outdoors.

United States

Brazil

Walt Disney 1901–1966

Character Trait: Inventiveness

Walt Disney is best known as a builder of theme parks. However, a **biography** about him, or story of his life, would also tell of his interest in communities. Disney planned EPCOT as a prototype, or model, community. The letters *EPCOT* stood for Experimental Prototype Community of Tomorrow. EPCOT's citizens were to enjoy the newest inventions in housing, transportation, and communication. However, Walt Disney did not live to make this dream a reality, and EPCOT became a theme park instead.

© Disney Enterprises, Inc.

MULTIMEDIA BIOGRAPHIES
Visit The Learning Site at
www.harcourtschool.com/biographies
to learn about other famous people.

LESSON 1
Review

1 **Main Idea**   What are three reasons that people live in communities?

2 **Vocabulary**   Write a short paragraph that uses the vocabulary words **goods**, **business**, and **community**.

3 **Reading Skill—Main Idea and Supporting Details**   Give two details to support the main idea that people live in communities for many reasons.

4 **Your Community**   Describe some of the businesses in your community that provide the goods you and your family use.

 Performance—Make a Postcard   Make a postcard that shows a place in your community where your family goes to have fun. On one side, draw the place. On the other side, write a description of the place. Share your postcard with your family.

2

Main Idea
People in a community have different jobs and depend on one another.

Vocabulary

needs

natural resource

depend

service

People Work at Many Jobs

In a community, the different jobs that people do help all citizens meet their needs. **Needs** are the things we all must have, such as food, clothing, and a place to live.

People Have Different Skills

Think about how busy you would be if you had to meet all your needs by yourself. You would have to grow your own vegetables. If you wanted meat, eggs, and milk, you would have to raise animals. You would not be able to get water from a faucet.

These shoppers can meet their needs for food, clothing, and other goods all in one store.

Instead, you would have to dig a well or take a pail to a river or lake.

You would have to make your own clothing, too. You could not even buy the cloth. You would have to make it and then sew it together to make a shirt or pair of pants.

You would have to build your own house, too. You could not go to a store to buy the nails and boards for it. You would have to make your own.

In a community, people use their different skills in their jobs. Some grow or sell food. Others make or sell clothing. Some build homes. Others get the **natural resources**, or materials from nature such as wood and stone, needed for building them. This way, nobody has to do every job. Living in a community helps people save time.

Review How can people's special skills help their community?

Growing vegetables

Sawing wood

Weaving cloth

People Depend on One Another

Members of a community **depend**, or rely, on one another for safety. Police officers work to keep people safe. Firefighters also protect people and the things they own. Firefighters, like everyone else in the community, depend on the police to keep their families safe. Police officers depend on firefighters for their families' safety, too.

Doctors, nurses, and other workers provide health services. A **service** is work that someone does for someone else. Health service workers help people stay well. They also care for those who are ill.

Police officer in
Los Angeles, California

Firefighters in Indianapolis, Indiana

Schools and libraries are important to the citizens of every community. Schools are places where people of all ages can learn. Libraries are also places where people can learn. A library keeps books and other materials for the members of a community to use.

Review Who helps keep a community safe and healthy?

At a public library in Orlando, Florida, a librarian helps this boy search for information on a computer.

LESSON 2
Review

1 **Main Idea** What are some of the services people provide for others in a community?

2 **Vocabulary** Make a word web to show how **natural resources** and **needs** are related.

3 **Reading Skill—Main Idea and Supporting Details** Give two details that show how people depend on others for the services they need.

4 **Your Community** Name three school service workers and tell what they do.

 Performance—Create a Hall of Fame Help create a class Hall of Fame for service workers in your community. You might show your doctor, your teacher, a park worker, and others. Draw and cut out pictures of these people to add to the Hall of Fame. Your class might invite younger classes to see the display. Explain who the people are and why they were chosen.

Read Graphs

Vocabulary

picture graph   bar graph

▶ Why It Matters

When you need to compare sets of numbers, a graph can often make the job easier. Graphs are drawings that show how numbers of things compare.

▶ What You Need to Know

Two kinds of graphs are shown on page 21. Both show the same information. These graphs show how many books were checked out of a small public library in one week.

The first graph shown is a picture graph. A **picture graph** uses small pictures or symbols to stand for the numbers of things. This picture graph has a title and a key that explains what the pictures show.

The second graph is a bar graph. A **bar graph** uses bars of different lengths to stand for the numbers of things. This bar graph has a title and labels that explain what the bars show.

▶ Practice the Skill

Use the picture graph and the bar graph to answer these questions.

1 How many books were checked out on Tuesday?

2 On which day were the fewest books checked out?

3 How many books were checked out on Wednesday, Thursday, and Friday?

4 On which day were the most books checked out?

5 Look at the picture graph. What is the symbol that stands for 10 books?

▶ Apply What You Learned

Think of some information about your community that you could show on a graph. Using this information, create both a picture graph and a bar graph. Explain your graphs to a family member.

Picture Graph of Books Checked Out in One Week

DAY OF WEEK	NUMBER OF BOOKS
Monday	📕📕📕📕📕📕
Tuesday	📕📕📕📕📕📕📕📕
Wednesday	📕📕📕📕
Thursday	📕📕📕📕🔖
Friday	📕📕📕📕📕📕📕
Saturday	📕📕📕📕📕📕📕📕📕📕
Sunday	📕📕📕📕📕

📕 =10 books

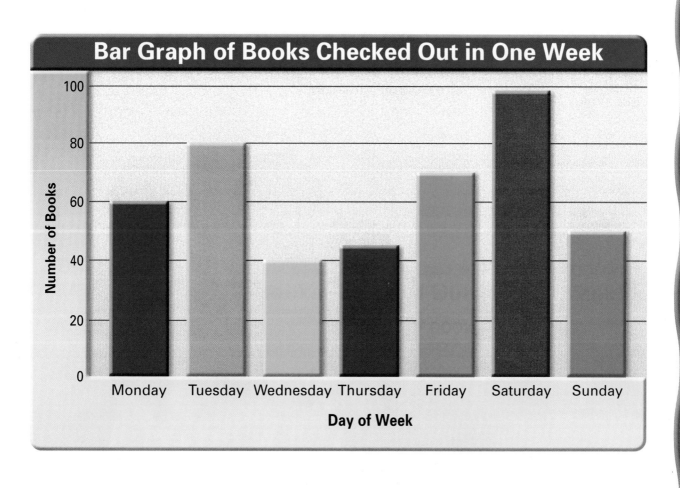

Bar Graph of Books Checked Out in One Week

Many People, One Community

Main Idea
Communities are made up of groups of people with different customs and cultures.

Vocabulary

custom

culture

ethnic group

holiday

heritage

In most communities, people with the same interests or background form groups. These groups make life interesting for all members of a community.

People Share Customs

People who live in or come from the same place often share customs. A **custom** is a way of doing something. For example, people in different countries have different customs for greeting one another.

Customs are a part of culture. The **culture** of a group is made up of the customs and beliefs that its members share. Culture can be seen in their clothing and heard in their language and music.

Review What are some ways members of a group show their culture?

In the United States, people shake hands when they meet. In Japan, they bow.

Friends from different ethnic groups enjoy a meal at this German restaurant.

People Are Different

The different ethnic groups in a community have different cultures. An **ethnic group** is a group of people who have the same language and culture and share a way of life. Each ethnic group brings some of its culture to the community. This gives everyone the chance to enjoy other ways of life.

Review What does an ethnic group bring to a community?

The Community Celebrates

Although the members of each ethnic group follow their own customs, they also share in many community customs. They take part in celebrating national and local holidays. A **holiday** is a special day for remembering a person or an event that is important to the people of a community.

The citizens of Eagle, Colorado, enjoy "Flight Days" each June. This holiday celebrates the time when young bald eagles get their flight feathers.

The bald eagle is a symbol of our nation's strength and freedom.

The Flight Days parade in Eagle, Colorado, is a time for all members of the community to celebrate.

The townspeople gather to watch a colorful parade. Then they visit booths set up in the park to buy food and look at handmade crafts. Some take part in softball games in which the players wear costumes. The members of the different ethnic groups in the town enjoy being members of the whole community as well.

Review How can people in a community share some of their customs?

· HERITAGE ·

Fourth of July

The Fourth of July holiday is an important part of our American heritage. A **heritage** is a set of values and traditions handed down to a group from those who lived before them. On July 4, 1776, our newly formed nation adopted the Declaration of Independence. This document announced that the Americans would no longer be ruled by England. Instead, they would rule themselves. Each year, we celebrate this date because it stands for the freedom we value. All over the country, people display the United States flag, hold parades, and end the day with fireworks.

LESSON 3
Review

❶ **Main Idea** How may the groups that make up a community be different from one another? How may they be the same?

❷ **Vocabulary** Compare and contrast the terms **custom** and **culture**.

❸ **Reading Skill—Main Idea and Supporting Details** Give two details to support the main idea that different ethnic groups make life interesting for all members of a community.

❹ **Your Community** What do people in your community celebrate?

Performance—Make a Drawing Choose a holiday or an event that your community celebrates each year. Make a drawing that shows how the holiday or event is celebrated. Then add your picture to a bulletin board titled "Our Community."

People Getting Along

Main Idea
People need to work together to have a safe community.

Vocabulary

cooperate
law
consequence
government
mayor
judge
fair
responsibility
peace

Most of the time people in communities get along with one another, but sometimes they do not. People need to **cooperate** (koh•AH•puh•rayt), or work together, to keep their community a safe and peaceful place to live.

Community Laws

To keep people safe, communities have rules. The rules that a community makes are called **laws**. Traffic laws help people travel safely through the streets of a community. Without traffic laws, many people would be hurt in accidents. They might ride their bicycles without stopping at stop signs and be hit by cars.

The boy and bus driver are both obeying traffic laws.

People who break laws face consequences. A **consequence** (KAHN•suh•kwens) is what happens because of what a person does. One consequence is being hurt in an accident. Another is having to pay a fine, or an amount of money to be paid as a punishment. If a person breaks a law, he or she may even have to go to jail.

Review **What are some consequences of breaking a law?**

Community Government

Each community has a way to make laws and to see that they are followed. In Eagle, Colorado, as in other communities, a group of people called the **government** makes the laws. The government members meet to talk about problems and decide how to solve them.

The leader of some community governments is called a **mayor**. The mayor's job is to see that the community's problems are solved.

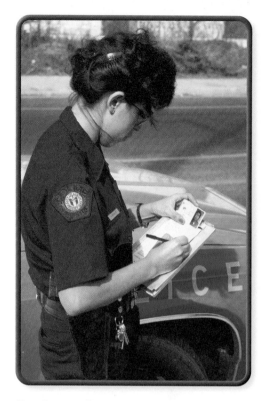

Paying a fine is one consequence of breaking a traffic law.

Courts are part of a community's government. **Judges** are people from the community who are chosen to work as leaders in the courts. Judges decide whether a person has broken the law. They also decide the consequences for those who have broken the law. Judges must be **fair**, or treat everyone in a way that is right and honest.

Review **What are some of the responsibilities of a community government?**

This judge in Eagle, Colorado, is a leader in the court system.

This courthouse in Eagle, Colorado, is where many of the government leaders work.

Being Responsible Citizens

Each citizen in a community has responsibilities. A **responsibility** is something a person should do because it is necessary and important. Citizens should understand and obey the laws. When people obey the laws, they keep their community safe and peaceful. **Peace** is a time of quiet or calm.

Some responsibilities are things citizens must do by law. Others are things that they should choose to do, such as work hard and treat others fairly. Good citizens help make their community a good place to live.

Review **What is one responsibility a citizen has?**

Opening a door for someone is one way to be a good citizen.

LESSON 4
Review

❶ **Main Idea** What are some ways a community helps people get along with one another?

❷ **Vocabulary** Write a paragraph to compare and contrast the meanings of the words **law** and **consequence**.

❸ **Reading Skill—Main Idea and Supporting Details** What details support the idea that good citizens help make their community a good place to live?

❹ **Your Community** Find out the name of a government leader of your community. Write a paragraph about how that person has helped your community.

Performance—Design a Button Make "Good Citizen" buttons. With your classmates, make up a list of titles for Good Citizen awards. You may decide to present awards for Responsible Behavior, Friendliness, or Helpfulness. Award one button each day.

Skills
CITIZENSHIP

Solve a Problem

Vocabulary

problem   solution

▶ Why It Matters

In a community government, citizens work together to find solutions to problems. A **problem** is something difficult or hard to understand. A **solution** is an answer to a problem. People need to be able to find solutions to their own problems, too. Knowing how to find a solution to a problem is an important skill that you can use now and in the future.

▶ What You Need to Know

There are steps you can follow to solve a problem.

Step 1 Identify the problem.

Step 2 Gather information about it and think about possible solutions.

Step 3 Choose the best solution and try it.

Step 4 Think about how well your solution worked.

Step 1

Step 2

▶ Practice the Skill

1. Look at the pictures.
2. Identify a problem that you think needs a solution.
3. Think of some possible solutions to the problem.
4. Follow the steps for finding a solution.

▶ Apply What You Learned

Read or listen to news reports, and identify a problem in your community that you could do something about. Talk with a family member about how a solution might be found. Share your problem and solution with a classmate.

Step 3

Step 4

1 Review and Test Preparation

Use Your Reading Skills

Complete this graphic organizer to show that you understand the main idea and details of each lesson. A copy of this graphic organizer appears on page 7 of the Activity Book.

Why People Live in Communities

MAIN IDEAS	SUPPORTING DETAILS
People live in communities for many reasons.	_____ _____ _____
_____ _____ _____	People share their skills. People depend on one another for safety.
People with the same interests form groups.	_____ _____ _____
_____ _____ _____	Laws keep people safe. The mayor leads the community government.

THINK & WRITE

Write a Persuasive Paragraph
Write a paragraph to persuade readers that all citizens in your community should follow the laws.

Write a Speech Think of a problem in your community that needs a solution. Write a speech telling what action you think should be taken.

Use Vocabulary

Write the word that correctly matches each definition.

> citizen (p. 12)   natural resource (p. 17)
> holiday (p. 24)   law (p. 26)
> judge (p. 28)   solution (p. 30)

1 a leader in the courts

2 a material from nature that people can use to meet a need

3 a special day for remembering a person or event

4 person who lives in a community

5 the answer to a problem

6 rule that a community makes

Recall Facts

Answer these questions.

7 Why do many people live where they do?

8 How does living in communities help people save time?

9 What are some services that people in a community provide for one another?

10 What are some consequences of not following traffic laws?

Write the letter of the best choice.

11 **Test Prep** People may honor a special person or event by—
  A going to court.
  B celebrating a holiday.
  C starting a business.
  D sharing natural resources.

12 **Test Prep** Communities have laws because citizens—
  F like old customs.
  G like to do things for one another.
  H want to remember an important event.
  J want to keep their community safe and peaceful.

Think Critically

13 How might your life be different without laws?

14 What are some of your responsibilities in your community?

15 Why is it important for a community to have places where people can have fun?

Apply Skills

Read Graphs

16 The numbers below tell how many cartons of milk were sold. Make a bar graph and a picture graph that show this information.

| Monday | 200 | Tuesday | 185 |
| Wednesday | 195 | Thursday | 175 |

Solve a Problem

17 Imagine that you forgot to bring your homework to school. Think of one or more solutions to your problem.

Pineville from Pine Mountain State Park

The community of Pineville, Kentucky, can be seen from Pine Mountain State Park in the eastern Kentucky mountains. This small city is located on the Cumberland River, the sixteenth-longest river in the United States.

Locate It

KENTUCKY

Pineville

2

Communities Are Places

❝ When we see land as a community to which we belong, we may begin to use it with love and respect. ❞
—Aldo Leopold, *A Sand Country*, 1949

CHAPTER READING SKILL

Draw Conclusions

A **conclusion** is something you figure out from clues in what you are reading.

As you read the chapter, list the clues and conclusions.

CLUES → CONCLUSIONS

Main Idea
Places on Earth can
be shown on maps
and globes.

Vocabulary

location
mountain range
continent
globe
hemisphere
equator
map
nation
border

Where on Earth Is Your Community?

Communities are different in many ways. One is
their **location**, or the place where they are found.
Communities may be near rocky mountains or on flat
plains. They may be next to flowing water or on dry
desert land.

Water and Land

If someone asked you to describe where your
community is located, how would you do it? You
might start by saying what body of water or kind
of land it is near.

Town Lake in Austin, Texas,
and the city skyline

FAST FACT

Austin was first
named Waterloo
because it had
many springs and creeks.
The city was renamed in
1839 to honor Stephen F.
Austin, an important
leader in Texas.

Himalaya Mountains, Asia

The Himalaya mountain ranges include the highest mountains in the world.

Your community may be near a river, a body of water that flows across the land. It may be near a lake, a body of water with land all around it. It may be near an ocean, a huge body of water that covers a large part of the planet. Earth's four oceans are the Pacific, Atlantic, Indian, and Arctic Oceans.

Your community may be located on highlands or lowlands. It may be near a **mountain range**, a large group of mountains. Mountains are the highest kind of land. They rise high above the land around them. Plains are the largest kind of lowland. They are flat or almost flat.

The largest land areas on Earth are called **continents**. The seven continents are Africa, Antarctica, Asia, Australia, Europe, North America, and South America.

Review How might you describe the location of a place?

Locate It

Kenya, Africa

Plains in Africa can stretch for miles.

On a Globe

To show someone which continent you live on, you might use a globe. A **globe** is a model of the planet Earth. Because it is round like the Earth, a globe shows the true shapes of the oceans and continents.

A globe can be divided in half to describe locations on it. Another way of saying "half of the globe" is to use the word **hemisphere** (HEH•muh•sfir). *Hemi* means "half." *Sphere* means "ball," the shape of the globe.

One way to divide the globe in half is to cut it along the equator. The **equator** is an imaginary line that is halfway between the North Pole and the South Pole. If you cut the globe this way, you get a northern hemisphere and a southern hemisphere.

These students are using a globe to find the location of their community.

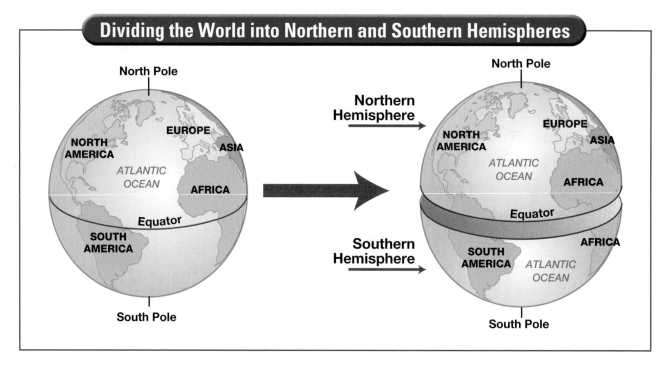

Dividing the World into Northern and Southern Hemispheres

North Pole

EUROPE

NORTH AMERICA

ASIA

ATLANTIC OCEAN

AFRICA

Equator

SOUTH AMERICA

South Pole

Northern Hemisphere

Southern Hemisphere

North Pole

EUROPE

NORTH AMERICA

ASIA

ATLANTIC OCEAN

AFRICA

Equator

SOUTH AMERICA

AFRICA

ATLANTIC OCEAN

South Pole

GEOGRAPHY THEME

Location This map shows how a globe can be divided along the equator.

In which hemisphere is North America?

Another way to divide the globe into two hemispheres is to cut it in half from the North Pole to the South Pole through the middle of the Pacific Ocean and the Atlantic Ocean. If you do this, you get a western hemisphere and an eastern hemisphere.

Every place on Earth is in at least two hemispheres. North America, for example, is in the Northern Hemisphere and also in the Western Hemisphere.

Review **What are two ways to divide a globe in half?**

Matthew Henson
1866–1955
Character Trait: Cooperation

On April 6, 1909, Matthew Henson and Robert Peary became the first explorers to reach the North Pole. Henson's friendly contact with the Inuit, the native people of the Arctic, had helped them reach their goal.

MULTIMEDIA BIOGRAPHIES
Visit The Learning Site at
www.harcourtschool.com/ biographies to learn about other famous people.

Dividing the World into Eastern and Western Hemispheres

North Pole
EUROPE
NORTH AMERICA
ASIA
ATLANTIC OCEAN
AFRICA
SOUTH AMERICA
South Pole

North Pole
Eastern Hemisphere
EUROPE
NORTH AMERICA
ASIA
ATLANTIC OCEAN
AFRICA
SOUTH AMERICA
South Pole

Western Hemisphere

Location **This map shows how a globe can be divided from the North Pole to the South Pole.**

In which hemisphere is South America?

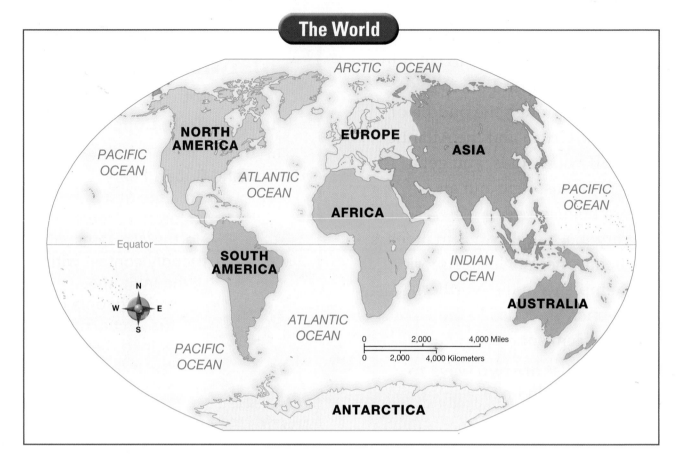

The World

ARCTIC OCEAN

NORTH AMERICA

EUROPE

ASIA

PACIFIC OCEAN

ATLANTIC OCEAN

PACIFIC OCEAN

AFRICA

Equator

SOUTH AMERICA

INDIAN OCEAN

N
W   E
S

AUSTRALIA

ATLANTIC OCEAN

0   2,000   4,000 Miles
0   2,000   4,000 Kilometers

PACIFIC OCEAN

ANTARCTICA

GEOGRAPHY THEME

Location This map shows Earth's continents and oceans.

❖ **Which ocean is between Africa and Australia?**

On a Map

A globe is a better model of the Earth than a map, but a map is easier to carry. A **map** is a picture that shows the location of things. A map can show the whole world—the planet Earth and all the places on it—or just a small part of it. Because a map of the world is flat, not round like a globe, it cannot show the true shapes of the oceans and continents.

On the map of North America, you can see that the continent is made up of both large and small nations. A **nation**, or country, is an area of land with its own people and laws.

North America

ARCTIC OCEAN

Greenland

ALASKA (U.S.)

CANADA

PACIFIC OCEAN

N
W E
S

UNITED STATES

ATLANTIC OCEAN

Gulf of Mexico

MEXICO

0   1,500   3,000 Miles
0   1,500   3,000 Kilometers

Place Canada, the United States, and Mexico are the largest nations in North America.

❖ With what nation does Alaska share a border?

The borders of a nation or state show its shape. A **border** is a line on a map that shows where a state or a nation ends. The map above shows state borders in the United States. It also shows some national borders.

Review Why is a globe a better model of the Earth than a map?

LESSON 1
Review

1 Main Idea What kinds of things do maps and globes show?

2 Vocabulary Use the words **globe** and **hemisphere** in a sentence about location.

3 Reading Skill—Draw Conclusions If you wanted to compare the sizes of Africa and Antarctica, would it be better to use a map or a globe? Why?

4 Your Community Describe the landforms and bodies of water near your community.

Performance—Write a Poem Write a poem that describes your community's location. Remember that a poem paints a picture with words. Give your poem a title and make it four lines long. It does not need to rhyme.

Read a Map

Vocabulary

map title	distance scale
map symbol	compass rose
map key	cardinal directions

▶ Why It Matters

Maps can tell you about a place. They can also help you find your way to a place.

▶ What You Need to Know

Most maps have the same parts. If you know how to use each part, you can read a map more easily.

Map Title—The **map title** tells you what the map is about.

Map Key—Most maps use **map symbols**. The meanings of these symbols are shown in the **map key**, also called the map legend.

Distance Scale—Most maps that you see have a **distance scale**. You can use it to measure the distance, or how far it is, between two places on a map. On the map on page 43, place a slip of paper just below City Park and the library.

Make one mark on the paper where City Park is and another where the library is. Place the first mark under the zero on the distance scale. Where is the second mark? You should find that the distance from City Park to the library is 500 feet.

Compass Rose—On a map, the **compass rose** is the drawing that shows the letters *N*, *S*, *E*, and *W*. These letters stand for the directions *north*, *south*, *east*, and *west*. Directions tell which way you need to go to get to a place. These four main directions are called **cardinal directions**.

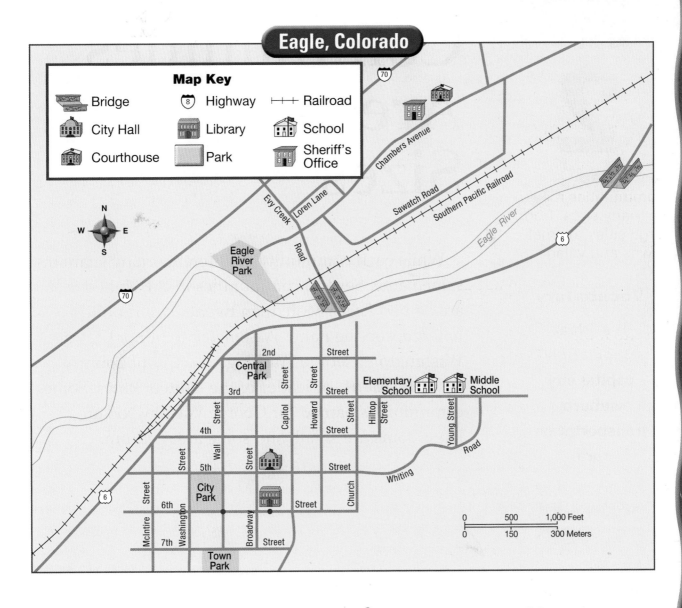

Eagle, Colorado

Map Key

- Bridge
- 🛡 Highway
- ├──┼──┤ Railroad
- City Hall
- Library
- School
- Courthouse
- Park
- Sheriff's Office

Practice the Skill

Use the map to answer these questions.

1 In the map key, what is the symbol for a school?

2 On this distance scale, 1 inch stands for 1,000 feet on the Earth. About how many feet is it from city hall to Central Park?

3 In which direction would you travel to go from Eagle River Park to the library?

Apply What You Learned

Draw a map of your community that includes a title, a compass rose with cardinal directions, a map key, and a distance scale. Share your map with a family member. Ask that person to use it to find a place, such as a park, school, library, or store, in your community.

Practice your map and globe skills with the **GeoSkills CD-ROM**.

Communities Are Different Sizes

Main Idea
Communities may be many sizes, from large cities to small towns and villages.

Vocabulary

President
population
capital city
suburb
transportation
rural

While each community is different, many share the same name. Several communities in the United States are named *Eagle*. More than twenty communities have chosen the name *Washington* to honor George Washington. George Washington was our country's first **President**, or leader of the United States. Some communities named for George Washington are large, some are small, and some are medium.

The skyline of Washington, D.C.

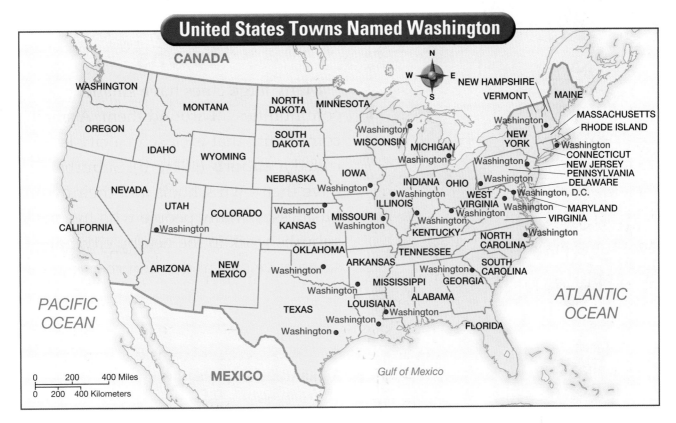

United States Towns Named Washington

CANADA

WASHINGTON
OREGON
IDAHO
MONTANA
NORTH DAKOTA
SOUTH DAKOTA
WYOMING
NEVADA
UTAH
COLORADO
CALIFORNIA
●Washington
ARIZONA
NEW MEXICO

MINNESOTA
WISCONSIN
Washington●
MICHIGAN
Washington●
IOWA
NEBRASKA
Washington●
INDIANA OHIO
Washington●
ILLINOIS
Washington●
Washington●
Washington
Washington
MISSOURI
KANSAS
Washington●
KENTUCKY

NEW HAMPSHIRE
VERMONT MAINE
Washington● MASSACHUSETTS
RHODE ISLAND
NEW YORK
●Washington
CONNECTICUT
NEW JERSEY
PENNSYLVANIA
Washington● DELAWARE
●Washington, D.C.
WEST VIRGINIA
Washington● MARYLAND
VIRGINIA
●Washington

OKLAHOMA
Washington●
ARKANSAS
Washington●
TENNESSEE
NORTH CAROLINA
●Washington
SOUTH CAROLINA
Washington●●
GEORGIA

Washington●
MISSISSIPPI
ALABAMA
TEXAS
Washington●
LOUISIANA
Washington●●
Washington●
FLORIDA

ATLANTIC OCEAN

PACIFIC OCEAN

MEXICO
Gulf of Mexico

0   200   400 Miles
0   200   400 Kilometers

N W E S

GEOGRAPHY THEME

Human–Environment Interactions **The dots on this map show the location of towns named Washington in the United States.**

❖ Are more towns named Washington in the western or eastern part of the United States?

Cities

A city is a large kind of community. Because it has a large **population**, or number of people, a city needs more schools and businesses than a smaller community does.

Cities cover large areas of land. Washington, D.C., is a very large city in the eastern part of the United States. It is an important city because it is the capital city of the United States. A **capital city** is a city in which government leaders meet and work. The leaders of our country's government, including the President, meet and work in Washington, D.C.

Review) **What is a large kind of community?**

George Washington was our country's first President.

Suburbs and Rural Towns

Many large cities have smaller communities all around them. A small community that is close to a city is called a **suburb** (SUB•erb). Suburbs have their own schools and their own businesses. Many people who live in suburbs work in the nearby city, but some have jobs in the suburbs.

Alexandria, Virginia, is a suburb of Washington, D.C.

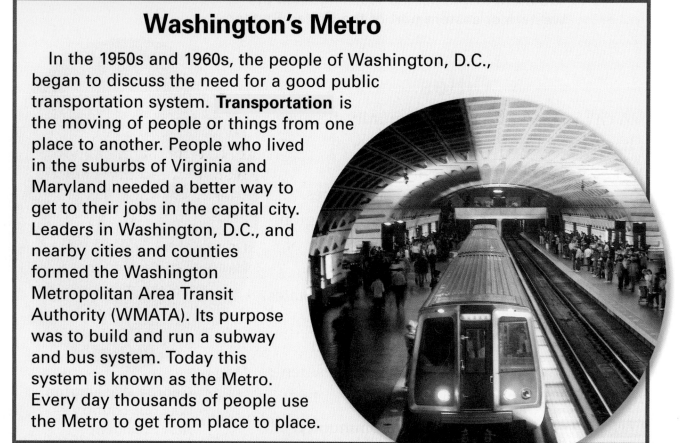

.SCIENCE AND TECHNOLOGY.

Washington's Metro

In the 1950s and 1960s, the people of Washington, D.C., began to discuss the need for a good public transportation system. **Transportation** is the moving of people or things from one place to another. People who lived in the suburbs of Virginia and Maryland needed a better way to get to their jobs in the capital city. Leaders in Washington, D.C., and nearby cities and counties formed the Washington Metropolitan Area Transit Authority (WMATA). Its purpose was to build and run a subway and bus system. Today this system is known as the Metro. Every day thousands of people use the Metro to get from place to place.

Farther from the cities, in rural areas, are small towns and even smaller villages. A **rural** area is the countryside, away from cities and large towns. Small towns and villages have their own schools, their own businesses, and their own governments.

Some people in small towns and villages work there, selling goods or providing services to their neighbors. Others work on the land nearby. They may cut trees for wood or raise plants or animals for food.

Review **How is a suburb different from a rural area?**

This photograph shows a rural area in the Shenandoah Valley in Virginia.

LESSON 2
Review

1 Main Idea Think about whether you would rather live in a place with a small or a large population. Write two or more reasons for your choice.

2 Vocabulary Write two sentences to explain how the words **President** and **capital city** are related.

3 Reading Skill—Draw Conclusions Why would a transportation system be important to people in cities and suburbs?

4 Your Community Decide whether you live in a city, a suburb, or a rural area. Then write a short paragraph giving three reasons to support your conclusion.

Performance—Make a Collage Divide a sheet of paper into three sections and label them *City*, *Suburb*, and *Rural Area*. Next, cut from magazines pictures that show each kind of community, and paste them where they belong. Finally, share your collage on a bulletin board.

Vocabulary

history
pioneer
ancestor
founder
settlement

Every Community Has a Story

Every community has its own history. A **history** is the story of what has happened in a place.

The Beginnings

The story often begins even before the community has a name. It may start long before there are any buildings. The community of Eagle, Colorado, which you read about at the beginning of the unit, has a history that begins a long time ago. It starts with the first Americans, known as Native Americans or American Indians. Native Americans have lived in the mountains around Eagle, Colorado, for more than 10,000 years.

One group, the Utes (YOOTS), lived in this part of Colorado until the late 1800s. They lived by hunting wild animals and gathering wild plants, nuts, and berries.

Review Who were the first people to live in the place where Eagle, Colorado, is now?

Ute leader Chief Ouray (OO·ray) and his wife Chipeta (cha·PEE·tah) around 1879

View of a Colorado iron and silver mine

FAST FACT An unexpected mining boom came to Eagle in 1913. In that year silver was discovered at nearby Horse Mountain. The Lady Belle Mine, as it was named, brought dozens of miners to the area.

Long Ago

In the 1880s silver was found in the sagebrush-covered mountains close to Eagle. Prospectors, or miners, came to work in the mines. Settlers also came and started ranching. Harvey Dice was one of the first pioneers to arrive. A **pioneer** is a person who helps settle a new land. At first Dice was a cattle rancher. Later he and his brother Tom built many of Eagle's important buildings including a bank, post office, and telephone office. After the mines closed, most of the miners left, but a few stayed and built homes.

Many of the people who live in and near Eagle today have ancestors who were ranchers and farmers long ago. They made their living by supplying the miners with meat and vegetables. An **ancestor** is someone in a person's family, such as a great-great-grandparent, who lived a long time ago.

Review How did the people who settled the land around Eagle make their living?

The Community Begins

These papers tell when William Edwards bought and sold his land.

William Edwards was the **founder** of, or person who started, the little settlement that later became Eagle. He chose to locate it where Brush Creek and the Eagle River meet so it would be near a source of water. Some people suggested naming the **settlement**, or new community, Brush. However, Edwards decided it should be called Castle. He built his home and ranch close to the railroad tracks so he could easily send and receive goods.

The first businesses in the tiny community were started by C. F. Nogal. He opened a store, a hotel, and a post office—all in tents! There was also a restaurant tent in which meals cost 25 cents. Nogal later put up buildings for his store and hotel. In 1890 the town's population was 25.

Review Why did Edwards choose a location near a creek and a river?

William Edwards's first home was a cabin like the one shown here. Pioneers used the natural resources around them to make their homes.

July 4, 1915, celebration at the Eagle train station

Changes Over Time

A few years later the settlement was renamed McDonald, to honor pioneer Alex McDonald. However, for years railroad workers had been calling it Eagle River Crossing. The railroad station was named *Río Águila* (REE•oh AH•gee•yah), which is Spanish for Eagle River. In 1896 the name of the small community was finally changed to Eagle.

Over time, the settlement of Eagle grew from a few homes into a town. Soon the town had a newspaper, schools, hotels, churches, markets, and shops. By 1940 the population had grown to 543.

A class at Eagle Elementary School in 1916

In the early 1960s, Eagle began to grow even faster. The airport was enlarged so that more visitors could come to this part of the Rocky Mountains to snow-ski. An interstate highway was also completed. This highway connects Colorado with other states.

In the last twenty years, many people have moved to Eagle, Colorado, from Mexico. Often they came to work and stayed to raise a family. Today, many families in Eagle have Mexican ancestors.

People of different ethnic groups now make Eagle their home. Their ancestors have come from countries around the world. They all have stories to tell about how they came to live and work in Eagle.

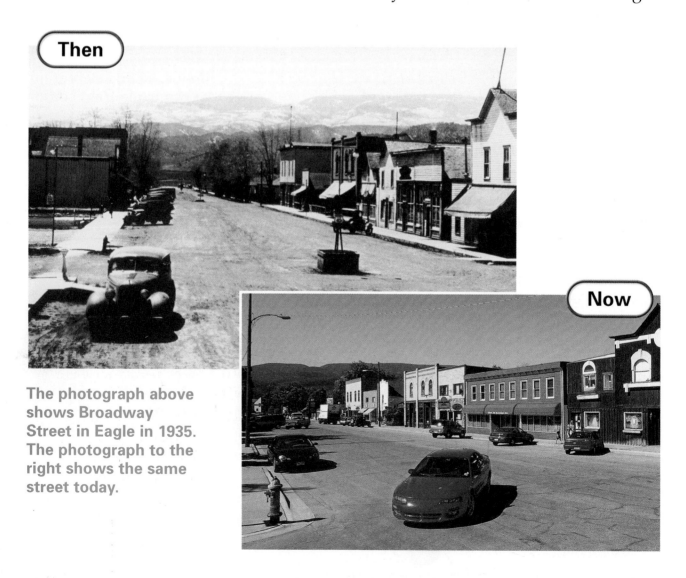

Then

Now

The photograph above shows Broadway Street in Eagle in 1935. The photograph to the right shows the same street today.

Although many changes have taken place in Eagle, much has stayed the same. People still live and work in this town in the Rocky Mountains. They raise their families and enjoy the beautiful mountain range near their homes.

In some ways Eagle is like all other communities. At the same time, its history makes it special to the people who live there. Nine-year-old Nicole sums up the way most of Eagle's citizens feel about their town.

"Eagle is a nice place to live. The people and land make it a special community."

This family in Eagle enjoys making a meal together.

Review **Describe some of the ways the community of Eagle has changed over time.**

LESSON 3
Review

1 **Main Idea** How do some communities begin, change, and grow?

2 **Vocabulary** Write a paragraph that includes the words **history**, **pioneer**, and **ancestor**.

3 **Reading Skill—Draw Conclusions** Communities change over time. What changes have taken place in Eagle, Colorado, and how have they affected the way people live there today?

4 **Your Community** Every community changes. Name one thing about your community that has changed in the last year.

Performance—Conduct an Interview Make a list of questions you would like to ask about how your community has changed. Then interview a community member to find out what changes he or she has seen. Share with your classmates the changes you learn about.

Skills

CHART AND GRAPH

Read a Time Line

▶ **Why It Matters**

When you learn about the history of a community, you need to be able to follow the events in order. A time line can help you. A **time line** is a drawing that shows when and in what order events took place.

▶ **What You Need to Know**

You read a time line from left to right. The events at the left end happened first. The events to the right of them happened later.

As you move from left to right, you follow the events in **sequence**, or time order.

Time Line of Eagle's Early History

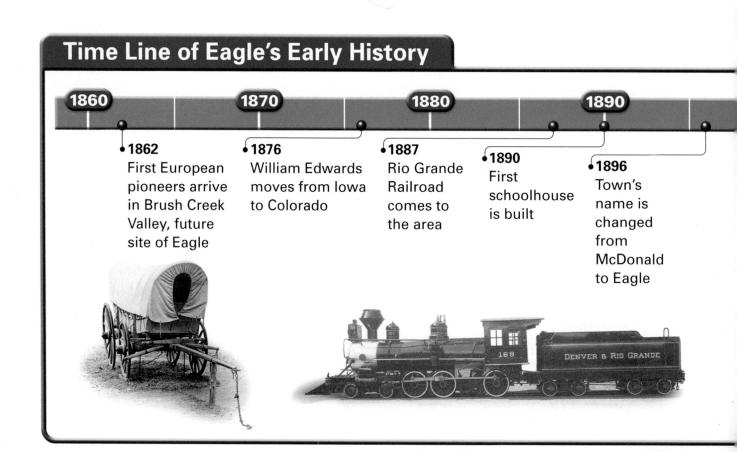

1860

1870

1880

1890

1862
First European pioneers arrive in Brush Creek Valley, future site of Eagle

1876
William Edwards moves from Iowa to Colorado

1887
Rio Grande Railroad comes to the area

1890
First schoolhouse is built

1896
Town's name is changed from McDonald to Eagle

▶ Practice the Skill

Use the time line to help you answer these questions about the early history of Eagle.

1 When did the first pioneers come to the valley where Eagle is now located?

2 Did the Rio Grande Railroad come to the area before or after telephone service to Eagle began?

3 How many years passed between the building of the first school and the first celebration of Flight Days?

▶ Apply What You Learned

Create a personal time line. Show your date of birth, the date you started school, and a milestone from each year after that. A milestone is something important that you did or that happened to you.

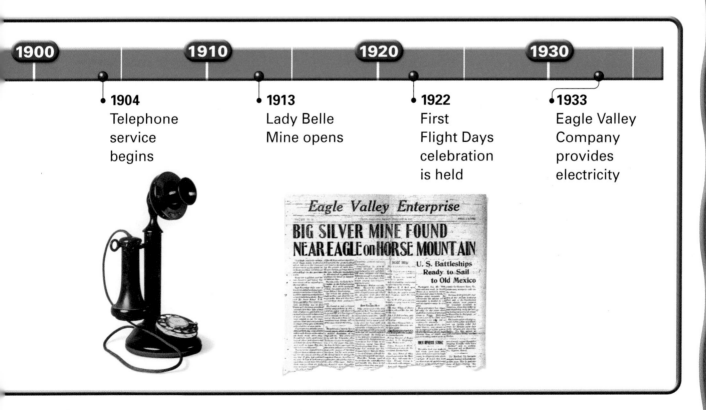

| 1900 | 1910 | 1920 | 1930 |

1904
Telephone service begins

1913
Lady Belle Mine opens

1922
First Flight Days celebration is held

1933
Eagle Valley Company provides electricity

Eagle Valley Enterprise
BIG SILVER MINE FOUND NEAR EAGLE on HORSE MOUNTAIN

U. S. Battleships
Ready to Sail
to Old Mexico

A History Museum

Imagine that you have been asked to write the history of your community. How should you begin? First, think of yourself as a historian. Historians are history detectives. Like detectives, they use sources to look for clues to the past. JoAnn Riggle has a special interest in history. She uses primary sources in museums to form a picture of what life was like long ago.

 FROM THE COLORADO HISTORY MUSEUM

Primary Source

Primary sources are records made by people who saw or took part in an event. Perhaps the people told their story in a newspaper or wrote it in their journal. They may have taken a photograph or painted a picture.

Secondary Source

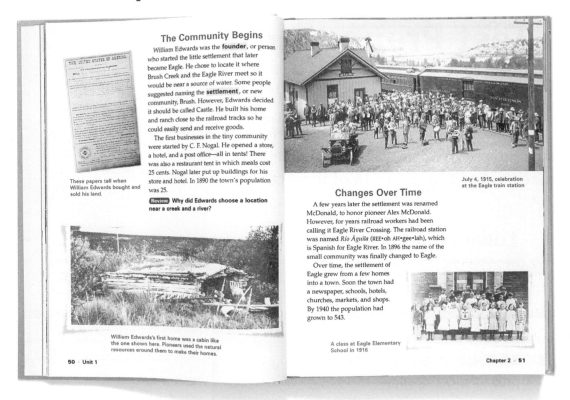

The Community Begins

William Edwards was the **founder**, or person who started the little settlement that later became Eagle. He chose to locate it where Brush Creek and the Eagle River meet so it would be near a source of water. Some people suggested naming the **settlement**, or new community, Brush. However, Edwards decided it should be called Castle. He built his home and ranch close to the railroad tracks so he could easily send and receive goods.

The first businesses in the tiny community were started by C. F. Nogal. He opened a store, a hotel, and a post office—all in tents! There was also a restaurant tent in which meals cost 25 cents. Nogal later put up buildings for his store and hotel. In 1890 the town's population was 25.

Review Why did Edwards choose a location near a creek and a river?

These papers tell when William Edwards bought and sold his land.

William Edwards's first home was a cabin like the one shown here. Pioneers used the natural resources around them to make their homes.

50 • Unit 1

July 4, 1915, celebration at the Eagle train station

Changes Over Time

A few years later the settlement was renamed McDonald, to honor pioneer Alex McDonald. However, for years railroad workers had been calling it Eagle River Crossing. The railroad station was named *Río Águila* (REE•oh AH•gee•lah), which is Spanish for Eagle River. In 1896 the name of the small community was finally changed to Eagle.

Over time, the settlement of Eagle grew from a few homes into a town. Soon the town had a newspaper, schools, hotels, churches, markets, and shops. By 1940 the population had grown to 543.

A class at Eagle Elementary School in 1916

Chapter 2 • 51

Riggle also uses information from primary sources to write reports. Her reports then become a secondary source. A **secondary source** is written by someone who was not there when an event took place.

Analyze the Primary Source

1. Why do you think historians are interested in both pictures and writings from the past?

2. How can primary and secondary sources be combined to describe the history of a place?

Activity

Write to a Historian   Gather two primary sources that describe or show life in your community today. Use each to write a sentence that would help a future historian know what life was like for you.

Research

Visit The Learning Site at **www.harcourtschool.com/ primarysources** to research other primary sources.

2 Review and Test Preparation

Use Your Reading Skills

Complete this graphic organizer to show the clues you used and the conclusions you reached as you read. A copy of this graphic organizer appears on page 14 of the Activity Book.

Location and History of Communities

CLUES   CONCLUSIONS

1. It helps you find your state.
2. You can see the four oceans on it.
3. It shows you the North and South Poles.

_____
_____
_____
_____

1. _____
2. _____
3. _____

The community of Eagle, Colorado, has changed over time.

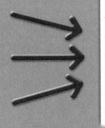

THINK & WRITE

Write a List   List all of the places on Earth where you could say you live. List them in order from greatest to smallest. Begin by asking yourself *In what hemispheres do I live? On what continent do I live?*

Write a Diary Entry   Imagine that you are a pioneer exploring the area where you live. Write a diary entry in which you tell why the area would or would not be a good place to start a community.

Use Vocabulary

Identify the word that correctly matches each definition.

1 a model of our planet that shows the true shapes of oceans and continents

   map (p. 40)   **globe** (p. 38)

2 half of a globe

   hemisphere (p. 38)   **equator** (p. 38)

3 the story of past events

   transportation (p. 46)
   history (p. 48)

4 record made by someone who saw or took part in an event

   primary source (p. 56)
   secondary source (p. 57)

5 a person who starts a community

   President (p. 44) **founder** (p. 50)

Recall Facts

Answer these questions.

6 Why are many towns and cities located near railroad tracks?

7 Why did some people rush to Eagle, Colorado, before there was a town there?

8 Antarctica, Europe, and Australia are three of the seven continents on Earth. Name the others.

9 Which continent is in both the Northern Hemisphere and the Western Hemisphere?

Write the letter of the best choice.

10 **Test Prep**   Who first lived where Eagle stands today?
   A shop owners
   B pioneers
   C American Indians
   D miners

11 **Test Prep**   Washington, D.C., is important because it—
   F is the largest city in our nation.
   G has the best transportation system in the world.
   H is in the center of our country.
   J is our nation's capital.

Think Critically

12 Would you take a map or a globe on a car trip? Why?

13 What might cause many of a town's citizens to move away?

14 Tell three ways your community and Eagle, Colorado, are alike and three ways they are different.

Apply Skills

Read Maps

15 Look at the map on page 43. If you were at City Park, in which direction would you go to reach the library?

Read Charts and Graphs

16 Use the time line on pages 54–55. How many years passed between the first Flight Days celebration and the year Eagle got electricity?

VISIT A Community Project

Get Ready

Many citizens take pride in the history of their community. In Austin, Texas, one group wanted to build a Mexican-style plaza. A plaza is an outdoor park or square where people gather for activities. In Mexico it forms the center of a city. The plaza in Austin celebrates the culture and history of the Hispanic community.

Locate It
United States

Austin, Texas

Plaza Saltillo is named for Austin's sister city in Mexico.

Statues honor Hispanic citizens who helped Austin grow.

The plaza is built with Mexican tiles.

Hispanic singers and dancers perform in the new plaza.

Take a Field Trip

GO ONLINE

A VIRTUAL TOUR
Visit The Learning Site at **www.harcourtschool.com/tours** to take virtual tours of other kinds of community projects.

A VIDEO TOUR
READING RAINBOW Check your media center or classroom library for a video featuring a segment from Reading Rainbow.

Use Vocabulary

Write the word that best completes each sentence.

> citizens (p. 12)
> natural resources (p. 17)
> holidays (p. 24)
> laws (p. 26)
> continent (p. 37)
> Hemisphere (p. 38)
> President (p. 44)
> capital city (p. 45)

1 The people who live in a community are its ___.

2 Wood and stone are materials from nature, ___ people can use to meet their needs.

3 Communities make ___ to keep their citizens safe.

4 Communities in our country celebrate ___, such as the Fourth of July.

5 Washington, D.C., was named in honor of our first ___.

6 Washington, D.C., is important because it is the ___ of the United States.

7 The United States is on the ___ of North America.

8 We live in the Northern ___ because we live north of the equator.

Recall Facts

Answer the questions.

9 Where do the leaders of our country work?

10 What has happened to the population of Eagle, Colorado, since the 1800s? Explain.

11 What are some of the ways a community's citizens can share or celebrate their culture?

12 Why are businesses important to communities?

Write the letter of the best choice.

13 **Test Prep** The first people to settle in a place are called—
A ancestors.
B pioneers.
C miners.
D mayors.

14 **Test Prep** Which is <u>not</u> a service worker?
F librarian
G doctor
H farmer
J police officer

15 **Test Prep** It is a responsibility of every citizen to—
A read the newspaper.
B eat a healthful diet.
C plant a garden.
D obey the laws.

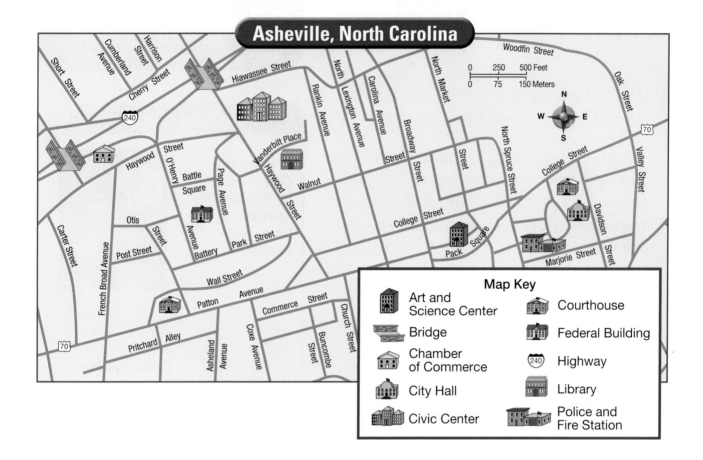

Asheville, North Carolina

Woodfin Street

0 250 500 Feet
0 75 150 Meters

Map Key

Art and Science Center

Courthouse

Bridge

Federal Building

Chamber of Commerce

 Highway

City Hall

Library

Civic Center

Police and Fire Station

---

16 Test Prep Every place on Earth is in at least—

F one hemisphere.

G two hemispheres.

H four hemispheres.

J two continents.

Think Critically

17 What are three places in your community where people can go to enjoy themselves?

18 Why is it important for people to be responsible citizens?

19 What are some ways you can help make your community a better place to live?

Apply Skills

Read a Map

Use the map of Asheville, North Carolina, on this page to answer the following questions.

MAP AND GLOBE SKILLS

20 If you were at the Library, in which direction would you go to reach the Art and Science Center?

21 In the map key, what is the symbol for the Civic Center?

22 How many bridges are shown on the map?

Unit Activities

 GO ONLINE

Visit The Learning Site at
**www.harcourtschool.com/
socialstudies/activities**
for additional activities.

Honor a Community Leader

Make a poster about a person you admire in your community. Do research on him or her and write a short biography. Draw pictures or take photographs of that person to illustrate your poster. Add captions to the pictures that tell how that person is a leader. Share your poster with the rest of the class. Then add it to a display titled *Leaders of Our Community*.

Complete the Unit Project

A Class Magazine   Work with a group of classmates to complete the unit project— a class magazine about your community. Decide which events and people you want to include in your magazine. Then write short paragraphs about them. Make maps, time lines, and charts for your magazine. You and the members of your group can take turns reading your items aloud to the other groups.

Visit Your Library

■ *What Is a Community?* by Bobbie Kalman. Crabtree Publishing.

■ *Two Days in May* by Harriet Peck Taylor. Farrar, Straus and Giroux.

■ *Nothing Ever Happens on 90th Street* by Roni Schotter. Orchard.

Citizenship and Government

A Native American
beaded waist pouch, 1950

Recital of the Pledge of Allegiance

2

Citizenship and Government

❝ Ask not what your country can do for you—ask what you can do for your country. ❞

—President John F. Kennedy,
in a speech on January 20, 1961

Preview the Content

Before you study the unit, write a few sentences telling what you already know about government. Then organize your sentences in a two-column chart with the headings **Citizenship** and **Government**.

Citizenship	Government

common good Something that is good for all people in a community. (page 75)

vote A choice made by citizens that gets counted. (page 111)

volunteer A person who chooses to work without getting paid. (page 76)

governor The leader of a state's government. (page 94)

government services The work that is done for a city or town by departments run by the government. (page 84)

patriotism The feeling of pride that citizens have for their country. (page 122)

The star-spangled banner.

ay, can ye see by the dawn's early light so proudly we hail'd by the twilight's ght stars & broad stri

PEACE and BREAD:

The Story of Jane Addams

by Stephanie Sammartino McPherson

From the front windows of her large house in Cedarville, Illinois, young Jane Addams could see wildflowers, trees, and sheep. She wondered what life might be like for people in other places. Soon Jane had answers to some of her questions. On a trip with her father, she saw people who worked very hard but were still poor. Their houses were run-down. Their children had no place to play. After that trip, Jane told her father she had a plan to help others. "When I grow up," she said, "I will have a large house right in the midst of houses like these." She was six years old at the time. Read to find out how Jane Addams carried out her childhood plan.

This photograph of Jane Addams was taken when she was six years old.

Chicago, Illinois, in 1889 seemed a perfect place for Jane's plan to help others. Sometimes Chicago was called "a city of a million strangers." Many of the people had left their old home and countries to find a better life. But when they got to the United States, they often had to take low-paying jobs and live in crowded run-down houses.

First, Jane had to find a place to live. It had to have one or two large rooms where many people could gather. Most important of all, it had to be located right in the midst of the people she wanted to help. She heard about a house built by a wealthy businessman named Charles Hull. The once beautiful house had fallen on hard times. But Jane saw beyond the dirt and disorder. Hull-House had everything she was looking for.

Jane Addams had this photo taken after she graduated from college.

This is what Hull-House looked like when Jane Addams and her friend Ellen Starr moved in.

Many women who came to visit Hull-House brought their small children with them. Sometimes the children were left to visit by themselves while their mothers hurried to jobs. Jane realized neighborhood children needed a place to play and learn. Older people in the neighborhood had problems, too. Often they were lonely, sick, and unable to work. From morning to night, there was always something for Jane to do—a neighbor to talk to, a child to tend to, a call for help to answer. As the house filled up with neighbors, it also attracted new volunteers. Jane was certain Hull-House could be as important to the volunteers as it was to the people in the neighborhood.

Jane greets her new neighbors.

The first public playground in Chicago was started by Hull-House in 1893.

But some neighbors continued to wonder why Jane and her friends would choose to live and to work here. One puzzled old man told Jane it was the strangest thing he could imagine. But Jane did not feel strange in her new home. She felt happy and energetic and useful. What could be more ordinary and right than helping people? Gradually Jane's neighbors came to look on her as someone they could count on.

The people in this Hull-House room are taking classes to become United States citizens. At Hull-House people could take other classes in English, reading, dancing, art, and music.

Think About It

❶ As a young girl, what plan did Jane have?

❷ What are some ways people help others today? Look in magazines and newspapers or on the Internet. From your search list three of the ways of helping others.

Read a Book

Start the Unit Project

Patriotic Medal With your classmates, create a medal that shows your patriotism, the love that you have for your country. As you read this unit, make a list of things you might want to show. Your list will help you decide what to include on the medal.

Use Technology

Visit The Learning Site at **www.harcourtschool.com/ socialstudies** for additional activities, primary sources, and other resources to use in this unit.

Tarrant County Courthouse

The Tarrant County Courthouse in Fort Worth, Texas, was built in 1895. The building was modeled after the state's capitol building in Austin and restored by architect Ward Bogard in 1983. The pink-granite courthouse was one of the first steel-framed buildings in the southwestern United States.

Locate It

TEXAS

Fort Worth

3

People and Their Local Government

" . . . with other people you can change things. **"**

—Virginia Ramirez,
from an interview in August 2000

CHAPTER READING SKILL

Categorize

To **categorize** means to divide into groups.

As you read this chapter, categorize the information about citizenship and government.

CATEGORY	INFORMATION
Reasons for Government	
Levels of Government	
People in Government	

Leaders in the Community

Main Idea
Good leaders can make a difference in a community.

Vocabulary

public service
common good
volunteer
elect
appoint
authority

United States President Franklin Roosevelt once called Jane Addams "Chicago's most useful citizen." Addams earned that praise by doing something for her community that its people could not do on their own. She started what became the best-known community center in the United States—Hull-House.

Community Leaders

Jane Addams was a person who believed in public service. **Public service** is doing work for the good of the community. Another person who made a difference in her community was Virginia Ramirez of San Antonio, Texas.

FAST FACT Jane Addams's Hull-House had the first public playground, first public swimming pool, and first kindergarten in the city of Chicago.

Hull-House in Chicago, Illinois

Members of the C.O.P.S. organization work together to create change in their neighborhood.

Virginia Ramirez worked with C.O.P.S. to make her community a better place.

Her neighbors' houses were falling apart, and she decided to do something about this. She began working with a community group called C.O.P.S., which stands for Communities Organized for Public Service. Along with other citizens, Ramirez learned how to work for the good of her community. She learned to speak out at public meetings and work with others to solve problems.

Ramirez had good citizenship skills. She also believed in fair and equal treatment for all citizens. Through her efforts, new houses were built and old houses were repaired. People like Jane Addams and Virginia Ramirez make important contributions to the **common good**— the good of everyone in a community.

Review How can organizations serve the common good of a community?

Oscar Arias Sanchez
1941–

Character Trait: Civic Virtue

Oscar Arias Sanchez was the president of Costa Rica from 1986–1990. He worked with leaders of other countries in Central America to improve the lives of their citizens. With his help, they gained the right to vote, freedom of the press, good schools, and better pay. In 1987 Sanchez won the Nobel Peace Prize for his work for the people of Central America.

MULTIMEDIA BIOGRAPHIES
Visit The Learning Site at
www.harcourtschool.com/
biographies
to learn about other famous people.

GO ONLINE

People Make a Difference

Public service includes many ways of helping a community. One way is to work as a volunteer. A **volunteer** is someone who chooses to work without being paid. Volunteers can help in a community in times of trouble. After an earthquake or a flood, volunteers collect food, clothing, and blankets for those who need them. In some communities, volunteers help by building or fixing up homes.

Another kind of public service is acting as a community leader. All over the United States, leaders help citizens solve community problems.

Review **What are two ways people can help a community as volunteers?**

A community's water may be unsafe to drink after a flood. Here members of the National Guard help people get clean water from special water tanks.

Government Leaders

The leaders of a community are its government leaders. The people of a community **elect**, or choose by voting, many of their government leaders. These leaders include the mayor, judges, and other members of the city or town government.

Some leaders are not elected. They are chosen by the elected government leaders to do certain jobs, such as to run the police and fire departments. Government leaders can **appoint**, or name, people to do these jobs. The citizens have given them the authority to do this. **Authority** is the right leaders have to give orders, make decisions, and take action.

This woman is getting an award for doing well in the job she was appointed to do.

Review What are two ways government leaders are chosen?

LESSON I
Review

1 Main Idea How do good leaders help a community?

2 Vocabulary Write a sentence about Jane Addams or Virginia Ramirez, using the vocabulary words **common good** and **volunteer**.

3 Reading Skill—Categorize Read the lesson again. Make a chart with the headings *Elected*, *Volunteer*, and *Appointed*. List some types of community leaders that belong in each category.

4 Your Community Write two sentences about the person who serves as mayor or city manager of your community.

Performance—Plan an Interview Make a list of good citizenship skills. Then think of someone who has these skills. The person could be someone in your community or a well-known American leader. Write a list of questions you would like to ask that person. Then, with a partner, role-play an interview with that leader.

2

Main Idea
Communities have governments to keep order and to protect citizens and their property.

Vocabulary

conflict
court
jury
public property
private property

Communities Have Governments

Every community has a government, a group of citizens that leads the community. The government works to keep order, manage disagreements, and protect people and their property.

To Keep Order

The government makes laws about how citizens should behave and makes sure laws are obeyed. Laws help people know what to do and what not to do.

Following traffic laws helps keep order in a community.

Many laws are made to keep people safe. There are speed limits on the streets and highways. There are laws about wearing a seat belt when driving or riding in a car.

Review **For what reasons do governments make laws?**

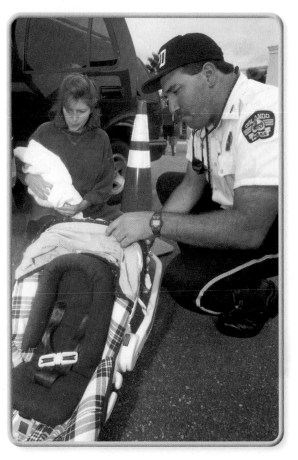

In some communities, there are laws about wearing bicycle helmets.

There are laws about special car seats for infants. This car seat is being checked for safety.

A police officer uses special equipment to find out if drivers are obeying the speed limit.

Democratic Values
Justice

SERVING ON A JURY

Being selected to serve on a jury has been counted as an honor for more than 1,000 years. Today, serving on a jury is one of the rights and responsibilities of every American adult. A **jury** is a group of citizens, usually 6 to 12, who sit in a courtroom and listen to the facts of a case.

The jury members then leave the courtroom and discuss the facts. If they decide a person is guilty, the judge decides his or her punishment. Juries are an important part of our government.

Analyze the Value

❶ Why is serving on a jury both a right and a responsibility?

❷ **Make It Relevant** Explain why juries are important in our courts. Then do research on court systems in other countries of the world. How do their systems compare to ours?

To Manage Conflict

A **conflict** is a disagreement. When people live together in communities, there are always some conflicts. For example, one family enjoys playing loud music. The family living next door does not enjoy listening to the loud music. These two neighbors find themselves in conflict.

The neighbors may be able to settle the conflict by themselves. Sometimes the conflict is settled in a **court** by a judge, who listens to both sides of the argument. The judge then tells the neighbors what they must do to get along.

Review **How do governments help settle conflicts?**

A jury listens as a lawyer explains the facts of a case.

To Protect People and Property

Community governments protect the public, or all the people. They set up police and fire departments to keep both citizens and property safe.

One kind of property is public property. **Public property** belongs to everyone in the community. Parks, streets and roads, and some libraries and museums are public property.

Another kind of property is private property. **Private property** belongs to one person or a group of people. Homes, businesses, and farms are examples of private property.

Review What is the difference between public and private property?

The land shown here is private property.

LESSON 2
Review

1 **Main Idea** Why does every community need to have a government?

2 **Vocabulary** Use the vocabulary words **court** and **jury** to tell how communities settle conflicts.

3 **Reading Skill—Categorize** Categorize examples of public property and private property in your community.

4 **Your Community** What might happen if the government in your community stopped working?

Performance—Write a Letter Write a letter to a person who lives in another country. In your letter, explain how your community government helps manage conflict and keep order.

CITIZENSHIP

Resolve Conflict

Vocabulary

compromise
mediator

▶ Why It Matters

One of the jobs of a government is to help citizens resolve, or settle, conflicts. Most of the time, people can settle disagreements on their own. Knowing how to resolve conflicts can help you get along with others.

▶ What You Need to Know

You can follow these steps when you are in a conflict. Remember that the same steps may not work every time. You may need to try more than one.

- **Walk Away**—Let some time pass. After a while, both people may feel less strongly about the conflict.

- **Smile About It**—Make things seem less serious. People who can smile together are more likely to work out their problem.

- **Compromise**—In a compromise (KAHM·pruh·myz), each person gives up some of what he or she wants. Each person also gets some of what he or she wants.

- **Ask for Help**—A mediator is a person who helps people settle a disagreement. The mediator may show them a new way of looking at the problem.

▶ Practice the Skill

Imagine that there is a conflict between two people in your class. Role-play what happens when they try the steps. Write what each classmate says and does.

1 What happens when one person walks away?

2 What happens when one person offers a compromise?

3 What happens when one person asks a mediator to help resolve the conflict?

▶ Apply What You Learned

Describe some ways people at your school resolve conflicts. Talk with a teacher or family member about how those ways compare with the steps in this lesson.

3

Main Idea
Citizens in a community need many services.

Vocabulary

government service

recreation

public works

tax

property tax

sales tax

council

Community Governments Provide Services

Community governments provide many services to citizens. A **government service** is work that is done by the government for everyone in a city or town.

Safety and Health

All cities and most towns have police and fire departments. A department is a part of a government with a special job to do. Some communities have a health department, which makes sure the community is a healthful place to live in. Large communities have hospitals that care for people who are sick or hurt. Many communities have clinics, where doctors and dentists help citizens stay healthy.

Review How do governments help citizens stay safe and healthy?

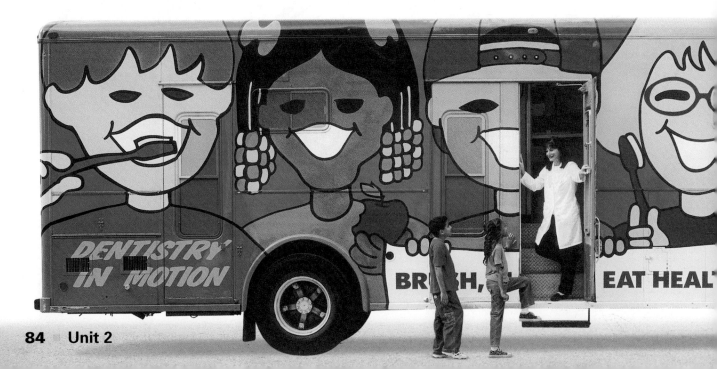

Public Education

One government service you know about is the public school system. Most communities have a board of education, or school board. Its members make decisions and solve problems for the community's schools.

In many communities, the school board helps choose teachers. The board decides how the schools should be run. This is an important job because a good education gives people a good start in life.

To help people continue their education, many communities provide public libraries. Libraries have the books and other materials people need for lifelong learning.

Review **How do governments make sure that children get a good education?**

Teachers help provide your education.

People can have their teeth checked on this bus from a county health department in Florida.

Central Park in New York City

Understanding Environment and Society

Central Park in New York City was one of the United States' first landscaped public parks. It was designed in 1858 by Frederick Law Olmsted to look like a beautiful natural setting. Its rolling hills, open meadows, and forests of thousands of trees seemed to stretch as far as the eye could see. Today the park includes a zoo, an ice-skating rink, trails for horseback riding, ball fields, and a lake.

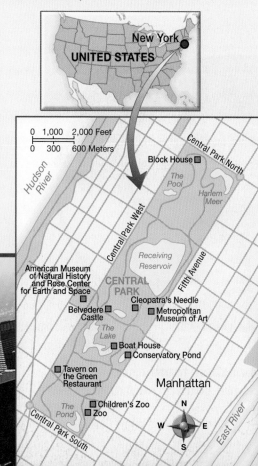

Parks and Recreation

Many communities have parks and public gardens. Citizens can go to these places to enjoy nature and open space. Parks give people a place for recreation (rek•ree•AY•shuhn), too. **Recreation** is any activity, hobby, or sport done for enjoyment after working. Reading, playing games, and exercising are all kinds of recreation.

A parks and recreation department provides many services. It takes care of community swimming pools, public softball diamonds, basketball and tennis courts, and golf courses. In the summer, a parks and recreation department may offer special programs for children.

Review What resources do governments provide to help citizens enjoy themselves?

Public Works

The **public works** department of a community government provides services to meet day-to-day needs. It sees that garbage is collected and that streets are kept clean and in good repair. It makes sure that the community has clean water.

The public works department also takes care of wastewater from homes, businesses, and streets. This wastewater is carried in pipes to buildings called water treatment plants. There it is cleaned before it is returned to the rivers and lakes. That way the wastewater does not harm people, plants, or animals.

Review **What are two of the jobs of a public works department?**

These workers check equipment in a water treatment plant.

Brushes turn under this street sweeper to clean the city's roads.

Taxes Pay for Services

All of these government services cost money. Equipment, such as police cars and fire engines, must be bought. Workers must be paid. Most of the money for government services comes from taxes that citizens living in the community pay. A **tax** is money that citizens pay to run the community government and provide services.

One kind of tax that brings money to the government is the property tax. **Property tax** is money paid by people who own land and buildings in the community.

Another kind of tax is the sales tax. **Sales tax** is the extra money that all people pay each time they buy something. For example, in some places the sales tax is five cents for every dollar the item costs. At this rate, when a person buys something for $10.00, the tax is fifty cents. The total cost of the item is then $10.50.

A worker in a "cherry picker," a crane mounted on a truck, repairs electrical wiring high above the ground.

This girl will pay a sales tax on the item she is buying.

Large communities usually get more tax money than small ones because they have more people, properties, and stores. That is why large communities can often provide more government services than small communities can.

A community government, just like a family, must decide how to spend its money. In some communities, members of a city or town **council**, the group that makes laws, meet to make these decisions. A community government must make choices based on the needs and interests of its citizens. If a government does not collect enough money in taxes, it will not be able to pay for all the services its citizens want.

A tax assessor's job is to assess, or determine, the values of property in the community. Property taxes are based on property values.

Review How do community governments pay for services?

LESSON 3
Review

1 **Main Idea** What are four kinds of services that community governments provide for their citizens?

2 **Vocabulary** Write a sentence that explains **property tax**.

3 **Reading Skill—Categorize** Read the lesson again. Make a table with two headings, *Government Services* and *Taxes*. List the types of services and the types of taxes.

4 **Your Community** Choose one kind of government service you read about in the lesson. Tell why this service is important to you and your community.

Performance—Make a Map Draw a map of your community or a nearby community. On your map, show locations where education and recreation take place. Also include the locations of schools, parks, and libraries. Display your map.

Main Idea
The three branches and three levels of government do different jobs and provide different services.

Vocabulary

legislative

executive

judicial

county

county seat

parish

governor

capitol

Branches and Levels of Government

In communities everywhere, citizens work with their governments to keep their towns safe and peaceful. In some small communities, everyone takes part in the community government by attending town meetings. In larger towns and cities, problems are discussed and solved by leaders elected by the citizens or appointed by government leaders.

The Branches of Government

Most governments are made up of three branches, or parts, each with a different job to do. The parts are called branches because, like the branches of a tree, they are separate but connected.

In this small New Hampshire town meeting, neighbors discuss ways to solve problems in the community.

TOWN MEETING TONIGHT

The Branches of the United States Government

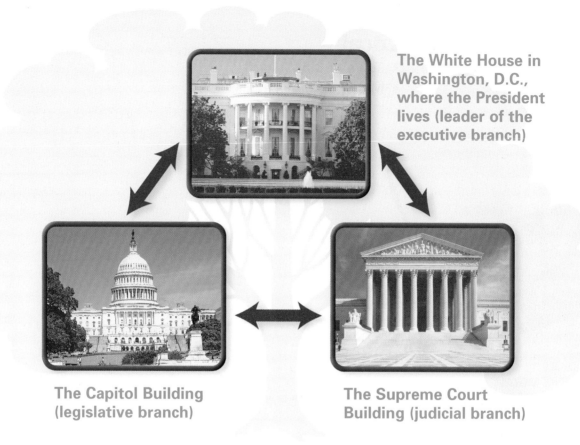

The White House in Washington, D.C., where the President lives (leader of the executive branch)

The Capitol Building (legislative branch)

The Supreme Court Building (judicial branch)

Analyze Drawings This drawing shows how the branches of government are connected.

◆ Which photograph shows the building that represents the judicial branch?

One part of the government is called the **legislative** branch. This branch makes laws. Another part is called the **executive** branch. This branch sees that laws are obeyed. The third part is called the **judicial** branch. This branch decides whether laws are fair. It also decides whether they have been carried out fairly.

Review What are the three branches of government called?

President George W. Bush signs a law to lower taxes.

Levels of Government

Local
- Town or City Council
- Mayor or City Manager

County
- Board of Supervisors
- Courts

State

Legislative
- Senate
- House of Representatives or Assembly

Executive
- Governor
- Departments of Education and Health

Judicial
- Supreme Court
- Local Courts

Nation

Legislative
- Senate
- House of Representatives

Executive
- President

Judicial
- Supreme Court

Analyze Diagrams This diagram shows the different levels of government.

◆ What are the branches of state government?

Local Governments

Community governments are one kind of local government. They make laws and solve problems for a small community, a town, or a city. In some local governments, all citizens decide things at a town meeting. In others, a mayor or city manager meets with a town or city council.

County governments are another kind of local government. A **county** is a part of a state. A county board of commissioners meets in a town or city known as the **county seat**. The board members discuss and solve the problems that affect the county.

Cochise County Courthouse in Tombstone, Arizona

Review What is the leader of a city or town called?

· HERITAGE ·

Louisiana Parishes

France was the first European country to make Louisiana a colony. In 1762, France gave Louisiana to Spain, which ruled the colony until France took it back in 1800. During Spanish and French rule, the Roman Catholic Church was part of the government of the colony. Each church served a small group of people called a parish. The church is no longer a part of the government, but Louisiana still calls its local governments **parishes**. There are 64 parishes in Louisiana today. The group that makes decisions for a parish is called a police jury. It works in much the same way as does a county board of commissioners in other states.

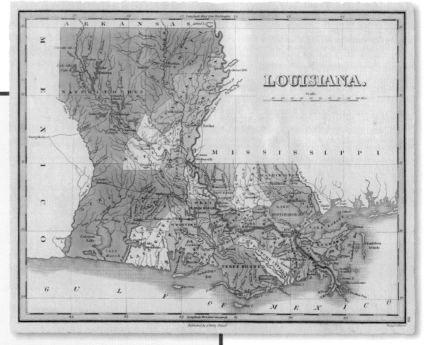
Historic map of Louisiana

State Governments

In each state, voters elect a leader called a **governor**. The governor's job is like the job of a mayor or city manager in many ways. The governor suggests laws that he or she thinks will be good for the state.

Almost every state has two groups of lawmakers. The lawmakers meet in the state's capital city in a building called the **capitol**.

State governments also have judges who decide whether the state's laws are fair. In some states, judges are chosen by the governor or the lawmakers. In others, they are elected.

Review In what special kind of building do state lawmakers meet?

Michael F. Easley, governor of North Carolina

Locate It

Raleigh, North Carolina

Old state capitol building in Raleigh, North Carolina

Governments Have Different Responsibilities

Community and state governments and the national government all do certain things. All make laws and collect taxes from citizens. All use tax money to provide services and to buy property that the public will own.

Each level of government also has its own responsibilities, or jobs to do. The community governments provide services such as fire protection and garbage collection. The state governments provide driver's licenses, build state highways, and care for state parks. They also provide for the education of their young citizens.

The national government deals with matters that affect the entire country. It is responsible for the nation's safety, which depends on keeping peace with other nations. It also works for the health and rights of all citizens.

Review **How are the three levels of government alike?**

Boise State University in Boise, Idaho, provides an education to college students.

LESSON 4
Review

① **Main Idea** Choose one of the three levels of government. Give two examples of the services it provides to citizens.

② **Vocabulary** Where would you expect to find a **capitol**? Why?

③ **Reading Skill—Categorize** Under what level of government would you place counties and parishes?

④ **Your Community** Write a few sentences describing your state's capitol building.

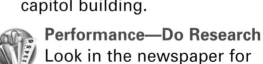 **Performance—Do Research** Look in the newspaper for articles about local and state problems. Your articles should also include solutions to the problems. Find one article for each category and share it with the class.

Identify State Capitals and Borders

Vocabulary

boundary

▶ Why It Matters

The map of the United States on these pages shows the states and their capitals. You can use this map to find the location and shape of your state. You can also use it to identify your state's capital city.

▶ What You Need to Know

A star is the map symbol that tells you a city is a state capital. A star in a circle shows the national capital. Find both symbols in the map key, or legend. Then find them on the map.

The map shows state and national borders. A border is also called a **boundary**. Find the symbols for state and national borders in the map key. Then find them on the map.

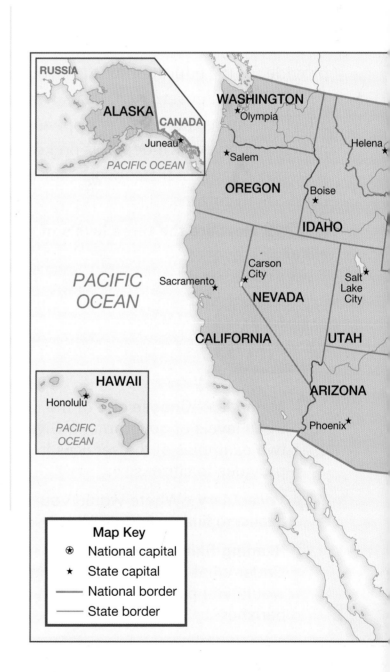

Practice the Skill

Use the map and the map key to help you answer these questions.

1 Where is your state?

2 What is your state's capital city?

3 What are the capital cities of the states that share borders with your state?

Apply What You Learned

Find a map of your state showing counties and county seats. Find the city or town in which you live. What county is it in? Look for your county seat. How many counties are there in your state?

Practice your map and globe skills with the **GeoSkills CD-ROM**.

States and Their Capitals

MAP AND GLOBE SKILLS

3 Review and Test Preparation

Use Your Reading Skills

Complete this graphic organizer to show that you understand how to categorize information from the chapter. A copy of this graphic organizer appears on page 22 of the Activity Book.

Parts of and Reasons for Government

CATEGORY	INFORMATION
Reasons for Government	To maintain order and security in our country
Parts of Government	_____ _____ _____
_____ _____ _____	National, state, and local
People in Government	_____ _____ _____

THINK & WRITE

Write a Persuasive Letter Think about the kinds of public service that members of a community can volunteer to do. Write a letter to an adult you know to persuade him or her to volunteer.

Write a Paragraph That Explains Imagine that you have been asked to explain community government to a younger student. Write a paragraph that tells what the community government does.

Use Vocabulary

Write the word that correctly matches each definition.

> volunteer (p. 76) capitol (p. 94)
> conflict (p. 80) boundary (p. 96)
> executive (p. 91)

1 The lawmakers of each state meet in a ____ building.

2 The border between two states is a ____.

3 Someone who offers to work without pay is a ____.

4 Governors are in the ____ branch of state government.

5 A disagreement is a ____.

Recall Facts

Answer the questions.

6 What did Jane Addams do for the common good of her community?

7 What are three ways volunteers can help their community?

8 How are mayors and city council members chosen for their jobs?

9 How is public property different from private property?

Write the letter of the best choice.

10 **Test Prep** A mediator is—
  A an imaginary line around a globe.
  B a government leader.
  C a person who makes laws.
  D a person who settles conflicts.

11 **Test Prep** United States citizens have a responsibility to—
  F exercise and eat healthful food.
  G pick up trash in public places.
  H pay taxes, obey laws, and vote.
  J use the public libraries.

12 **Test Prep** The branch of government that makes laws is the ____ branch.
  A executive
  B legislative
  C judicial
  D appointed

Think Critically

13 What would you say to a person who does not want to pay taxes?

14 How can volunteers help a community after a flood?

15 What are some ways you could help two friends resolve a conflict?

Apply Skills

Resolve Conflict

16 Look at the information on page 82. What are the four steps that you can use to help resolve a conflict?

Identify State Capitals and Borders

17 Look at the map on pages 96–97. What is the capital of Colorado?

Jefferson Memorial

The Jefferson Memorial, located in Washington, D.C., was completed in 1943. It was created to honor Thomas Jefferson, the third President of the United States. Made of white marble, it is one of the city's most visited landmarks. Inside it is a bronze statue of Jefferson. On the walls are quotations from his writings that express the beliefs of one of our nation's great leaders.

Locate It

MARYLAND

Washington, D.C.

VIRGINIA

Jefferson Memorial

Our Nation's Government

66 We, the people of the United States, in order to form a more perfect union . . . **99**

—*Constitution of the United States of America*, signed on September 17, 1787

CHAPTER READING SKILL

Generalize

To **generalize** is to make a statement that is based on what you know about a group of ideas.

As you read this chapter, collect ideas about citizenship. Then make some generalizations about the role of citizens.

IDEAS		GENERALIZATION
—————— —————— ——————	→	—————— —————— ——————

Main Idea
Laws are made by the national government for the entire nation.

Vocabulary

federal
constitution
Congress
representative
Supreme Court

The National Government

The government of the United States of America is our national, or **federal**, government. It is located in Washington, D.C., our nation's capital. Like other levels of government, the national government is made up of three branches. The Constitution of the United States describes the job of each branch. A **constitution** is a written set of laws that describes how a government is to work.

The signing of the Constitution of the United States on September 17, 1787, as painted by Howard Chandler Christy in 1940

President George W. Bush speaks to Congress in the Capitol Building in Washington, D.C.

Congress Makes the Laws

Congress is the legislative branch of the national government. It decides on new laws for the nation. Congress has two parts, the Senate and the House of Representatives. A **representative** is a person chosen to act or speak for others.

Members of the Senate and the House are elected by the citizens of the United States. They work to solve national problems much as the members of a city council do to solve local problems.

Each of the 50 states, no matter how many people live in it, has two members in the Senate. The number of members a state can have in the United States House of Representatives depends on its population. Population is the number of people living in a place. The greater the population a state has, the more members it can have in the House of Representatives.

United States Senator from Texas, Kay Bailey Hutchison

The Capitol Building, Washington, D.C.

The members of the Senate and House of Representatives work in the United States Capitol Building in Washington, D.C. They meet in two large chambers, or rooms, called the Senate Chamber and the House Chamber. The members of each group discuss problems and vote on how to solve them. They write new laws and decide how tax money should be used. Before a new law can pass, the members of the Senate and the House must agree on it. Then the President must sign it.

Review **What are the two parts of Congress?**

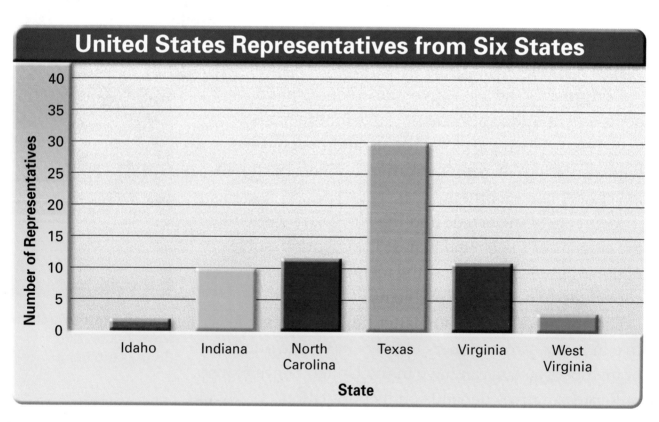

Analyze Bar Graphs This bar graph shows the number of United States Representatives from six states.

❖ Which of the states shown here has the most representatives? Why?

President Ronald Reagan communicates with citizens.

President George Bush greets the troops.

President Bill Clinton works with leaders of other nations.

President George W. Bush speaks to Congress.

The President Leads the Nation

The President of the United States leads the executive branch of the national government, which enforces the laws of the whole country. The Constitution says that the most important responsibility of the President is to "take care that the laws be faithfully executed," or carried out. The President also has other jobs. The pictures show some United States Presidents doing these jobs.

Review What are three jobs the President has?

The Supreme Court Judges Laws

This painting shows John Jay, the first Supreme Court chief justice, who served from 1789 to 1795.

The courts make up the judicial branch of the national government. The **Supreme Court** is the highest, or most important, court in the United States. Nine judges, called justices, serve on the Supreme Court. Their leader is the chief justice.

The justices of the Supreme Court study laws that have been made by the legislative branch. When cases are brought to the Supreme Court, they decide whether the laws have been used fairly.

Chief Justice John Marshall said long ago that our nation's Constitution is "the outline of a government." This outline often does not tell lawmakers exactly what they need to know. The Supreme Court answers their questions when the Constitution is not clear about a subject.

The nine justices of the Supreme Court are shown here. Standing: Ruth Bader Ginsburg, David Souter, Clarence Thomas, Stephen Breyer; Seated: Antonin Scalia, John Stevens, William Rehnquist, Sandra Day O'Connor, Anthony Kennedy

Supreme Court justices are not elected. They are appointed, or named, by the President and must be approved by the Senate. A Supreme Court justice may serve for the rest of his or her life or until he or she retires. A person who is chosen to serve on the Supreme Court promises to "do equal right to the poor and to the rich."

Review What do Supreme Court justices do?

LESSON 1
Review

1. **Main Idea** Describe the three branches that make up the federal government.

2. **Vocabulary** Use the words **Constitution** and **federal** to write a sentence about our nation's government.

3. **Reading Skill—Generalize** Tell in a short paragraph what you think it would be like to be President of the United States.

4. **Your Community** Describe two or more ways the federal government affects your community or state.

Performance—Make a Poster Draw three large circles on a poster, and label them for the three branches of government. In each circle, draw a symbol, or small picture, that stands for that branch of the government.

Skills

CHART AND GRAPH

Read a Table

Vocabulary

table

▶ Why It Matters

A **table** is a drawing that is used to organize information. Knowing how to use a table will help you compare numbers and other kinds of information more easily.

▶ What You Need to Know

Like charts and graphs, tables have titles that describe what they show. They use columns and rows to organize information.

Columns go up and down, and rows go across. The table below shows this. On the table below, you can see there are four columns and three rows.

The table on the next page gives information about the offices, or jobs, in the national government. It lists the name of each office; its term, or length; the age requirement; and any other qualifications needed.

To find information about each office, look for its name in the first column. Then read across that row.

Title			
Column 1	Column 2	Column 3	Column 4
Row A			
Row B			
Row C			

Practice the Skill

Use the table to help you answer these questions.

1 How old must a person be to run for President?

2 What is the greatest number of years a President can serve?

3 How long is the term of office for a Supreme Court Justice?

4 How long must a member of the Senate have been a citizen?

Apply What You Learned

Work with a partner to list the titles of tables you find in the newspaper. Cut out three tables that interest you. Share your list and the tables with your class.

Offices in the National Government

OFFICE	TERM	AGE REQUIREMENT	OTHER QUALIFICATIONS
Member of the House	2 years	25 or older	U.S. citizen for 7 years; Must live in state for which elected
Member of the Senate	6 years	30 or older	U.S. citizen for 9 years; Must live in state for which elected
President	4 years; Can be elected twice	35 or older	Citizen born in U.S.; Must have lived in U.S. for 14 years
Supreme Court Justice	Life Appointed by President	None	None

CHART AND GRAPH SKILLS

Citizens Have Rights and Responsibilities

Main Idea
Citizens have responsibilities as well as rights.

Vocabulary

rights
Bill of Rights
religion
vote
election
ballot
majority rule
minority rights

The Constitution of the United States of America is more than 200 years old. It is still our nation's most important document, or official paper. It describes how the national government is to work. It also names some of the **rights**, or freedoms, all citizens are to have.

Citizens have the right to speak in public about their ideas. The Constitution, shown here, names our rights.

The Rights and Responsibilities of Citizens

A very important part of the Constitution of the United States is the Bill of Rights. The **Bill of Rights** names many of the rights and freedoms that belong to all Americans. It says that citizens have the right to speak in public about their ideas and beliefs, including religion. A **religion** is a belief in a god or a set of gods. The Bill of Rights also names the freedoms that the government cannot take away.

American citizens have the right to vote. To **vote** is to make a choice that gets counted. Voting is also a responsibility. By making their choices known, citizens keep their government strong. Citizens are also responsible for obeying the laws the government makes. Another important responsibility citizens have is to pay their taxes. This gives the government the money to pay for the services citizens need.

Review **What are two responsibilities that American citizens have?**

FAST FACT "Freedom of the Press" is the right of United States citizens to write, read, and speak freely. Today the press includes not only newspapers and magazines but also films, television, radio, and the Internet.

This student follows the country's important events by reading the newspaper.

Campaign Buttons

Analyze Primary Sources

Many people like to wear buttons to show which person they support in an election. Such buttons often have photographs and symbols that tell something about the people and their ideas.

1 This button is from Harry S. Truman's campaign, or try, for United States President in 1948.

2 This button is from Walter Mondale and Geraldine Ferraro's 1984 campaign.

3 This button is from Ronald Reagan and George Bush's campaign in 1984.

◈ Why do you think the colors red, white, and blue are often used on campaign buttons?

Citizens Make Choices

Voting allows citizens to help make choices in the government. To vote, people must be 18 years old and meet the qualifications required by their state.

Citizens vote when an **election**, or voting time, is held. They go to special voting places where votes are counted. They mark their choice on a ballot or use a machine to record it. A **ballot** lists all the possible choices. When the voting time is over, the votes are counted and the winner is named.

When more than half of the voters vote in the same way, they are the majority. In **majority rule**, these people rule, or get what they want.

The smaller group of voters, those who did not vote for the winner, are the minority. In the United States, those who did not vote for the winner still keep their rights. This idea is called **minority rights**.

The votes in an election are kept secret. Only the results are announced. At a voting booth, people can make their choice without anyone watching. Voters do not put their names on ballots. This way, people can vote without worrying about what other people may think of their choices.

This man makes his choice by voting.

Review What is majority rule?

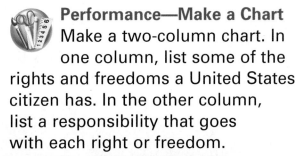

LESSON 2
Review

1 **Main Idea** Why is it important for citizens to understand their rights and responsibilities?

2 **Vocabulary** Write a sentence that compares **majority rule** and **minority rights**.

3 **Reading Skill—Generalize** An important characteristic of our government is that it protects minority rights. Write a short paragraph telling why this idea is important.

4 **Your Community** Choose one of the rights or freedoms of United States citizens. Then write a paragraph describing what life would be like in your community if that right or freedom were taken away.

Performance—Make a Chart Make a two-column chart. In one column, list some of the rights and freedoms a United States citizen has. In the other column, list a responsibility that goes with each right or freedom.

Make a Choice by Voting

Vocabulary
democracy   candidate

▶ Why It Matters

When you vote in an election, you are making a choice. Our form of government, called a **democracy**, gives each adult citizen the right to vote. This allows everyone to take part in running the country. The laws that get passed and the people who get elected to office are the ones the most citizens choose.

Understanding the choices you are given in an election will help you be a more thoughtful voter.

▶ What You Need to Know

Before you vote on something, you should learn as much as you can about the choices you are offered. Think about the good and not-so-good things about the candidate or the law. A **candidate** is someone who is running for office. Be a careful listener, and ask questions.

Step 1

Step 2

▶ Practice the Skill

Hold a mock, or pretend, election. Name three candidates who will run for office. Have them make speeches about what they will do if they are elected. The photographs on these pages show the four steps.

Step 1 Prepare the ballots.

Step 2 Vote in secret.

Step 3 Count the ballots.

Step 4 Announce the winner.

▶ Apply What You Learned

Many students belong to clubs in which they can practice voting. The members of the club can elect their own leaders. In many schools, the students elect leaders to offices such as Student President.

Step 3

Step 4

3

Main Idea
Many American citizens have worked hard for the common good.

Vocabulary

justice
slave
communicate
hero
civil rights

Models of American Citizenship

A good citizen follows the laws of the nation, pays taxes, and takes part in the government by voting. He or she also believes that freedom and **justice**, or fairness, are important. These are the ideas upon which the United States was founded. A good citizen works for the common good.

Some citizens become leaders in the government and bring big changes to the lives of the people. Others work with their neighbors to solve problems in their communities.

These new citizens promise in a citizenship ceremony to be true to the United States.

Thomas Jefferson
(1743–1826)

Thomas Jefferson was the third President of the United States. Before that, he was Vice President of the United States, Secretary of State, a member of Congress, and the governor of Virginia. Thomas Jefferson worked hard to make sure that Americans would enjoy many freedoms. Freedom of speech, freedom of the press, and freedom of religion are ideas he thought were important.

Review **For which state did Jefferson serve as governor?**

Portrait of Thomas Jefferson, painted in 1791 by Charles Willson Peale

President Jefferson was a talented architect. He designed his home, Monticello, in Charlottesville, Virginia.

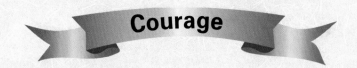

Harriet Tubman
(1820–1913)

Harriet Tubman was born on a plantation in Dorchester County, Maryland, around the year 1820. She and her family were slaves. A **slave** is someone who is forced to work for another person without pay. In 1849 Tubman ran away from the plantation and went to Philadelphia. Soon she went back to Maryland to help other slaves escape to freedom. She risked her life again and again to help more than 300 people escape from slavery.

Photograph of Harriet Tubman taken around 1865

Review **For what reason did Tubman risk her life?**

Routes, or paths, of the Underground Railroad

Helen Keller
(1880–1968)

A serious illness caused Helen Keller to lose both her sight and her hearing before she was two years old. She had not yet learned to talk, and now she had no way to **communicate**, or share information about the world. When she was six years old, a woman named Anne Sullivan came to be her teacher. Sullivan was able to communicate with Helen by using the sense of touch. She made letters in the palm of Helen's hand. Soon Helen could communicate with her teacher and her parents. She later went to college and became a public speaker and an author.

Helen Keller read and studied by using her sense of touch.

Although she could not see or hear, Helen Keller never gave up. She encouraged other people to meet their challenges, too. She was a good citizen who worked hard to help others succeed.

Review How was Keller able to communicate?

First Lady Eleanor Roosevelt greets Helen Keller (right) in 1936 on the 25th anniversary of the opening of the National Library for the Blind.

Dr. Martin Luther King, Jr.
(1929–1968)

Dr. Martin Luther King, Jr., made his living as a minister in a Baptist church. He never held an elected office, but he is an American hero. A **hero** is someone whose courage sets an example for others. King spoke out against the laws that he thought were unfair. What he said made some people angry, but King encouraged his followers to remain peaceful.

In 1963 Dr. Martin Luther King, Jr., made a speech before 200,000 people in the nation's capital. His words inspired those who believed in **civil rights**, or rights of personal freedom, for all. Dr. Martin Luther King, Jr., won the Nobel Peace Prize for his efforts to gain these rights for all Americans.

Dr. Martin Luther King, Jr., delivers his "I Have a Dream" speech in Washington, D.C., on August 28, 1963.

Review Why is Dr. Martin Luther King, Jr., a hero to many people?

· HERITAGE ·

Dr. Martin Luther King, Jr., Day

Each year, on the third Monday of January, Dr. Martin Luther King, Jr., Day is celebrated. It is a time for our nation to remember the changes King helped bring about. Schools and federal offices are closed across the United States in order to celebrate the birth, life, and dream of Dr. Martin Luther King, Jr.

"I have a dream that one day this nation will rise up and live out the true meaning of its creed..."

Community Heroes

Americans have many heroes. Some work in our communities to help people who are in danger. Police officers, firefighters, and emergency medical technicians risk their own lives to save others.

On September 11, 2001, the World Trade Towers fell after an attack on New York City. Many people died. Rescue workers helped to save the lives of many others who were injured.

Review What kinds of community heroes risked their lives to help others after the September 11, 2001, attack on New York City?

Retired Fire Chief Joseph Curry organizes rescue teams after the attack on New York City.

LESSON 3
Review

1 **Main Idea**   How did the people you read about in this lesson work for the common good?

2 **Vocabulary**   Choose two of the people you read about in this lesson. Use the vocabulary word **hero**, and write a paragraph that tells how each person was a good citizen.

3 **Reading Skill—Generalize**   How can citizens work for change?

4 **Your Community**   Write down two ideas for ways that people in your community could help one another.

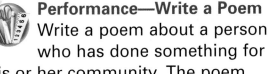 **Performance—Write a Poem** Write a poem about a person who has done something for his or her community. The poem may be about any hero—famous or ordinary. Share the poem with your class.

Symbols of National Pride

Main Idea
Our nation's symbols help citizens express their pride in their country.

Vocabulary
patriotic symbol

patriotism

Pledge of Allegiance

anthem

There are many kinds of flags. Some stand for cities or states. Others stand for businesses or teams. Of all the kinds of flags, a nation's is the most important. It is a **patriotic symbol** that stands for the ideas the people believe in, such as freedom. The feeling of pride that citizens have for their country is called **patriotism**.

Our Country's Flag

The design of the flag of the United States has changed over time. On early United States flags, the number of both stars and stripes showed the number of states in the nation.

Time Line of Our Country's Flags

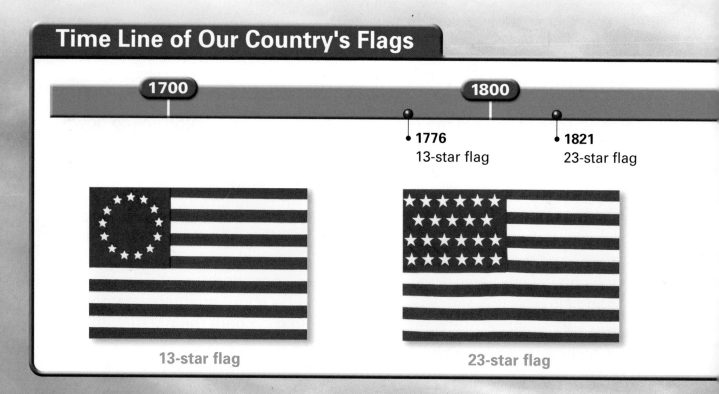

1700

1800

• 1776
13-star flag

• 1821
23-star flag

13-star flag

23-star flag

The country grew, and soon there were too many states to show as stripes. Congress decided that only a star should be added to the flag when a new state joined the United States. The number of stripes stayed at 13, to stand for the first 13 states.

Congress did not say how the stars should be grouped, so there were different designs. In 1912 the President ordered that the stars should always be grouped in straight rows. The latest change to the nation's flag was in 1960. In that year the fiftieth star was added to stand for the state of Hawaii.

Review **What do the stars on the American flag stand for?**

The present United States flag has 50 stars.

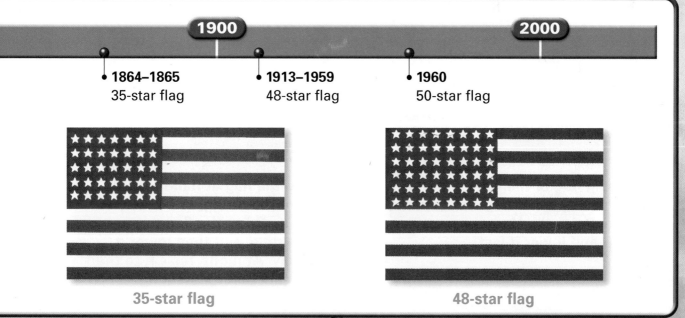

1900   2000

1864–1865
35-star flag

1913–1959
48-star flag

1960
50-star flag

35-star flag

48-star flag

There are rules about how the United States flag should be respected and displayed.

❖ How should you salute the flag when you are wearing a hat?

SALUTING THE FLAG

❶ Stand and look at the flag. Place your right hand, open, over your heart.

❷ If you have a hat on, remove it and hold it at your left shoulder with the hand that is over your heart.

DISPLAYING THE FLAG

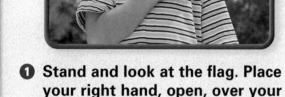

❸ Fly the flag of the United States above any other flag on the same pole. Raise the United States flag first, and lower it last.

❹ Flying the flag at half-mast is a sign of mourning, or sorrow for a death. Raise the flag to the top of the pole, and then lower it halfway. At night, raise it to the top again before lowering it.

The Pledge of Allegiance

Citizens show their respect for the flag and what it stands for by saying the **Pledge of Allegiance**. To pledge allegiance is to promise to be true. When you pledge allegiance to the flag, you are promising to be true to the flag and all that it stands for.

The Pledge of Allegiance was said for the first time in 1892 by children in public schools. Students all across the United States now join in this salute to the flag every school day.

Review **What does it mean to pledge allegiance to the flag?**

Schoolchildren say the Pledge of Allegiance with their teacher.

The Pledge of Allegiance

"I pledge allegiance

to the flag of

the United States of America

and to the Republic

for which it stands,

one nation under God,

indivisible,

with liberty and justice

for all."

I promise to be true

to the flag of

my country

and to the nation

it stands for,

one country led by God,

which cannot be divided,

with freedom and fairness

for everyone.

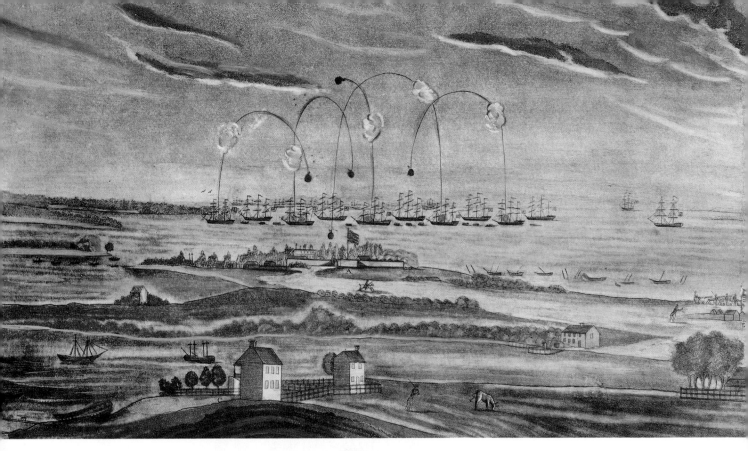

This painting shows the bombing of Fort McHenry.

Francis Scott Key

Our National Anthem

When many people look at the flag, they think of the freedom for which it stands. They also think about the people who fought and died in wars to protect the nation's freedom. "The Star-Spangled Banner" is our nation's **anthem**, or song of patriotism. It was written because of the flag.

Francis Scott Key was a lawyer from Washington, D.C. He watched from a ship as the British attacked Fort McHenry, in Baltimore, Maryland, during the War of 1812. The battle, which had started during the day, went on into the night. Key had to wait through the hours of darkness to learn which side had won.

As the sun rose the next morning, Key could see the American flag still flying above the fort. He knew then that the United States had won. His feeling of patriotism was so strong that he wrote a poem. That poem became the words to "The Star-Spangled Banner."

Most flags are flown only in the daytime. Over Fort McHenry and over the grave of Francis Scott Key, the nation's flag flies day and night.

Review What event led to Key's writing the poem that became the national anthem?

· HERITAGE ·

The Liberty Bell

The Liberty Bell cracked the first time it was rung in 1753. A new bell was made and it, too, cracked! Even though it no longer rings, the bell is still a symbol for freedom. It is on display near Independence Square in Philadelphia, Pennsylvania.

LESSON 4
Review

1. **Main Idea** What are some of the ways people can express pride in their country?

2. **Vocabulary** Give one example of a **patriotic symbol**, and tell why it makes citizens feel proud.

3. **Reading Skill—Generalize** Write a paragraph telling why you think people create flags, songs, and other patriotic symbols.

4. **Your Community** Share with the class a photograph or object that shows your pride in your town or community.

 Performance—Create a Flag Use construction paper to create a flag for your classroom, club, or sports team. Use colors and symbols that would help someone new learn about your group. Then present and explain your flag to the class.

Patriotic Symbols

The powerful bald eagle is the national bird of the United States and is used on many objects and documents. This early drawing of the Great Seal was the model for the Great Seal used today. The Great Seal is an important symbol to our country. It is used on government papers and on government buildings in the nation's capital.

FROM THE NATIONAL ARCHIVES

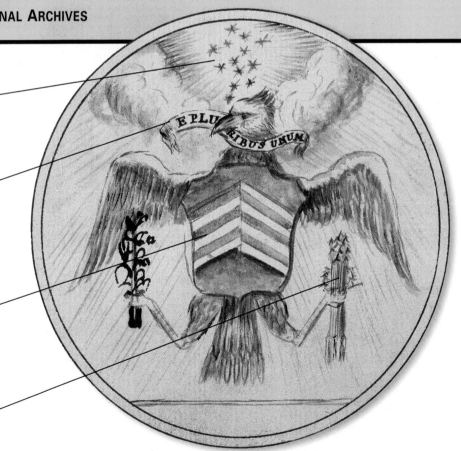

The stars represent the thirteen colonies.

E Pluribus Unum is a motto for the United States that means "out of many, one."

The red, white, and blue colors used in the shield stand for freedom and strength.

Arrows, which are a symbol for strength

On June 20, 1782, Congress approved this drawing by Charles Thomson, which became the model for the Great Seal.

A mold for the Great Seal of the United States used today

Analyze the Primary Source

1 **Why do you think the eagle in each seal is wearing a shield?**

2 **What objects are being held by the eagles in all three seals?**

3 **Why do you think the eagle is shown with its wings spread apart?**

Olive branch, which is a symbol for peace

Treaty Seal from 1825

The Great Seal and the Treaty Seal both have symbols that came from the drawing on page 128.

Activity

Create a Classroom Seal With your classmates, make a list of objects that stand for, or symbolize, your class. Then design a seal for your class using one of the objects in your design. Share your seal with other classes.

Research

Visit The Learning Site at **www.harcourtschool.com/ primarysources** to research other primary sources.

4 Review and Test Preparation

Use Your Reading Skills

Complete this graphic organizer to show that you understand how to generalize information about the responsibilities of citizens. A copy of this graphic organizer appears on page 30 of the Activity Book.

What a Responsible Citizen Does

IDEAS → GENERALIZATION

Obeys the laws
_____
_____

Becomes a leader in his or her community
_____
_____
_____

Chooses to vote
_____
_____

→

_____
_____
_____
_____

THINK & WRITE

Write an Election Speech   Imagine that you want to be president of your student council. Recall the character traits of the American leaders featured in this chapter. Then write an election speech to present to your classmates that will persuade them to vote for you.

Write a Poem   Francis Scott Key was inspired to write a poem to express his patriotism. Think about what you have learned about our nation. Write a rhymed or an unrhymed poem that expresses your feelings about the United States.

Use Vocabulary

Write the word or words that correctly match each definition.

> **Bill of Rights** (p. 111)   **hero** (p. 120)
> **justice** (p. 116)   **patriotism** (p. 122)

1 a feeling of pride in one's country

2 a paper that lists the rights and freedoms of all Americans

3 someone whose courage sets an example for others

4 fairness

Recall Facts

Answer the questions.

5 Who was Harriet Tubman, and what did she do to help others?

6 What are the three branches of our federal government?

7 What does our flag stand for?

Write the letter of the best choice.

8 **Test Prep**   The stars on the U.S. flag stand for the number of—
   A representatives in Congress.
   B United States Presidents.
   C colonies our country had.
   D states in the United States.

9 **Test Prep**   Congress meets in the—
   F White House.
   G Washington Monument.
   H Capitol Building.
   J Supreme Court Building.

10 **Test Prep**   The leader of the executive branch of the United States government is the—
   A chief justice.
   B governor.
   C President.
   D mayor.

Think Critically

11 If you could work in government, which branch would you choose to work in? Explain.

12 What is something that you think Congress should do?

13 What are some of the beliefs that good citizens share?

14 Who are some of the everyday heroes in your community? Explain what makes them good citizens.

Apply Skills

Read a Table

15 Study the chart on page 109. How old must a person be to be a member of the House?

CHART AND GRAPH SKILLS

Make a Choice by Voting

16 Look over the information on page 115. What are the four steps in the process of holding an election?

VISIT

Young Active Citizens

✫ ✫ ✫ ✫ ✫

Get Ready

Across the United States, young citizens are helping in their communities. Some organize food drives or collect and mend things. Others work with the city government. While their activities may be different, they all want to make their community a better place to live.

Locate It
United States

Washington, D.C.

Shaverton, Pennsylvania

Boston, Massachusetts

What to See

Youth Mayor Helps Her Community

Crystal is the youth mayor of Washington, D.C. She helps her community as an elected member of a group that works with the mayor. Her job is to tell the mayor about the problems of young people.

Sisters Repair Bicycles for their Community

Ashley and her sisters turn broken bicycles into shiny ones ready to ride. People in the community of Shaverton, Pennsylvania, give them old bicycles to fix. Each bicycle is delivered to its new owner with a helmet.

Brother and Sister Help Local Food Bank

In Boston, Massachusetts, Danny and Betsy collect money to pay for food donations. The brother-and-sister team buys food and donates it to a local food bank.

Take a Field Trip

GO ONLINE

A VIRTUAL TOUR
Visit The Learning Site at **www.harcourtschool.com/tours** to take virtual tours of other kinds of community projects.

READING RAINBOW

A VIDEO TOUR
Check your media center or classroom library for a video featuring a segment from Reading Rainbow.

2 Review and Test Preparation

Use Vocabulary

Write the word that matches the definition.

1 the set of laws that tells how our government is to work

Congress (p. 103)
Constitution (p. 102)

2 the branch of government that decides whether a law is fair

judicial (p. 91)   **executive** (p. 91)

3 a border between two countries

boundary (p. 96) **parish** (p. 93)

4 a time for voting

recreation (p. 86)
election (p. 112)

5 the legislative branch of the national government

Congress (p. 103)
Supreme Court (p. 106)

6 a person chosen to speak and act for others

representative (p. 103)
volunteer (p. 76)

7 fair and equal treatment for all

patriotism (p. 122)
justice (p. 116)

Recall Facts

Answer these questions.

8 What are two jobs of Congress?

9 What do you call the leaders of your community government, of your state government, and of your national government?

10 Why is Francis Scott Key a famous American?

11 Why are laws important?

Write the letter of the best choice.

12 **Test Prep**   Which does <u>not</u> work in public service?

A mayor
B banker
C judge
D senator

13 **Test Prep**   Two kinds of property are public and—

F private.
G national.
H local.
J forests.

14 **Test Prep**   Our national anthem is—

A the Pledge of Allegiance.
B the Bill of Rights.
C the Constitution.
D "The Star-Spangled Banner."

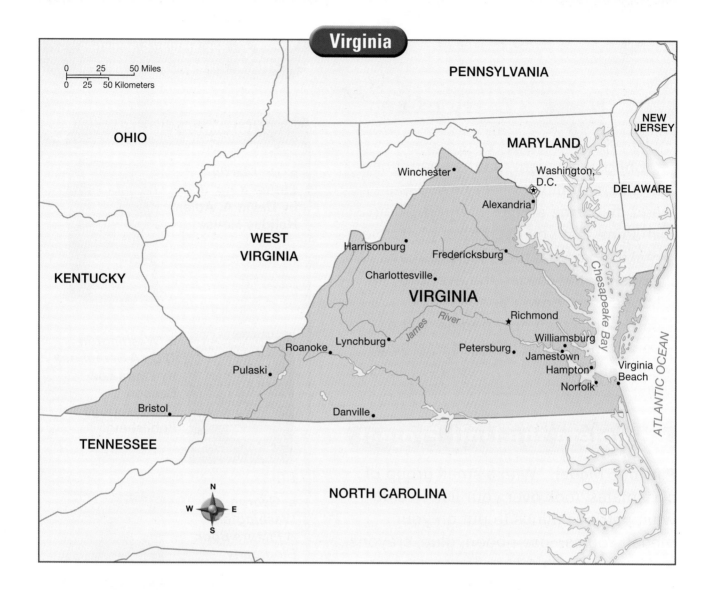

Virginia

PENNSYLVANIA

NEW JERSEY

OHIO

MARYLAND

WEST VIRGINIA

KENTUCKY

DELAWARE

Winchester

Washington, D.C.

Alexandria

Harrisonburg

Fredericksburg

Charlottesville

VIRGINIA

James River

Richmond

Lynchburg

Roanoke

Williamsburg

Petersburg

Jamestown

Hampton

Virginia Beach

Pulaski

Norfolk

Chesapeake Bay

ATLANTIC OCEAN

Bristol

Danville

TENNESSEE

NORTH CAROLINA

0 25 50 Miles
0 25 50 Kilometers

Think Critically

⑮ How would you describe the characteristics of a good citizen?

⑯ What did Dr. Martin Luther King, Jr., do that makes you think he was a good citizen?

⑰ Why is it important for citizens to obey laws and vote?

⑱ What are some of the ways organizations can take action to improve a community?

Apply Skills

Use the map to answer the following questions.

MAP AND GLOBE SKILLS

⑲ What is the state capital of Virginia?

⑳ Is the state capital north or south of the nation's capital in Washington, D.C.?

㉑ What are the names of the states that border Virginia?

㉒ On which ocean is Virginia Beach located?

Unit Activities

 GO ONLINE Visit The Learning Site at www.harcourtschool.com/socialstudies/activities for additional activities.

Make a Diary of an Event

Choose an event that has happened in a community. Collect newspaper and magazine articles about it. Then imagine that you lived through it, and make a diary about it. In your diary, explain what caused the event to happen and how it affected the community. Tell how people in the community worked together to help each other.

Complete the Unit Project

Patriotic Medal   With a small group of classmates, look over your list. Decide what patriotic things to put on your medal. You can use ribbon, glue, crayons, markers, and other supplies to decorate your medal. Display your medal around your neck or on your shirt. Wear your medal with pride.

Visit Your Library

- *Dr. Martin Luther King, Jr.* by David A. Adler. Holiday House.

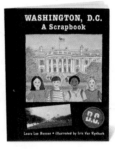

- *Washington D.C.: A Scrapbook* by Laura Lee Benson. Charlesbridge Publishing.

- *George Washington: A Picture Book Biography* by James Cross Giblin. Scholastic Trade.

Communities Are Everywhere

A globe and inkpot,
late 1800s

The Mississippi River in Minneapolis, Minnesota

Communities Are Everywhere

" The richest thing is the earth, for out of the earth come all the riches of the world. "

—Parker Fillmore, *Clever Manka*, 1920

Preview the Content

Think of what you know about geography. Then create a K–W–L chart like the one below. In the first column, write what you know about geography. In the second column, write what you want to know. When you have finished reading this unit, write in the last column what you learned.

K-W-L Chart

What I Know	What I Want to Know	What I Learned

climate   The kind of weather a place has over a long period of time. (page 150)

geographers   Scientists who study the Earth and its people. (page 172)

geography   The study of Earth's features. (page 146)

human feature Something that people add to the landscape, such as a building, bridge, or road. (page 154)

landform Natural features, or shapes, of the land including mountains, valleys, plateaus, and plains. (page 147)

region An area with at least one feature that makes it different from other areas. (page 174)

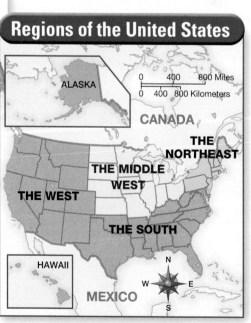

Regions of the United States

ALASKA

CANADA

THE NORTHEAST

THE MIDDLE WEST

THE WEST

THE SOUTH

HAWAII

MEXICO

0 400 800 Miles
0 400 800 Kilometers

N W E S

ROBINSON CRUSOE

WRITTEN BY DANIEL DEFOE
ADAPTED BY PLEASANT DESPAIN
ILLUSTRATED BY RICH NELSON

The story of Robinson Crusoe was written nearly three hundred years ago. It is based on the adventures of a real man named Alexander Selkirk. In the story, Crusoe's ship is wrecked after a terrible storm. Read on to discover how he reaches land and where he decides to build a shelter.

provisions
supplies

navigated
sailed

I made a strong raft out of wooden beams and a topmast or two from the ship. Then I filled seaman's chests with <u>provisions</u> of food, clothes, and tools. It was with great difficulty that I <u>navigated</u> the heavy raft nearly a mile to reach the shore.

I climbed to the top of a steep hill and discovered that I had landed on an <u>uninhabited</u> island. My next work was to seek a place to live. There was a little plain on the hillside with a hollow, like the entrance to a cave. I pitched my tent on the flat green, just before the hollow. Here I had water, shelter from the sun, protection from hungry creatures and a view to the sea.

I drove two rows of six-foot long stakes in the ground in a half circle before the hollow. It cost me much work, and many days, before things were brought to perfection. I entered by a short ladder. Once inside, I lifted the ladder over after me. Now I was <u>fortified</u>, and neither man nor beast could get over this strong fence.

uninhabited
not lived in

fortified
protected

It required several days more to survey the island. I went
up the creek about two miles and found meadows covered
with green grass and sugar cane. Farther on I discovered
wild goats, which brought me great satisfaction. I came
into a valley that was so fresh, and so green, it looked like
a spring garden. Melons lay upon the ground and ripe
grapes hung from vines. Cocoa trees, orange, lemon and
lime trees grew wild.

I so liked the hills and woods in the center of the island
that I built a little shelter, and surrounded it with a tall and
strong fence. Now I fancied that I had my country house
and my seacoast house.

CRUSOE'S ISLAND

- ⚪ country home
- ⚫ creek
- ⚫ where Crusoe lands
- ⚪ wild goats
- ⚫ seacoast home
- ⚪ shipwreck
- ⚫ steep hills
- ⚪ meadow
- ⚫ woods

A mapmaker created this map of Crusoe's Island by using information from the story.

Think About It

1. How did Robinson Crusoe discover that he was on an island?

2. If you were going to start a new community in an unfamiliar place, what kinds of supplies would you want to have with you? Why?

Read a Book

Start the Unit Project

Physical Features Model With your classmates, make a model of the land around your community. As you read the unit, make a list of the physical features and bodies of water in your community. Also list features that people have built. Your list will help you plan how to build your own group model.

Use Technology

Visit The Learning Site at **www.harcourtschool.com/ socialstudies** for additional activities, primary sources, and other resources to use in this unit.

Mount Hood, near Portland, Oregon

The city of Portland is located in northwestern Oregon. Although it is the largest city in the state, Portland has preserved many of its natural areas. On a clear day, Mount Hood can be seen from the city.

Locate It

Portland

OREGON

A Community's Geography

66 Geography, the world is in it. **99**

—Walt Whitman, *Leaves of Grass*, 1855

CHAPTER READING SKILL

Make Inferences

When you make an **inference**, you decide what you think the writer is telling you, based on the facts and hints you read.

As you read this chapter, collect facts about communities and their geography. List what you know about your community's geography. Make an inference about communities.

FACTS AND HINTS	WHAT I KNOW	MY INFERENCE

Describing a Place

Main Idea
Earth is made up of many kinds of places.

Vocabulary

geography
physical feature
landform
valley
plateau
climate
desert
growing season

In Daniel Defoe's story, Robinson Crusoe lands on an island and builds a home there. Before he builds his shelter, Crusoe has to think about the land's geography. **Geography** is the study of Earth's features. All places on Earth have features, or things that are special about them. You can describe a place by telling about its **physical features**—its land, water, climate, and plant life.

The Fitz Roy peaks in Argentina form a part of the Andes range in South America.

Landforms

Earth is made up of many kinds of places. One way to describe a place is to talk about the **landforms**, or kinds of lands, it has. Landforms include mountains, valleys, plateaus, and plains.

South America has one of the highest and longest mountain ranges on Earth. These mountains are called the Andes. The United States has many mountain ranges, too. The Rocky Mountains in the west are tall and sharply pointed. The Appalachian Mountains in the east are lower and more rounded.

The Appalachian Mountains begin in Massachusetts and stretch southward into Alabama.

FAST FACT

The Andes Mountains stretch along the western coast of Central America and South America from Panama to Chile. Covering a distance of 4,500 miles (7,242 km), they form the world's longest continuous chain of mountains. Mount Fitz Roy, located in Los Glaciares National Park in Argentina, is 11,073 feet (3,375 m) high.

From the Bitterroot Trail a valley stretches to the National Bison Range of mountains in Montana.

Valleys are lowlands that lie between mountain ranges. Valleys are often good places for communities because water runs down to them from mountains. Many valleys have very rich soil, so they are good places to grow crops.

Plateaus (pla•TOHZ) are landforms that have steep sides and a flat top. Plains are also flat, but they do not drop off steeply. They may stretch for miles in every direction.

Review What are the physical features of a place?

A Closer Look
Landforms and Bodies of Water

There are many different kinds of landforms and bodies of water. In this drawing you can compare how they are the same and different.

1 A desert is dry land with few plants.

2 An island is land that has water on all sides.

3 The area of flat land along a sea or ocean is a coastal plain.

4 The source of a river is the place where the river begins.

5 Land along a river is a riverbank.

6 A peak is the top of a mountain.

◆ Which of these landforms or bodies of water are near your community?

Bodies of Water

Earth has many bodies of water. The oceans are the largest. They cover the spaces between Earth's continents. The continents have many smaller bodies of water. These include lakes, ponds, rivers, and streams.

Review **What are the largest bodies of water?**

Opaekaa Falls in Kauai (kah·WY), Hawaii, is a feature of the thick rain forest on the island.

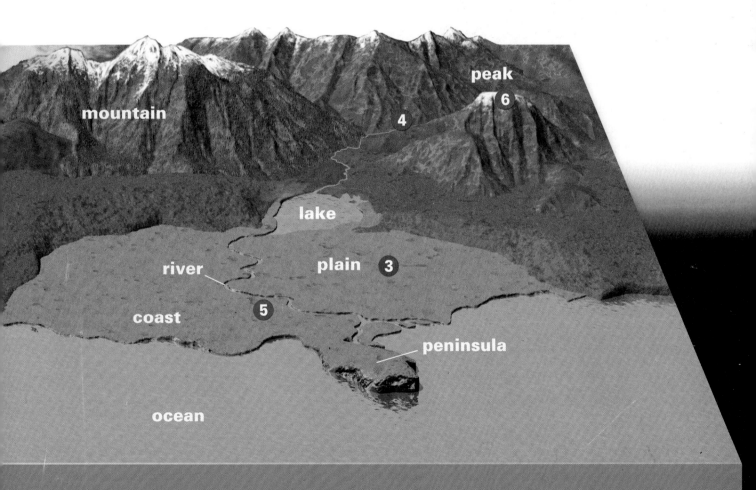

peak
6

mountain

4

lake

river

plain   3

coast

5

peninsula

ocean

Climate and Plant Life

Climate and plant life are also physical features. **Climate** is the pattern of weather a place has over a long period of time. This pattern is affected by how close the place is to the equator and to a large body of water. Climate includes how hot or cold the temperatures are and how much rain falls.

Because the United States is so large, it has many different climates. **Deserts** are places with very dry climates. Forests grow in places that get much more rain.

Children have fun making a snow figure in Arkansas.

The hot, dry desert of Arizona is a beautiful place to go hiking.

The plant life in a place depends on the climate and the soil. With the right amount of rain and the right temperatures, plants can grow. Without water, the land is bare. Climate also affects how long plants can grow each season. The time in which crops can grow is known as the **growing season**. In places with long, cold winters, the growing season is short. Where winters are shorter and warmer, the growing season is longer.

Review **What is the climate of a place?**

Bananas grow well in the hot, moist climate of the Canary Islands, off the coast of Africa.

A saguaro (sah·WAHR·oh) cactus can survive in the hot, dry climate of northern Mexico.

LESSON 1
Review

1 **Main Idea** What are some of the landforms on Earth?

2 **Vocabulary** Write a paragraph that uses the vocabulary word **desert** to describe where cactus grows.

3 **Reading Skill—Make Inferences** What can you guess about the plant life in a place that is hot and dry?

4 **Your Community** What landforms are near your community or home? How do they affect the way you live?

Performance—Make a Weather Chart Keep track of the weather in your community for several weeks. Record the temperature and the rainfall amounts. Make a bar graph for your weather chart.

Read a Landform Map

Vocabulary

landform map

▶ Why It Matters

There are many kinds of maps, each with a special use. For example, to find where a friend lives, you can use a street map. If you want to know about the geography of a place, you can use a **landform map**. This kind of map shows you a region's physical features, such as mountains, plains, plateaus, lakes, rivers, and oceans.

▶ What You Need to Know

On a landform map, the different physical features are indicated by different colors or patterns. The map key tells you what color stands for each kind of physical feature.

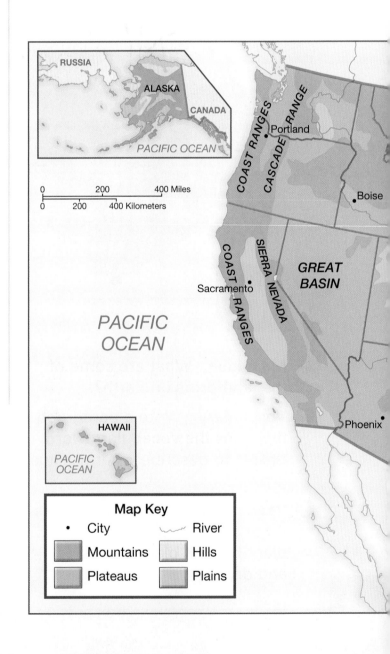

▶ Practice the Skill

Use the map and map key to answer these questions.

1 Which city is on higher ground, Orlando, Florida, or Boise, Idaho?

2 Are the Coast Ranges in the eastern or western part of the United States?

3 Which major body of water is close to St. Louis?

▶ Apply What You Learned

Look at the landforms shown on a map of your state and a bordering state. In a paragraph, describe the landforms of your state. In a second paragraph, compare your state's landforms to those of the bordering state you picked.

 Practice your map and globe skills with the **GeoSkills CD-ROM**.

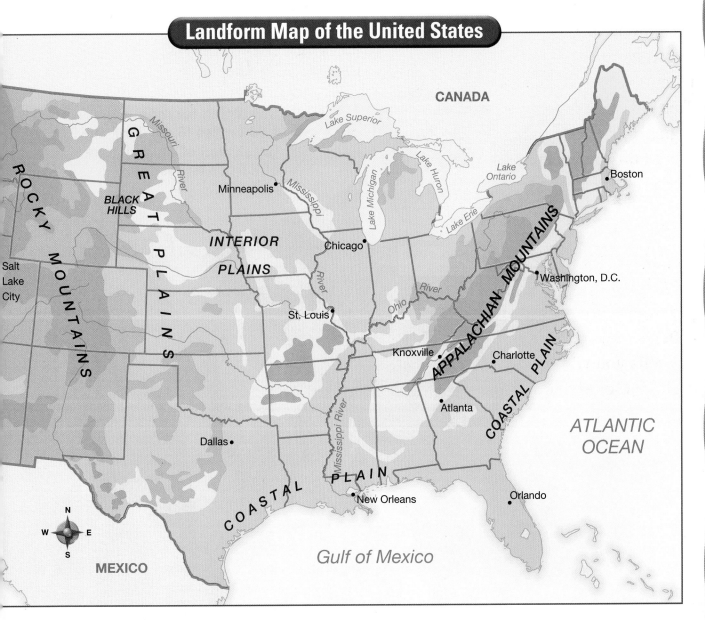

Landform Map of the United States

What People Add to Places

Main Idea
People add human features to Earth.

Vocabulary

human feature
route
crossroads
mineral

When you describe a place, you might mention some things that people have added there. These are called **human features**. For example, when Robinson Crusoe built a shelter to live in, he added a human feature to the island. Buildings, bridges, roads, farms, and mines are all examples of human features.

Locate It

The Great Wall of China

Stretching for more than 4,000 miles (6,437 km), the Great Wall of China is one of Earth's largest human features.

The buildings and bridges of Philadelphia, Pennsylvania, one of America's oldest cities, make it a very modern city today.

Locate It

Philadelphia, Pennsylvania

Buildings, Bridges, and Roads

When people first come to a place, they often add buildings to it. Perhaps they want to live near natural resources, such as water or land, and decide to build their homes there. New settlements begin with homes for people to live in. Soon those people need other buildings for their work. In time, some communities build places where people can have fun.

Some of the most beautiful features humans have built are the bridges that connect one part of the land with another. Today much of the surface of Earth is covered with bridges, roads, highways, and railroad tracks. These **routes**, or paths between one place and another, make possible the movement of people and goods.

Emmanuel "Manny" Gentinetta rode a bicycle much of the length of the Pan-American Highway—from the U.S./Mexico border to the southern tip of Chile.

One of the longest highways in the world is the Pan-American Highway. It runs from Canada through the United States and all the way to southern Chile in South America. This highway connects the capitals of 17 countries and joins the east and west coasts of South America.

Along the Pan-American Highway are several **crossroads**, or places where two routes meet. It is at these meeting points where people, goods, and ideas come together and then move on. Many communities have started at a crossroads.

Review **What are human features?**

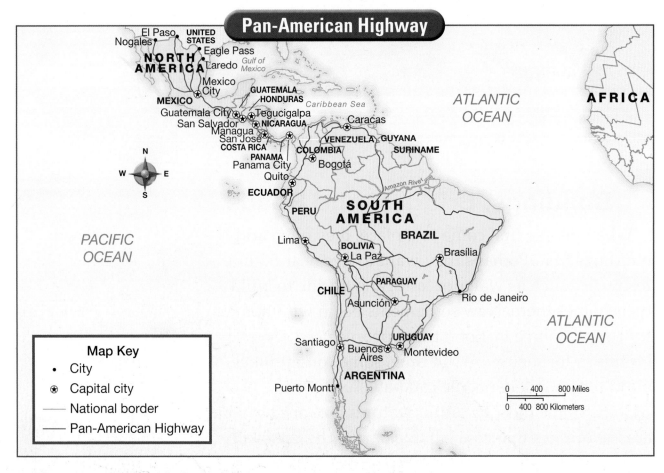

Pan-American Highway

Map Key
- • City
- ⊛ Capital city
- — National border
- — Pan-American Highway

Movement This map shows the part of the highway from the United States to Argentina.

❖ What are the capital cities in South America that the highway goes through?

Farms and Mines

Farms are also human features. Long ago, people discovered ways of growing the plants and raising the animals they needed for food. In some places, farming is still very simple. Families work with handmade tools and grow just enough food for themselves. In other places, farms are owned by large companies. These farms grow huge food crops with the help of modern machinery. The large crops from these companies provide food for millions of people around the world.

Mines are another kind of human feature. People create mines to get the minerals that lie beneath Earth's surface. **Minerals** are natural resources such as iron and gold.

In some places, such as on this farm in Catalunya (kah·tah·LOO·nyah), Spain, people harvest their crops by hand.

In farm areas such as Quincy, Washington, huge irrigation machines allow farmers to grow many hundreds of acres of corn.

Some mines are deep tunnels dug into the ground. Others are open pit mines, carved out of Earth's surface by heavy machinery.

Mining is important in many states. Many kinds of natural resources are mined. Coal dug from mines is used to provide heat and energy. Iron and copper are minerals used to make products. Salt is used for seasoning food. Gold, silver, and diamonds are used in making jewelry.

Review **What human features are built to provide people with food?**

At this mine in West Virginia, important mineral resources are being dug out of the ground.

LESSON 2
Review

1 Main Idea What are some of the human features that people have added to Earth?

2 Vocabulary Use the words **crossroads** and **route** in a paragraph that explains what human features are.

3 Reading Skill—Make Inferences As automobile usage increases, what do you think happens to streets and highways?

4 Your Community What are some of the human features in your community?

Performance—Build a Bridge Using cardboard, string, a box of wooden toothpicks, and glue, design and build a model bridge. The bridge can be for people on foot or for automobiles. Add your work to a classroom display of bridges.

Predict a Likely Outcome

▶ Why It Matters

When you **predict** something, you tell what you believe will happen in the future. If you can predict what will happen, you won't be caught unprepared. Predicting can help you plan for things.

▶ What You Need to Know

If you knew that your community would grow, you could predict that there would be more children. That would lead to a need for more schools. It would be wise for the community to start building them to meet the future need.

▶ Practice the Skill

Use the information in the chart to answer these questions.

1 If the island's growth continues, would you expect more or fewer people?

2 If the number of people continues to grow, would you expect the number of cars and houses to grow as well?

▶ Apply What You Learned

Work with a small group of classmates. Using answers to the questions above, brainstorm what the island might be like in the year 2100. Write a newspaper story to report your predictions.

Island Growth Rate Information				
	1990	2000	2010	2020
Number of People	300	500	1,500	3,000
Number of Cars	50	90	150	250
Number of Homes	450	800	1,800	2,500
Number of Businesses	25	50	100	200

READING SKILLS

People and Their Environments

Main Idea
The environment affects the way people live in a community.

Vocabulary

environment
adapt
fuel
harbor
canal
port

There are many kinds of landforms on Earth and many kinds of climates. All of these affect the way people live in their environments. An **environment** is made up of all the physical features, human features, and conditions of a place. People have developed technologies that allow them to live in nearly every place in the world.

Locate It

Alaska, North America

In cold climates people heat their homes. They wear warm clothing when they go outdoors.

Adapting to Climate

Climates in the United States range from very cold to hot. People have found ways to **adapt**, or change, to suit the climate.

From earliest times, people have adapted their clothing. The Inupiat people in Alaska wear thick parkas outdoors to stay warm. In the deserts of Arabia, people wear long, loose robes. They cover their heads and faces with cloth to keep the sun from burning their skin.

Humans have discovered how to heat and cool their environments. They burn **fuels**, or natural resources such as oil, coal, and wood, to get energy for heat or electricity.

Review **What are some ways people can adapt to the climate in which they live?**

In hot climates people build homes that allow breezes to pass through and keep them cool. Outdoors they wear clothing that protects them from the sun.

Using Resources

People use natural resources to meet their needs. Natural resources include water, soil, plants, minerals, and animals.

Communities are often built to be near certain natural resources. Portland, Maine, is located beside a natural harbor on the Atlantic coast of the United States. A **harbor** is a protected place with deep water that allows ships to come close to the shore.

Portland's natural harbor has made the city one of the largest fishing centers in the United States. Each morning, hundreds of

Lobster is a popular seafood in Maine.

Locate It

Portland, Maine

boats leave the harbor to fish along the coast. They return loaded with fish, such as grey sole and Atlantic salmon, and shellfish, such as scallops and lobsters. Some of the seafood is sold in Portland, but more of it is shipped to other cities around the world.

Besides the harbor, Portland has thick forests nearby. The hard wood of these trees is used for shipbuilding. The growing season in Maine is short, but some crops can be grown in the summer months.

Review How does the harbor affect the way people in Portland, Maine, live?

This Portland fisher is getting his lobster traps ready for a day's work.

In Portland, Maine, fishing boats share the harbor with boats people use for recreation.

Now

Today more than 30 ships pass through the canal every day.

The Panama Canal was very difficult to build. It took thousands of workers ten years to complete it.

Changing Physical Features

People have found ways to change the physical features of Earth. They have cut tunnels through mountains to build railroads. They have made mountaintops flat to build farms and cities. One of the largest projects ever carried out was the building of a canal between the Atlantic and Pacific Oceans in Central America. A **canal** is a waterway built by people.

The Panama Canal, completed in 1914, made it possible for ships to go from the Atlantic Ocean to the Pacific Ocean in a short time. The slogan of the canal builders was "The Land Divided, the World United." By using the canal, ships could shorten the distance between **ports**, places where ships dock to pick up goods or passengers. The journey of 13,000 miles (20,921 kilometers) from New York to San Francisco was shortened to just 5,200 miles (8,368 kilometers).

Review How did the Panama Canal change shipping between California and New York?

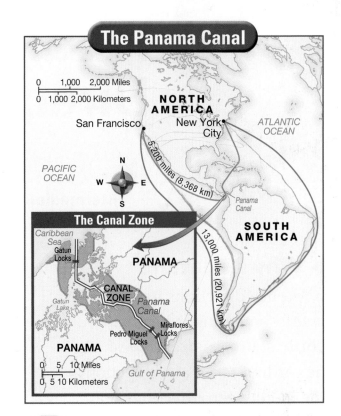

The Panama Canal

The Canal Zone

Location The inset map here shows a close-up of the location of the Canal Zone and the locks.

❖ The Panama Canal begins and ends with which oceans?

LESSON 3
Review

1 **Main Idea** How does the environment affect the way people live?

2 **Vocabulary** Use the vocabulary words **port** and **canal** in a sentence to explain how people make changes to physical features.

3 **Reading Skill—Make Inferences** Explain how changing physical features can make it easier to get from one place to another.

4 **Your Community** Write a paragraph to explain how the environment in your community affects the way you and your family live.

 Performance—Make a Diorama Choose a place in another part of the world. Do research in the library to find out how people there live. Then make a diorama to show the kinds of homes people live in and the kinds of clothing they wear. Invite other classes to view your dioramas.

Find Intermediate Directions

Vocabulary

intermediate direction

▶ Why It Matters

You use directions to find where something is located. North, south, east, and west are the cardinal, or main, directions. The in-between directions that give more exact information about the location of a place are called **intermediate directions**.

▶ What You Need to Know

The compass rose below shows both cardinal directions and intermediate directions. The four intermediate directions are northeast, southeast, northwest, and southwest. Each intermediate direction is halfway between two of the cardinal directions.

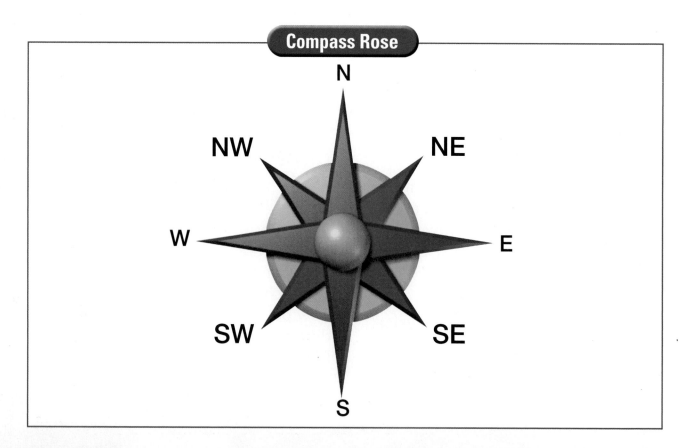

Compass Rose

▶ Practice the Skill

Use the compass rose on the map to answer these questions.

1 Is Washington, D.C., southwest or southeast of New York City?

2 In which direction would you travel from St. Louis, Missouri, to get to San Diego, California?

3 If you were traveling from Chicago, Illinois, to Denver, Colorado, in what direction would you be going?

▶ Apply What You Learned

Use the compass rose to help you identify objects in your classroom that are northeast, southeast, northwest, and southwest from where you sit. List them in a four-column chart with the directions as headings.

Practice your map and globe skills with the **GeoSkills CD-ROM.**

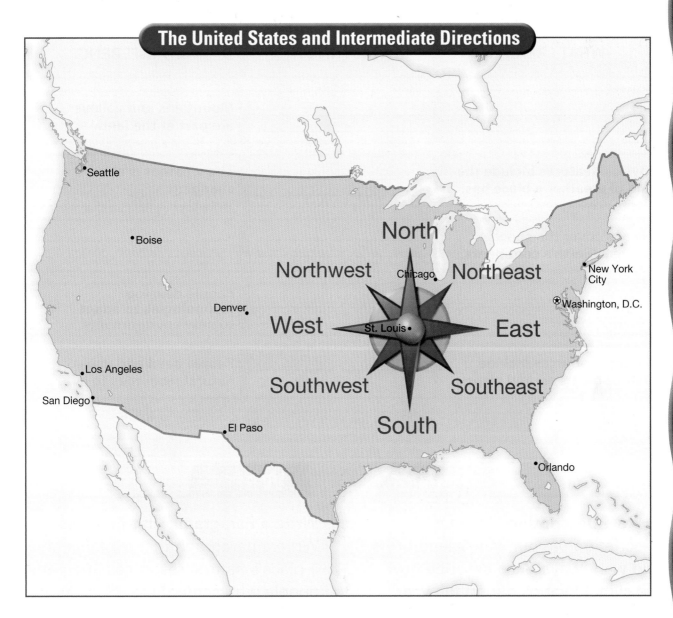

The United States and Intermediate Directions

MAP AND GLOBE SKILLS

Chapter

5 Review and Test Preparation

Use Your Reading Skills

Complete this graphic organizer to show that you understand how to make inferences based on what you have read and what you already know. A copy of this graphic organizer appears on page 38 of the Activity Book.

Inferences Based on What I Read and What I Know

WHAT I READ	WHAT I KNOW	MY INFERENCE
_____ _____	_____ _____	Mountains and valleys are part of the land.
Physical features include the kind of weather a place has.	_____ _____	The weather is always changing.
Oceans cover the space between Earth's continents.	_____ _____	_____ _____
_____ _____	_____ _____	People develop technologies to adapt to new environments.
Natural resources include water, soil, trees, and plants.	_____ _____	People need and use natural resources to live.

THINK & WRITE

Write a Description Write a description of your state's landforms and waterways. Also describe how the climate varies during the year.

Write a Paragraph That Explains Write a paragraph that explains how a place's natural resources affect the people who settle there.

Use Vocabulary

Write the missing word.

plateau (p. 148)	fuel (p. 161)
climate (p. 150)	harbor (p. 162)
desert (p. 150)	canal (p. 164)

1. A natural resource that is burned to get energy is called a ___.

2. The pattern of weather a place has over time is its ___.

3. A protected place with deep water where ships can come close to the shore is a ___.

4. A landform that has steep sides and a flat top is a ___.

5. A waterway that is built by people is a called a ___.

6. A place with a very dry climate is a ___.

Recall Facts

Answer the questions.

7. What are some of the effects humans have in shaping the landscape?

8. Why is the Pan-American Highway an important human feature?

9. How do people adapt to the environment in Alaska?

Write the letter of the best choice.

10. **Test Prep** ___ are human features that provide the food people need.

A Plants and animals
B Farms and ranches
C Soil and minerals
D Rain and sunshine

11. **Test Prep** Many communities began in places near—
F natural resources.
G human resources.
H places to work.
J landmarks.

Think Critically

12. Describe the landforms where you live. How do they affect the people in your community?

13. What is an environment that is very different from yours? How would you adapt to living there?

Apply Skills

14. Look at the landform map on pages 152–153. Where are the Appalachian Mountains?

15. Look at the chart on page 159. If the number of people continues to grow, would you expect the number of businesses to grow?

16. Use the map and compass rose on page A4. Is the Amazon River in South America located northwest or southeast of the Brazilian Highlands? In which intermediate direction are the Himalayas from Thar Desert?

Statewide Operations Center (SOC)

The Statewide Operations Center, or SOC, in Baltimore, Maryland, watches over 375 miles (603 km) of the state's highways. The Center uses television cameras to spot accidents or traffic jams. When workers see a problem on one of the screens, they immediately send a message on the radio and on electronic traffic signs alerting drivers to use a different route.

Locate It

Baltimore
MARYLAND

Thinking Like a Geographer

66 A map is a picture of where we are going. 99

—Goldie Capers Smith, *Instructor*, 1964

CHAPTER READING SKILL

Predict a Likely Outcome

When you make **predictions**, you combine your own knowledge with information you are reading to guess what the likely outcome, or result, will be.

As you read this chapter, make some predictions based on the information you are reading and on your own knowledge.

Main Idea
Using directions and identifying regions can help you understand the geography of a place.

Vocabulary

geographer
relative location
region
satellite

Highway signs help people find their way.

The World in Geographers' Terms

Robinson Crusoe had to find places by the positions of the sun and the stars. With no tools to use, he had to think like a geographer. A **geographer** is a person who studies Earth and its people.

Finding Locations

When you describe where a place is located by comparing it to another place, you are describing its **relative location**. Perhaps you would like to know if Toronto, in Canada, is north of Philadelphia. To find out, you could look at a map. After checking the compass rose on the map, you would see that Toronto is northwest of Philadelphia.

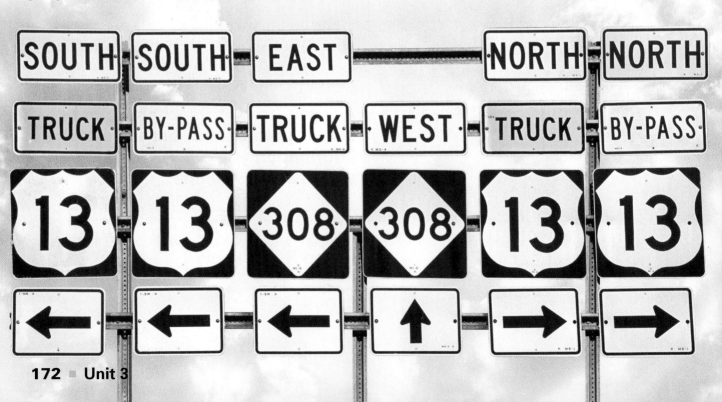

To describe a relative location, you need a point of reference, or something to which you can compare the location you are interested in. Once you have your reference point, you can ask a question about relative location. For example, from Spain, would Sweden be to the north or to the south? By using a map or a globe, you would see that the location of Sweden is to the northeast of Spain.

Both globes and maps can be used to determine a relative location. However, because a globe shows the entire world, it cannot show the small details of a city. If you wanted to know the location of a city's museum, you would need to use a street map. Geographers use both maps and globes to help them describe locations.

Review **What part of a map can help you find the relative location of a place?**

The theodolite was a tool used by mapmakers of long ago.

William Doolittle 1947–

Character Trait: Cooperation

William Doolittle is a geography professor at the University of Texas in Austin, Texas. He helps students explore not only the physical characteristics of Earth but also where and how people live. Doolittle specializes in studies of the American Southwest and Mexico. He has taken students to northern Mexico to study the land and culture there. He makes friends with people all over the world in order to learn how members of different cultures live.

MULTIMEDIA BIOGRAPHIES
Visit The Learning Site at
www.harcourtschool.com/biographies
to learn about other famous people.

GO ONLINE

Identifying Regions

Once you know the relative location of a place, how else might you describe it? You could identify the region it is in. A **region** is an area with at least one feature that makes it different from other areas.

Geographers sometimes divide the United States to study the land and people. One way to divide the states is into four large regions—the Northeast, the South, the Middle West, and the West. The states in each region are all located in the same part of the country.

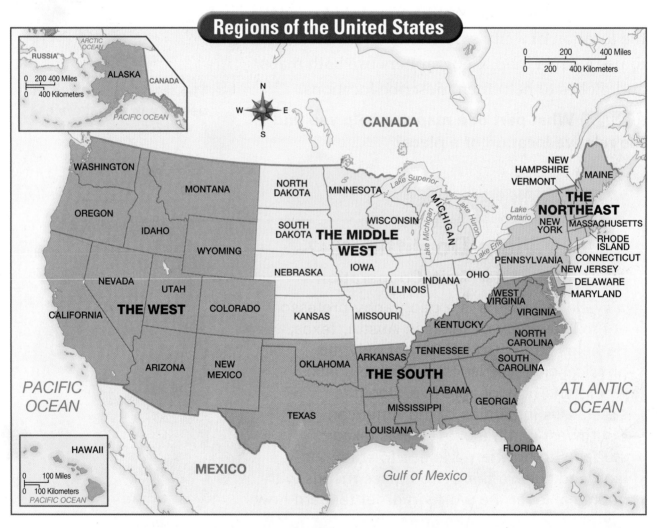

Regions of the United States

Regions   Geographers often divide the 50 states into four regions. All the states in each region are in the same part of the United States.

❖ In which region of the United States is your state located?

They may have the same kinds of landforms, natural resources, and climate. The people who live in those states often earn their living in the same ways and may share a culture.

The states in the Middle West are: Illinois, Indiana, Iowa, Kansas, Michigan, Minnesota, Missouri, Nebraska, North Dakota, Ohio, South Dakota, and Wisconsin.

The states in the Northeast are: Connecticut, Delaware, Maine, Massachusetts, New Hampshire, New Jersey, New York, Pennsylvania, Rhode Island, and Vermont.

THE WEST

THE MIDDLE WEST

THE NORTHEAST

THE SOUTH

The states in the West are: Alaska, Arizona, California, Colorado, Hawaii, Idaho, Montana, Nevada, New Mexico, Oregon, Washington, Utah, and Wyoming.

The states in the South are: Alabama, Arkansas, Florida, Georgia, Kentucky, Louisiana, Maryland, Mississippi, North Carolina, Oklahoma, South Carolina, Tennessee, Texas, Virginia, and West Virginia.

A region that is described by one main feature may still share features with other regions. Look at the three maps here to see how a place can be included in more than one region.

Review **Why do geographers group states into regions?**

One State, Three Regions

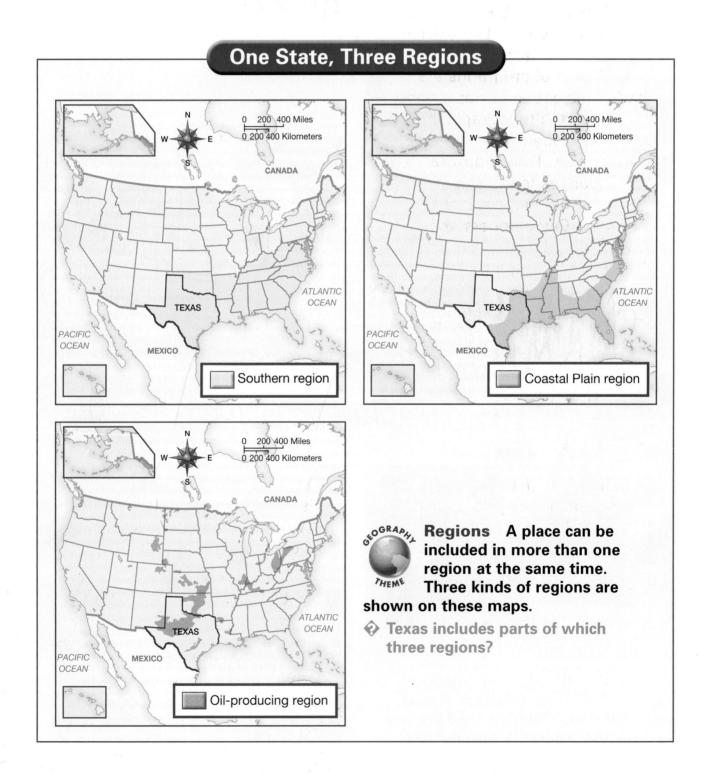

Southern region

Coastal Plain region

Oil-producing region

GEOGRAPHY THEME

Regions A place can be included in more than one region at the same time. Three kinds of regions are shown on these maps.

◇ Texas includes parts of which three regions?

Mapping from Space

Satellites help people make maps of Earth's surface. A **satellite** is a spacecraft without a crew that orbits Earth. It uses cameras and computers to take pictures of the landforms on Earth. These photographs are used in many ways. Maps made from satellite photographs help scientists study climate change in Antarctica. They measure small changes in the size of the ice sheets that cover that continent. City planners, too, can use maps made from satellite photographs.

This photograph taken from space shows the United States at night.

LESSON 1
Review

1 Main Idea What can help you understand the geography of a place?

2 Vocabulary Use the vocabulary words **region** and **relative location** in a sentence to explain the tools a geographer uses to study Earth.

3 Reading Skill—Making Inferences Why do you think geographers divide the United States into different regions?

4 Your Community What region is your community located in? Which of the other regions would you like to visit?

Performance—Study a Map Cameras can take pictures of the moon and use them to create maps of the lunar surface. Do research in the library to find a map of the moon. Compare the moon's features with the features of Earth. What things are the same? What things are different?

Skills

Use a Map Grid

Vocabulary

exact location
grid system

▶ Why It Matters

One way to find **exact location** is to use a map that has a grid system. A **grid system** is a set of lines the same distance apart that cross one another to form boxes. Knowing how to use a grid makes it easier to quickly find locations on a map. For example, you can find the exact location of a street on a city map. You can find out exactly how far north, south, east, and west a place is on a world map.

▶ What You Need to Know

Look at the grid on this page. Find the row labels—the letters along the sides of the grid. Now look for the column labels—the numbers at the top and at the bottom of the grid.

Put your finger on the purple box. Now slide your finger to the left side of the grid. You will see that the purple box is located in row C. Go back to the purple box. Slide your finger to the top of the grid. The purple box is in column 3. To describe the exact location of the purple box, you would say that it is at C-3.

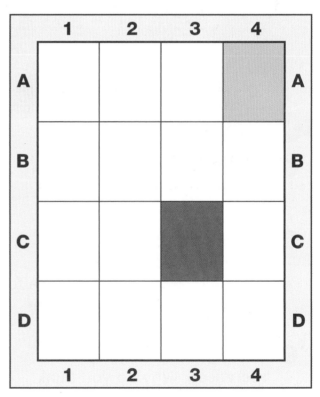

178 ▪ Unit 3

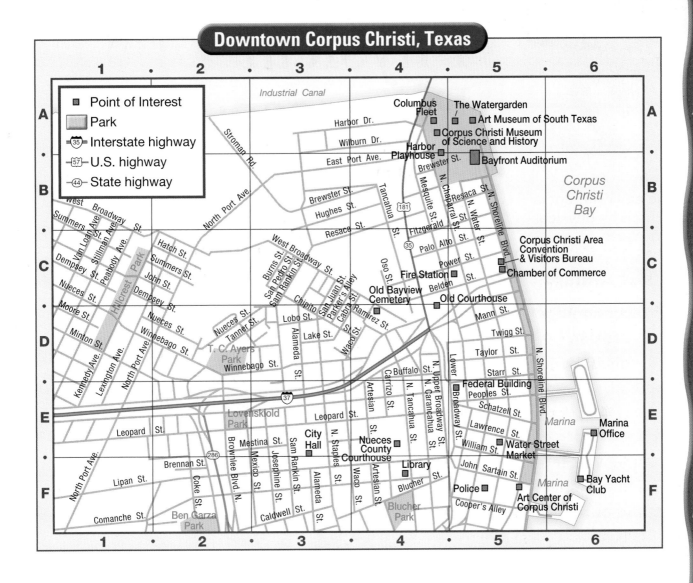

Downtown Corpus Christi, Texas

Legend:
- ■ Point of Interest
- Park
- 🛡35 Interstate highway
- 🛡57 U.S. highway
- 🛡44 State highway

Practice the Skill

Look at the map above of Corpus Christi, Texas. It has a grid. Use the map and its grid to answer these questions. Give a letter and a number when you are asked for a location.

1 Where is city hall?

2 What buildings do you see in the box at C-5?

3 Where is the Art Center of Corpus Christi?

Apply What You Learned

Draw a map of a place you know, such as your neighborhood, your school, or your classroom. Add a grid so people can find places on your map. Then share your map with a classmate or a family member.

Practice your map and globe skills with the **GeoSkills CD-ROM.**

Main Idea
The environment is formed by physical processes.

Vocabulary

ecosystem

erosion

disaster

Physical Processes

Earth has been changing for millions of years. Most of the changes are slow, but some happen quickly. The changes, whether they are fast or slow, affect all living things on Earth.

Life in an Ecosystem

Plants and animals and the environment in which they live make up an **ecosystem**. The members of an ecosystem affect one another in many ways.

This forest in Washington State is an ecosystem.

In a forest, for example, the trees provide shelter and food for birds, insects, and other animals. They also provide shade for other plants. The birds and animals help spread the trees' seeds, and the insects help break down fallen logs. The environment provides the soil and the weather the trees need to grow.

If a forest is cut down, the environment changes. Without the trees, plants that need shade die. Birds and animals must move on to find new homes. With no roots to hold the soil in place, it washes and blows away. When one part of an ecosystem disappears, all the other parts are affected.

Review **What is an ecosystem?**

A bald eagle lives high in the trees of the forest.

A marmot lives on the forest floor.

A mushroom gets moisture from the soil.

A fossil on a rock found in Wyoming shows a fish that lived millions of years ago.

Slow Changes to the Earth

Some physical processes that affect Earth are slow and take millions of years to change things. For example, scientists know that at one time there was just one huge continent. Over time, it broke into several smaller ones, which are still slowly drifting apart. Humans living on the continents today are hardly aware that this movement is happening.

Another very slow physical process is erosion. **Erosion** is the wearing away of Earth's surface. The Grand Canyon was formed by millions of years of water erosion. The Colorado River wore away its rocky bed to form a canyon one mile deep.

Review What are two natural processes that are slowly changing Earth?

The Grand Canyon

Understanding the World in Spatial Terms

Worn through layers of rock by water erosion, the Grand Canyon is more than one mile deep in some places. The rocks at the bottom of the canyon are two billion years old.

UNITED STATES

Map Key

35	Interstate highway
57	U.S. highway
44	State highway
▨	Park
•	City
■	Point of interest

Virgin R.
Virgin Mountains
Grand Wash
Lake Mead
Shivwits Plateau
Rampart (Sloth) Cave
Colorado R.
GRAND
Toroweap Point
Vulcans Throne
Lava Falls Rapids
Separation Canyon
Kaibab
Pipe Spring Natl. Mon.
Kanab Cr.
Colorado R.
CANYON
Granite Gorge
Supai
Pt. Sublime
Hermits Rest
Grand Canyon Village
Coconino Plateau
Havasu Cr.
Tusayan
Lees Ferry
Colorado R.
Jacob Lake
Kaibab Plateau
NORTH RIM
Marble Canyon
Kaibito Plateau
Pt. Imperial
Bright Angel Pt.
Cape Royal
Phantom Ranch
SOUTH RIM
Little Colorado R.
Quivero
Red Lake
ARIZONA
Truxton
Seligman
Williams
Flagstaff

0 10 20 Miles
0 10 20 Kilometers

Sudden Changes to the Earth

Some physical processes that affect Earth happen very quickly. Activity taking place beneath Earth's surface can cause earthquakes and the eruption of volcanoes.

Floods, powerful storms, forest fires, and other disasters can change an area in a matter of days. A **disaster** is an event that causes great harm or damage.

FAST FACT

When Mount Saint Helens erupted thousands of years ago, the lava flowed out of the volcano. It left behind Ape Cave, the longest lava tube in the United States.

This photograph shows the eruption of Mount Saint Helens, a volcano in Washington State, in 1980.

Natural disasters can cause great harm to plants and animals. When they happen where people live, they destroy property and make life difficult. People need to learn how to prepare for natural disasters.

Review **What are two kinds of natural disasters?**

A forest fire, like this one in Yellowstone National Park, is a natural disaster that can quickly change the environment.

LESSON 2
Review

1 **Main Idea** What are some of the natural processes that form the environment?

2 **Vocabulary** Use the vocabulary word **ecosystem** in a sentence to describe plant and animal life in a forest.

3 **Reading Skill—Making Inferences** In the ecosystem of a pond, what might happen to plants and animals if there is a lack of rain?

4 **Your Community** How have natural processes and changes affected your community?

 Performance—Diagram an Ecosystem Find a photograph of an ecosystem. It could be a forest, a desert, a swamp, a rain forest, a pond, or an ocean. Then do some research so you can draw pictures of the plants and animals that live in the ecosystem. Paste your pictures around the photograph of the ecosystem.

Compare Bar Graphs

▶ Why It Matters

Scientists keep records about natural disasters so that they can discover patterns. They can show these records in a number of ways. One way they do this is by using bar graphs.

▶ What You Need to Know

Scientists use the Richter scale, a table of numbers, to measure the magnitude, or strength, of an earthquake. The scale is named for its inventor, Dr. Charles F. Richter of the California Institute of Technology.

Earthquakes with a Richter number of 2 are usually the smallest that can be felt. Earthquakes with a magnitude of 6 or higher are very strong and may cause great damage.

The bar graphs on the next page show earthquake activity in the United States between 1990 and 2000. Bar Graph A shows earthquakes with a magnitude of 5. Bar Graph B shows earthquakes with a magnitude of 3.

▶ Practice the Skill

Use the bar graphs to help you answer these questions.

1 In Bar Graph A, what year had the most earthquakes?

2 In Bar Graph B, what year had the fewest earthquakes?

3 How many earthquakes with a magnitude of 5 happened in 1992?

4 How many earthquakes with a magnitude of 3 happened in 2000?

▶ Apply What You Learned

Bar graphs can be used to compare numbers of things. Think of some numbers you want to compare. One example might be the number of baskets that each member of a team made during a basketball game. Collect the information, and use the numbers to create a bar graph. Share your bar graph with your family.

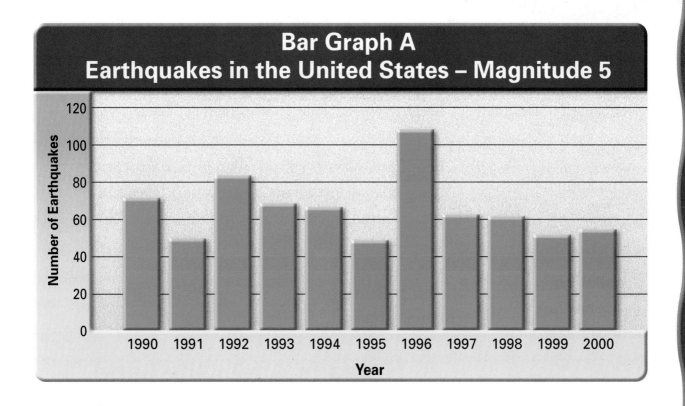

Bar Graph A
Earthquakes in the United States – Magnitude 5

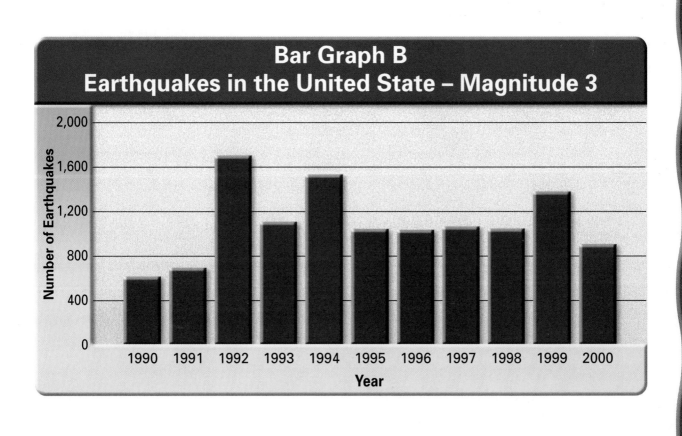

Bar Graph B
Earthquakes in the United State – Magnitude 3

3

Human Processes

Main Idea
Human processes affect the natural environment.

Vocabulary

pollution
conservation
natural hazard

People use Earth's land, water, and air in many ways. They set up farms to grow foods and ranches to raise animals. They use some land for factories and other land for homes and shopping centers. They make some land into places where people can enjoy themselves. All of these changes to the land can create problems.

Humans Affect the Land

To get the things they need, people often use up most or all of the nearby natural resources.

A housing development in the desert near Palm Springs, California

Locate It

Palm Springs, California

Scientists test the water after an oil spill near the Galapagos Islands.

Locate It

Galapagos Islands, Ecuador

They cut down forests to get wood for fuel, for building houses, and for making furniture. It takes many years for a forest to grow again.

People also cause pollution. **Pollution** is anything that makes a natural resource, such as air, soil, or water, dirty or unsafe to use. If water is polluted with oil, it is unsafe to drink. Oil in the water affects animals, too.

People can prevent pollution, and they can replace and protect the natural resources that they use. One way to protect resources is through conservation. **Conservation** means working to save resources and make them last longer.

Review What is pollution?

Planting new trees is a way that people can replace some of the resources that they use.

Julia Morgan
1872–1957

Character Trait: Responsibility

In 1904 Julia Morgan became the first woman architect in California. She designed schools, churches, stores, and homes. Her buildings were made with extra-strong materials. In 1906 an earthquake destroyed most of the city of San Francisco. But some of Morgan's buildings were still standing! So people asked her to design more buildings. Julia Morgan cared very much about her work. She said, "My buildings will be my legacy [gift to the world]. . .they will speak for me long after I'm gone."

MULTIMEDIA BIOGRAPHIES
GO ONLINE
Visit The Learning Site at **www.harcourtschool.com/biographies**
to learn about other famous people.

Protection from Natural Hazards

A **natural hazard** is a possible harmful event that is not caused by humans. It may be difficult or impossible to predict. Earthquakes, tornadoes, blizzards, hurricanes, forest fires, floods, and eruptions of volcanoes are examples of natural hazards.

People need to be prepared to survive if a natural hazard becomes a natural disaster. California has had many earthquakes in the past. Many communities there have passed laws requiring buildings to be made stronger. These communities also teach their citizens what to do if an earthquake happens.

This photograph shows the damage after the 1906 San Francisco earthquake.

People who live where tornadoes are a natural hazard prepare safe shelters. People who live where forest fires are a hazard cut down dry grasses around their homes.

Many riverside communities build dams across the rivers. The dams allow them to control the flow of water to prevent flooding.

Review What can people who live where there are natural hazards do to prepare themselves?

Recent earthquake damage in California

Disaster Plan Tips

● Have supplies on hand such as flashlights, extra batteries, first aid kits, and water.

● Memorize emergency contacts such as 9-1-1.

● Tune in to local radio or television stations or go on the Internet for news and information.

Analyze Charts

❖ What preparations can you make?

LESSON 3
Review

❶ **Main Idea** How can human actions lead to changes in the environment?

❷ **Vocabulary** Write a sentence about a **natural hazard** that you would like to know more about.

❸ **Reading Skill—Making Inferences** What do you think happens to the environment if people conserve, or wisely use, natural resources?

❹ **Your Community** What are the ways people in your community work together to improve the environment?

Performance—Recycling Research Set up a "recycling center" in your class. Then research what kinds of products can be recycled. For example, you might collect and sort newspapers and aluminum cans. Add the items to the recycling center and invite other classes to see it.

EXAMINE Primary Sources

Many Kinds of Maps

The Library of Congress, in our nation's capital, has a huge collection of maps. There are many different kinds of maps in this collection. Some of the maps are hundreds of years old. The maps on these pages were drawn by George Washington.

FROM THE MAP ROOM OF THE LIBRARY OF CONGRESS IN WASHINGTON, D.C.

This map drawn in 1766 is of River Farm, land that George Washington purchased next to his home in Mount Vernon.

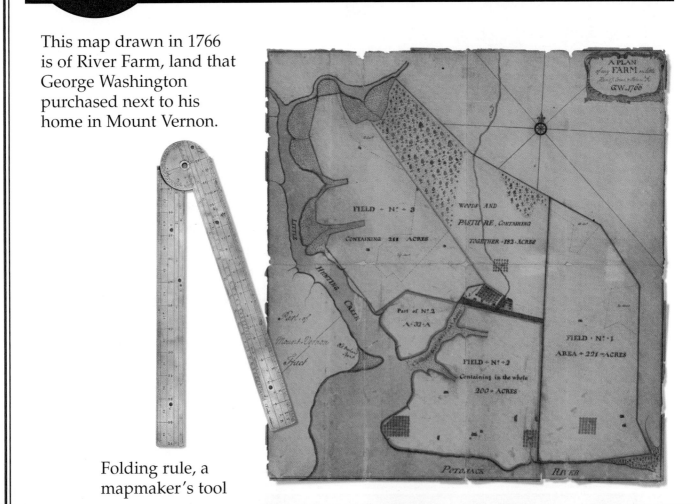

Folding rule, a mapmaker's tool

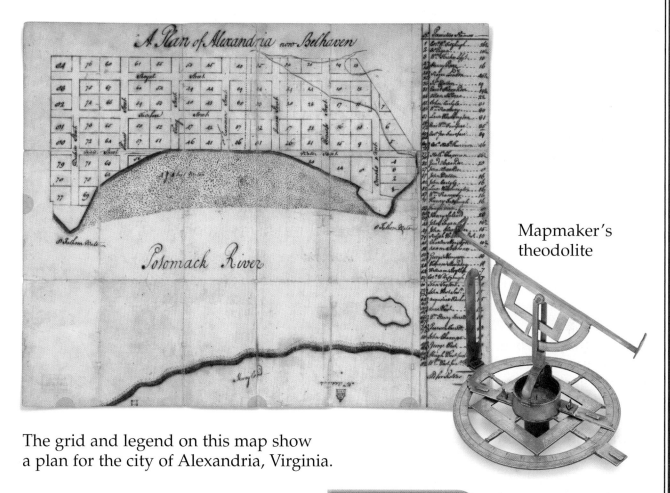

The grid and legend on this map show
a plan for the city of Alexandria, Virginia.

Mapmaker's
theodolite

Analyze the Primary Source

① How are the 1766 map of
River Farm and the city plan
for Alexandria, Virginia,
different?

② What body of water is
shown on both maps?

③ Have you ever seen tools
like the ones shown?
How might mapmakers
use these tools?

Activity

Draw a Map   With a small group,
imagine that you are building a new
restaurant. Decide where in your
community you think the restaurant
should be built. Draw a map that
shows how to get to the new
restaurant from your school. Add a
map key to explain the symbols you
used and a compass rose for
directions. Then give your map a title.

Research

Visit The Learning Site at
**www.harcourtschool.com/
primarysources** to research other
primary sources.

6 Review and Test Preparation

Use Your Reading Skills

Complete this graphic organizer to show that you understand how to make predictions about geographers. A copy of this graphic organizer appears on page 45 of the Activity Book.

Predictions About Geographers

WHAT YOU READ	WHAT YOU KNOW	PREDICTIONS
A geographer is a person who studies Earth and its people. Geographers divide areas of the United States into regions.		

THINK & WRITE

Write a List Using a map of your state, write a list of relative positions that describe your community's location. Use the compass rose to help you determine directions.

Write a Paragraph That Compares Choose one natural process that is slow and one that is fast. Write a paragraph that compares those two processes.

Use Vocabulary

Write the word that correctly matches each definition.

> **geographer (p. 172) disaster (p. 184)**
> **region (p. 174)   conservation (p.189)**

1 Working to save resources or make them last longer is ___.

2 A person who studies Earth and its people is a ___.

3 A large area with at least one feature that makes it different from other areas is called a ___.

4 A ___ is a happening that causes great harm or damage.

Recall Facts

Answer the questions.

5 What are three types of pollution?

6 Name a natural hazard that could affect your community. What can people do to prepare for it?

7 Why are trees important in a forest ecosystem?

Write the letter of the best choice.

8 **Test Prep** When you describe where a place is located by comparing it to another location, you are describing its—
A exact location.
B relative location.
C ecosystem.
D region.

9 **Test Prep** ___ is a slow physical process that affects Earth's surface.
F Erosion
G Fire
H Exploring
J Recycling

10 **Test Prep** ___ is made up of plants and animals living together in an environment.
A Agriculture
B Conservation
C An ecosystem
D A growing season

Think Critically

11 A forest is an ecosystem. Name and describe another ecosystem.

12 Explain the relative location of your community to that of Orlando, Florida.

13 Compare your region with another region of the country. What is one feature that makes your region different from the other one?

Apply Skills

14 On the map on page 179, what point of interest is at F-4?

15 In Bar Graph A on page 187, what year had the fewest number of earthquakes? How many did that year have?

Get Ready

Niagara Falls is located on the Niagara River, which forms a natural border between New York State and Canada. For 12,000 years rushing water has worn away rock and soil. This has caused the waterfalls to move seven miles (about 11 kilometers) upstream. These waterfalls include the Canadian Falls, also called the Horseshoe Falls, and the American Falls.

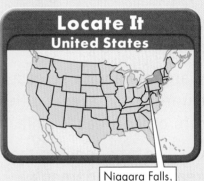

Locate It
United States

Niagara Falls, New York

What to See

Most of the Niagara River's water rushes over the Horseshoe Falls. 600,000 gallons (2,271,240 liters) pour over the rocky ledge per second!

Nearby power plants use the energy of the falling water to turn machines that produce electricity.

Visitors to the Hurricane Deck are provided with raincoats. Without the raincoats, they would be soaked by the blowing spray. The waterfall is just 25 feet (about 8 meters) from the deck.

Since 1848, boats have taken visitors through the foaming waters at the base of the waterfalls.

Take a Field Trip

A VIRTUAL TOUR
Visit The Learning Site at **www.harcourtschool.com/tours** to take virtual tours of other parks and scenic areas.

A VIDEO TOUR
Check your media center or classroom library for a video featuring a segment from Reading Rainbow.

Use Vocabulary

Write the word that matches each definition.

1 landforms that have steep sides and a flat top

plateaus (p. 148) **valleys** (p. 148)

2 a waterway that is built by people

harbor (p. 162) **canal** (p. 164)

3 the pattern of weather a place has over time

climate (p. 150)
environment (p. 160)

4 low land that lies between mountains or hills

desert (p. 150) **valley** (p. 148)

5 the wearing away of Earth's surface

pollution (p. 189) **erosion** (p. 182)

6 a possible harmful event not caused by humans

conservation (p. 189)
natural hazard (p. 190)

7 a large area with at least one feature that makes it different from other areas

region (p. 174)
grid system (p. 178)

Recall Facts

Answer the questions.

8 How do people change the land they live on?

9 Many natural resources are mined in the United States. Give four examples.

10 What are some natural hazards people need to be prepared for?

Write the letter of the best choice.

11 **Test Prep** A bridge is an example of a—
A human feature.
B natural feature.
C landform.
D natural resource.

12 **Test Prep** A crossroads is a place where—
F you can walk across a road.
G a road crosses over a stream.
H two routes meet and continue on.
J a road splits into two roads.

13 **Test Prep** Four regions of the United States are—
A mountains, hills, valleys, plains.
B Northeast, South, Middle West, West.
C Iowa, Arizona, Oregon, Maine.
D states, cities, suburbs, rural areas.

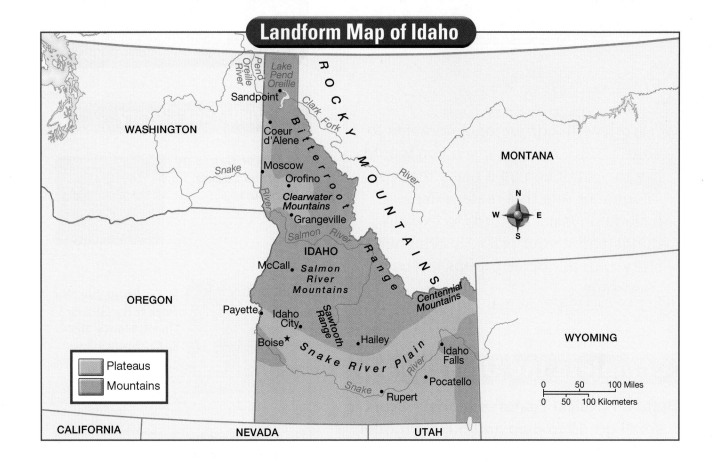

Landform Map of Idaho

Plateaus
Mountains

Think Critically

14 Compare the growing seasons of two communities that have different climates. One of the communities can be your own.

15 What is the relative location of your community to Washington, D.C.?

16 What kind of natural disaster could happen where you live? What could people in your community do to prepare for it?

Apply Skills

Read a Landform Map
Use the landform map of Idaho to answer the following questions.

17 Through which landform does the Salmon River flow?

18 Is Boise closer to the Sawtooth Ranges or to the Centennial Mountains?

19 Use the distance scale on the map. About how many miles is it from Boise to Coeur d'Alene? About how many kilometers is it?

Unit Activities

GO ONLINE

Visit The Learning Site at
www.harcourtschool.com/
socialstudies/activities
for additional activities.

Write a Story

Work with a group of classmates to write a story about a place you would like to visit. It can be a place that you imagine or one that really exists. Include physical features to explain things about your place. Share your story with the other groups in your classroom.

Complete the Unit Project

Build a Physical Features Model Work in a small group to plan and build a model of the land around your community. Study your list of physical features to decide what things to include. Use clay to show the shape of the land. Then put the clay on a thick piece of cardboard. Next, paint the bodies of water on the cardboard. Now label the physical features. Share your model with other classes and explain it to them.

Visit Your Library

■ *Water Dance* by Thomas Locker. Harcourt.

■ *Fighting for the Forest* by Gloria Rand. Henry Holt & Company, Inc.

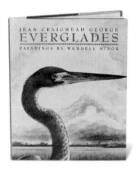

■ *Everglades* by Jean Craighead George. Scott Foresman.

Many Kinds of People

A Korean wolgeum

The Korean Moon Festival in Los Angeles, California

Many Kinds of People

66 We are more alike than unalike. 99

—Maya Angelou, *The New York Times*, January 20, 1993

Preview the Content

Quickly read over the headings, captions, graphs, maps, and charts in each lesson. Then write predictions about what you will learn in the unit. Do this by answering the "five W's." **Who** and **What** will the unit be about? **Where** are the locations you will study? **When** did the events happen? **Why** are they important? After you have read the unit, review your predictions.

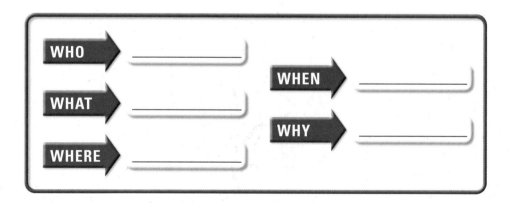

WHO ⟶ _____

WHAT ⟶ _____

WHERE ⟶ _____

WHEN ⟶ _____

WHY ⟶ _____

opportunity The chance to find a job, get an education, or have a better way of life. (page 242)

immigrant A person who comes to live in a country from somewhere else in the world. (page 242)

language The words or signs people use to communicate. (page 252)

tradition A custom, or way of doing something, that is passed on in a family. (page 245)

monument Something created to honor and remember a person or an event. (page 228)

JOHN HENRY

retold and illustrated by
Ezra Jack Keats

The story of John Henry is a folktale, a traditional story that tells about someone who does something impossible. Starting in the 1870s, railroad workers sang songs and told stories about John Henry. In this part of the story, he is working on digging a tunnel for the railroad. Workers bring in a steam drill, a machine they say can dig the tunnel faster. Find out what happens when John Henry decides to race the steam drill.

Down the tunnel came a group of men with a strange machine.

"This is a steam drill. It can drill more holes faster than any six men combined," a new man bragged. "Who can beat that?"

John Henry stepped forward. "Try me!"

A hoarse voice counted, "One, two—THREE!"

The machine shrieked as it started. John Henry swung his hammer—and a crash of steel on steel split the air!

Clang! Bang! Clang!

Hiss! Whistle! Rattle!

Men frantically heaved coal into the hungry, roaring engine and poured water into the steaming boiler.

Whoop! Clang! Whoop! Bang!

John Henry's hammer whistled as he swung it.

Chug, chug! Clatter! rattled the machine. Hour after hour raced by. The machine was ahead!

> **boiler**
> a large tank in which water is heated to make steam used for running engines

Great chunks of rock fell as John Henry ripped hole after hole into the tunnel wall. The machine rattled and whistled and drilled even faster. Then John Henry took a deep breath, picked up two sledge hammers, and swung both mighty hammers—faster and faster. He moved so fast the men could only see a blur and sparks from his striking hammers. His strokes rang out like great heart-beats.

At the other side of the tunnel the machine shrieked, groaned, and rattled, and drilled. Then all at once it shook and shuddered—wheezed—and stopped. Frantically men worked to get it going again. But they couldn't. It had collapsed! John Henry's hammering still rang and echoed through the tunnel with a strong and steady beat.

Suddenly there was a great crash. Light streamed into the dark tunnel. John Henry had broken through! Wild cries of joy burst from the men. Still holding one of his hammers, John Henry stepped out into the glowing light of a dying day. It was the last step he ever took. Even the great heart of John Henry could not bear the strain of his last task. John Henry died with his hammer in his hand.

If you listen to the <u>locomotives</u> roaring through the tunnels and across the land, you'll hear them singing—singing of that great steel-driving man—John Henry.

Listen!

locomotives (loh•kuh•MOH•tivz) engines used to pull the cars of railroad trains

Think About It

1 Why do people create folktales?

2 Use the illustrations to retell the story of John Henry.

Read a Book

TIME FOR KIDS READERS
The Amish
Harcourt   by Jeri Cipriano

TIME FOR KIDS READERS
Ancient **Egypt**
Harcourt   by Jeri Cipriano

TIME FOR KIDS READERS
Sights, Sounds, **Celebrations**
Harcourt   by Jeri Cipriano

Start the Unit Project

Story Scrapbook Use the library to find out what stories are told in other countries and what each says about that country's culture. Make a list of these stories and the ways in which they are similar to stories you already know. Your list will help you select stories for your scrapbook.

Use Technology

GO ONLINE

Visit The Learning Site at **www.harcourtschool.com/ socialstudies** for additional activities, primary sources, and other resources to use in this unit.

Orlando, Florida

People travel from across the United States to visit Orlando, Florida. On a boat at one of the city's theme parks, they celebrate America's culture.

Locate It

FLORIDA

Orlando

Chapter 7

American Culture

> **" America is . . . something only if it consists of all of us. "**
>
> —President Woodrow Wilson,
> from a speech in January 1916

CHAPTER READING SKILL

Summarize

When you **summarize**, you retell the main events and ideas of a passage in your own words.

As you read this chapter, list some important topics, along with events and ideas based on that topic. Then use that list to summarize what you have read.

TOPIC	EVENTS AND IDEAS	SUMMARY

Stories People Tell

Main Idea
Myths and legends are important to every community.

Vocabulary

literature
myth
tall tale
character trait
legend

People express their culture, or customs and beliefs, in many ways. One way to express culture is through literature. **Literature** includes the stories and poems that people write to share their ideas.

Greek and Roman Myths

The Greeks and Romans, who lived thousands of years ago, told stories known as myths. A **myth** uses the actions of gods and goddesses to explain why something in nature is the way it is. Myths were important in the culture and religion of both ancient peoples.

Locate It

Rome, Italy

Athens, Greece

The Parthenon in Athens, Greece, was built to honor the goddess Athena.

Zeus
(Greek name)
Jupiter
(Roman name)
Ruler of the gods

Hera
(Greek name)
Juno
(Roman name)
Protector
of humans

Poseidon
(Greek name)
Neptune
(Roman name)
God of the sea

Demeter
(Greek name)
Ceres
(Roman name)
Goddess of
growing things

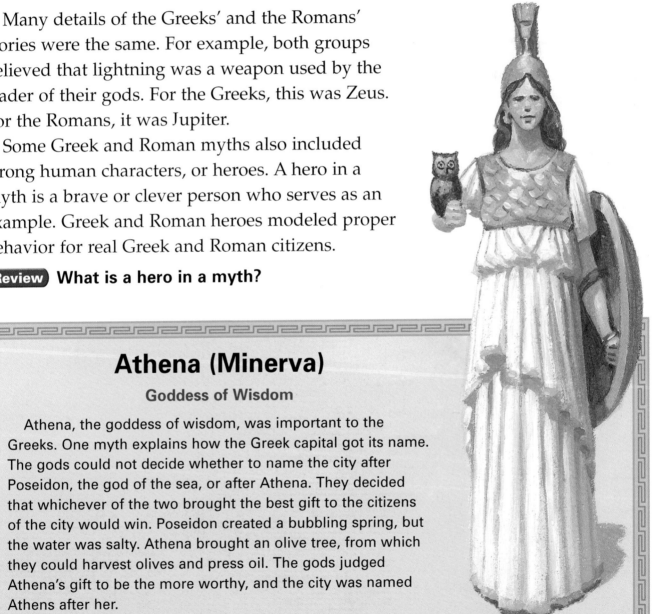

Many details of the Greeks' and the Romans' stories were the same. For example, both groups believed that lightning was a weapon used by the leader of their gods. For the Greeks, this was Zeus. For the Romans, it was Jupiter.

Some Greek and Roman myths also included strong human characters, or heroes. A hero in a myth is a brave or clever person who serves as an example. Greek and Roman heroes modeled proper behavior for real Greek and Roman citizens.

Review What is a hero in a myth?

Athena (Minerva)

Goddess of Wisdom

Athena, the goddess of wisdom, was important to the Greeks. One myth explains how the Greek capital got its name. The gods could not decide whether to name the city after Poseidon, the god of the sea, or after Athena. They decided that whichever of the two brought the best gift to the citizens of the city would win. Poseidon created a bubbling spring, but the water was salty. Athena brought an olive tree, from which they could harvest olives and press oil. The gods judged Athena's gift to be the more worthy, and the city was named Athens after her.

Paul Bunyan

Americans share tall tales for some of the same reasons the Greeks and Romans told myths. A **tall tale** uses humorous exaggeration to explain how something came to be the way it is. One of the best-known heroes in American tall tales is Paul Bunyan.

Paul Bunyan is a make-believe giant with great strength. In one story, he digs a hole in the ground that becomes Puget Sound, a body of water in Washington State. In another story, he clears trees from North Dakota and South Dakota to get the land ready for settlers. Many stories about Paul Bunyan include his great blue ox, Babe. In one, the giant logger scoops out the Great Lakes to provide water for Babe!

Review According to one tall tale, how was Puget Sound formed?

Pecos Bill

Pecos Bill is a tall-tale hero of the American Southwest. His superhuman deeds illustrated the **character traits** of strength, courage, and humor. The stories say that Pecos Bill was born in Texas in the 1830s. When he fell out of his parents' wagon near the Pecos River, coyotes found him and raised him. When he grew up, he rode a mountain lion and used a rattlesnake as a whip. One dry year, he drained the Rio Grande to water his ranch—the entire state of New Mexico.

Edward O'Reilly wrote the first stories about Pecos Bill in 1923. Other writers retold his tales and added more of their own. O'Reilly claimed that the stories came from tales told by real cowhands.

Review **Why was Pecos Bill a hero to people settling the land?**

Casey Jones

Casey Jones

Unlike myths and tall tales, legends often are based on fact. A **legend** is a tale that may have started as a true story about a real person or event. However, as it was repeated over time, details were added that did not really happen.

One such American legend is the story of John Luther "Casey" Jones. Jones was a railroad engineer who worked for the Illinois Central Railroad. On April 30, 1900, he volunteered to take the place of another engineer who had become ill.

Casey Jones was driving a train like this one the night of the accident.

Near Vaughan, Mississippi, Casey Jones saw two freight trains blocking the tracks ahead. He could have jumped to save his life, but instead he stayed on board to apply the brakes. When his train smashed into the other two, Jones was the only person to die. If he had not stayed in the engine to slow his train, many others would have lost their lives.

That train wreck might have been forgotten if it had not been for Wallace Saunders. Saunders was a railroad worker who wrote a song about Casey Jones and the Mississippi train wreck. Over time, it became a legend in song form about the brave engineer.

Review **What is a legend?**

Lanterns like this one were used to signal trains at night or in bad weather.

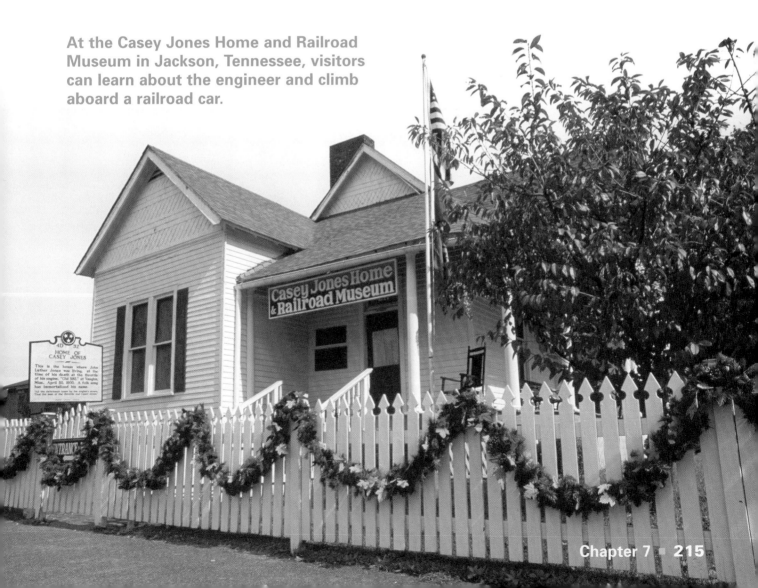

At the Casey Jones Home and Railroad Museum in Jackson, Tennessee, visitors can learn about the engineer and climb aboard a railroad car.

Daniel Boone

The story of Daniel Boone is another legend in American culture. Boone opened the West to settlement by clearing a path through the Appalachian Mountains. He was the first to lead groups of settlers through the Cumberland Gap from Virginia to what is now Kentucky. There they found lands that were good for farming and hunting. As more settlers followed Boone to Kentucky, the path he used came to be called the Wilderness Road.

Daniel Boone proved his courage often in the wilderness, where he kept the settlers safe from many dangers. The stories of his many brave deeds and daring adventures made him a national hero. Daniel Boone became a model of courage and leadership.

Review **How did Daniel Boone open the West to settlement?**

This powder horn for holding gun powder was owned by Daniel Boone.

This painting by George Caleb Bingham shows Daniel Boone leading a group of settlers through the Cumberland Gap.

The Cumberland Gap

Understanding Places and Regions

Daniel Boone used the Cumberland Gap several times before he cleared the Wilderness Road and led settlers through it. This low spot in the Appalachian Mountains is found at the point where present-day Kentucky, Tennessee, and Virginia come together. Between 1775 and 1800, more than 200,000 settlers passed through this "gap" on their way to the West.

LESSON I
Review

1 **Main Idea**   Why are myths and legends an important part of a community's culture?

2 **Vocabulary**   Write a paragraph that tells about your favorite **tall tale** or **legend**.

3 **Reading Skill—Summarize** America's legendary heroes have many qualities in common. Write a paragraph summarizing the character traits that the heroes you have read about share.

4 **Your Community**   Choose a physical feature in your community, and make up a tall tale that might explain how it got there.

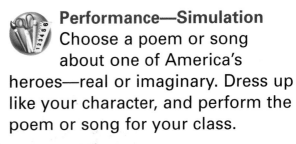

Performance—Simulation Choose a poem or song about one of America's heroes—real or imaginary. Dress up like your character, and perform the poem or song for your class.

Skills
READING

Tell Fact from Fiction

▶ ## Why It Matters

Legends are tales that often begin with real people and real events. As they are retold over time, more and more details are added.

Sometimes facts turn into fiction. It is important, when you are reading, to be able to tell one from the other.

▶ ## What You Need to Know

Facts are statements that can be proved. In stories about real people, things, or events, there are often dates and place names that can be checked.

In **fiction**, the story is made up. It may be based on a real person or event, but many of the details are imaginary.

"The Ballad of Davy Crockett"

Born on a mountaintop in Tennessee
Greenest state in the land of the free
Raised in the woods so he knew every tree
Killed him a bear when he was only three.
Davy, Davy Crockett, king of the wild frontier!

He went off to Congress and served a spell
Fixing up the governments and laws as well
Took over Washington so we heard tell
And patched up the crack in the Liberty Bell.
Davy, Davy Crockett, seeing his duty clear!

Grateful acknowledgment is made to Wonderland Music Company, Inc., for permission to reprint lyrics by Tom Blackburn from "The Ballad of Davy Crockett" (music by George Bruns). © 1954 by Wonderland Music Company, Inc.

Practice the Skill

On these pages are two selections about Davy Crockett. One is a song, and the other is an article. Use the selections to answer the following questions.

1 Which selection contains *facts*? How do you know?

2 Which selection is *fiction*? What details helped you decide?

3 In which selection do you learn more about Davy Crockett?

Apply What You Learned

Use what you have learned to think about what you read. As you read, you can ask yourself these questions.

- Is this fact or fiction?
- Can this be proved?
- How can it be proved?
- Which details are imaginary?

David "Davy" Crockett
(1786–1836)

David Crockett, one of America's most famous symbols of the Western frontier, was born in Greene County, Tennessee. In 1813 he became a scout for the United States Army. From 1821 to 1825 Crockett served in the Tennessee legislature. He served in the U.S. House of Representatives in 1827, 1829, and 1833.

In early February of 1836, Davy Crockett went to San Antonio, Texas, to help American soldiers. He died there just a month later, at the Battle of the Alamo, on March 6, 1836.

Lesson

2

Main Idea
Some real American heroes have been important to our country.

Vocabulary

disease

vaccine

Real American Heroes

Some people have helped our country grow and change in important ways. These people are real American heroes.

Frederick Douglass

Born into a family of enslaved Africans, Frederick Douglass did not have much chance for a good life. He lived with his grandmother because his mother had to work on a farm many miles away.

Young Frederick was given an unexpected opportunity few enslaved children had—the chance to learn to read and write. When he read about freedom, he knew that was what he wanted more than anything.

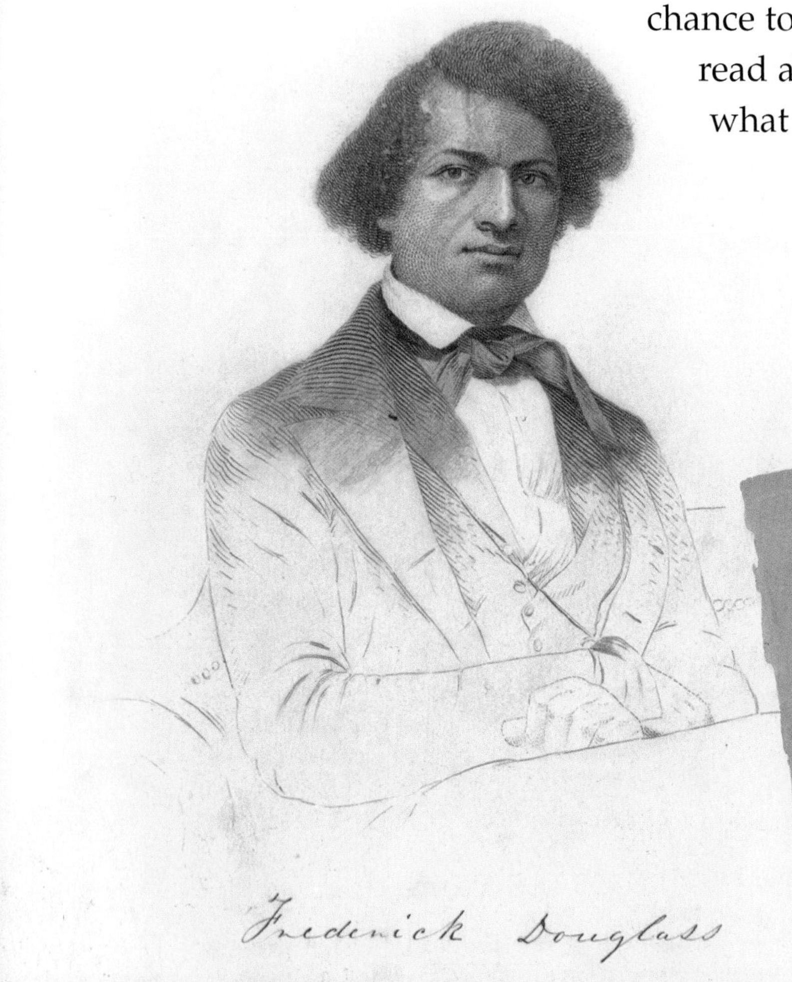
Frederick Douglass

In 1845 Frederick Douglass published this book. It tells the story of his life as a slave.

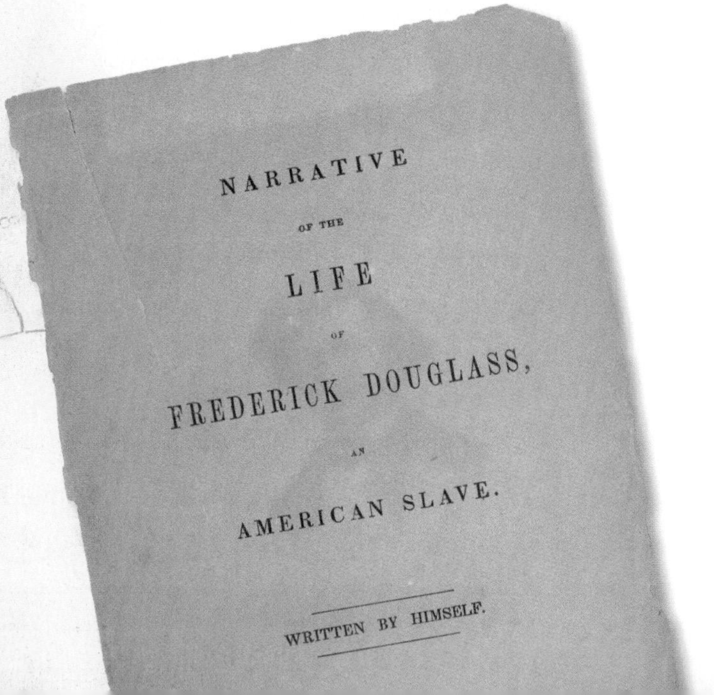
NARRATIVE
OF THE
LIFE
OF
FREDERICK DOUGLASS,
AN
AMERICAN SLAVE.
WRITTEN BY HIMSELF.

Beginning in 1847 in Rochester, New York, Douglass published the *North Star* newspaper.

When he was still a young man, Frederick Douglass escaped to the North, where he could be free. He continued his education, becoming a speaker for the Massachusetts Antislavery Society. He spoke out against slavery wherever he went. Soon he began publishing a newspaper called the *North Star*, in which he wrote about slavery.

Review **Why was learning to read important to Frederick Douglass?**

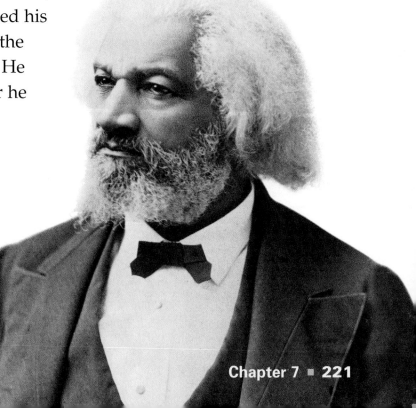

Frederick Douglass spent most of his life speaking and writing about freedom.

Chief Plenty Coups

In the late 1850s, a Crow Indian boy named Plenty Coups (KOO) had a dream in which the buffalo disappeared. In his dream a storm destroyed all the trees except for one.

The leaders of the boy's tribe believed that the storm stood for the power of the white newcomers. The trees were the Indian tribes that fought against it. The single tree was the Crow nation, which did not fight. Because of the dream, the Crows protected travelers who passed through their lands. Later, as chief of one of the largest Crow bands, Plenty Coups remembered his boyhood dream, which reminded him to look for peaceful solutions to problems.

Review **What did Plenty Coups dream?**

Chief Plenty Coups wears the traditional clothing of a Crow leader.

In 1879, Chief Plenty Coups (front row, second from the right) made the first of many trips to Washington, D.C., to speak to leaders in the U.S. government.

Jonas Salk

Jonas Salk worked in medical research, looking for the causes of illness. In the early 1950s, people were very frightened of a disease called polio. A **disease** is an illness or other condition that harms a living thing. Polio spread from one person to another and left people partly or completely paralyzed.

Salk and his research partners developed a **vaccine**, or medicine, that could keep people from getting the disease. To prove that the new vaccine was safe, Salk and his family were the first to use it. In 1955, it was given to more than one million schoolchildren in the United States. At last people were free of the fear of this disease.

Review How did Jonas Salk free people from the fear of polio?

In 1955, schoolchildren in San Diego, California, lined up to get their polio shots.

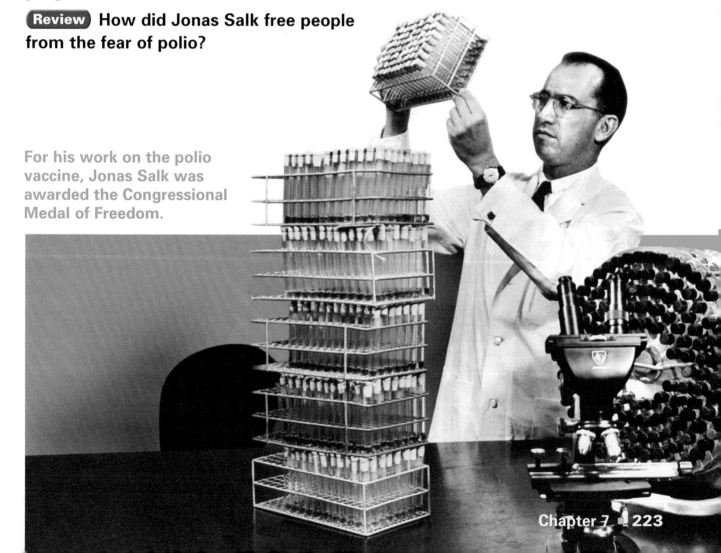

For his work on the polio vaccine, Jonas Salk was awarded the Congressional Medal of Freedom.

Rosa Parks

Rosa Parks did not set out to be a hero. Born in 1913, she grew up in Alabama when many states had separate rules for black people and white people. If a white person got onto a crowded bus, a black person had to give up his or her seat.

On December 1, 1955, Rosa Parks was riding a crowded bus home from work in Montgomery, Alabama. When a white man got on, the driver asked Parks to give up her seat to him. When Parks refused, she was arrested. She decided to fight the unfair charges in court.

Rosa Parks had the courage to take an important step against unfair treatment. Her action made a difference to Montgomery, to Alabama, and to the entire United States.

Review **How did Rosa Parks show her courage?**

Rosa Parks receiving an award during a ceremony in Washington, D.C.

Rosa Parks riding on a bus after black people could no longer be forced to give up their seats

Cesar Chavez

Cesar Chavez was a Chicano, or Mexican American, who was born near Yuma, Arizona. He lived with his grandparents, who moved to the United States from Mexico, and his parents. In 1937 Cesar's parents lost their farm in Arizona, and the family moved to California. There they worked in the fields for others instead of for themselves. They had to move from place to place as the fields were planted and harvested.

An eagle is the symbol for the NFWA organization.

Mexican American farmworkers were very poor. Cesar Chavez started an organization called the National Farm Workers Association to protect their rights. The NFWA also worked to get them better pay and living conditions. Today the lives of Mexican American farmworkers are better than they were in the past. Cesar Chavez made a difference in the lives of many thousands of people.

Review **How did Cesar Chavez help Mexican American farm workers?**

Cesar Chavez speaks to a group of people about the need for better working conditions for farmworkers.

Eleanor Roosevelt

Although she was shy as a child, Eleanor Roosevelt became one of the most admired women of her time. In 1933 her husband, Franklin D. Roosevelt, was elected President of the United States. As First Lady, she worked to end poor living conditions.

In her newspaper column "My Day," Eleanor Roosevelt wrote about her ideas for change. When her husband was disabled by polio, she traveled around the world to speak for him. She once said, "If anyone were to ask me what I want out of life, I would say the opportunity for doing something useful, for in no other way, I am convinced, can true happiness be attained (reached)."

Eleanor Roosevelt rides on a coal car with miners to learn about their working conditions.

President Franklin D. Roosevelt and First Lady Eleanor Roosevelt on their way to dinner

After World War II, Eleanor Roosevelt was elected to lead the Human Rights Commission in the newly formed United Nations. On December 10, 1948, under her leadership, the Universal Declaration of Human Rights was published. This document states the basic rights of all people in the world. These include the rights to free speech, a fair trial, and an education.

Review **What did Eleanor Roosevelt write about in her newspaper column?**

Eleanor Roosevelt holds a document she helped publish.

LESSON 2
Review

1 Main Idea How have real heroes been important to our country?

2 Vocabulary Use the vocabulary word **vaccine** in a sentence to tell about scientific research.

3 Reading Skill—Summarize Choose one of the heroes you read about in this lesson. Write a short summary of what he or she did. In your summary, include one of the person's heroic character traits.

4 Your Community Make a list of two or three people you think are real heroes. Then interview adult family members to see who their heroes are. Talk about the reasons for your choices.

Performance—Write an Article Choose a person who has made a difference in your state or in the nation. Research the person on the Internet. Use the facts you find to write a short article to add to a class album of heroes.

Main Idea
People celebrate their heritage in many ways.

Vocabulary

monument

sculpture

memorial

At the National Statuary Hall in Washington, D.C., visitors can see sculptures of leaders from each state.

Our American Heritage

The United States was built by people who came to this land from all over the world. Our heritage, the values and ways of life passed down to us from our ancestors, blends many cultures. Americans celebrate their heritage in many ways.

Monuments and Memorials

One way people celebrate their heritage is by building monuments to honor their leaders and the ideas they stand for. A **monument** is something created to honor and remember a person or event. It may be a sculpture, wall, fountain, or other lasting marker. A **sculpture** is a piece of art carved from stone or made from metal or other materials. One place to see sculptures is at the National Statuary Hall in Washington, D.C.

Elisabet Ney
1833–1907

Character Trait: Self-Discipline

Elisabet Ney dreamed of becoming a sculptor. Although people tried to discourage her, she did not give up. In 1890, Ney moved to Texas from Germany. She sculpted a statue of Sam Houston, the first president of the Republic of Texas. She also sculpted one of Stephen Austin, another important early Texas leader. Both sculptures are now part of the National Statuary Hall.

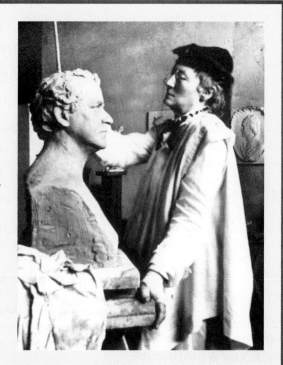

MULTIMEDIA BIOGRAPHIES
Visit The Learning Site at www.harcourtschool.com/biographies
to learn about other famous people.

The House of Representatives first met in a beautiful hall. However, the country grew, and in time there were too many representatives to fit in that hall. When a new hall was opened, a use for the old space was found. It was turned into the National Statuary Hall, in which citizens are honored. Each state was invited to choose two people who have made a difference within the community. Sculptures were made of these people and sent to Washington, D.C. Today visitors to the nation's capital can view lifelike statues of these citizens who have been honored by their states.

This marble sculpture of Sam Houston was sculpted by Elisabet Ney.

Many communities remember their special members with memorials. A **memorial** is something that keeps a memory alive. It may be a monument, or it may be something different, such as an event. In Val-Kill, New York, people have created a "living memorial" that honors Eleanor Roosevelt.

Each summer, the Girls' Leadership Workshop is held in what was once Roosevelt's home. Dozens of young women from high schools around the country are chosen to attend. They learn ways to give community service and to work for human rights. An event that passes on the values Eleanor Roosevelt felt were important seems like the kind of memorial she would have liked best.

At the end of the workshop, each young woman receives a certificate.

Review What is the "living memorial" to Eleanor Roosevelt?

The Staff and Members of the Board of Directors of
The Eleanor Roosevelt Center at Val-Kill (ERVK)

certify to all that

Bailey Lewis

has participated fully and actively in the

Girls Leadership Workshop

July 28 - August 5, 2001 at the Eleanor Roosevelt
National Historic Site, Val-Kill
Hyde Park, New York

August 5, 2001

Date

ERVK Girls Leadership Workshop Coordinator

At the Girls' Leadership Workshop in Val-Kill, New York, young women gather to talk about events and ideas important to all citizens.

Places That Celebrate Our Heritage

On the banks of the Mississippi River in St. Louis, Missouri, the Gateway Arch rises 630 feet (192 meters) above the city. Eero Saarinen (AIR•oh SAR•uh•nuhn) was the architect who designed it. He wrote that he wanted to create a monument that would be "a landmark for our time." Construction on the arch was completed in October 1965.

His slim stainless-steel arch honors the brave pioneers who settled the West. St. Louis, often called the Gateway to the West, was the place from which they set out on their journeys. Some people still think of St. Louis as a gateway to the West for business and trade.

Architect Eero Saarinen looks at a model of the Gateway Arch.

The Gateway Arch rises above the city of St. Louis and the Mississippi River.

Gutzon Borglum and workers during the building of Mount Rushmore

The faces of the American Presidents George Washington, Thomas Jefferson, Theodore Roosevelt, and Abraham Lincoln are carved in the cliffs of Mount Rushmore.

In the Black Hills of South Dakota, a rocky cliff has been turned into a huge sculpture. Mount Rushmore National Memorial shows the faces of American Presidents George Washington, Thomas Jefferson, Theodore Roosevelt, and Abraham Lincoln. They were selected because they stand for the birth, growth, and development of our nation.

Before sculptor Gutzon Borglum began work on the memorial, he had to find the right spot. When he found what he was looking for, he said, "Here is the place! American history shall march along that skyline." Borglum and his workers used dynamite and drills to carve the faces into the cliff. The work began in 1927 and was completed by Borglum's son, Lincoln Borglum, in 1941.

Review **What does the memorial at Mount Rushmore honor?**

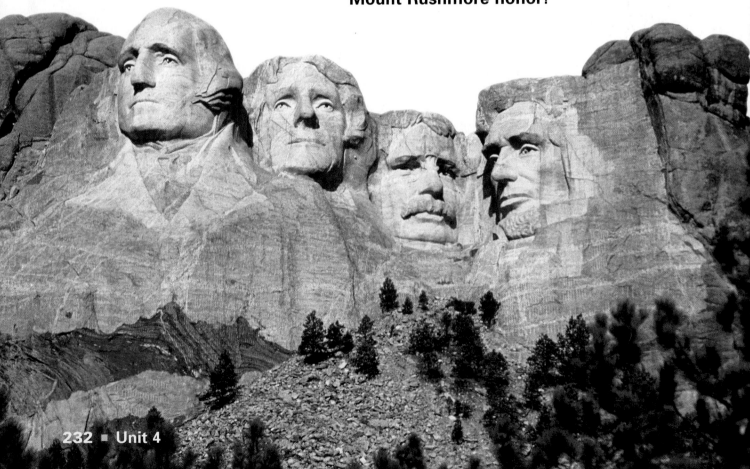

Holidays That Celebrate Our Heritage

No matter where citizens of the United States are from, they share a common identity as Americans. People from all cultures and ethnic groups come together to celebrate American holidays.

In November, Americans give thanks on Thanksgiving Day. The Pilgrims of Plymouth, Massachusetts, celebrated their first harvest in 1621. Many people think of that event as the first-ever Thanksgiving celebration. However, Native Americans had been celebrating their harvests for thousands of years.

This painting by artist Jennie Augusta Brownscombe shows the Pilgrims celebrating Thanksgiving.

• BIOGRAPHY •

Sarah Josepha Hale 1788–1879

Character Trait: Perseverance

Sarah Josepha Hale believed Thanksgiving should be a national holiday. For years she sent letters about this to the governors of all the states. In 1863 she wrote to President Abraham Lincoln. She asked him to name a day when Thanksgiving would be celebrated each year. President Lincoln chose the last Thursday of November, and the holiday was celebrated on that day until 1939. Thanksgiving Day has been held on the fourth Thursday of November since that time.

MULTIMEDIA BIOGRAPHIES
Visit The Learning Site at
www.harcourtschool.com/biographies
to learn about other famous people.

In May, Americans celebrate Memorial Day. The holiday began in Waterloo, New York, on May 5, 1866. On that day, people there gathered to lay flowers and American flags on the graves of those who had died in war. Now Memorial Day is held near the end of May. The entire nation remembers the citizens who have given their lives for their country.

Another holiday Americans celebrate is the Fourth of July. On this holiday we celebrate our country's birthday. On July 4, 1776, the United States government adopted the Declaration of Independence, which said America would no longer be ruled by the king of England.

In Chattanooga, Tennessee, people gather to celebrate Memorial Day.

The Fourth of July is a time to feel pride in our community, in our government, and in our country. Red, white, and blue are the colors of the day. Flags fly everywhere, and parades, picnics, and fireworks make our country's birthday celebration fun for all.

Review **What are the names of three holidays Americans celebrate?**

Fireworks (above) explode over the Washington Monument on the Fourth of July. People in Marietta, Georgia, enjoy a Fourth of July picnic (left).

LESSON 3
Review

1 Main Idea What are some ways people celebrate their heritage?

2 Vocabulary Use the vocabulary words **sculpture** and **memorial** in a sentence that tells the importance of artists in celebrating heritage.

3 Reading Skill—Summarize Write a short summary of the lesson. Include the names of places and events that celebrate our heritage.

4 Your Community Give two examples of monuments or memorials in your town or state.

Performance—Plan a Class Picnic Think of a food that is a part of your heritage, and write down the name of the food and its main ingredients. Then work with other classmates to combine your food ideas and plan a class picnic.

Read a Cutaway Diagram

Vocabulary

cutaway diagram

▶ Why It Matters

Knowing how to read a diagram can help you learn about something quickly. A **cutaway diagram** shows the outside and inside of an object at the same time.

▶ What You Need to Know

On a cutaway diagram, part of the object has been "cut away" to make a kind of window. A cutaway diagram can let you see the inside of something such as a computer or a monument.

The Statue of Liberty is one of our country's most famous monuments. It was given to the people of the United States by the people of France in 1884. French sculptor Frédéric-Auguste Bartholdi designed the statue and chose the location for it. The statue is displayed on an island in Upper New York Bay.

▶ Practice the Skill

Look at the cutaway diagram on page 237. It lets you see inside the Statue of Liberty. Use the diagram to answer the questions below.

1 Where is the elevator located?

2 How can people get from the pedestal to the crown?

3 Can people reach the tablet? How can you tell?

▶ Apply What You Learned

Use library books to find out what something is like inside. Draw a cutaway diagram of that object, and add a title and labels. Then use your diagram to explain to classmates what the object is like inside.

The Statue of Liberty

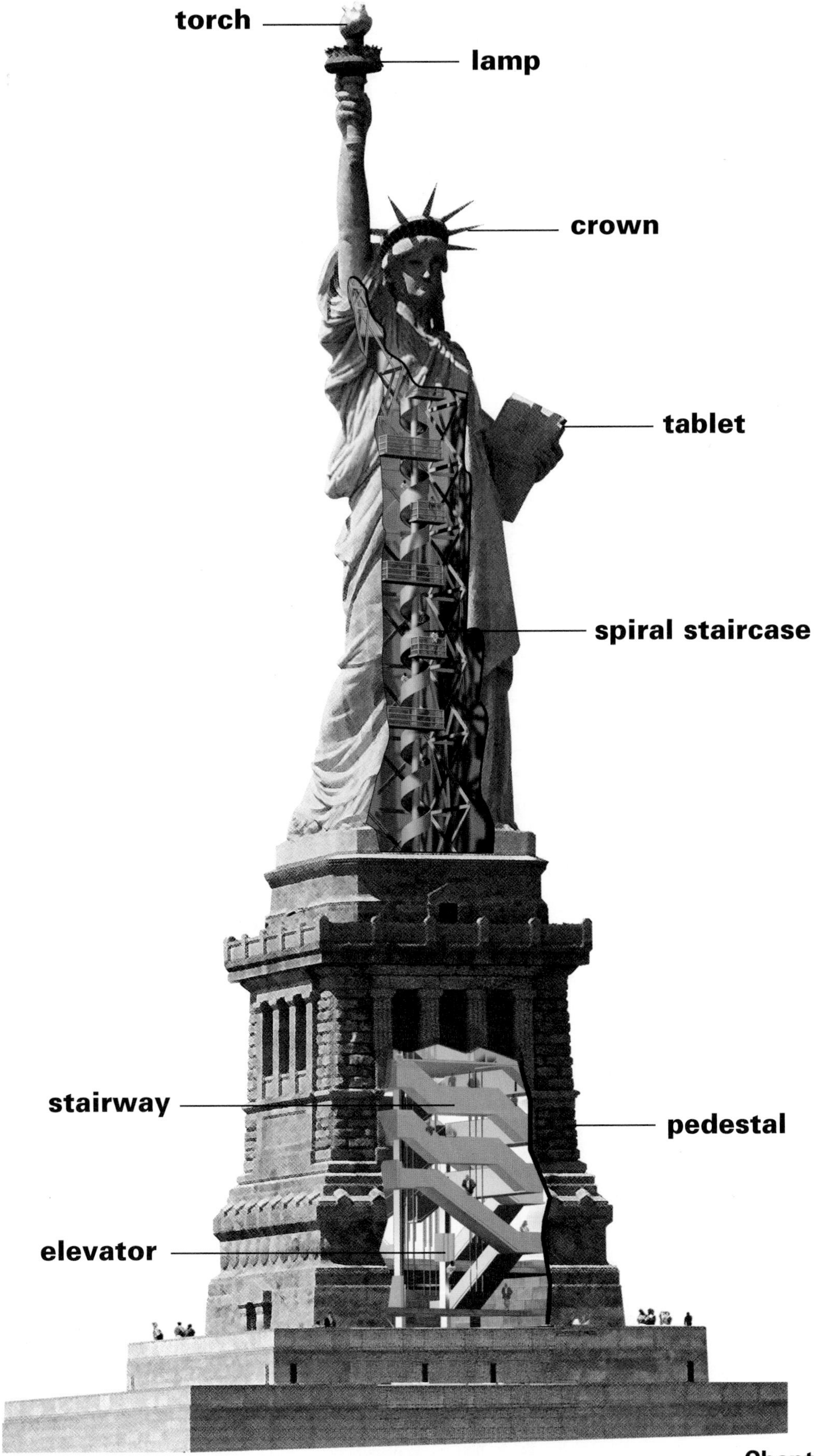

torch —

lamp

crown

tablet

spiral staircase

stairway

pedestal

elevator

7 Review and Test Preparation

Use Your Reading Skills

Complete this graphic organizer to show the events you summarized as you read. A copy of this graphic organizer appears on page 52 of the Activity Book.

Real American Heroes

HERO	ACTS	SUMMARY
Cesar Chavez	1. Started an organization called the National Farm Workers Association. 2. _____ 3. _____	_____
Eleanor Roosevelt	1. Helped publish a document stating the basic rights of all people. 2. _____ 3. _____	_____

THINK & WRITE

Write a Short Play Choose one of the heroes you read about in this chapter or another hero you know about. Write a short play, with dialogue and stage directions, that shows why he or she is a hero.

Write an Invitation Choose a local hero or community leader to be honored at a ceremony. Write an invitation in the style of a friendly letter to invite that person to the ceremony.

Use Vocabulary

Write the word that correctly completes each sentence.

literature (p. 210) fact (p. 218)
myth (p. 210) disease (p. 223)

1 Another word for *illness* is ___.

2 Stories and poems are two kinds of ___.

3 A story that uses the actions of gods to explain something in nature is a ___.

4 A ___ is a statement that can be proved.

Recall Facts

Answer these questions.

5 How did Athens, the Greek capital, get its name?

6 How did Daniel Boone show leadership and courage?

7 Why is Mount Rushmore a national monument? What does it honor?

8 **Test Prep** Which is <u>fiction</u> about Davy Crockett?

   A He was born in Tennessee.
   B He killed a bear when he was only three.
   C He served in Congress.
   D He died at the Battle of the Alamo.

9 **Test Prep** Jonas Salk became a national and international hero when he freed people from the fear of—

   F slavery.
   G polio.
   H unfair treatment.
   J lack of money.

Think Critically

10 Explain why Pecos Bill and Paul Bunyan are tall tales. Retell in your own words a story about one of these characters.

11 Do you think it was a good idea to create a National Statuary Hall to honor two people from each state? Explain your answer.

12 Name one of your heroes. What character traits does this person have that you admire?

Apply Skills

Tell Fact from Fiction

13 "The Ballad of Davy Crockett" on page 218 has both fact and fiction. Identify one example of each and tell why you made the choices you did.

Read a Cutaway Diagram

14 Use the cutaway diagram on page 237. Which section of the statue do people enter first to begin their tour?

Central Square in Boston

Many cultures are celebrated in this mural painted on a wall in Central Square in Boston, Massachusetts. The mural shows many groups of people that are part of this diverse community.

Locate It

Boston

MASSACHUSETTS

8

The Many People of a Community

66 We must be part of the community in which we live and not apart from it. 99

—Paul R. Williams,
The Will and the Way, 1994

CHAPTER READING SKILL

Determine Point of View

Point of view is the way a person feels about something.

As you read the chapter and the point-of-view feature, identify the different points of view.

SUBJECT	PERSON'S POINT OF VIEW

A Nation of Immigrants

Main Idea
Immigrants come to the United States from all over the world for many different reasons.

Vocabulary

immigrant
opportunity
tradition

Immigrants come to the United States for many reasons. An **immigrant** is someone who comes to live in a country from somewhere else in the world.

Many People Come to the United States

Most immigrants come to the United States for better **opportunity**. This means the chance to find a job, get an education, or have a better way of life.

FAST FACT Many immigrants came to the United States in the late 1800s and early 1900s. For those arriving by ship, the first thing they saw in New York harbor was the Statue of Liberty.

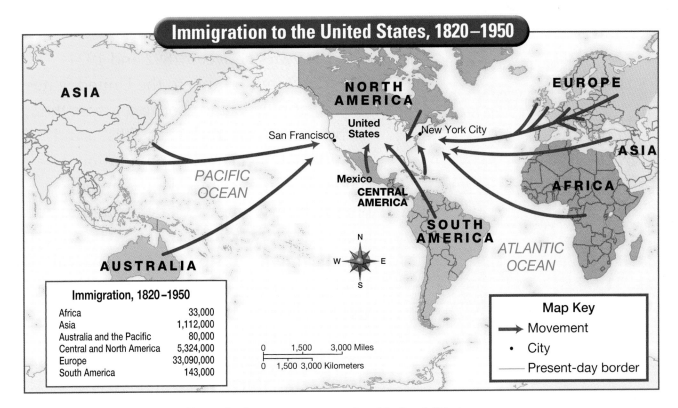

Immigration to the United States, 1820–1950

ASIA

NORTH AMERICA

EUROPE

United States

San Francisco

New York City

ASIA

PACIFIC OCEAN

Mexico

CENTRAL AMERICA

AFRICA

SOUTH AMERICA

ATLANTIC OCEAN

AUSTRALIA

N
W   E
S

Immigration, 1820–1950

Africa	33,000
Asia	1,112,000
Australia and the Pacific	80,000
Central and North America	5,324,000
Europe	33,090,000
South America	143,000

0   1,500   3,000 Miles
0   1,500 3,000 Kilometers

Map Key
→ Movement
• City
— Present-day border

GEOGRAPHY THEME

Movement People have come to the United States from all over the world. Between 1820 and 1950, most immigrants came from Europe.

❖ What part of the United States did most of these immigrants from Europe reach first?

Some people come for the freedoms our country offers. They may not be allowed to vote for their leaders or follow their religion in their home country.

Some of the first immigrants came from England in the 1600s. They joined the millions of Native Americans who were already living here. Then, in the 1700s, hundreds of thousands of enslaved Africans were brought to the colonies to work on large farms called plantations.

In the 1800s, many more people came from Europe. From 1881 until 1920, more than 23 million immigrants entered the United States from countries all around the world.

A ticket from 1913 for a family of Polish immigrants traveling by ship to New York

Review From which country did some of the first European immigrants come?

Arriving at Ellis Island

In the years between 1892 and 1924, many new immigrants to the United States arrived at Ellis Island. Located across the harbor from New York City, Ellis Island was the nation's largest immigration center. The immigrants waited in long lines to be examined by doctors and to be interviewed by officials.

If the immigrants passed the physical examination and the interview, they were allowed to enter the United States. First, they took a ferryboat to New York City. From there they began the journey to their new community in the United States.

Review **What did the immigrants do on Ellis Island?**

Many immigrants came to the United States aboard crowded ships.

At the Registry Hall on Ellis Island, immigrants wait to be interviewed.

Immigration Today

Today the largest immigrant groups are from Asia, Mexico, and Central America. Many immigrants to the United States choose to learn English. Then, although they come from different cultures, they can communicate with other Americans.

Even though American people have a common identity as Americans, they also keep many of their own traditions. A **tradition** is a custom, or way of doing something, that is passed on by families to their children. Many families eat special foods, follow their own religions, and celebrate their own holidays. The blending of many cultures lets all Americans enjoy ways of life from other parts of the world.

A young boy practices Chinese writing with the help of a family member.

> **Review** **What are the largest immigrant groups today?**

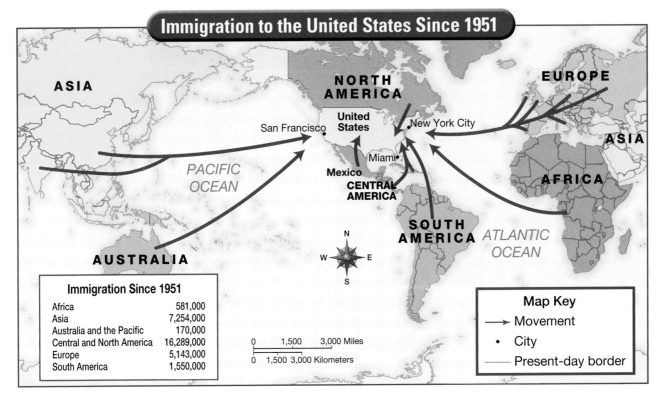

Immigration to the United States Since 1951

ASIA

NORTH AMERICA

EUROPE

United States

San Francisco

New York City

PACIFIC OCEAN

Miami

ASIA

Mexico

CENTRAL AMERICA

AFRICA

AUSTRALIA

SOUTH AMERICA

ATLANTIC OCEAN

N W E S

Immigration Since 1951	
Africa	581,000
Asia	7,254,000
Australia and the Pacific	170,000
Central and North America	16,289,000
Europe	5,143,000
South America	1,550,000

0   1,500   3,000 Miles
0   1,500 3,000 Kilometers

Map Key
→ Movement
• City
— Present-day border

GEOGRAPHY THEME

Movement Since 1951, the largest number of immigrants have come to the United States from Asia, Mexico, and Central America.

❖ From Asia, which city do immigrants reach first?

Madeleine K. Albright came to the United States from Czechoslovakia. She served as Secretary of State for the U.S. government. She used her skills as a leader to improve communication between the United States and other countries in the world.

Albert Einstein was a professor in Germany, where his work earned him the Nobel Prize for Physics in 1921. In 1933 he moved to the United States. He made many important contributions to the fields of science and mathematics.

I. M. Pei came to the United States from China to study architecture. He has designed many beautiful buildings that are located all over the world. He stands next to his model for the Regent Hotel in New York City.

Newcomers Have Made a Difference

The many immigrants to the United States have brought with them their own cultures. They have also brought their own skills and talents, which have helped make our country unique. The people shown on these pages have made contributions in many different areas, including science, mathematics, medicine, politics, literature, and architecture.

Review How can immigrants make a difference in our country?

Elizabeth Blackwell came to the United States from England as a young girl. In 1849 she became the first woman to earn a medical degree in the United States. Each year an award in her name is given to the woman who has contributed the most to the field of medicine.

Elijah McCoy came to the United States from Scotland. While working at the Michigan Central Railroad, he invented a cup that slowly dripped oil into machinery on trains. Trains no longer had to be stopped to be oiled. His time-saving invention was later used in other engines in mines and factories.

Pura Belpré came to the United States from Puerto Rico. She became the first Hispanic librarian at the New York Public Library. As a writer and librarian, she shared the traditions of her culture. Every year an award is given in Belpré's name to Hispanic writers of children's books.

LESSON 1 Review

1 Main Idea What are three reasons people come to live in the United States?

2 Vocabulary Use the vocabulary word **tradition** in a sentence to explain how people can celebrate their culture.

3 Reading Skill—Determine Point of View Write a paragraph from the point of view of a newcomer to the United States as he or she enters New York harbor and arrives at Ellis Island.

4 Your Community Write a paragraph to describe the contributions of immigrants in your community or state.

 Performance—Create an Immigrants' Hall of Fame List the names of people who have immigrated to the United States. Choose people who have made a difference in the fields of science, government, or the arts. Put a list of their achievements on a bulletin board in the classroom.

The Potato Famine

Main Idea
More than a million Irish immigrants came to the United States between 1840 and 1850.

Vocabulary

famine

voyage

Between 1840 and 1850, more than a million people from Ireland entered the United States. Most of the Irish immigrants came to escape the potato famine in their homeland. **Famine** is a time of hunger when there is little food.

Ireland in the 1800s

In the early 1800s most people in Ireland were very poor. They survived by growing their own fruits and vegetables, living mostly on potatoes.

County Kerry, Ireland, is still a place where many Irish people make a living as farmers.

Locate It

Ireland, Europe

In the 1840s, for several years in a row, a plant disease killed all the potato crops. With no potatoes to eat, people began to go hungry. Many sold everything they owned and left Ireland for the United States. They left on a **voyage** across the rough Atlantic Ocean on overcrowded sailing ships.

Many of the Irish immigrants settled in New York and Boston. Although most had been farmers in Ireland, they began their new lives here as workers in the cities.

Review What kind of transportation did immigrants from Ireland use to reach the United States?

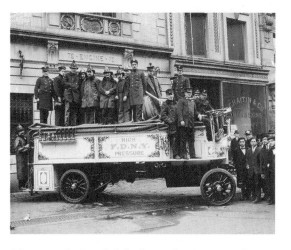

Many of the Irish immigrants who came to the United States became firefighters and police officers.

Ireland's President Mary McAleese at the launching of the *Jeanie Johnston*.

This United States postage stamp honors Irish immigrants to the United States.

Ireland and the United States Today

In May of 2000 Ireland's president, Mary McAleese, helped launch a large wooden sailing ship. The *Jeanie Johnston* is a copy of a ship that carried Irish immigrants to the United States and Canada. The first *Jeanie Johnston* was a cargo ship that had been remodeled so that it could carry 200 passengers. Ireland and the United States have joined to remember the immigrants from Ireland in another way. Both countries have created a postage stamp showing an immigrant sailing ship.

Review **What did Ireland and the United States do together to remember the immigrants from Ireland?**

LESSON 2
Review

1 Main Idea Why did many people leave Ireland and immigrate to the United States?

2 Vocabulary Use the words **famine** and **voyage** to tell about the immigrants who came to the United States from Ireland.

3 Reading Skill—Determine Point of View Many Irish immigrants who had been farmers had to find jobs in factories and live in crowded buildings in the city. From the point of view of a new Irish immigrant, describe what a day might be like.

4 Your Community Research ways that Irish culture has influenced your community or another community in your state. Share your examples with other students in your class.

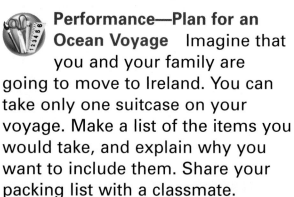 **Performance—Plan for an Ocean Voyage** Imagine that you and your family are going to move to Ireland. You can take only one suitcase on your voyage. Make a list of the items you would take, and explain why you want to include them. Share your packing list with a classmate.

CITIZENSHIP

Make a Thoughtful Decision

Vocabulary

decision

▶ Why It Matters

You make many decisions every day. A **decision** is a choice. Some decisions are easy, but others can be difficult. When you make a thoughtful decision, you think about the consequences before you act.

▶ What You Need to Know

In the 1840s, many people living in Ireland made a thoughtful decision to move their families to the United States. To make a thoughtful decision, the people in Ireland, like people everywhere, followed these steps.

Step 1 Identify the choices.

Step 2 Think about possible consequences.

Step 3 Make a choice and act.

▶ Practice the Skill

Mark is trying to decide whether to do his homework before or after the basketball game. He creates a chart to help him make a thoughtful decision. Copy his chart, and list two consequences for each choice.

▶ Apply What You Learned

Think about a decision you have made. Create a chart that shows the choices and consequences you faced.

CHOICES	→	CONSEQUENCES
Do homework and then go to the game.	→	
Go to the game and then do homework.	→	

CITIZENSHIP SKILLS

3

Main Idea
Living near others from their country helps immigrants feel at home.

Vocabulary

language

manufacture

Locate It

Los Angeles, California

Cities of Many Cultures

Many immigrants feel homesick when they first arrive in their new country. They miss their home and family and also the language and customs of their culture. **Language** is the words or signs people use to communicate. Often people move to neighborhoods where others from their home country have lived for a time. There they can speak their own language and follow the customs of their culture. The people in these neighborhoods help the newer immigrants learn about this country. They also help the newcomers not to miss their home country so much.

Los Angeles, California

Los Angeles, on the Pacific coast in southern California, is one of the largest cities in the United States. Many of those who live there have come from somewhere else. They may be from other parts of the United States or from other countries. These people have moved to Los Angeles to find new opportunities.

Many Spanish speakers in Los Angeles were born in the United States. Their ancestors, however, were immigrants from Mexico, Central America, and South America.

Many large cities have neighborhoods where immigrants from different countries can feel at home.

Olvera Street

You don't have to go to Mexico to hear the sound of a *mariachi* band. In Los Angeles, you can just go to Olvera Street. Named for Agustin Olvera, the county's first judge, it is a place to enjoy Mexican culture and tradition. *La Placita Olvera*, as the street is called in Spanish, is located in one of the oldest parts of the city. It has historic buildings, a traditional Mexican-style plaza, and many small shops that sell Mexican handcrafts.

A sign identifying
Koreatown in Los Angeles

Los Angeles is also home to a growing number of immigrants from Asia. There are new families from the Philippines, Japan, China, and Korea. Koreatown is a Korean American neighborhood that is growing fast. Thousands of Koreans live there already. New immigrants feel at home, thanks to the area's Korean-language newspapers, radio stations, and television stations. The streets of this neighborhood are busy with Korean-speaking shoppers.

Every fall, as in Korea, neighbors gather to make a pickled vegetable treat called *kimchi*. Chopped cabbages and white radishes are mixed with red pepper and garlic. Then the mixture is set aside for several months. When the *kimchi* is ready, it has become very hot and spicy!

Review **What helps new immigrants from Korea feel at home in Los Angeles?**

Kimchi (above) is a
spicy vegetable dish.

People share a meal in one of Koreatown's
many Asian restaurants.

Chicago, Illinois

Chicago, Illinois, on the shore of Lake Michigan, is another large city. African Americans form its largest ethnic group. Many African Americans live in the Avalon Park and South Shore neighborhoods, as well as on the West Side.

Many groups of Europeans live in Chicago, too. There are neighborhoods of people from Poland, Germany, Italy, and Ireland. Many Poles live in an area of Chicago called the Northwest Side. On Polonia Street, they still speak Polish with the shopkeepers. Some shops there sell several kinds of Polish sausage.

People enjoy outdoor dining at one of the restaurants in the Little Italy neighborhood.

A mural in the Avalon Park neighborhood celebrates dance.

Locate It

Chicago, Illinois

In this Chicago neighborhood, a bakery sells Polish breads and desserts.

German and Scandinavian families built farms on the edges of the city. Their rural communities have now become suburbs of Chicago. Like many other American cities, Chicago has an area called Chinatown and one called Little Italy. There is also a Greektown.

Spanish speakers make up the fastest-growing group in Chicago. People of Mexican, Puerto Rican, and Cuban heritage live in the neighborhoods of Pilsen and Little Village. Colorful murals form a background for the excellent Mexican restaurants and *taquerías* (tah•keh•REE•ahs)—places to buy tacos and burritos. Visitors to the Mexican Fine Arts Center Museum can enjoy Mexican paintings, drawings, and sculptures.

Review **Why do you think Chicago has so many ethnic neighborhoods?**

Musicians perform at the opening of a Mexican restaurant in Chicago.

Paterson, New Jersey

Paterson, New Jersey, is one of the oldest cities in the United States. It was built near a waterfall to be a manufacturing center. To **manufacture** is to make something with machines. The water provided the energy to run the machines.

Many ethnic groups make up Paterson's population. There are immigrants from a number of countries in Europe and Asia. Many people speak Arabic, so some shops in Paterson have Arabic signs. There are stores where immigrants can shop for food, clothing, and other items imported from their home countries.

Review Why did Paterson become a manufacturing center?

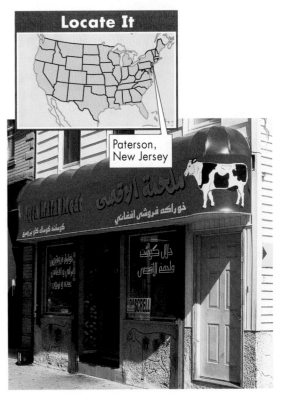

Locate It

Paterson, New Jersey

A butcher shop in a Paterson neighborhood

LESSON 3
Review

1 Main Idea Why do ethnic groups form neighborhoods in a large city?

2 Vocabulary Use the word **language** in a sentence to explain what can make immigrants feel at home in some of the neighborhoods in cities.

3 Reading Skill—Determine Point of View Write a paragraph from a new immigrant's point of view, telling why learning to speak English is important.

4 Your Community In a grocery store in your neighborhood, find examples of food that may be part of the cultural traditions of different ethnic groups.

Performance—Create a Travel Brochure Write about the neighborhood in which you live. Describe some interesting restaurants, shops, and other places. Include enough details to make people want to visit your neighborhood. Add photographs or drawings to illustrate your brochure.

Use a Population Map

Vocabulary

population density

▶ Why It Matters

Like natural resources, people are not spread out evenly around Earth. Many people live in large cities, and others live in small communities. A population map can show you where people live.

▶ What You Need to Know

Different areas have different population densities (DEN•suh•teez). **Population density** is the number of people living in an area of a certain size, usually 1 square mile. A square mile is a square piece of land that is 1 mile wide and 1 mile long.

Population density affects the way people live. In places where 10 people live on each square mile of land, the population density is 10 people per square mile. Where 100 people live on each square mile, the population density is 100 people per square mile. The land there is more crowded.

▶ Practice the Skill

The map on page 259 shows population density in Mexico. Use the map to answer these questions.

1 The map key shows four population densities. What color is used to show the lowest population density?

2 What color shows the highest population density?

3 Find Mexico City on the map. Like other large cities, it has a population of more than 250 people per square mile. How do you think Mexico City's high population density affects the lives of people living there?

4 Why do you think population density is higher along the coasts than along the northern border?

Apply What You Learned

Find a population map of your state in an encyclopedia or an atlas. What is the population density where you live? In which part of your state is the population density the lowest?

Practice your map and globe skills with the **GeoSkills CD-ROM**.

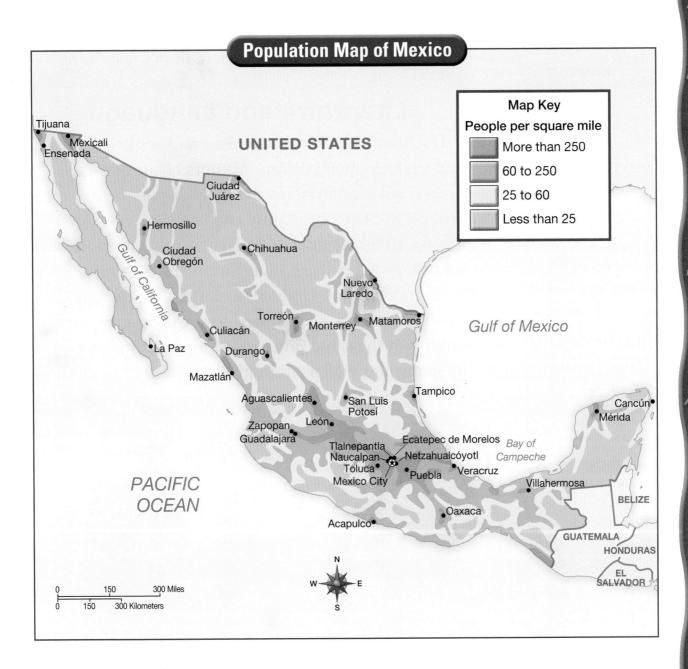

Population Map of Mexico

Map Key

People per square mile

More than 250

60 to 250

25 to 60

Less than 25

UNITED STATES

Tijuana
Mexicali
Ensenada
Ciudad Juárez
Hermosillo
Ciudad Obregón
Chihuahua
Gulf of California
Nuevo Laredo
Torreón
Monterrey
Matamoros
Culiacán
La Paz
Durango
Mazatlán
Tampico
Aguascalientes
San Luis Potosí
Zapopan
León
Guadalajara
Tlalnepantla
Naucalpan
Ecatepec de Morelos
Netzahualcóyotl
Toluca
Mexico City
Puebla
Veracruz
Oaxaca
Acapulco

Gulf of Mexico

Bay of Campeche

Cancún
Mérida
Villahermosa

BELIZE
GUATEMALA
HONDURAS
EL SALVADOR

PACIFIC OCEAN

0   150   300 Miles
0   150   300 Kilometers

N W E S

MAP AND GLOBE SKILLS

People Express Their Culture

Many of the things we do every day express our culture. The foods we eat, the clothing we wear, and the stories we write are all part of our culture. Because people in the United States come from all over, we have the chance to share in many cultures.

Literature and Language

The literature that people read and write is important to their culture. Authors create stories, plays, books, and poems that help to pass on a group's heritage. Literature can help us experience life in a different time and place. It helps keep the traditions of a culture alive. Since Amy's family immigrated to the United States from Guatemala, in Central America, she learned to speak Spanish and English at the same time. She enjoys reading stories in Spanish as well as in English.

Locate It

Guatemala, Central America

Amy likes to read folktales from different cultures.

The language that people speak is also a part of culture. Many families from other parts of the world speak one or more other languages before they learn to speak English. Because language is something that people learn when they are very young, it becomes a part of their culture at an early age. Even though most immigrants learn English to communicate with others in their new home, they still enjoy hearing and speaking the language they learned as a child.

Cameron's grandparents came to the United States from Vietnam and China. He is learning to write a character in the Chinese language. A character is like a small picture, drawn with a brush. It has meaning, much like a word in English does. It takes many hours of practice to make a character properly.

Review **When do most people learn to speak a language?**

Locate It

China, Asia   Vietnam, Asia

Cameron writes the Chinese character that means "big."

Art

Art is an important part of a culture as well. Through drawing, painting, and sculpture, artists can create a piece of art that expresses meaning. Works of art often give pleasure to others and help express the values that are important in a culture.

Larissa's grandparents came to the United States from Russia. Her father is an artist who makes religious paintings for churches. These paintings are called icons. Larissa is learning to paint like her father. Sometimes he lets her paint the backgrounds of his paintings. Larissa enjoys helping her father make something beautiful.

Review **Why is art an important part of a culture?**

Locate It

Russia, Europe

Larissa paints the background on one of her father's paintings.

Music

Sounds made with instruments or voices create **music**, another important part of culture. Music involves the participation of many people. There are those who write the music, those who perform it, and those who listen to it and enjoy it.

Drums often provide the beat for music. In African cultures, there are many kinds of drums and many ways to play them.

Robert plays a *kalungu*, or "talking drum." This drum comes from Nigeria in Africa. The sounds from the drum can be changed by pressing on the strings around the middle to tighten them. Robert can make the drum sound high or low, and the combination sounds like someone talking.

Review **What instrument often provides the beat in music?**

Robert enjoys playing the *kalungu*, or "talking drum."

Locate It

Nigeria, Africa

Places of Worship

Most people who follow a religion like to worship together. For this reason, there are special places in our communities where people can worship. People who follow Christianity go to services at a church or cathedral. Those who follow Judaism go to a synagogue (SIN•uh•gahg), or temple, to pray. Followers of Islam pray in a masjid (MAHS•jid) or mosque. Churches, synagogues, and masjids serve as places for people to gather. Sometimes people eat special meals there. Some places of worship also include schools.

Trinity Church in Newport, Rhode Island

th Elohim Synagogue in arleston, South Carolina

Masjid Omar Ibn Al-Kattah in Los Angeles, California

Religion

Religion is an important part of the culture of many groups. People in the United States follow many different religious traditions. There are those who follow Christianity and others who follow Judaism. Still others follow the teachings of Buddhism, Hinduism, or Islam. Some people choose not to follow any religion. Freedom of religion is one of our rights as citizens of the United States.

Review What are some of the religions people in the United States follow?

Followers of Five Religions in the United States

RELIGION	NUMBER OF FOLLOWERS
Buddhism	401,000
Christianity	151,225,000
Hinduism	227,000
Islam	527,000
Judaism	3,137,000

Analyze Tables This table shows the number of followers of five religions in the United States.

◈ Which religious group has the greatest number of followers?

LESSON 4
Review

1 Main Idea What are some of the ways people express their culture every day?

2 Vocabulary Use the vocabulary word **music** in a sentence to tell something about your own culture.

3 Reading Skill—Determine Point of View Although there are many different songs or poems in the world, they often share similar ideas or subjects. Choose a subject, and then research it to find two poems or songs about the topic.

4 Your Community What are some of the ethnic celebrations that are held in your state? Find out when and where some of these festivals are held, and explain which one you would most like to attend.

Performance—Hold an Art Fair Bring in to class or draw some examples of art that tell something about the culture of a group. Display the artwork around the classroom, and invite other classes to view it while you explain its meaning.

Determine Point of View in Pictures

Vocabulary

point of view

▶ Why It Matters

Two pieces of art about the same subject may be quite different. If you know what to look for, you can understand what the artist is saying to you. A person's **point of view** is the way he or she feels about something. For example, one artist's painting of a scene may show it as exciting and colorful, but another artist's painting of the same scene may show it as calm and quiet.

▶ What You Need to Know

People have different points of view. What is important to one person may not be important to someone else. Here are some things you can do to practice finding the point of view of artists.

❶ Identify the artist's feelings. How does the artist seem to feel about the subject of the piece of art? Does the work show excitement or calmness? Do you see humor or sadness?

❷ Think about the information the artwork gives. What does the artist want people to know about the subject?

❸ Compare two pieces of art. Look at either two paintings or two photographs of the same subject, such as a beach scene. What is different about the way each artist shows that subject?

▶ Practice the Skill

Look at the paintings below. One was painted by Jacob Lawrence. The other was painted by Mary Cassatt. These paintings are self-portraits because the artist has painted himself or herself.

1 What is Lawrence doing in the painting? What feeling does his face show?

2 Now look at the painting of Cassatt on this page, and ask yourself the same questions.

3 Did the artists use bright or dull colors? How do these colors make you feel?

4 What do the paintings tell you about the artist's point of view toward himself or herself?

▶ Apply What You Learned

Look at the front cover of your social studies book. Take some time looking at what the artist has chosen to display on the cover. Then write a short paragraph. Tell why you think the artist chose to show these pictures. What messages did he or she want to give you, the reader?

Self-Portrait by Mary Cassatt

Self-Portrait by Jacob Lawrence

Main Idea
People express their culture through holidays and celebrations.

Vocabulary

festival

Holiday Customs and Traditions

Another way people express their culture is in their holidays and celebrations. Each holiday you will read about comes from a different culture, but all are celebrated by Americans. They have become part of our American heritage.

Saint Patrick's Day

Saint Patrick's Day is celebrated each year in Ireland on March 17. It is also celebrated in the United States and in other countries to which Irish people have immigrated. Saint Patrick's Day began as a religious celebration. Over the years, its meaning has grown to include a sense of Irish pride.

New York City has many citizens whose ancestors were Irish immigrants. On Saint Patrick's Day, it honors them with a parade down Fifth Avenue.

Review Where is Saint Patrick's Day celebrated?

On Cinco de Mayo, dancers in bright costumes perform Mexican folk dances.

The flag of Mexico

Cinco de Mayo

In Mexican American communities across the United States, people celebrate Cinco de Mayo. The name of this holiday means the "Fifth of May" in Spanish. This date marks an important event in Mexican history. On this day in 1862, the Battle of Puebla took place in Mexico. A small army of Mexicans fought bravely against a French army that was much larger, and won. Today Cinco de Mayo is celebrated with performances by dancers in bright costumes, music by bands of *mariachis*, and lots of good Mexican food.

Review What happened at the Battle of Puebla on May 5, 1862?

Kwanzaa

The celebration of Kwanzaa is a new tradition. It was begun in the 1960s by an African American teacher named Maulana Karenga. Kwanzaa is a holiday that celebrates African culture and values. For seven days following Christmas, African Americans focus on a different value, or principle, each day.

Some communities hold a Kwanzaa festival. A **festival** is a joyful gathering for celebration. At Kwanzaa festivals, people listen to speeches, eat special foods, and enjoy music and entertainment.

Review **What is Kwanzaa?**

People celebrate Kwanzaa with family gatherings, special foods, and the daily lighting of a *kinara*. There is one new candle for each of the seven days.

New Year's Day Celebrations

New Year's Day is a holiday celebrated by people throughout the world. Although people celebrate the same event, the way they celebrate might be different. In the United States, people welcome the New Year by staying up until midnight. In Europe, children in Belgium write New Year's messages to their parents on decorated pieces of paper and read them aloud on New Year's Day. In South America, the Andean Indians of Peru celebrate the New Year with music and dance.

A New Year's Day celebration in Cuzco, Peru

LESSON 5
Review

❶ **Main Idea** Why are holidays and celebrations important to communities?

❷ **Vocabulary** Use the vocabulary word **festival** in a paragraph to tell about a cultural celebration you have learned about in this lesson.

❸ **Reading Skill—Determine Point of View** Why is Kwanzaa an important celebration for African Americans?

❹ **Your Community** Write a descriptive paragraph about a holiday you enjoy.

Performance—Put on a World Festival Choose a holiday or celebration. Plan a party to celebrate the cultures represented by the students in your classroom. Bring in a poem, story, song, food, music, or work of art to help you share your holiday or celebration with the class.

Cultural Objects

People have moved to the United States from all over the world. Who are these people? How do they express their cultures? You can find out the answers to these questions by examining the objects that people make and use. Each culture's contributions can be seen in many places throughout a community.

FROM COMMUNITIES LIKE YOUR OWN

Mexican painting on bark

Russian nesting dolls

African kente cloth

Analyze the Primary Source

1. Compare and contrast the pottery and the cloth. What do they tell you about each culture?

2. What does the painting mean to you?

3. Why do you think people express their cultural heritage in different ways?

Moroccan jewelry

Navajo pottery

Activity

Create a Cultural Object Think of an object you could create to show something about your culture. Then write about the object or draw details of it. Share your work with the class. How are your class's objects alike? How are they different?

Research

Visit The Learning Site at **www.harcourtschool.com/primarysources** to research other primary sources.

8 Review and Test Preparation

Use Your Reading Skills

Complete this graphic organizer to show the points of view of the people you have read about. A copy of this graphic organizer appears on page 62 of the Activity Book.

Points of View

Speaker and Statement	Reason for Statement	Speaker's Point of View	Words Which Show That Point of View

THINK & WRITE

Write a List of Questions Imagine that you are going to interview a classmate whose family traditions are different from those of your family. Write a list of questions for the interview. Be sure to ask why the tradition is continued in the family.

Write a Letter Expressing a Point of View Why is it important for people to respect others' rights to continue their traditions and religions? Write a letter to a friend or family member that expresses your point of view.

Use Vocabulary

Write the word that correctly matches each definition.

1 a custom, or way of doing something, that is passed on in a family

> **opportunity** (p. 242)
> **tradition** (p. 245)

2 sounds made by instruments or voices

> **voyage** (p. 249)
> **music** (p. 263)

3 words or signs people use to communicate

> **language** (p. 252)
> **manufacture** (p. 257)

4 a joyful gathering of people to celebrate something

> **famine** (p. 248)
> **festival** (p. 270)

Recall Facts

Answer these questions.

5 Who were the first immigrants to arrive in the 1600s, and what people were already here when they came?

6 What are three reasons that immigrants come to our country?

7 What parts of their culture do immigrants often keep in their new country?

Write the letter of the best choice.

8 **Test Prep** During the 1800s, the largest group of immigrants came from—

A Australia.
B Asia.
C Europe.
D South America.

9 **Test Prep** Today, the largest groups of immigrants come from—

F Russia and countries in Europe.
G Mexico, Central America, and countries in Asia.
H England, Ireland, and Scotland.
J Canada and countries in Africa.

Think Critically

10 How are churches, synagogues, and mosques alike?

11 If you were a new immigrant to the United States, what part of the country would you choose to live in? Explain.

Apply Skills

12 Use the map on page 259. What is the population density of Tampico?

13 What decision did many of Ireland's citizens make during the potato famine?

14 Look at the two paintings of Davy Crockett on pages 218–219. What is different about the way each artist shows Crockett?

VISIT

A Powwow

Get Ready

Many cultures express themselves through celebrations, holidays, or ceremonies. A powwow is a Native American event that celebrates a tribe's history and culture. Visitors to a powwow in Livingston, Texas, learn about the tribe through dance, song, music, and crafts.

Locate It
United States

Livingston, Texas

What to See

Tribe members play a ceremonial drum whose shape represents the shape of the Earth.

Native American crafts are made from natural materials, bones, and feathers.

Dancers wear brightly
colored traditional clothing
and headresses.

Metal ornaments,
ribbons, and
beadwork
decorate
a jingle dress.

Take a Field Trip

GO ONLINE

A VIRTUAL TOUR
Visit The Learning Site at
www.harcourtschool.com/tours
to take virtual tours of
other cultures.

 READING RAINBOW.

A VIDEO TOUR
Check your media
center or classroom library
for a video featuring a segment
from Reading Rainbow.

4 Review and Test Preparation

Use Vocabulary

Write the word that correctly completes each sentence.

myth (p. 210)	immigrant (p. 242)
legend (p. 214)	opportunity (p. 242)
fact (p. 218)	tradition (p. 245)
memorial (p. 230)	festival (p. 270)

1 A monument or an event that keeps a memory alive is a ____.

2 A ____ is a custom, or way of doing something, that is passed on in a family.

3 Someone who comes to live in a country from someplace else is an ____.

4 A story that uses the actions of gods to explain something in nature is a ____.

5 A ____ is a statement that can be proved.

6 A ____ is a tale that may have started as a true story but now has added details that did not really happen.

7 The chance to find a better job, get an education, or have a better way of life is an ____.

8 A ____ is a joyful gathering of people to celebrate something.

Recall Facts

Answer the questions.

9 Choose one of the people you read about in this unit. How did she or he make a difference in the lives of others?

10 What did Daniel Boone do to open the western frontier to settlement?

11 Give an example of a festival. What does it celebrate?

Write the letter of the best choice.

12 **Test Prep**   The first group of immigrants to arrive in the 1600s came from—
  A Mexico.
  B Russia.
  C China.
  D England.

13 **Test Prep**   Which statement is a fact? Rosa Parks is admired because she—
  F helped pass the first laws that allowed women to vote.
  G fought for the basic rights of all people as First Lady of our country.
  H refused to give up her seat on a bus to a white person.
  J was a leader in the United Nations.

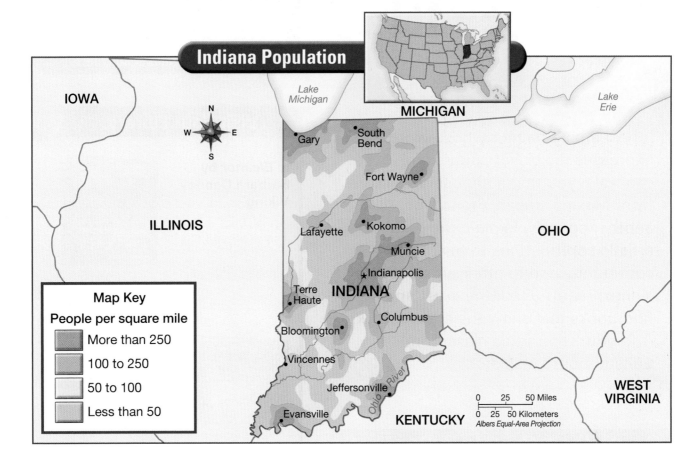

Indiana Population

Map Key
People per square mile
- More than 250
- 100 to 250
- 50 to 100
- Less than 50

IOWA

ILLINOIS

Lake Michigan

MICHIGAN

Gary

South Bend

Fort Wayne

Lafayette

Kokomo

Muncie

Indianapolis

Terre Haute

INDIANA

Columbus

Bloomington

Vincennes

Jeffersonville

Evansville

Ohio River

KENTUCKY

OHIO

Lake Erie

WEST VIRGINIA

0   25   50 Miles
0   25   50 Kilometers
Albers Equal-Area Projection

---

14 **Test Prep**   Memorial Day is a national holiday that honors—
 A the Presidents of the United States.
 B our independence from England.
 C Americans who have died in war.
 D the landing of the Pilgrims.

Think Critically

15 What message do you think the Statue of Liberty communicated to immigrants sailing into New York Harbor?

16 Why do you think most immigrants settle in the largest cities in our country?

17 Compare St. Patrick's Day with Cinco de Mayo.

18 Name a person from your state whose statue you would like to add to the National Statuary Hall in Washington, D.C. Why does this person deserve to be honored?

Apply Skills

Use a Population Map
Use the map above to answer these questions.

19 What is the population density of Indianapolis?

20 Which city has the greater population density, Lafayette or South Bend?

Unit Activities

GO ONLINE

Visit The Learning Site at
**www.harcourtschool.com/
socialstudies/activities**
for additional activities.

Research an Artist

Research a painter whose work expresses his or her culture. For example, you might choose a painter from Mexico, Japan, France, or another country. Explain the person's artistic contributions to his or her community and to other artists. Write a short report about the artist and find books that show the artist's work. Add your report to a classroom bulletin-board display.

Complete the Unit Project

A Story Scrapbook Work with a group of your classmates to complete the unit project. Decide which folktales, tall tales, myths, or legends from around the world you will include in your scrapbook. Then write short paragraphs that retell each story. Make drawings that will help explain the stories. What does your story explain or teach? You and the members of your group can take turns reading the entries to the other groups.

Visit Your Library

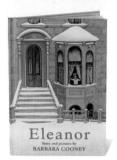

- *Eleanor* by Barbara Cooney. Viking.

- *A Picnic in October* by Eve Bunting. Harcourt.

- *Dear Juno* by Soyung Pak. Viking.

Communities
Over Time

Explorer James Cook's
timekeeper, 1774

Union Station in Nashville, Tennessee

Communities Over Time

❝ People, human beings with all their diversity, are the makers of history. ❞

—Mikhail Gorbachev, *Perestroika*, 1987

Preview the Content

With a partner, read each chapter's lesson titles and Main Idea statements. Then make a web for each chapter. Write the chapter's main topic in the center of the web. As you read, fill in the webs with supporting details. Use words and phrases that relate to the chapter's main topic.

ancient   From a time very long ago. (page 314)

colony   A settlement that is ruled by another country. (page 306)

The Thirteen Colonies

Lake Superior

UNITED STATES

MAINE (part of Massachusetts)

Lake Michigan

Lake Huron

Lake Ontario

NEW HAMPSHIRE

NEW YORK   MASSACHUSETTS

Lake Erie

RHODE ISLAND

PENNSYLVANIA   NEW JERSEY   CONNECTICUT

DELAWARE

VIRGINIA   MARYLAND

Chesapeake Bay

NORTH CAROLINA

ATLANTIC OCEAN

SOUTH CAROLINA

GEORGIA

N W E S

0   200   400 Miles
0   200   400 Kilometers

revolution   A fight for a change in government. (page 338)

landmark   A natural or human feature that helps people find their way. (page 351)

explorer   A person who goes to find out about a place. (page 332)

HOW WE CROSSED THE WEST:
The Adventures of
LEWIS AND CLARK
by Rosalyn Schanzer

In 1803 President Thomas Jefferson and the United States Congress wanted to know more about the land and rivers west of St. Louis. They asked Meriwether Lewis to lead the journey, and Lewis invited his friend William Clark to join him. The two soon found many others eager to join them on this great adventure. The daring explorers called themselves "The Corps of Discovery." Read the words of Lewis and Clark to find out what happened on their journey.

MERIWETHER LEWIS

WILLIAM CLARK

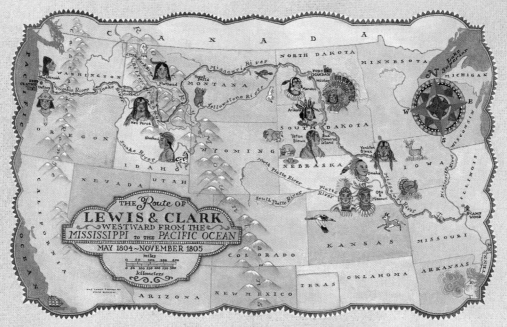

This map shows the route taken by The Corps of Discovery.

A FEW MEMBERS OF THE CORPS OF DISCOVERY

SHIELDS

YORK

SHANNON

SACAGAWEA
(sak•uh•juh•WEE•uh)

CHARBONNEAU
(shar•buh•NOH)

CRUZATTE
(croo•ZAT)

SEAMAN

MAY 14, 1804
CAMP WOOD NEAR ST. LOUIS

Set out at 4 o'clock p.m. in the presence of many of the neighboring inhabitants, and proceeded on under a gentle breeze up the Missouri.

SUMMER, 1804
WILDLIFE OF THE PLAINS

Discovered a village of small animals that burrow in the ground. The village covers about four acres and contains great numbers of holes on the top of which those little prairie dogs sit erect. They make a whistling noise when alarmed and step into their holes.

BUILDING FORT MANDAN

On November 2, we went down the river to look for a proper place to winter and found a place well supplied with wood. The next morning we commenced the building of Fort Mandan, named in honor of our neighbors, on the east bank of the Missouri.

A Mr. Toussaint Charbonneau came down to see us, and wished to be hired as an interpreter. This man has a wife called Sacagawea. She is from the Shoshoni [Snake] nation. The Shoshonis live by the Rocky Mountains and own many horses.

APRIL 7, 1805
WE CONTINUE ON

At 4 p.m. we dismissed the barge and crew with orders to return to St. Louis with our dispatches to the government, letters to our friends, and several articles to the President of the United States. Our party to continue the Voyage of Discovery now consists of 33 individuals.

WE MEET THE SHOSHONIS
AUGUST 17, 1805

A fair cold morning. I saw Indians on horseback coming toward me. Sacagawea danced for the joyful sight and made signs to me that they were her nation. The Great Chief Cameahwait of this nation proved to be the brother of Sacagawea! We spoke to the Indians about our want of horses to cross the mountains. They said the route was unfavorable, with immense waterfalls and steep cliffs, and that there were no deer, elk, or game to eat.

LATE SUMMER, 1805
CROSSING THE BITTERROOT MOUNTAINS

On August 30, we set out on our route. Traversed some of the worst roads that a horse ever passed on the sides of steep and stony mountains, some covered with snow.

To our inexpressible joy, saw a prairie 60 miles distant. We should reach its borders tomorrow. Spirits of the party much revived, as they are weak for want of food.

RUNNING THE RAPIDS
OCTOBER 1805

Built dugout canoes and set out past many bad rapids between rugged rocks and cliffs 200 feet high. One canoe split open and sank; another turned over. A great many articles lost. All our powder, some bedding, and half our food prepared in the Indian way wet. Nothing to eat but roots.

After 17 days, this great roaring river compressed between 2 rocks not 45 yards wide. Determined to pass this horrid swelling, boiling, and whorling in every direction, we rode with great velocity and passed safe, to the astonishment of all the Indians who viewed us from atop the rocks.

CLOSER AND CLOSER TO THE GREAT PACIFIC!

NOVEMBER 7, 1805

We were encamped under a high hill when the morning fog cleared off. Ocean in view! Oh! The joy. This great Pacific Ocean which we have been so long anxious to see, and the roaring noise made by waves breaking on rocky shores may be heard distinctly.

Immense swells from the main ocean immediately in front of us. All the men who wish to see the main ocean prepare themselves to set out early tomorrow morning.

NOVEMBER 18, 1805

OUR GOAL IS REACHED AT LAST!

We behold with astonishment the waves dashing against the rocks & this immense Ocean!

Think About It

1 What was the name of the river on which Lewis and Clark started their journey?

2 Imagine that you are a member of The Corps of Discovery and are about to write in your journal. For today's entry, write about some of the things you saw and heard during your exploration.

Start the Unit Project

Make a Museum Make a classroom museum about communities long ago. Choose a topic, such as art, technology, or history, to be the focus. As you read the unit, list important people, places, and events related to your topic. Your list will help you create a museum that will be displayed in your classroom.

Use Technology

Visit The Learning Site at **www.harcourtschool.com/ socialstudies** for additional activities, primary sources, and other resources to use in this unit.

Plimoth Plantation

Visitors to Plimoth (Plymouth) Plantation's Pilgrim Village in Massachusetts seem to travel back in time to 1627. Museum workers called interpreters act out what it was like to live and work in a pilgrim community. This living museum brings the past to life.

Locate It

MASSACHUSETTS

Plimoth Plantation

Learning About the Past

66 We are tomorrow's past. **99**

—Mary Webb, *Precious Bane*, 1926

CHAPTER READING SKILL

Sequence

Noticing the sequence of events helps you understand what you read. **Sequence** is the order in which events happen. Words such as *first*, *next*, *then*, and *last* help you put events in order.

As you read this chapter about our ever-changing communities, put events in the order in which they happened.

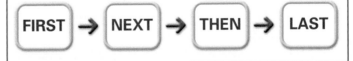

FIRST → NEXT → THEN → LAST

Continuity and Change

Main Idea
Some things in a community change over time, and others stay the same.

Vocabulary

decade
century
continuity
ghost town

Communities change every day. New buildings and roads are built. Old buildings are torn down to make way for new shopping malls. New shops open for business in old buildings. To see the changes, you can compare photographs that have been taken of the same place at different times.

Over Time

The changes that take place in a community may take a day, a year, a decade, or a century. A **decade** is 10 years. A **century** is 100 years. Here are three photographs of Atlanta, Georgia. What changes can you see in this community after 50 years? What changes can you see after a century?

Today

Using the same set of pictures, you also can see continuity in the community. **Continuity** is continuing without changing. In communities everywhere, some things stay the same. Many old buildings are still used, but they have new things in them, such as computers. The kind of work people do in the community may be the same as it was 50 years or a century ago.

Review What is continuity?

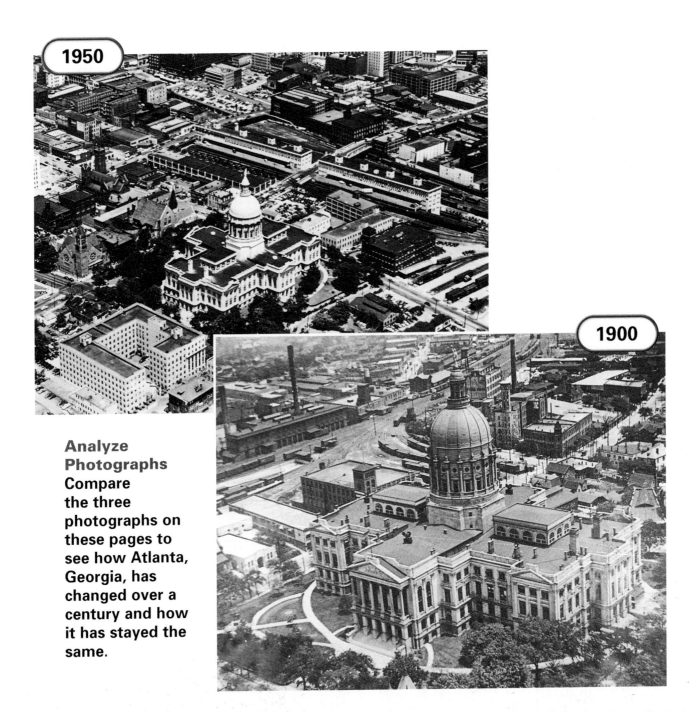

1950

1900

Analyze Photographs Compare the three photographs on these pages to see how Atlanta, Georgia, has changed over a century and how it has stayed the same.

Fast Change in Idaho

Some communities change very quickly. Some changes cause a community to grow rapidly and then disappear.

In the 1860s, gold and silver were found in Idaho. Soon thousands of people moved there. Some worked in the mines to get the gold and silver out of the ground. Others came to sell food and clothing to the miners. With all these people moving into the area, towns near the mines grew fast.

One of these towns was Silver City. Between 1863 and 1889, it grew from a few tents into a big town. When the gold and silver ran out, however, people began to move away. By 1914, all the mines had closed, and Silver City had become a **ghost town**. The buildings were there, but no people lived in them.

These photographs show the Idaho Hotel in Silver City in 1890s and today. People can visit the ghost town to find out what life was like there long ago.

Now

Review Why do some places become ghost towns?

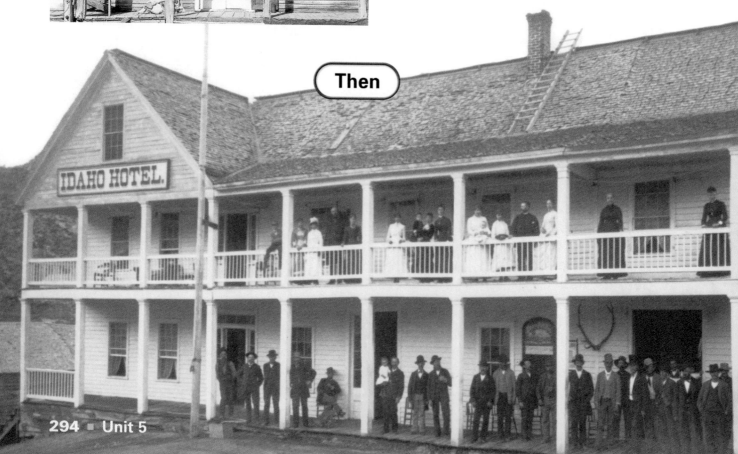

Then

Unplanned Change in Texas

Sometimes a change happens that is unplanned. It may be caused by a natural disaster, such as a hurricane, a flood, or an earthquake. Natural disasters can cause great damage and change.

On September 8, 1900, a powerful hurricane hit the United States, slamming into Texas. It struck the city of Galveston with winds as high as 120 miles per hour. The Galveston hurricane was one of the most powerful storms ever to strike the United States mainland. It destroyed businesses and homes and killed more than 6,000 people.

This photograph shows hurricane damage in Galveston to the area south of Broadway, which was approximately 16th Street.

The Galveston Daily News.

69TH YEAR—NO 173.   GALVESTON, TEXAS, THURSDAY.- SEPTEMBER 13, 1900   ESTABLISHED 1842

STORY OF THE GREAT DISASTER AT GALVESTON

These people are preparing this house for a hurricane by putting boards over the windows.

Before the storm, Galveston had been one of the largest cities in Texas. After the storm, it was rebuilt, but it was never the same again. Many people decided to move farther inland to nearby Houston.

Hurricanes can still hit Texas each year between the months of June and October. Texans need to know what to do before a hurricane hits and after the storm is over. Being prepared for natural disasters can save people's lives.

Review **How can hurricanes cause change?**

This photograph shows the hurricane damage to the Marx and Blum Building between 23rd and 24th Streets.

Unseen Change

The buildings in communities are not the only things that change. The lives of the people change, too. For example, new discoveries in health care help people have healthier, longer lives.

One person who brought better health to communities all over the world was Louis Pasteur. Pasteur, who lived in France in the 1800s, made discoveries that changed the way people thought about disease. It was Pasteur who proved that many diseases are caused by living things called germs. His work has helped people realize how important it is to keep clean. Pasteur also found a way to kill the germs in milk. This way, called pasteurizing, has made milk a safe food for people all over the world.

Louis Pasteur made discoveries that brought better health to people.

Review How did Pasteur's work change people's lives?

LESSON 1
Review

1 Main Idea Describe some of the ways a community can change.

2 Vocabulary Write a paragraph describing the changes in an imaginary town over the years. Use the vocabulary words **decade**, **century**, **continuity**, and **ghost town**.

3 Reading Skill—Sequence Read the paragraphs about Silver City, Idaho, again. Then make a list of the things that happened there in sequence.

4 Your Community How has your community changed over the past year?

Performance—Make a Time Line Mural Research scientific discoveries that people made during each decade of the 1900s. Divide a long sheet of mural paper into decade sections. Work in a group of two or three students for each decade, and draw the scientists and their discoveries. The finished mural will show change through scientific discovery over the century.

Skills

READING

Identify Cause and Effect

Vocabulary

cause   effect

▶ Why It Matters

Changes take place every day. To understand these changes, you need to identify cause and effect. A **cause** is what makes something happen. What happens is an **effect**.

Understanding cause and effect can help you make predictions. If you understand how something happened in the past, you can predict how it will happen in the future. You can use a graphic organizer to help you understand causes and their effects.

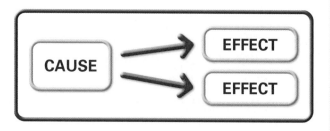

▶ What You Need to Know

Sometimes the weather can cause serious effects. The effects of the hurricane that hit Galveston, Texas, included great damage to homes and businesses. The damage caused some people to decide to move farther inland. Experts who have studied the causes and effects of hurricane damage can help us prevent such damage in future storms.

Use the following steps to help you understand an event.

Step 1 Look for the cause or causes of the event.

Step 2 Look for the effect or effects of the event.

Step 3 Think about how the causes and effects are connected.

▶ Practice the Skill

Read the following paragraph. Then copy the chart below, and use the information in the paragraph to complete it.

One sunny day in Stormville, the sky suddenly grew dark. The radio and television stations announced a tornado warning. In a very short time, the tornado roared through the town. Houses were destroyed, electricity was lost, and cars were damaged.

▶ Apply What You Learned

Imagine that a new school has opened in your neighborhood. What might have caused the building of the new school? What might be some of the effects of adding this school to the community? Use the chart below as a model to help you answer the questions. Share your answers with a partner.

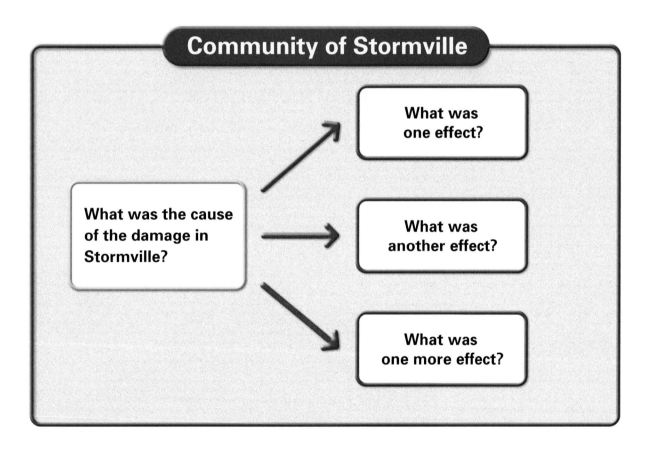

Community of Stormville

What was the cause of the damage in Stormville?

What was one effect?

What was another effect?

What was one more effect?

Main Idea
There are many sources people can use to learn about their community's history.

Vocabulary

oral history
historical society
artifact

Exploring Your Community's Past

Imagine that you have been asked to discover the history of your community. How should you begin? First, think of yourself as a historian. Historians are history detectives. They look for clues in all kinds of things, from the biggest events to the smallest details. Then they put all of the information together to form a picture of the past.

Learning from People

There are many ways you can learn about the history of your community. One place to start is with your family and neighbors. Older family members can tell you what life was like before you were born. You can learn history from the stories they tell.

A grandmother shares her photographs and stories with her grandson.

These students are interviewing a park manager about the history of a community park.

These stories make up the oral history of your community. An **oral history** is a story of the past that is spoken rather than written. Family members may also have photographs showing life in your community long ago.

Asking people questions, or interviewing them, is another good way to get information about your community's past. To learn what daily life was like long ago, you can ask an older member of your community. To find out about your community's government or businesses, you can interview leaders and store owners.

An old newspaper is one kind of artifact you might see at a historical museum.

Review What is an oral history?

Places to Go

Many communities have special places where you can learn about their history. Your community may have a museum or a historical society. A **historical society** is a group of people who have a special interest in the history of a community. Museums and historical societies may have collections of old photographs, newspapers, books, and artifacts. An **artifact** is an object that was used by people in the past.

Students learn about an early printing press from a worker at a historical museum.

The library is a good place to look for information. A library has reference works for finding facts. Reference works include books such as almanacs, dictionaries, atlases, and encyclopedias in print or on CD-ROM. They also include magazines and newspapers. At many libraries, you can use a computer to search for more information on the Internet. It may be that someone has already written a history of your community. In such a book, you might find drawings or photographs of people, places, and events important in your community's past.

Review What kinds of things does a historical society collect?

Many communities have monuments or historic markers. These tell about people or events important in the community's history.

History Is Everywhere

You may find that the history of your community is everywhere you look. The name of your community may tell you the name of its founder. Streets may be named for people who were leaders in your town. Landmarks, memorials, and historic sites are also good places to learn about the history of communities. Some towns have set up places that re-create their history. You can experience what it was like to live there long ago. Re-creating earlier times in the present gives people a chance to learn history in a new way.

These people learn what it was like to be a pioneer by traveling the Oregon Trail in covered wagons.

Review Where might you look to learn about the history of your community?

LESSON 2
Review

1 Main Idea What are some ways people can learn about their community's history?

2 Vocabulary Write a description of your favorite way to learn history. Use the vocabulary words **oral history**, **artifact**, and **historical society**.

3 Reading Skill—Sequence List the sequence of steps you would use at the library to find information about the history of a place.

4 Your Community What sources in your community could help you learn the history of your community?

Performance—Oral History Create an oral history of your family, your neighborhood, or your school. Interview people, taking notes about what they say or using a tape recorder. Then write a short summary of the things they tell you. Share your oral history with the class.

A Time Capsule

Some groups of people make time capsules to show our world to people of the future. They collect objects that are important today and place them in a container to be opened in the future.

The Rochester Museum and Science Center in Rochester, New York, buried a time capsule in 1873. Here worker Ralph Wiegent takes the lid off the time capsule. Inside the time capsule were a variety of artifacts and documents.

 FROM THE ROCHESTER MUSEUM AND SCIENCE CENTER

This time capsule was buried in 1873 and opened in 1999.

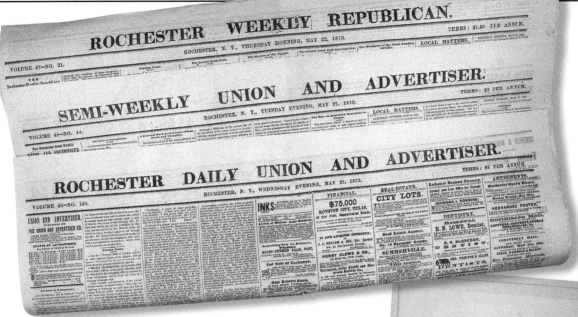

Rochester newspapers from 1873

Analyze the Primary Source

1. Why do you think newspapers were put in the time capsule?

2. Why might a medal be an important artifact to place in a time capsule?

Union League of America medal

Postcard of Rochester City Hall in the mid-1870s

Activity

Create a Time Capsule Make a drawing about something that is going on in the world right now. Then fold your paper and put it into a shoebox with the drawings of your classmates. The shoebox will be opened by next year's students.

Research

GO ONLINE Visit The Learning Site at **www.harcourtschool.com/primarysources** to research other primary sources.

Main Idea
Many communities
began as
settlements.

Vocabulary

colony

settler

factory

Tracing a Community's History

Jamestown, a community in the colony of Virginia, was the first settlement built by the English. A **colony** is a region that is ruled by another country. The colony of Virginia was ruled by England. We can learn about the newcomers to Virginia by asking the questions *Who? What? When? Where?* and *Why?*

The first settlers came to Jamestown, Virginia, from England aboard sailing ships like these restored ships in the Jamestown harbor.

Who Came to Virginia, and When?

The first settlers were 105 men and boys from London, England. **Settlers** are the first people to live in a new place. They brought the supplies they would need to build a settlement in Virginia. The group was led by Captain John Smith.

On May 24, 1607, the settlers arrived in three sailing ships. They landed near a river they called the James River to honor King James I, the English king. The Jamestown settlers started the first lasting English settlement in the Americas.

All around the settlement were villages where Native Americans had lived for centuries. Powhatan was the leader of a group of Native Americans living in Virginia at the time. The Powhatan nation was made up of more than thirty tribes, or groups. Some of the tribes helped the newcomers. Other tribes fought with the settlers and tried to drive them away.

Captain John Smith

Review When did the settlers arrive in Virginia?

The Powhatans lived in villages like the one shown here.

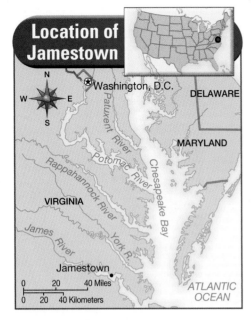

Washington, D.C.

DELAWARE

MARYLAND

Patuxent River

Potomac River

Rappahannock River

Chesapeake Bay

VIRGINIA

James River

York R.

Jamestown

ATLANTIC OCEAN

0   20   40 Miles
0   20   40 Kilometers

Movement

❖ What ocean did the settlers cross to reach the James River?

Where Did They Live?

The settlers built Jamestown, also named for King James I, at the mouth of the James River. The settlement was built as a walled fort that faced the river. Inside were houses made of wood with straw roofs. There were also a storehouse, a guardhouse, and a church.

However, the settlers soon found that the location was not a good one. Mosquitoes from the swamps around it carried disease. Also, there were no sources of fresh drinking water nearby. Many of the settlers died.

Review **Where did the settlers choose to build Jamestown?**

This map shows the walled fort built by the settlers. Chief Powhatan is shown in the upper right corner of the map.

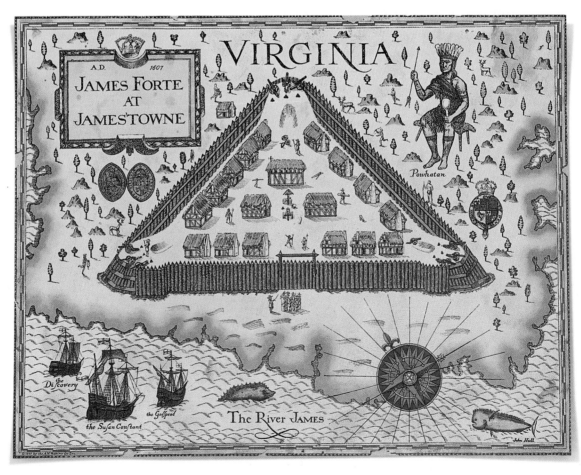

VIRGINIA

A.D. 1607
JAMES FORTE AT JAMESTOWNE

Powhatan

Discovery

the Godspeed

the Susan Constant

The River JAMES

John Hull

Why Did They Come?

The Virginia Company of London had paid for the ships and supplies. It wanted the settlers to find a way to make money for the company. The company thought Captain John Smith and his men would find gold and silver. It also hoped the settlers would find a water route to the Pacific Ocean. Such a route would make the company's trade with India and China easier and cheaper.

The settlers came for their own reasons. Some wanted to share their religious beliefs with the Native Americans. Others came for the adventure of living in a new place.

Review **For what reasons did settlers come to Virginia from England?**

Land Granted to The London Company and The Plymouth Company

Analyze Primary Sources

The Virginia Company of London was also known as The London Company. The Plymouth Company, which was formed at the same time, also sent settlers to the area. Land was granted, or given, to both companies, but The Plymouth Company's map settlements did not last. This shows how the land along the Virginia coast was divided between the two companies in 1606. It also shows land that either company could use.

1 This part of the map shows land granted to The London Company and the place where Jamestown was started.

2 This part of the map shows land granted to The Plymouth Company.

3 This part of the map shows land that could be used by either company.

Along which river was the settlement of Jamestown started?

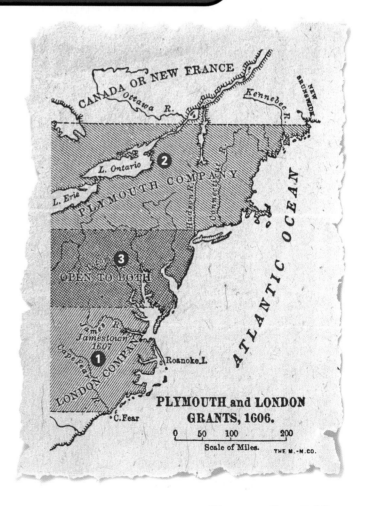

PLYMOUTH and LONDON GRANTS, 1606.

0   50   100   200
Scale of Miles.   THE M.-N.CO.

What Did They Do?

John Smith mapped Chesapeake Bay and the land around it. He also wrote books about Virginia, which led more people in England to decide to become settlers.

The settlers tried different ways to make money for the Virginia Company. In 1608, they built the first glass factory in America. A **factory** is a building in which people use machines to make goods. Tobacco, however, proved to be the best money maker. The plant grew well in Virginia. In 1614, the first shipload was sent to England. Three years later, tobacco had become the main crop of the colony.

A few years later, Dutch ships began bringing Africans to Virginia to work as slaves. The slave trade provided workers for the tobacco fields of Virginia.

Jamestown continued to grow until 1698, when the government building burned down. The government moved up the river to Williamsburg, and Jamestown began to fail.

This small glass pitcher was made at Jamestown.

John Smith's 1612 map of Virginia

Today Jamestown has been re-created so people can see what the settlement was like in the 1600s. Although it is no longer a real community, it is a good place to learn about the past.

Review **What did the Virginia Company hope the settlers at Jamestown would do?**

Pocahontas, the daughter of Chief Powhatan, married a settler named John Rolfe. She traveled with him to England, where she had this portrait painted.

The buildings at Jamestown have been re-created to appear as they looked in 1607.

LESSON 3
Review

1 **Main Idea** Explain how the beginning of the community of Jamestown is similar to the beginnings of many other communities.

2 **Vocabulary** Write two sentences and include the words **colony** and **settler**.

3 **Reading Skill—Sequence** List in sequence at least five events in the founding of Jamestown.

4 **Your Community** Do research to find out how your community began.

Performance—Create a Diorama Using wooden sticks, modeling clay, and found objects, create a diorama of the fort at Jamestown. Use the drawing of the fort and John Smith's map in this lesson as references.

Understand Time Periods

▶ Why It Matters

As you read about people in the past, you will learn about things that happened over long periods of time. You will need to know about the different periods into which time can be divided. Understanding time periods will give you a better idea of when things happened.

▶ What You Need to Know

Time lines can show events that happened during any period of time. For example, a time line might show events that happened during a day, a week, a month, a year, or any number of years.

All time lines are divided into smaller parts. These parts can stand for different time periods. A part may stand for a decade, a period of 10 years, or for a century, a period of 100 years. Time Line A shows a century divided into decades.

Time Line B shows a greater period of time. Each smaller part of Time Line B stands for 1,000 years. A period of 1,000 years is called a **millennium** (muh•LEH•nee•uhm).

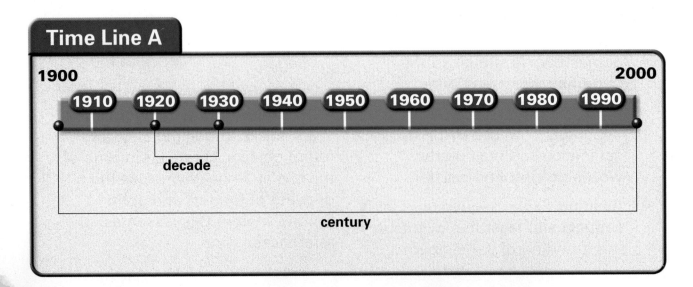

Time Line A

1900									2000
1910	1920	1930	1940	1950	1960	1970	1980	1990	

decade

century

Many people today identify years by whether they took place before or after the birth of Jesus Christ.

Notice that some of the dates on Time Line B have the letters B.C. after them. This stands for "before Christ." For example, something that happened in 2000 B.C. took place 2,000 years before Jesus Christ was born.

Some dates have the letters A.D. before them. These letters stand for the Latin words that mean "in the year of the Lord." For example, something that happened in A.D. 1000 happened 1,000 years after Jesus Christ was born. Sometimes dates are shown without letters. A date without letters is always A.D. For example, the dates 750, 1492, and 2010 are all dates after the birth of Jesus Christ.

▶ Practice the Skill

Use the time lines to help you answer these questions.

1 Which time line covers the greater amount of time?

2 How many centuries are shown on Time Line A?

3 How many decades are shown on Time Line A?

4 How many millenniums are shown on Time Line B?

5 How many years are shown on Time Line B?

▶ Apply What You Learned

Draw a time line that starts with 1901 and ends with the present year. Show three important world events on your time line. Choose one from about a year ago, one from a decade ago, and one from a century ago.

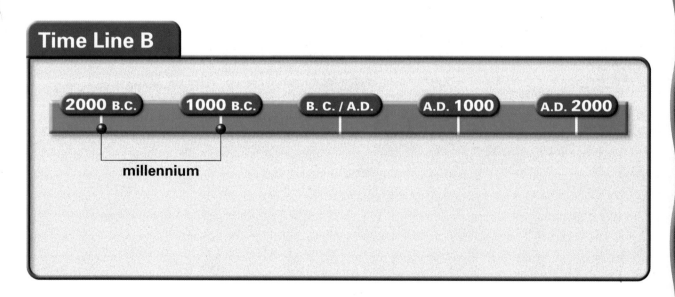

Time Line B

2000 B.C. 1000 B.C. B. C. / A.D. A.D. 1000 A.D. 2000

millennium

Main Idea
Many ideas from long ago are still used today.

Vocabulary

ancient

civilization

modern

invention

pyramid

pharaoh

republic

empire

Communities in Ancient Times

Since **ancient** times, or the time long ago, people have lived together in communities. In even the earliest groups, they shared a government, a place to live, a culture, and more. Some of those communities grew to become great civilizations. A **civilization** is a large group of people living in a well-organized way. Ideas from some of the ancient civilizations are still used in **modern** times, or the time we live in today.

This scene from a stone carving called the *Standard of Ur* shows Mesopotamian soldiers and a wheeled cart.

Sumerian Cuneiform

MEANING	PICTOGRAPH	CUNEIFORM
Star		
Bird		
Grain		

Analyze Tables The Sumerians wrote first with pictographs. Later they used cuneiform symbols that stood for sounds. Why do you think the Sumerians started to use cuneiform?

The Sumerians wrote on clay tablets in cuneiform (kyoo·NEE·uh·fawrm).

Locate It

Ancient Mesopotamia, Asia

Ancient Mesopotamia

One of the world's earliest civilizations began in southwestern Asia. It was in a place called Mesopotamia (meh·suh·puh·TAY·mee·uh). The world's first cities grew in a part of Mesopotamia called Sumer (SOO·mer).

The Sumerians developed many important ideas and inventions. An **invention** is something that has been made for the first time. One important Sumerian invention was the wheeled cart. Their wheeled carts made it easier to move things from place to place.

Another important idea developed by the Sumerians was writing. Before they invented writing, they had to keep track of everything by remembering. Writing gave them a way to record their thoughts and their history.

Review What are some Sumerian inventions that are still important today?

Ancient Egypt

The ancient civilization of Egypt, in Africa, is known for its pyramids. An Egyptian **pyramid** is a tomb, or burial place, for a dead king or queen.

Of the pyramids that are still standing, the Great Pyramid is the largest. It stands more than 450 feet (137 m) high. This pyramid was built about 4,500 years ago for an Egyptian **pharaoh**, or king, named Khufu.

The pyramids were made by stacking stone blocks in layers. Some of the blocks in the Great Pyramid weigh 5,000 pounds (2,268 kg). Wheels and pulleys for moving things were unknown to the ancient Egyptians. They put the giant blocks into place by pushing them up ramps on log rollers. The Great Pyramid took 20 years to build, with up to 10,000 people working on it at all times.

Review How was the Great Pyramid of Egypt made?

Hatshepsut (hat·SHEP·soot) was one of Egypt's leaders.

The pyramids at Giza still stand today.

Locate It

Ancient Egypt, Africa

Ancient China, Asia

In ancient China, scribes recorded the country's history.

Ancient China

Every Fourth of July, fireworks light up the night sky all across the United States. Yet fireworks are not an American invention. They were invented thousands of years ago in China.

The ancient Chinese also invented paper and printing. They pounded tree bark to make a pulp, or mush. They spread this out to dry into sheets of paper, on which they wrote by using brush and ink. Later they invented a way to print copies of pages. They carved the writing for a page on a wooden block. Then they put ink on the block and pressed paper against it to make a print. This let them make many copies of a page much faster than they could write them by hand.

Chinese wooden printing block

Review What inventions made in ancient China are still used today?

Ancient Greece

The Greek civilization began in what is now the country of Greece, in Europe. Athens was one of its most important communities.

About 2,500 years ago, the government of Athens was the world's first democracy. In a democracy, citizens make the decisions. All free men over the age of 18 could take part in the democracy of Athens. Women, children, and slaves could not. The male citizens met in a large group, or assembly, where each had the right to speak. There they discussed ideas for new laws and voted on them.

The people of Athens loved the arts and learning. Ancient Greece is still known for its sculptors, potters, painters, builders, and writers.

Review What form of government did Athens have?

This vase shows early Greeks harvesting olives.

Analyze Drawings
The drawing shows how the Acropolis, or religious center, may have looked in ancient Athens.

◈ What was the largest building of the Acropolis?

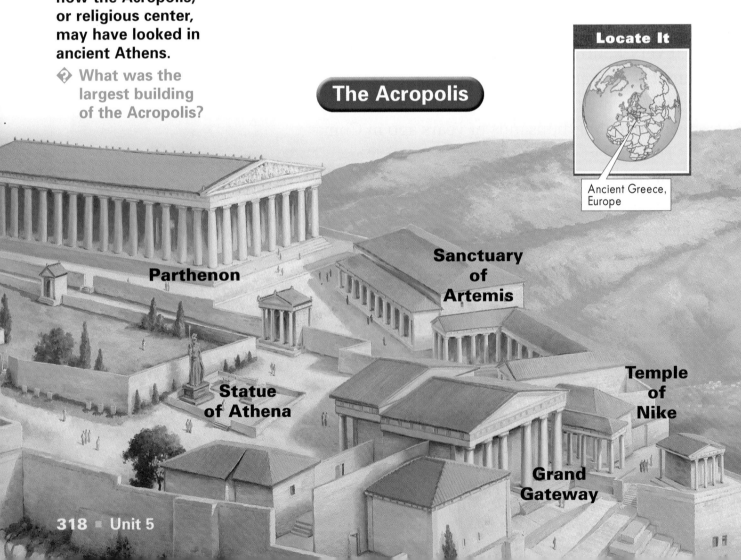

The Acropolis

Locate It

Ancient Greece, Europe

Parthenon

Sanctuary of Artemis

Statue of Athena

Temple of Nike

Grand Gateway

At the center of Rome was a public square called the Forum. Romans met there to talk about government or to buy and sell goods and services.

Locate It

Ancient Rome, Europe

Ancient Rome

The Roman civilization developed from a number of tiny villages. These were scattered over seven hills above the Tiber (TY•ber) River in what is today the country of Italy. As the villages grew, they combined to form the city of Rome.

The people of ancient Rome created the world's first republic. In a **republic**, citizens vote for leaders to make decisions for them in the government.

Rome's leaders, working to make the city stronger, ordered new roads and public buildings. Over time, Rome grew to become one of the richest cities in the world.

Sculpture of Roman leader Caesar Augustus

Review What form of government did Rome have?

Mali

The great empire of Mali in Africa was among the richest in the ancient world. An **empire** is all the land and people under the control of a powerful nation. For many hundreds of years, between 700 and 1400, Mali and other empires were important trading centers. Traders exchanged gold and slaves for salt and cloth that came by camel caravan from the Mediterranean coast. A caravan is a traveling group of traders.

Although some buildings from ancient times still stand, Mali is no longer a powerful trading center. Modern shipping routes do not come through Mali, which has no seaport or good roads. Dry weather makes farming difficult, and there are few natural resources. Mali today is among the world's poorest countries.

Review **What caused Mali to fail as a trading center?**

Locate It

Ancient Mali, Africa

The Great Mosque at Timbuktu in Mali

Mansa Musa

Character Trait: Cooperation

In 1324, Mansa Musa, the ruler of Mali, made an important journey. Mansa Musa was a Muslim. He followed the way of life and religion of Islam. His trip was a religious journey to the Islamic city of Mecca. On his way he exchanged goods with people he met, and they never forgot him. Trade with Mali increased, and Muslim teachers and students began to come to Timbuktu. This city in Mali soon became a cultural center for Muslims.

MULTIMEDIA BIOGRAPHIES
Visit The Learning Site at **www.harcourtschool.com/ biographies**
to learn about other famous people.

GO ONLINE

LESSON 4
Review

1 Main Idea What ideas from civilizations of the past are still used today?

2 Vocabulary Write a few sentences about one of the **ancient** cultures you read about.

3 Reading Skill—Sequence Reread the section on ancient China. Then list the steps of the processes the ancient Chinese used to make paper and to print pages.

4 Your Community Write about a place in your community that shows an idea from one of the ancient civilizations.

 Performance—Create a Radio Interview With a partner, write a radio interview with an imaginary person living in one of the ancient civilizations. Tape-record your interview, and play it for the class.

9 Review and Test Preparation

Use Your Reading Skills

Complete this graphic organizer to show that you understand the sequence of events in the Virginia Colony and Jamestown. A copy of this graphic organizer appears on page 70 of the Activity Book.

Sequence of Events in the Virginia Colony and Jamestown

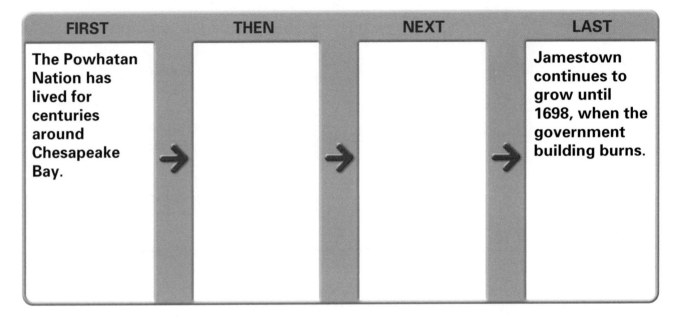

FIRST	THEN	NEXT	LAST
The Powhatan Nation has lived for centuries around Chesapeake Bay.			Jamestown continues to grow until 1698, when the government building burns.

THINK & WRITE

Write an Advertisement When the government of Virginia moved to Williamsburg, the colony of Jamestown failed. Write an advertisement that the government leaders might have written to persuade Jamestown residents to move to Williamsburg.

Write a Thank-You Letter Suppose you could write a letter to an inventor in an ancient civilization. Write a thank-you letter, explaining how his or her invention has affected later civilizations. Include details about how the invention affects your life today.

Use Vocabulary

Write the missing word.

decade (p. 292)	civilization (p. 314)
century (p. 292)	pyramid (p. 316)
ancient (p. 314)	pharaoh (p. 316)
modern (p. 314)	

1 A large group of people living in an organized way is a ___.

2 The times we live in today are called ___ times.

3 A ___ is an Egyptian king.

4 A ___ is an ancient tomb, or burial place, for Egyptian kings and queens.

5 The times thousands of years ago are called ___ times.

6 Ten years is a ___.

7 One hundred years is a ___.

Recall Facts

Answer these questions.

8 What are some sources of information about the history of a community?

9 Why was life difficult in the Jamestown colony?

10 What happened in Galveston, Texas, in 1900 that changed the city? Why has Galveston never been the same since then?

11 How did Louis Pasteur bring better health to people all over the world?

Write the letter of the best choice.

12 **Test Prep** ___ had the world's first democracy.
   A The United States
   B Greece
   C China
   D Mali

13 **Test Prep** In a democracy, citizens—
   F vote to make decisions.
   G are ruled by kings and queens.
   H share the same religious beliefs.
   J can do whatever they want.

Think Critically

14 How would you find information about what your community was like a decade ago?

15 Name an important ancient invention. How do you think it changed people's lives?

16 Compare ancient Egypt with ancient Greece. How were they alike? How were they different?

Apply Skills

Identify Cause and Effect

17 What natural disaster caused damage to the town of Stormville?

Understand Time Periods

18 How many years are shown on Time Line A on page 312?

Fort Massac State Park

History comes alive at Fort Massac in Metropolis, Illinois. Visitors can explore this copy of the real fort, which was built in 1794. They can also watch costumed workers reenact scenes of pioneer life in the 1700s. Fort Massac became the first state park in Illinois in 1908.

Locate It

Lake Michigan

ILLINOIS

Ft. Massac State Park

10

Our Nation's History

66 Our history sings of centuries
Such varying songs it sings!
It starts with winds, slow
moving sails, it ends with
skies and wings. 99

—Catherine Cate Coblentz,
Our History, 1957

CHAPTER READING SKILL

Identify Cause and Effect

A **cause** is something that makes some-thing else happen. An **effect** is something that happens as a result of a cause.

As you read this chapter, look for clue words such as *because* and *as a result*. They will help you identify the causes and effects of important events in the United States. List the causes and effects you discover.

CAUSE	EFFECT

Main Idea
People have lived in North America and South America for many thousands of years.

Vocabulary

nomad

America's Earliest Communities

Who were the first Americans? No one knows the answer to that question. However, historians agree that humans have lived on the continents of North America and South America for thousands of years.

Over hundreds of thousands of years, Earth's continents have changed. Once there was a strip of land connecting Asia and North America. It joined what is now Russia with present-day Alaska. When large mammals crossed that land bridge, the people who hunted them followed. These hunters were the ancestors of the Native Americans, also called American Indians.

Hunting Communities

The first people to cross from Asia to North America were used to the harsh climate of the Far North. In winter, the weather is very cold there, and it is dark even in the daytime. In summer, the weather is warmer, and it stays light day and night. The early hunters survived by hunting caribou on land and catching seals, walrus, and whales in the ocean.

As the people moved farther south, the land changed, and there were different animals to hunt. In the dense forests, they found deer, elk, and bear. On the Great Plains, there were great herds of buffalo.

Early North American hunters

FAST FACT Early people spent much of their time hunting for food. They probably walked about 20 miles (32 km) every day.

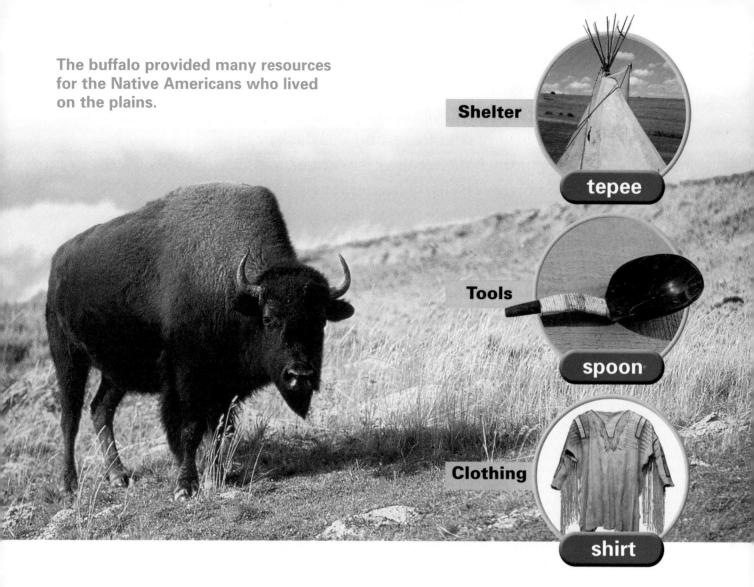

The buffalo provided many resources for the Native Americans who lived on the plains.

Shelter
tepee

Tools
spoon

Clothing
shirt

Native Americans used a travois to move their belongings from place to place.

The groups who settled on the plains made the buffalo the center of their lives. These Native Americans, ancestors of the Sioux Indians, were **nomads**. They did not settle in one place but followed the buffalo herds. They used movable homes called tepees and dragged their belongings on a travois (truh•VOY).

When the hunters killed a buffalo, they used every part of it. They ate the meat and made the bones into tools. They used the skin to make their clothes, their tepees, and the travois. The buffalo was so important to them that it became part of their religion.

Review What is a nomad?

Farming Communities

When they reached the dry land of the desert Southwest, early people became farmers in order to survive. Once people began to farm, they could store extra food to live on in bad years and to use in trade. For example, when they met with Indians who hunted buffalo, they would trade corn for meat and skins.

Because farmers settled in one place, they could own more than hunters, who had to keep moving. The Pueblo Indians used clay to make pottery and dishes. They also used adobe (uh•DOH•bee), or sun-dried clay bricks, to build the *pueblos*, or villages, that gave them their name.

Review **How did life change for Native Americans after they began farming?**

This woman is wearing traditional Pueblo clothing. Adobe bricks were used to build homes like these in Taos, New Mexico.

Cities and Empires

The Native Americans who settled and farmed developed many technologies. In time, these led to a rich and well-organized way of life.

Around A.D. 700, a civilization grew up where the Missouri River meets the Mississippi River. This place, called Cahokia, was once the home of nearly 40,000 people. Cahokia reached this size because the people had learned how to grow enough food to feed a large population.

The Cahokians came to be called the Mound Builders because they created large mounds of soil to honor their leaders. On the flat tops of these mounds, they built temples.

The climate of Cahokia was pleasant, and the land was rich in animal and plant resources. The location on the two rivers made it easy for the people to trade with other communities far away.

This dish is an artifact from Cahokia Mounds State Historic Site.

This painting shows how Native Americans lived and worked in the community of Cahokia.

This early American civilization lasted for about 700 years. Historians are not sure why it disappeared. Some think that the population may have grown too large and that overcrowding may have led to disease.

Review Why were the Cahokians called Mound Builders?

Native Americans used canoes like this one for transportation on the Missouri and Mississippi Rivers.

LESSON I
Review

1. **Main Idea** Where did the first people to come to North and South America come from?

2. **Vocabulary** Use the vocabulary word **nomad** in a sentence to describe the way of life of the buffalo hunters.

3. **Reading Skill—Cause and Effect** What were some things that made the civilization at Cahokia possible?

4. **Your Community** Do research in a library to learn about the Native Americans who live in or near your community. Share the information you find.

Performance—Make a Display of Cultures Research a Native American tribe. Bring to class something that relates to that group—an object, a picture, a poem, or a song. Add your item to a bulletin board display.

Main Idea
The voyage made by Christopher Columbus opened up the Americas to settlement by Europeans.

Vocabulary

explorer
claim

Newcomers Arrive

Long ago, only Native Americans lived in North America. Then, in 1492, the Italian explorer Christopher Columbus sailed from Spain. An **explorer** is a person who goes to find out about a place. He thought he could sail west around the world to the part of Asia that Europeans called the Indies. Instead, he reached a continent that people in Europe did not know about. It was part of what we now call the Americas, the continents of North America and South America.

Ships built to look like those used by Christopher Columbus enter Corpus Christi harbor in Texas.

In this painting, Columbus claims the Americas for the king and queen of Spain.

Cultures Meet

The people already living in the Americas belonged to hundreds of groups, or tribes. Each had its own name, language, and culture. Because Columbus thought he had reached the Indies, he called the people he met Indians.

News of Columbus's discovery spread through Europe. Explorers from Spain, France, Portugal, and England sailed to the Americas. They took home stories of the rich natural resources, such as gold, that they discovered there. Soon their kings and queens claimed parts of the Americas for their own countries.

Columbus Day

Each year on the second Monday of October, many Americans celebrate Christopher Columbus's voyage. Columbus Day was started by Italian immigrants in New York City on October 12, 1866. In 1937 President Franklin Roosevelt made the holiday official. Today it is celebrated with parades in many American cities with large Italian American populations.

Fort Castillo de San Marcos in St. Augustine, Florida

The oldest school in St. Augustine

To **claim** something is to say that it belongs to you. Spain claimed what is now the Southwestern part of the United States, Mexico, and most of South America. France claimed what is now Canada and most of the Middle Western United States. Portugal claimed present-day Brazil. England claimed a strip of North America along the coast of the Atlantic Ocean.

Soon people began coming from those European countries to settle these lands. In 1565 the Spanish started St. Augustine, the first long-lasting European settlement, in what is now Florida. In 1607 the English started Jamestown in what is now Virginia.

Review Which country started St. Augustine?

The Time of the Colonies

Over time, many settlements were started in what is now the United States. Willing settlers came from England and other parts of Europe. There were also people who came against their will. Africans were captured in their own countries and sold to traders. Some were brought to Jamestown in 1619 to work in the fields as slaves.

Most of the settlements along the eastern coast of North America were colonies of England. The colonies had their own laws, but England made laws for them, too. By the 1700s, there were 13 English colonies along the Atlantic Ocean from present-day Maine to Georgia. These colonies were the beginning of what is now the United States of America.

Review **Where were the colonies located?**

Location **This map shows the locations of the 13 colonies.**

◇ **Why do you think the colonies were built along the coast?**

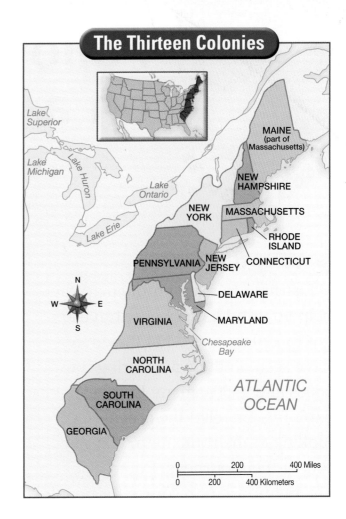

The Thirteen Colonies

MAINE (part of Massachusetts)
NEW HAMPSHIRE
NEW YORK
MASSACHUSETTS
RHODE ISLAND
CONNECTICUT
PENNSYLVANIA
NEW JERSEY
DELAWARE
VIRGINIA
MARYLAND
Chesapeake Bay
NORTH CAROLINA
SOUTH CAROLINA
GEORGIA
ATLANTIC OCEAN

Lake Superior
Lake Michigan
Lake Huron
Lake Ontario
Lake Erie

0   200   400 Miles
0   200   400 Kilometers

LESSON 2
Review

1 **Main Idea** What event in history opened the Americas to settlement by Europeans?

2 **Vocabulary** Use the vocabulary word **claim** in a sentence to explain why Europeans came to the Americas.

3 **Reading Skill—Cause and Effect** The need to find a faster trade route to Asia caused Columbus to sail on a voyage of discovery. What was one effect of his voyage?

4 **Your Community** Look around at home and in your community to find the name *Christopher Columbus*. You might find it on signs, packaging, and more. Share the examples you find.

 Performance—Write a Letter Imagine that you are a sailor on one of Columbus's ships. Write to your family, describing what it was like to come ashore in this new land. Illustrate your letter with drawings, if you wish, and share it with your class.

Follow Routes on a Map

▶ Why It Matters

Learning to read a route map can help you understand how travelers got to a place and what they may have seen on the way. During the 1500s and 1600s, many European explorers traveled the ocean. By looking at the route map, you can follow their journeys. Route maps are an important resource for people who want to make the same journey.

▶ What You Need to Know

The routes the explorers took are marked with different colors on the route map. The color blue is used for Columbus's route, green for Magellan's, pink for Dias's, yellow for da Gama's, and red for Vespucci's.

▶ Practice the Skill

Look at the route map and answer the questions.

1. What oceans did Magellan travel on his journey?
2. Which explorers traveled east on their journey?
3. Which explorer traveled the shortest distance?

▶ Apply What You Learned

Make a route map from your home to a store in your community. Draw at least two ways to get there, using a different color for each route. Label all the important landmarks, and include a map key.

 Practice your map and globe skills with the **GeoSkills CD-ROM**.

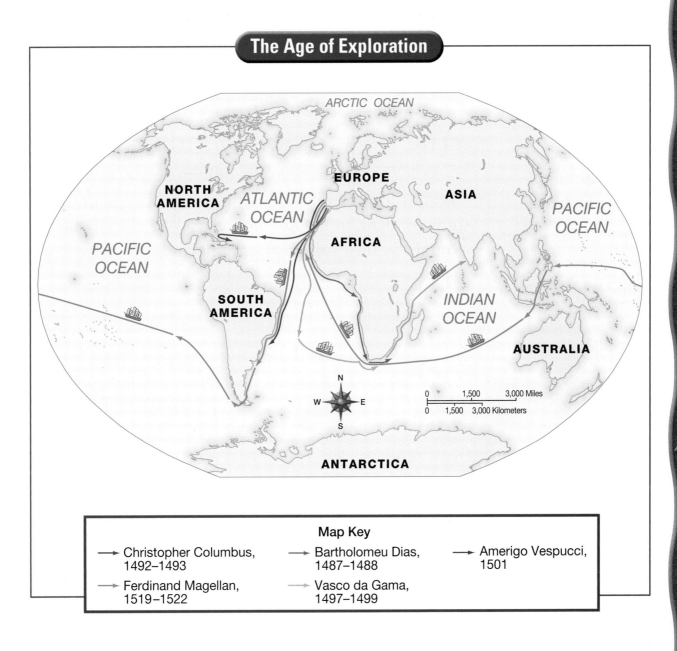

The Age of Exploration

ARCTIC OCEAN

EUROPE

ASIA

NORTH AMERICA

ATLANTIC OCEAN

PACIFIC OCEAN

AFRICA

PACIFIC OCEAN

SOUTH AMERICA

INDIAN OCEAN

AUSTRALIA

ANTARCTICA

N
W · E
S

0   1,500   3,000 Miles
0   1,500   3,000 Kilometers

Map Key

→ Christopher Columbus, 1492–1493

→ Ferdinand Magellan, 1519–1522

→ Bartholomeu Dias, 1487–1488

→ Vasco da Gama, 1497–1499

→ Amerigo Vespucci, 1501

A New Nation

Main Idea
The thirteen English colonies decided to fight for independence from England.

Vocabulary

colonist
revolution
independence

For a long time the **colonists**, or people living in the thirteen English colonies, did not mind being ruled by England. Then lawmakers in England began passing new laws for them that they felt were unfair. The colonists were angry that they were given no part in making these laws. They began talking about starting their own country.

The Declaration of Independence

In 1775 the American Revolution began. In a **revolution**, people are fighting for a change in government. In the Revolutionary War, the colonists fought against soldiers from England.

Benjamin Franklin, Thomas Jefferson, and John Adams are shown working on the Declaration of Independence.

Independence Hall in Philadelphia, Pennsylvania, is where the Declaration of Independence was signed in 1776.

Benjamin Franklin 1706–1790

Character Trait: Cooperation

Benjamin Franklin was one of the leaders who signed the Declaration of Independence in 1776. He was also a signer of the Constitution of the United States in 1787. Other leaders had fought in the war. Benjamin Franklin served his country with the power of his pen. He was good at writing ideas down clearly, talking with foreign leaders, and cooperating with fellow Americans. In these ways, he helped the new country reach its goals of independence and peace. Representing the United States in France, Benjamin Franklin signed the Treaty of Paris, which ended the Revolutionary War.

MULTIMEDIA BIOGRAPHIES
Visit The Learning Site at www.harcourtschool.com/biographies
to learn about other famous people.

GO ONLINE

In 1776, John Adams, Benjamin Franklin, Thomas Jefferson, and other leaders wrote down the reasons the colonies wanted independence. **Independence** is freedom from another country's control. The statement they wrote is called the Declaration of Independence. In it they said that the colonies had decided to form a new government and be free from England. They wrote that all people are "created equal" and have the right to "Life, Liberty, and the pursuit of Happiness."

On July 4, 1776, the leaders of the thirteen colonies voted to accept the Declaration of Independence. It told everyone that the colonies no longer belonged to England. They were now states in the new nation of the United States of America.

Review **What is a revolution?**

This ink stand was used by the signers of the Declaration of Independence.

Points of View
Declaring Independence

WILLIAM PITT, a member of the English Parliament

❝Be it declared . . . the colonies and the people of America are [English] subjects . . ., in all cases whatsoever.❞

RICHARD HENRY LEE, a member of the Continental Congress

❝That these united colonies are, and of right ought to be, free and independent states . . . and that all political connection between them [the colonies] and [England] is, and ought to be, totally dissolved.❞

Analyze the Viewpoints

❶ What views about the colonies' independence did each person have?

❷ **Make It Relevant** Look for the letters to the editor section of a newspaper. Find two letters that have different points of view about the same subject. Then write a short paragraph about the point of view expressed in each letter.

William Pitt

Richard Henry Lee

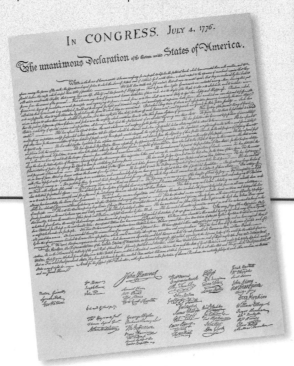

The Declaration of Independence

The War for Freedom

The Revolutionary War lasted for many years. George Washington was chosen to lead the American troops against the English. Washington's army was made up of colonists who wanted to help. They were not trained or paid, and they had to get supplies from the towns for which they were fighting. The English soldiers, on the other hand, were well trained and were paid to fight. Their supplies were shipped to them from England.

George Washington led the American soldiers in many battles. Some they won, and others they lost badly. In 1783, after a long struggle, the Americans finally won the war and their independence from England.

Revolutionary War drum

Review **Who was the leader of the American army in the Revolutionary War?**

This painting shows the Battle of Princeton, 1777.

A New Government

Americans fought the Revolutionary War because they felt that England's laws were unfair. For their new nation they wanted a government that would make fair laws. The leaders of the thirteen states got together and wrote a plan of government. We call it the Constitution of the United States.

The Bill of Rights is a part of the Constitution that names our rights and freedoms.

Here a woman views the Constitution in Washington, D.C.

George Washington, surrounded by other leaders, is sworn in as the nation's first President.

The states approved the Constitution by 1789. When Americans voted to elect their first President, they chose General George Washington. Washington became President on April 30, 1789, in New York City, which was the capital at that time.

Review **What is the Constitution of the United States?**

LESSON 3
Review

① Main Idea Why did the people in the thirteen colonies want independence from England?

② Vocabulary Use the word **independence** in a sentence about the Revolutionary War.

③ Reading Skill—Cause and Effect What caused the Revolutionary War?

④ Your Community Look around your home or community for ways in which pictures of leaders have been used.

For example, some American leaders can be found on the money we use.

 Performance—Write a Newspaper Article Write an article about the Revolutionary War. Tell about the event by answering the questions *Who? What? When? Where?* and *Why?* If possible, include pictures of the people and events. Add your article to those of your classmates to make a newspaper.

Main Idea
The nation's new capital city was built along the Potomac River between the states of Virginia and Maryland.

Vocabulary

District of Columbia

Building the Nation's Capital

The newly formed country needed a capital city, a city where government leaders could meet to make laws. Without one, they were meeting in different places. Some lawmakers thought that one of the country's largest cities, such as New York or Philadelphia, should be the capital. President George Washington, however, thought the capital should be a new city built in the geographical middle of the new country.

George Washington, as painted by Rembrandt Peale

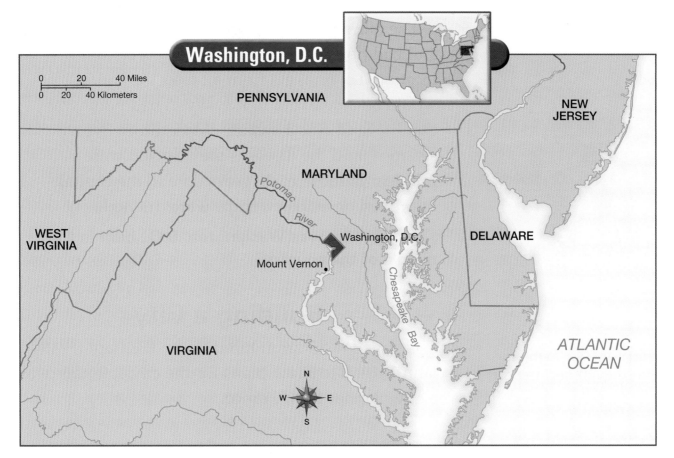

Washington, D.C.

0   20   40 Miles
0   20   40 Kilometers

PENNSYLVANIA

NEW JERSEY

WEST VIRGINIA

MARYLAND

Potomac River

Washington, D.C.

Mount Vernon

DELAWARE

Chesapeake Bay

VIRGINIA

ATLANTIC OCEAN

N W E S

Human-Environment Interactions This map shows the area along the Potomac River where the nation's capital city was built.

◆ Is George Washington's home, Mount Vernon, north or south of Washington, D.C.?

Selecting a Place

In 1791 the Potomac (puh•TOH•muhk) River was right in the middle of the United States. The states of Virginia and Maryland each gave some land along the Potomac River for the new capital. This land would belong to the nation, not to any state. It would be known as the **District of Columbia** (D.C.) in honor of Christopher Columbus.

The lawmakers asked George Washington to find a good place on this land to build the new city. Each day, Washington rode his horse along the riverbank. Finally, he chose the place where the country's capital, to be called Washington, would be built.

George Washington's compass

Pierre L'Enfant

The place that Washington chose had good points and bad points. A good point was its central location. Lawmakers from all over the country would be able to get to it easily. A bad point was that the land was a swamp. Mosquitoes live in swamps, and the diseases they carried were a problem in those early years. Life in the capital improved once the swamps were drained.

Review **Why was Washington, D.C., built in the middle of the country?**

Building a City

George Washington hired Pierre L'Enfant (PYAIR lahn•FAHNT) to draw plans for the city. L'Enfant was a city planner from France.

From this drawing by Pierre L'Enfant, the city of Washington, D.C., began to take shape.

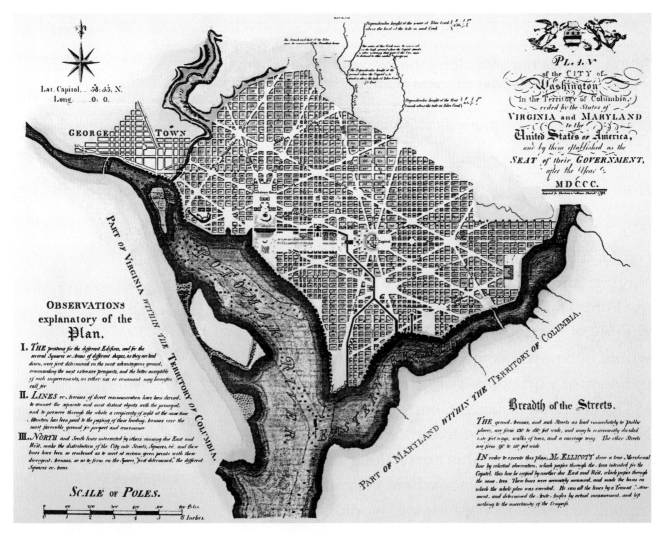

Benjamin Banneker
1731–1806
Character Trait: Creativity

At a time when many African Americans were still enslaved, Benjamin Banneker became a respected inventor and scientist. In 1791 and 1792 he helped to plan the new capital city of the United States, Washington, D.C. Banneker later became famous as the author of his own almanac. He also worked to end slavery.

MULTIMEDIA BIOGRAPHIES **GO ONLINE**
Visit The Learning Site at
www.harcourtschool.com/biographies
to learn about other famous people.

He decided he wanted the Capitol, or the building where lawmakers meet, to be the focus of the city. The President's house, later called the White House, would be built nearby.

L'Enfant lost his job before much of the city was built. George Washington fired him because he did not listen to directions and had too many disagreements with important people. L'Enfant also spent more money than the government had given him for the project.

L'Enfant's ideas, however, still guided the building of Washington, D.C. Two surveyors, Andrew Ellicott and Benjamin Banneker, made maps and plans based on L'Enfant's designs. The result is a city known for its wide streets and many beautiful parks.

Review Who planned the building of Washington, D.C.?

Early surveying tools

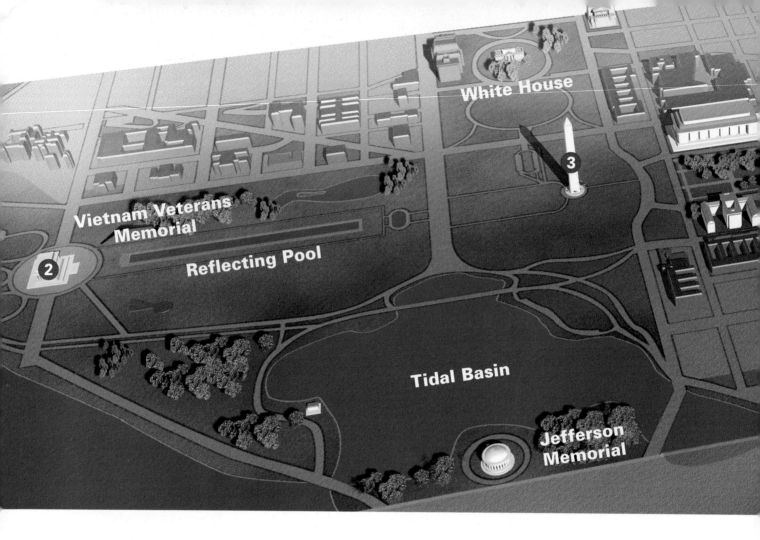

Vietnam Veterans
Memorial

Reflecting Pool

White House

2

3

Tidal Basin

Jefferson
Memorial

People visit the Capitol
Building in Washington,
D.C.

Washington Today

Today Washington, D.C., is known for the Capitol, the White House, and other government buildings. It is also known for its monuments to people and events important in our country's history. The District of Columbia has a population of more than half a million people. Many work for the government in offices located in the capital city.

Washington, D.C., is visited both by citizens of the United States and by people from around the world. Our capital city is a symbol of our nation's history.

Review Why is Washington, D.C., important today?

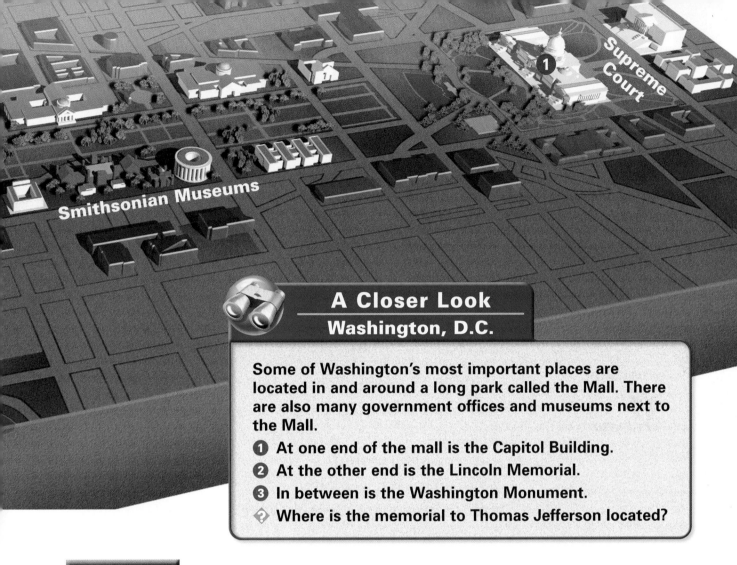

Smithsonian Museums

Supreme Court

A Closer Look
Washington, D.C.

Some of Washington's most important places are located in and around a long park called the Mall. There are also many government offices and museums next to the Mall.

1. At one end of the mall is the Capitol Building.
2. At the other end is the Lincoln Memorial.
3. In between is the Washington Monument.
? Where is the memorial to Thomas Jefferson located?

LESSON 4
Review

1. **Main Idea** Why did the nation's early leaders want to build a new capital city?

2. **Vocabulary** Use the vocabulary term **District of Columbia** in a sentence to describe the nation's new capital city.

3. **Reading Skill—Cause and Effect** Why did L'Enfant, the planner of Washington, D.C., lose his job?

4. **Your Community** Learn the location of the capital city of your state.

Use the Internet or books in the library to help you find an interesting fact about the location or the plan of your state capital. Share the fact with your class.

Performance—Make a Flag Choose a state you would like to know more about. Then use markers or crayons and construction paper to make that state's flag. Identify your flag, and add it to a display of flags around the classroom.

The Nation Grows

Main Idea
The boundaries of the United States changed as people began to settle the West.

Vocabulary

expansion
landmark
civil war
amendment

The American Revolution took place in the eastern part of our country, where most Americans then lived. Over time, more and more Americans moved west, and our nation grew in size.

Moving West

It was President Thomas Jefferson's dream that one day the United States would stretch from ocean to ocean. Soon westward expansion was more than a dream. **Expansion** is growth in size. In 1803, Jefferson purchased or bought the huge territory of Louisiana from the French. With the Louisiana Purchase, Jefferson added thousands of miles of land to the United States.

The Oregon coastline near Astoria

William Clark

Meriwether Lewis

Jefferson sent Meriwether Lewis and William Clark to explore the new lands and to map a route to the west coast. The Corps of Discovery, as the explorers and their crew called themselves, mapped their route and the landmarks along the way. **Landmarks** are important natural features that help people find their way.

In the explorers' journals were drawings of the plants, animals, and birds they saw along their way. The explorers also brought back information about the Native Americans who lived in these lands. The knowledge that explorers Lewis and Clark provided helped open the western lands to American settlement.

Review Why did President Thomas Jefferson send Lewis and Clark to the western lands?

· GEOGRAPHY ·

Rivers and Mountains
Understanding Physical Regions

The mountain ranges on the continent of North America were like barriers to people wanting to move west. The early pioneers had to find a way through the Appalachian Mountains. Later, settlers moving farther west had to get through the Rocky Mountains and the Sierra Nevada. Rivers could be crossed by floating the wagons like boats. Rivers also provided highways for explorers in canoes. The Mississippi, the Missouri, the Snake, and the Columbia Rivers were all important to settlement in the West.

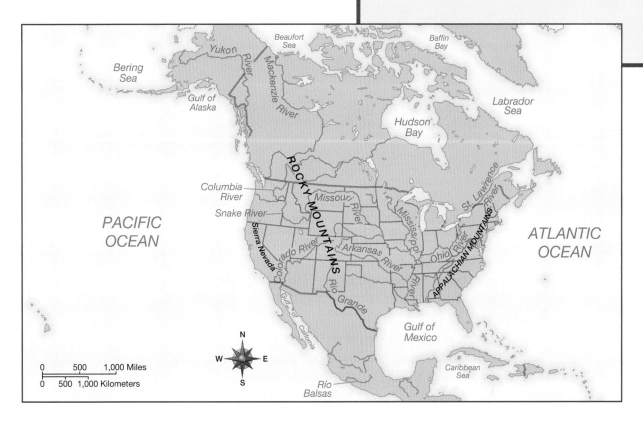

The Civil War

Beginning in 1861, Americans fought a terrible war. One half of the nation fought against the other half. This war between the North and the South is known as the Civil War. A **civil war** is a war in which two parts of one country fight each other.

Many people in the North thought that having slaves was wrong. They wanted a law saying that no one in our country could own slaves. Many people in the South disagreed. Their way of life was based on having slaves to help them on their plantations and farms.

The conflict over owning slaves was not the only reason for the war. There were other things on which people in the North and the South did not agree.

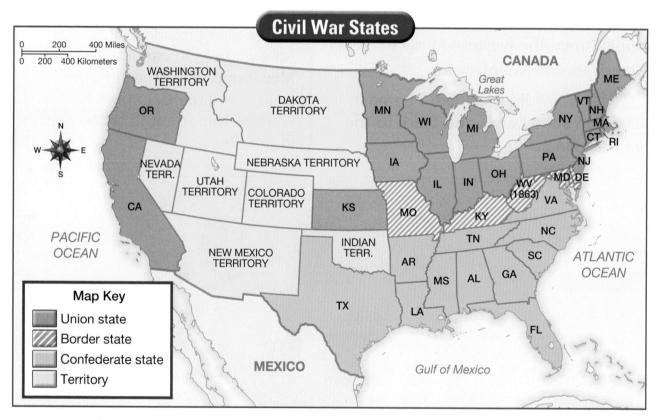

Civil War States

Map Key
- Union state
- Border state
- Confederate state
- Territory

Human-Environment Interactions This map shows the border states that did not support either the North or the South.

◈ A territory is land that belongs to a government but is not a state. Which territory borders a Union state, a Confederate state, and a border state?

Because of these disagreements, those in the South decided to start their own country. They separated from the rest of the United States, or the Union. They formed the Confederate States of America, also called the Confederacy. For a time these states had their own government, laws, and president. The president of the Confederacy was Jefferson Davis.

The Union's President Abraham Lincoln hoped that the North and the South would find a way to get together again. He felt strongly that the nation should remain united. He also felt that owning slaves was wrong. In 1863 President Lincoln signed a document that freed all slaves in the Confederacy.

In 1865 President Lincoln helped pass the Thirteenth Amendment to the Constitution of the United States. An **amendment** is a change to something that is already written. This amendment says that it is against the law to own slaves.

Lincoln hoped that the end of the Civil War in 1865 and the end of owning slaves would bring the country together. This did happen, but only very slowly.

Review **Why was the Civil War fought?**

Analyze Documents
Lincoln signed a document like this one that freed all slaves in the Confederate states.

❖ What do you think the eagle stands for?

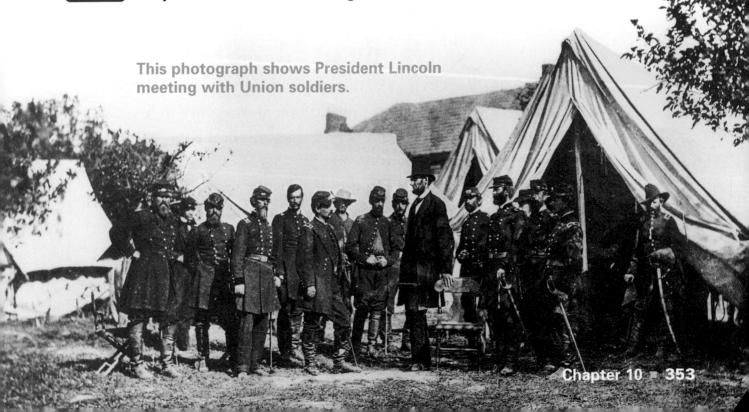

This photograph shows President Lincoln meeting with Union soldiers.

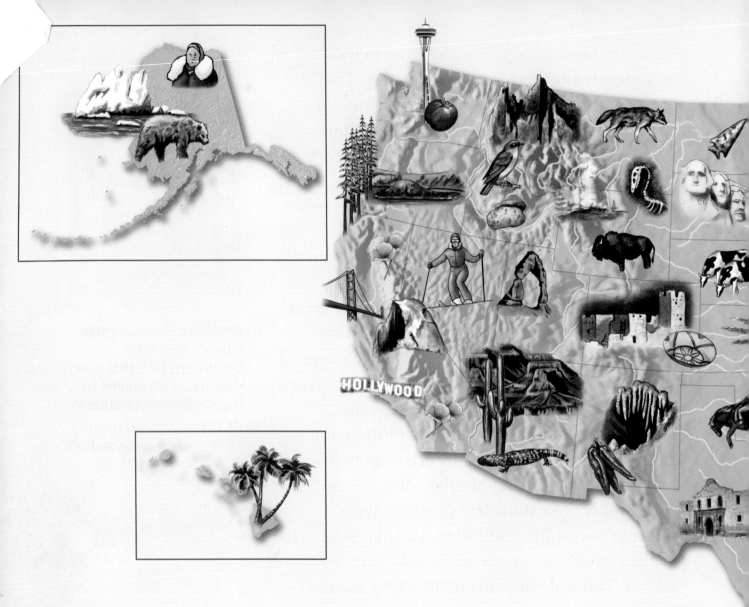

A Nation of Fifty States

After the Civil War, the country kept growing. What was once a tiny nation of thirteen states grew in less than 200 years to become a very large nation of fifty states. The United States now stretches across the continent from the Atlantic Ocean to the Pacific Ocean.

Review Which oceans does the United States stretch between?

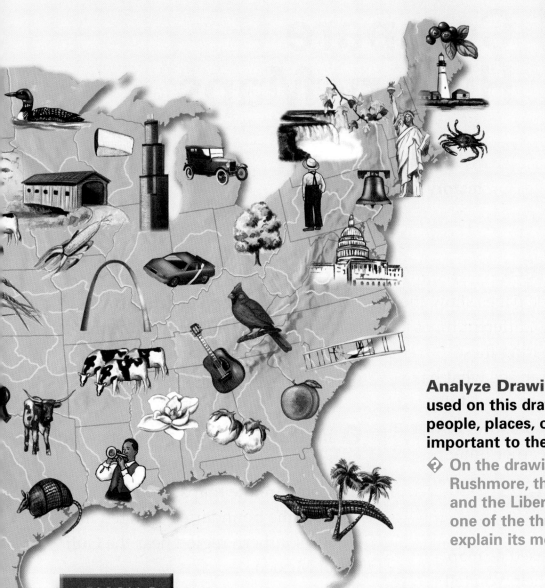

Analyze Drawings The symbols used on this drawing stand for people, places, or items that are important to the state or region.

◆ On the drawing, find Mt. Rushmore, the Statue of Liberty, and the Liberty Bell. Then choose one of the three symbols and explain its meaning.

LESSON 5
Review

1 **Main Idea** Which events led to the expansion of our country?

2 **Vocabulary** Write a sentence using either **civil war** or **amendment** from the vocabulary words to explain how our country has changed.

3 **Reading Skill—Cause and Effect** What caused the Southern states to form the Confederacy? What happened as a result?

4 **Your Community** Find out when your state became a part of the United States.

Performance—Make a Map Make a map that shows when your state became a part of the United States. Choose one color for your state. Choose another color to show all the states that were a part of the nation before your state.

Compare History Maps

Vocabulary

history map

▶ Why It Matters

The maps on these pages show the United States at two different times in history. By comparing these history maps, you can see what has changed and what has stayed the same. A **history map** shows how a place looked in an earlier time.

▶ What You Need to Know

Colors are often used as map symbols. They can help you tell water from land and show you the areas of states and countries. On these two maps, the color orange is used to show land that is part of the United States.

▶ Practice the Skill

Look at the map keys to see what each color shows. Then use the maps to answer these questions.

1 Which states were part of the United States in 1776?

2 By 1821, how many more states had been added to the nation?

3 Compare the maps and explain how the boundaries changed in the southern region near the Gulf of Mexico.

▶ Apply What You Learned

Compare and contrast an old map of your community with a newer map. What has changed? What has stayed the same?

Practice your map and globe skills with the **GeoSkills CD-ROM**.

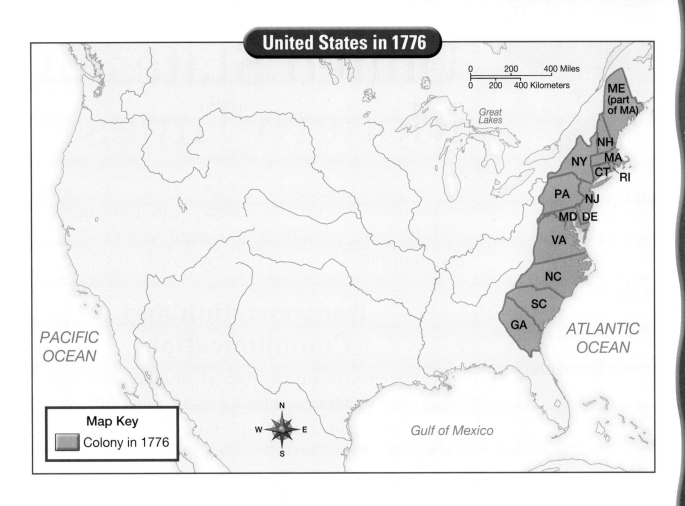

United States in 1776

0   200   400 Miles
0   200   400 Kilometers

Great Lakes

ME
(part of MA)

NH

NY   MA

CT   RI

PA   NJ

MD   DE

VA

NC

SC

GA

ATLANTIC OCEAN

PACIFIC OCEAN

Gulf of Mexico

Map Key

Colony in 1776

N   W   E   S

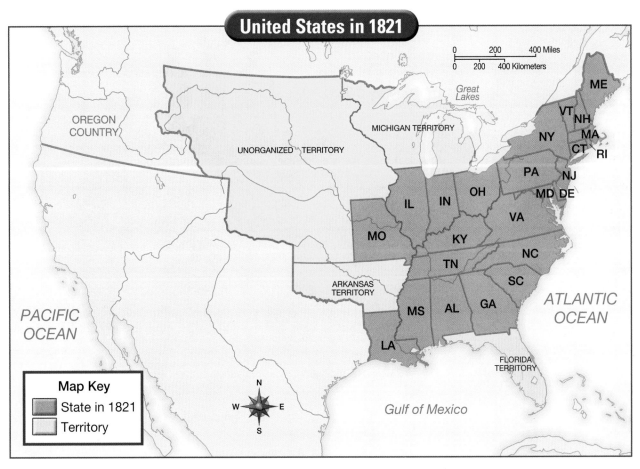

United States in 1821

0   200   400 Miles
0   200   400 Kilometers

Great Lakes

OREGON COUNTRY

MICHIGAN TERRITORY

ME

VT   NH

NY   MA

CT   RI

UNORGANIZED   TERRITORY

PA   NJ

MD   DE

IL   IN   OH

VA

MO   KY

NC

TN

SC

ARKANSAS TERRITORY

MS   AL   GA

ATLANTIC OCEAN

LA

FLORIDA TERRITORY

PACIFIC OCEAN

Gulf of Mexico

Map Key

State in 1821

Territory

N   W   E   S

Main Idea
Changes in forms of communication and transportation continue to change our country.

Vocabulary

transcontinental

United States in Modern Times

After the Civil War, the country kept growing and changing. New kinds of transportation and communication changed the way Americans lived.

Transportation and Communication

Railroads were already important in the East, but there were few trains in the West. Horses were mainly used there for transportation. In 1862 President Lincoln decided that a railroad should connect the whole country.

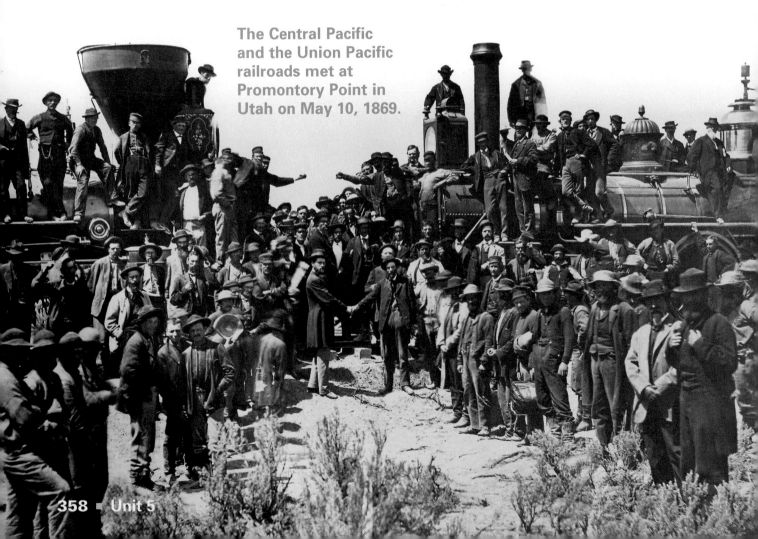

The Central Pacific and the Union Pacific railroads met at Promontory Point in Utah on May 10, 1869.

Alexander Graham Bell speaks into one of his inventions—the Centennial telephone.

Samuel Morse changed long-distance communication with the invention of the telegraph.

The telephone and the telegraph changed communication.

The Central Pacific Railroad was built eastward from Sacramento, California, as the Union Pacific Railroad was being built westward from the Missouri River. In 1869 the tracks met in Utah. At last, the Transcontinental Railroad was complete! The word **transcontinental** describes something that crosses a continent. Soon more railroads connected all the larger towns.

Samuel Morse's most important invention was the telegraph in 1840. The telegraph used electricity in a code of dots and dashes to send messages over wires. When telegraph wires were strung across the country, people could get news quickly to and from people far away.

In 1876 Alexander Graham Bell invented the telephone. People could use it to speak to and hear others who were far away. Since then, the telephone has changed in many ways.

Review Why was the transcontinental railroad important to the growth of the United States?

Astronauts John Curbeam, Jr., Thomas Jones, and Marsha Ivins wave before boarding the space shuttle *Atlantis*, which will take them to the International Space Station.

Today's World

In just one hundred years, the United States expanded its territory across the continent of North America. Soon there were towns and cities all over the land. In the 1960s Americans discovered another frontier, or new area to explore —space.

The United States was not the only country interested in exploring space. The first satellite was launched by the Soviet Union in October 1957. *Sputnik I* orbited, or circled, Earth once every hour and a half until January 1958. Soon the Soviets sent up *Sputnik II*. The Americans followed with the launch of *Explorer I*.

The International Space Station orbits Earth.

The first spacecrafts were satellites without crews. They were sent into orbit by powerful rockets. The challenge in putting people on board was planning how to get the spacecrafts back to Earth safely. In 1961 Soviet cosmonaut Yuri Gagarin orbited Earth once. Just eight years later, American astronauts Neil Armstrong and Edwin Aldrin walked on the moon.

Today, exploring space has become an international project. Twenty-two nations are cooperating to pay for, build, and run the International Space Station. Astronauts from many countries work together on the station to carry out science research.

Review **What frontier did Americans begin exploring in the 1960s?**

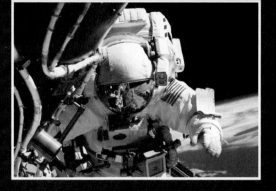

Astronaut Michael Lopez-Alegria makes a repair to the International Space Station.

Astronaut Susan J. Helms works on a computer keyboard inside the International Space Station.

LESSON 6
Review

1. **Main Idea** Name two forms of communication or transportation that have brought changes to our nation. Explain.

2. **Vocabulary** Use the vocabulary word **transcontinental** in a sentence telling what happened at Promontory Point in 1869.

3. **Reading Skill—Cause and Effect** What led to the building of the transcontinental railroad? Who made the decision?

4. **Your Community** What different kinds of communication systems are used in your school and in your community? How have they changed over time?

Performance—Research Transportation Systems What transportation systems does your community have? Choose one, and write a paragraph telling why it is important to people in your town or city. Share your paragraph.

10 Review and Test Preparation

Use Your Reading Skills

Complete this graphic organizer to show that you understand the causes and effects of early peoples' changes and growth. A copy of this graphic organizer appears on page 80 of the Activity Book.

Early Peoples' Changes and Growth

CAUSE EFFECT

CAUSE		EFFECT
Early people learned to survive by becoming farmers.		Native Americans who settled and farmed developed new technologies.
_____ _____ _____		The city of Cahokia was home to more than 10,000 people.
Native Americans living in Cahokia built large mounds to honor their dead leaders.		_____ _____ _____

THINK & WRITE

Write a Newspaper Story Imagine that you are a reporter for a colonial newspaper during the Revolutionary War. Write a newspaper story that explains the causes of the Revolutionary War to your fellow colonists.

Write a Speech The actions of many individuals affected the outcome of the American Revolution. Choose one individual and write a speech about that person. Be sure to tell in the speech how that person's actions affected the outcome of the revolution.

Use Vocabulary

Write the word that matches the definition.

nomads (p. 328)   colonists (p. 338)
explorer (p. 332)   revolution (p. 338)
independence (p. 339)
expansion (p. 350)

1 a person who goes to find out about a place

2 a fight for a change in government

3 freedom from another country's control

4 growth in size

5 the people who settled in the thirteen colonies

6 groups of people who roam the land and live in movable homes

Recall Facts

Answer the questions.

7 What did Columbus hope to find? What did he find instead?

8 What are three countries that claimed lands in the Americas?

9 Why did the ancestors of the Sioux Indians live in tepees and move from place to place?

Write the letter of the best choice.

10 **Test Prep** During the Revolutionary War, the leader of the American troops was—

A Benjamin Franklin.
B Abraham Lincoln.
C Jefferson Davis.
D George Washington.

11 **Test Prep** ____ was President of the United States during the Civil War.

F Benjamin Franklin
G Abraham Lincoln
H Jefferson Davis
J George Washington

Think Critically

12 Think about the explorers you read about in this chapter. Which one do you admire most? Explain your answer.

13 What are four ways Alexander Graham Bell's invention of the telephone in 1876 changed people's lives?

14 What words or thoughts come to mind when you think about our nation? List at least three.

Apply Skills

Follow Routes on a Map

15 Look at the map on page 337. Which explorer traveled the greatest distance?

Compare History Maps

16 Look at the maps on page 357. How many territories did the United States have in 1821?

VISIT

Monuments and Memorials in Washington, D.C.

Get Ready

A memorial is a reminder of the actions or beliefs of a person or group of people. In Washington, D.C., those who fought for our country's freedom are honored with memorials. The Vietnam Veterans Memorial, the Lincoln Memorial, the Washington Monument, and the Korean War Veterans Memorial all remind us of those who acted for our country's independence.

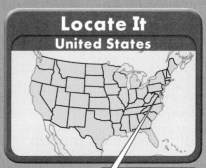

Locate It
United States

Washington, D.C.

What to See

Vietnam Veterans Memorial

This memorial, known as "The Wall," was completed in 1982. On it the designer, Maya Lin, listed the names of more than 58,000 Americans who were killed or missing in action during the Vietnam War.

Lincoln Memorial

The Lincoln Memorial opened in 1922. It was built by Daniel Chester French and Henry Bacon to honor the sixteenth President of the United States, Abraham Lincoln.

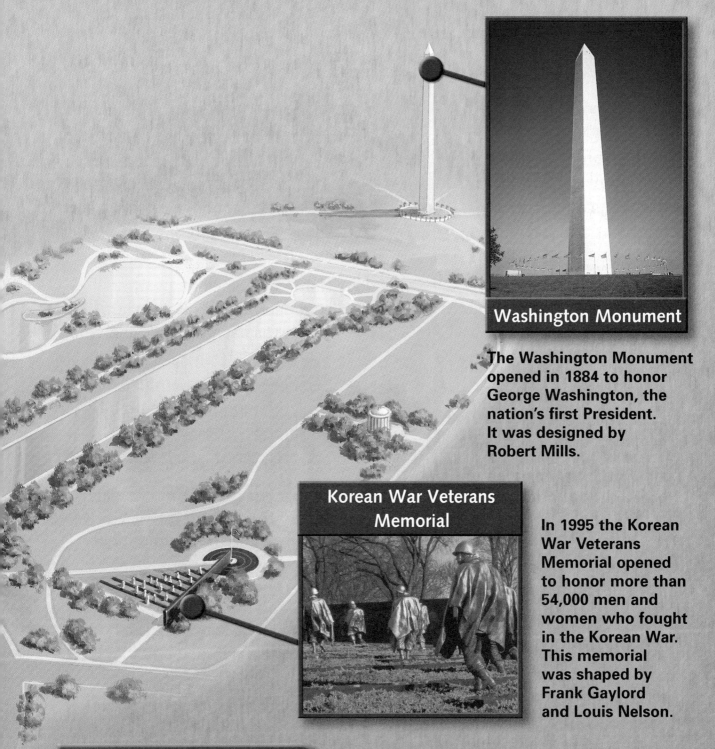

Washington Monument

The Washington Monument opened in 1884 to honor George Washington, the nation's first President. It was designed by Robert Mills.

Korean War Veterans Memorial

In 1995 the Korean War Veterans Memorial opened to honor more than 54,000 men and women who fought in the Korean War. This memorial was shaped by Frank Gaylord and Louis Nelson.

Take a Field Trip

A VIRTUAL TOUR
Visit The Learning Site at **www.harcourtschool.com/tours** to take virtual tours of other monuments and memorials.

A VIDEO TOUR
READING RAINBOW Check your media center or classroom library for a video featuring a segment from Reading Rainbow.

5 Review and Test Preparation

Use Vocabulary

Write the word or words that match the definition.

1 a word that describes times long, long ago

modern (p. 314) **ancient** (p. 314)

2 one hundred years

decade (p. 292) **century** (p. 292)

3 people who used movable homes and did not settle in one place

colonists (p. 338)
nomads (p. 328)

4 a natural or human feature that helps people find their way

claim (p. 334) **landmark** (p. 351)

5 a fight for a change in government

revolution (p. 338)
expansion (p. 350)

6 a change made to something already written

amendment (p. 353)
expansion (p. 350)

7 freedom from another country's control

independence (p. 339)
civil war (p. 352)

Recall Facts

Answer the questions.

8 What are some things that are likely to change in a community? What are some things that usually stay the same?

9 Name two cities that were changed by natural disasters. What was each disaster and what was its effect?

10 Explain how Abraham Lincoln and Jefferson Davis could be presidents at the same time.

Write the letter of the best choice.

11 **Test Prep** Benjamin Franklin served his country by—
   A fighting in the Revolutionary War.
   B becoming President of the United States.
   C helping to write the Declaration of Independence and the Constitution.
   D opening western lands to American explorers.

12 **Test Prep** The first long-lasting settlement built in North America by Europeans was—
   F Plymouth Colony.
   G Jamestown Colony.
   H Powhatan Nation.
   J St. Augustine.

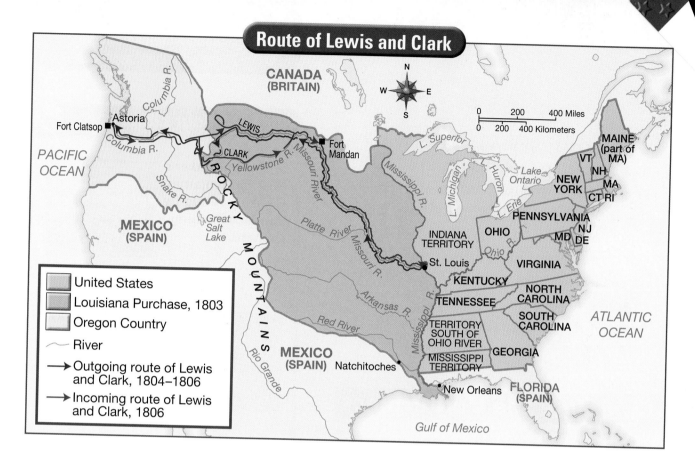

Route of Lewis and Clark

CANADA (BRITAIN)

Fort Clatsop
Astoria
PACIFIC OCEAN
Columbia R.
LEWIS
CLARK
Fort Mandan
Yellowstone R.
Missouri River
MEXICO (SPAIN)
Great Salt Lake
Snake R.
Platte River
Missouri R.
L. Superior
L. Michigan
Lake Huron
Lake Ontario
L. Erie
Mississippi R.
MAINE (part of MA)
VT NH
NEW YORK MA
CT RI
PENNSYLVANIA
NJ
OHIO MD DE
INDIANA TERRITORY
St. Louis
Ohio R.
VIRGINIA
KENTUCKY
NORTH CAROLINA
TENNESSEE
SOUTH CAROLINA
ATLANTIC OCEAN
Arkansas R.
Red River
Rio Grande
MEXICO (SPAIN)
Natchitoches
TERRITORY SOUTH OF OHIO RIVER
MISSISSIPPI TERRITORY
GEORGIA
New Orleans
FLORIDA (SPAIN)
Gulf of Mexico

Legend:
United States
Louisiana Purchase, 1803
Oregon Country
River
Outgoing route of Lewis and Clark, 1804–1806
Incoming route of Lewis and Clark, 1806

Scale: 0 200 400 Miles / 0 200 400 Kilometers

13 Test Prep Our country has grown from 13 colonies to—
A 22 colonies.
B 50 colonies.
C 50 states.
D 52 territories.

Think Critically

14 Compare the ancient Greek government with our present-day government. How are they alike? How are they different?

15 Why do you think some colonists did not want freedom from England?

16 What are four places you would like to visit in our nation's capital? Explain your choices.

Apply Skills

Follow Routes on a Map
Use the route map of Lewis and Clark to answer the following questions.

MAP AND GLOBE SKILLS

17 What symbol is used to show the route of Lewis and Clark?

18 Which river did Lewis and Clark follow through the Louisiana Purchase?

19 What color is used to show the Oregon Country?

20 From what city did Lewis and Clark start their journey?

21 What mountain range did Lewis and Clark have to cross?

Unit Activities

GO ONLINE

Visit The Learning Site at www.harcourtschool.com/socialstudies/activities for additional activities.

Present a Play

A play is a story you can act out. It has characters, a setting, and a plot. Work with a group to write and act out a play about a community of long ago. You can find information about the community in your textbook or at the library. Your group should practice acting out the play and then present it to the rest of your class.

Complete the Unit Project

Make a Museum With a small group of classmates, look at the information you have collected. Use maps, portraits, photographs, time lines, and models to present the people, places, and events you have chosen to show in your museum. Display these items on a table or bulletin board in your classroom. Invite other classes to visit your museum.

Visit Your Library

■ *The Hatmaker's Sign* by Benjamin Franklin, retold by Candace Fleming. Orchard.

■ *Old Home Day* by Donald Hall. Harcourt.

■ *Turn of the Century* by Ellen Jackson. Charlesbridge.

People Working in a Community

A brass cash register,
early 1900s

Purchase of goods from a supermarket

6

People Working in a Community

" So the more we work [and the less we talk] the better results we shall get. "

—Rudyard Kipling, *The Book of Virtues*, 1899–1902

Preview the Content

Think about what you already know about economics. Before you study the unit, create an outline chart with the two headings **Producer** and **Consumer**. As you read the unit, write each fact you learn under the correct heading.

Producer	Consumer

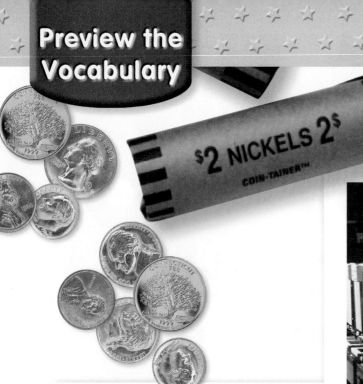

producer   A person who makes and sells a product. (page 378)

opportunity cost   What you give up in order to get what you want. (page 434)

consumer   A person who buys a product or service. (page 402)

income The money people earn for the work they do. (page 418)

free enterprise A system in which people can decide for themselves what products and services to produce and sell. (page 402)

Henry Ford's Dream

from *A Kid's Guide to the Smithsonian*

Long ago, a boy sat at a workbench and took apart a watch to see why it was broken. To everyone's surprise, he repaired the watch. Soon people were bringing their own broken watches to Henry Ford. Henry's curiosity and tinkering didn't end with watches. Instead, it started him dreaming about making something that would improve life for everyone. Read now to learn about Henry Ford's dream and how he made it come true.

In the late 1800s, a man named Henry Ford from Michigan had a dream. He wanted to make a car for everyone.

While other automakers were busy catering to the needs of the wealthy few, Ford saw an opportunity in marketing to everyday people, such as shopkeepers, farmers, and people working in offices. He dreamed of an automobile so easy to drive that a person with no experience could quickly master the controls. He dreamed of a car that would be easy to fix and affordable to practically everyone. He dreamed of millions of people driving this car everywhere, and their lives made easier and richer as a result.

catering
giving people
what they want

**Henry Ford as
a young man**

Ford's first car, the Model A, was built in his shop in 1903 and sold modestly well. Over the next five years, he continued to experiment with additional models. One thing he needed to create his ideal car was strong but cheap metal for the <u>chassis</u>. He finally found what he was looking for in a steel <u>alloy</u> called <u>vanadium</u> steel. In 1908, he used it to create his first Model T.

The Model T, or "Tin Lizzie" as it came to be known, was small, <u>homely</u>, and lightweight, with a folding top, big round headlights, and a top speed of 45 miles (72 kilometers) per hour. It was cheap and reliable, and the American people loved it.

A woman drives the Model A in front of the Ford Motor Company.

chassis
the frame of a car

alloy
a mixture of metals

vanadium
a gray metal used to make steel

homely
simple and plain

The first Model T which was built in 1908.

But Ford was still not satisfied. He continued to work on improving his manufacturing methods. His goal was to increase production efficiency of the Model T and lower costs. In 1913, he began using a conveyor belt to move cars along the assembly line, an idea he adapted from the meat-packing industry. This saved him a lot of money, and Ford passed the savings to his customers.

Much to everyone's delight, the price of a new Model T actually began to drop and continued to drop with each passing year! Eventually prices were so low that practically everyone could afford to buy a Ford. By 1927, fifteen million Model Ts had been produced. Henry Ford had made his dream come true.

People drove the Model T just about everywhere!

production efficiency
to make more products in less time

conveyor belt
a belt that carries items from worker to worker

The assembly line in 1913

It's amazing to consider where Ford's dream eventually led us. As automobiles became popular, roads were built and improved all over America. Stores, then towns, sprang up at crossroads where gas stations had been built. Motoring became one of America's favorite leisure-time activities. For the convenience of vacationing motorists, motels were established along the newly paved roads. Owing to the genius of Henry Ford, America became a country on wheels. And we remain so to this day.

"Cloverleaf" highway system of roads

Think About It

① How did Ford's dream help people and change the country?

② Today, many new items make people's lives easier. Name one new item you use, and make a drawing of it.

Henry Ford Museum

Located in Dearborn, Michigan, the Henry Ford Museum displays 200 years of inventions that made life easier. The museum, which receives more than one and a half million visitors a year, shows how Americans lived and worked in the past.

Locate It

MICHIGAN

Henry Ford Museum

Making and Selling Products

66 When you get an idea in which you believe with all your heart, work it out. **99**

—Henry Ford,
A Home for Our Heritage, 1979

CHAPTER READING SKILL

Compare and Contrast

When you **compare and contrast** people, places, ideas, or events, you think about how they are alike and how they are different.

As you read this chapter, look for ways the people and their ideas are alike and different.

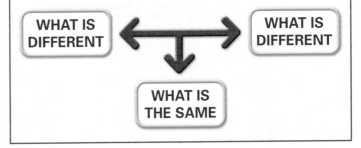

| WHAT IS DIFFERENT | | WHAT IS DIFFERENT |

WHAT IS THE SAME

Henry Ford Makes a Product

Main Idea
Henry Ford used several kinds of resources to make a product.

Vocabulary

producer
assembly line
industry
capital
human resource
raw material
capital resource

Henry Ford did not make the first automobile. Germany's Karl Benz built the first gasoline-powered automobile in 1885. Ford, however, was important as an automobile producer. A **producer** is someone who makes and sells a product. It was Ford who made the first automobiles cheap enough for many people to buy.

Ford Starts His Company

Henry Ford tried twice to start an automobile-making business before he got the Ford Motor Company running in 1903.

These workers check new cars at Ford's automobile factory in 1906.

FAST FACT

By 1908 there were more than 240 automobile factories in the United States. Many were in Detroit, giving the town the nickname "Motor City."

A Closer Look
Ford's Assembly Line

In an assembly line, work areas called stations are arranged in a specific order to make a product. The workers at each station do their task and then a moving conveyor belt carries the item to the next station.

1 Car bodies are placed on the assembly line.
2 The top and sides of car are attached.
3 Wheels are attached to cars.
4 Engine parts are added to car.

❓ Why do you think producing cars on an assembly line increased the number of cars a factory could make?

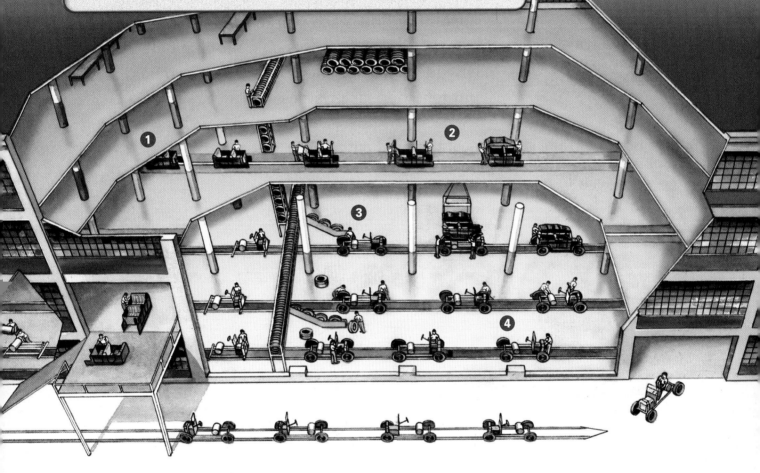

At first it was a small business that made only a few cars a day. Groups of two or three workers built the cars one at a time. They used parts made by other businesses. Building cars one at a time was very expensive. So these cars cost a lot of money.

In 1908 Ford's company produced its first Model T automobile. People liked it so much that they were willing to pay the $825.00 Ford asked—which was a lot of money in those days. By 1918 half of all cars driven in the United States were Model Ts.

To make more Model Ts to sell, Ford opened a bigger factory and tried out a new way of making his product. Up until that time, a few workers had built the complete automobile, doing every job themselves. Now Ford divided the jobs among many workers along an assembly line. On an **assembly line**, each worker adds one kind of part to a product as it passes on a moving belt. Ford's new idea allowed Model Ts to be assembled, or put together, faster at less cost.

Henry Ford in the 1930s. His signature was used to make the "Ford" nameplate placed on cars.

Smoke rises from the chimneys of this Ford automobile factory in Dearborn, Michigan. At the dock next to the factory, cargo ships wait to take the new cars away to be sold.

Instead of a few automobiles a day, Ford could now build one every 93 minutes. As a result, he could sell more cars and lower their price. In 1924, a Model T sold for only $265.00.

Review What new idea did Ford use to build automobiles faster for less money?

Ford's Company Grows

By 1927 Henry Ford's automobile company had grown into one of the biggest businesses in the car-making industry. An **industry** is all the companies that make the same product or provide the same service. Its success had brought him huge amounts of money. He used this money as **capital** to start a large new factory near Detroit, Michigan. It covered an area larger than many small towns!

This 1914 Ford Model T convertible could be driven with its top up or down.

In his new factory, Ford brought together all the resources needed to make automobiles. He hired more than 14,000 workers for the Detroit factory. Workers are the **human resources** needed to make and sell a product.

Ford also built railroads and bought ships to bring iron ore, coal, and other raw materials to his factory. **Raw materials** are the natural resources needed to make something.

Ford used his **capital resources** to buy the equipment to make iron into steel. He built factories that turned the steel into automobile parts, such as springs, axles, and car bodies.

Henry Ford had now reached his goal. He was producing automobiles that cost what people could pay. His ideas helped change the way businesses nearly 100 years ago made and sold their products. His ideas serve as models for factories even today.

Review **What raw materials did Ford use to make his automobiles?**

Thousands of workers gather outside the Ford Motor Company Building in Detroit, Michigan.

Industrial Robots

In automobile factories all over the world, robots help people build cars. A robot is a machine that is controlled by a computer. Most robots used in factories are just a big arm. These industrial robots can identify shape, light, sound, motion, and heat. They do jobs that are too heavy or dangerous for humans, such as lifting car frames or handling chemicals. Robots can do anything people program them to do. Best of all, they can do the same job hour after hour, day after day without getting tired—or bored!

LESSON I
Review

1 **Main Idea** What kinds of resources did Henry Ford use?

2 **Vocabulary** Write a paragraph that describes Henry Ford's role as a **producer**.

3 **Reading Skill—Compare and Contrast** Before Henry Ford used the assembly line, how were automobiles made?

4 **Your Community** Make a chart of community resources. Use the headings *Natural Resources, Human Resources,* and *Capital Resources.*

Performance—Simulation Work in a small group. First, each member should create an automobile from construction paper. Then divide the work into separate jobs. One member cuts out automobile bodies, all alike, for the number of group members. The others cut out wheels, headlights, and so on. Pass the automobile bodies along your "assembly line," with each person attaching a part. Compare the cars made by each method. What was lost by using the assembly-line method?

Read a Product Map

Vocabulary	
product map	agriculture

▶ Why It Matters

Not all businesses make and sell products made in factories. The map on page 385 shows where some products are raised on farms. When you can interpret, or explain, information on a **product map**, you can learn where products come from.

▶ What You Need to Know

Picture symbols are important on product maps. Each symbol stands for a different product. To find out what product each symbol stands for, look at the map key.

The map shows products from agriculture. **Agriculture** is the raising of crops and farm animals for sale. Look at the map key to find the symbols for agricultural products that are not planted.

▶ Practice the Skill

Use the map to answer these questions.

1 Is more corn grown north or south of Indianapolis?

2 Near which cities is transportation equipment manufactured?

3 Which farm animals are raised both north and south of Lafayette?

▶ Apply What You Learned

Draw a product map of your state or a nearby state. Use reference materials to find out what agricultural products are raised near you. Make a map key to explain the symbols you use. Share your map with a classmate or family member.

 Practice your map and globe skills with the **GeoSkills CD-ROM**.

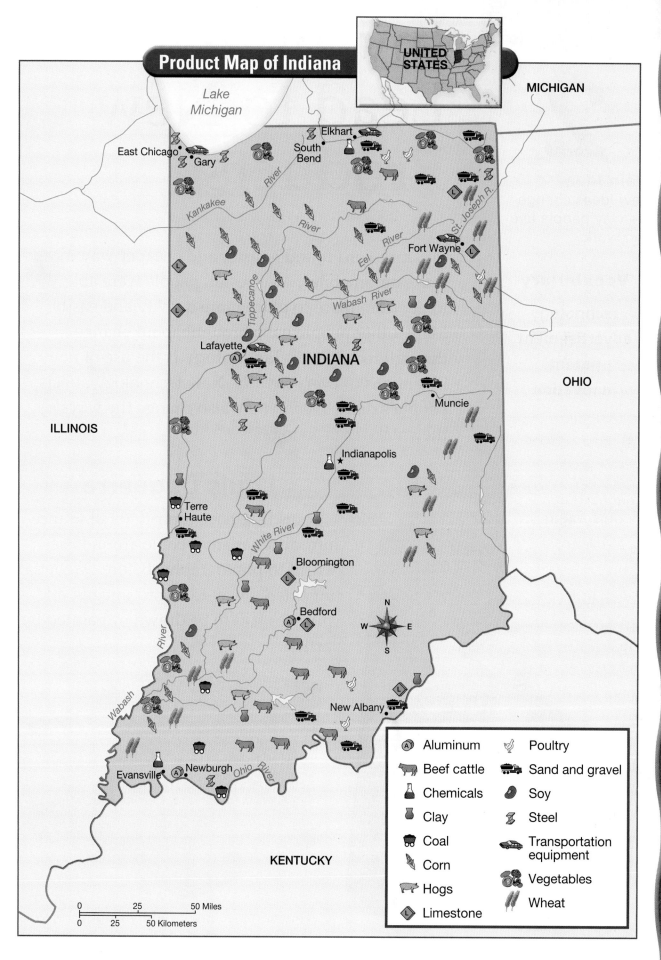

Product Map of Indiana

UNITED STATES

MICHIGAN

Lake Michigan

East Chicago
Gary
South Bend
Elkhart
Fort Wayne

ILLINOIS

Kankakee River
Tippecanoe River
Eel River
St. Joseph R.
Wabash River

Lafayette

INDIANA

Muncie

OHIO

Indianapolis

Terre Haute

White River

Bloomington

Bedford

N
W   E
S

Wabash River

New Albany

Evansville
Newburgh
Ohio River

KENTUCKY

| 0 | 25 | 50 Miles |
| 0 | 25 | 50 Kilometers |

Legend:
- Ⓐ Aluminum
- Beef cattle
- Chemicals
- Clay
- Coal
- Corn
- Hogs
- Ⓛ Limestone
- Poultry
- Sand and gravel
- Soy
- Steel
- Transportation equipment
- Vegetables
- Wheat

Main Idea
New ideas change the way people live and work.

Vocabulary

technology
advertisement
patent
innovation

Inventions Lead to New Products

Henry Ford found a faster and cheaper way to make automobiles. As a result, people were able to get from place to place more quickly and easily. Many other people have brought about change through technology. **Technology** is the use of new inventions in everyday life. New technology affects people's daily lives. It may also change the ways they make their living.

A daguerreotype portrait of Louis Daguerre

Louis Daguerre

Louis Daguerre (dah•GAIR) of France introduced many people around the world to photography. Before Daguerre invented a way to record images, all pictures had to be drawn or painted by artists.

This camera, invented by Daguerre, was the first one made for people to buy.

This daguerreotype shows the United States Capitol building in the 1840s.

While working with another inventor, Daguerre made a discovery. When he put a metal plate coated with chemicals in the light, an image formed. However, it soon faded. In 1837 Daguerre discovered that he could make the image stay by placing the plate in salt water. He named his new kind of image after himself, calling it a daguerreotype.

Daguerreotypes were a huge success. People had portraits made. Pictures of places showed what other parts of the world looked like. Daguerreotypes are no longer made, but they still have value, or worth. People collect them because they are important in the history of art and photography.

A daguerreotype of a mother and daughter

Review **What was Louis Daguerre's invention, and why was it important?**

Cyrus McCormick

Cyrus McCormick of Virginia was both an inventor and a business owner. His work changed the lives of farmers all across America. For a long time, people had used a scythe (SYTH) to harvest grain. This hand tool had a curved blade at the end of a long handle. Using a scythe was hard work. To make life easier for farmworkers, McCormick developed a new machine called a reaper. The reaper could harvest in one hour what it took one person several days to harvest with a scythe.

The reaper worked so well that McCormick opened a reaper factory in Chicago in 1847. He also began the use of advertisements to get customers. An **advertisement** is information that a business provides about its goods or services.

Review How did Cyrus McCormick's invention change farming?

Portrait of
Cyrus McCormick

The McCormick reaper was designed to be pulled by horses. Here it is being used to harvest wheat.

Granville T. Woods

Granville T. Woods of Columbus, Ohio, never had the chance to finish going to elementary school. At about the age of ten, he had to go to work. He spent his free time studying electricity and got a job as an engineer on an ocean ship.

By 1881 Woods had settled down in Cincinnati, Ohio. There he opened a factory that made telephones, telegraphs, and other electrical equipment.

Woods also became interested in steam power. In 1884 he got his first patent for a steam-boiler furnace that he invented. A **patent** is a government paper saying that only the inventor has the right to make or sell his or her invention.

Woods continued to invent. In 1887 his railroad telegraph made it possible to send messages between moving trains and between trains and stations. Woods also improved the air brake, which made train travel safer.

Review Why was it important for Woods to have patents on his inventions?

An early railroad telegraph

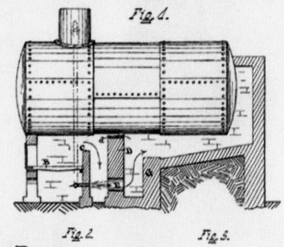

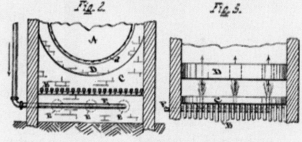

G. T. WOODS.
STEAM BOILER FURNACE.
No. 299,894.   Patented June 3, 1884.

These are diagrams of the furnace patented by Granville T. Woods. The inventor is shown below.

Jeanie Low

Jeanie Low and her invention

Most **innovations**, or new ideas and products, begin with a problem that needs to be solved. Jeanie Low of Houston, Texas, was looking for a better, safer step stool for children.

"When I was in kindergarten, I couldn't reach the bathroom sink," Low, now a young adult, explained. "We had a plastic stool, but it broke. I wanted to make a stool that folded up onto the door of the cabinet under the sink."

"My parents took me to a building supply store," she said. "I picked out some wood, and I told the man at the store how I wanted him to cut it and what it was for. He said my idea would not work."

That man was wrong. On March 10, 1992, Jeanie Low became the youngest female inventor to receive a United States patent. She was 11 years old!

Review What innovation, or new product, did Jeanie Low invent?

Low had to provide diagrams for her step stool to get a patent.

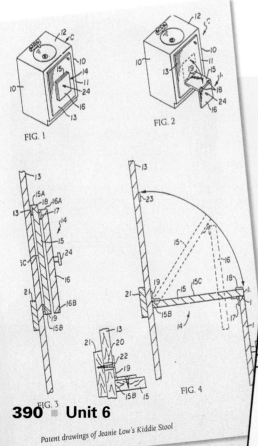

Patent drawings of Jeanie Low's Kiddie Stool

PATENT APPLICATION TRANSMITTAL LETTER   Docket Number (Optional)

To the Commissioner of Patents and Trademarks:
Transmitted herewith for filing under 35 U.S.C. 111 and 37 CFR 1.53 is the patent application of

entitled _____

Enclosed are:
- ☐ _____ pages of written description, claims and abstract.
- ☐ _____ sheets of drawings.
- ☐ an assignment of the invention to _____
- ☐ executed declaration of the inventors.
- ☐ a certified copy of a _____
- ☐ associate power of attorney.
- ☐ a verified statement to establish small entity status under 37 CFR 1.9 and 1.27.
- ☐ information disclosure statement
- ☐ preliminary amendment
- ☐ other: _____

CLAIMS AS FILED

	NUMBER FILED	NUMBER EXTRA	RATE	FEE
BASIC FEE			$730	$730
TOTAL CLAIMS	- 20 =	*	x $22	
INDEPENDENT CLAIMS	- 3 =	*	x $76	
MULTIPLE DEPENDENT CLAIM PRESENT			$240	

* NUMBER EXTRA MUST BE ZERO OR LARGER

If applicant has small entity status under 37 CFR 1.9 and 1.27, then divide total fee by 2, and enter amount here.	TOTAL	$	
	SMALL ENTITY TOTAL	$	

- ☐ A check in the amount of $ _____ to cover the filing fee is enclosed.
- ☐ The Commissioner is hereby authorized to charge and _____ No.

Hans Christiansen Lee

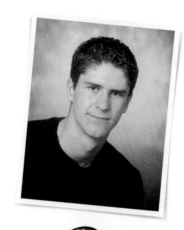

Automobiles are still being improved today. Hans Christiansen Lee was awarded a $20,000 college scholarship in 2000 for his engineering project on controlling spin in cars. Lee designed what he called a Differential Torque Control System, or DTCS. It uses torque, a twisting force, to improve control of a skidding car that begins to spin.

In road tests, cars were skidded until they went into a spin. Drivers were able to control the spinning far better in cars with DTCS than in those without it. Lee's invention may save many lives.

Review How does Lee's invention help control a car that begins to spin?

Hans Christiansen Lee and his invention

LESSON 2
Review

❶ **Main Idea** Choose one of the inventions you read about in this lesson. Tell how it changed the way people live.

❷ **Vocabulary** Write a sentence about an invention that has been important to you. Use the vocabulary word **innovation**.

❸ **Reading Skill—Compare and Contrast** Compare and contrast the ways grain was harvested before and after the invention of the McCormick reaper.

❹ **Your Community** Think of an invention that is important to the people in your community. What would life be like without it?

Performance—Draw an Invention With a partner, brainstorm a list of ideas for inventions that would make your lives easier or more comfortable. Choose one of your invention ideas. Then make a drawing of it. On your drawing include labels for the different parts of the invention. Share it with the class and explain how it could make their lives easier.

A Safer Bicycle

By the late 1800s more than 4 million Americans were riding bicycles. In about 1885 J. K. Starley, an English bicycle-maker, produced a safety bicycle. It had two wheels of equal size, a chain-driven pedaling system, a brake, and a movable handlebar.

Bicycles remained one of the most popular forms of transportation in the United States until the early 1900s. After that, since many more people owned cars, there was less interest in the bicycle. However, the bicycle continues to be important for both transportation and recreation.

 FROM THE COLLECTION OF THE AMERICAN BICYCLE MUSEUM

A Draisiene bicycle, about 1816

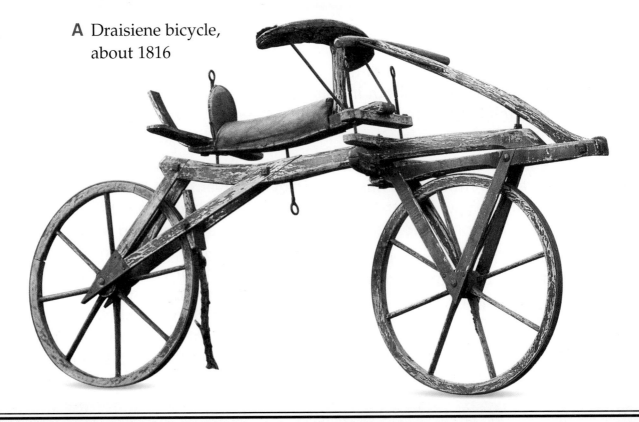

Analyze the Primary Source

1 **Compare and contrast these three early bicycles.**

   A **About 1816**

   B **About 1887**

   C **About 1891**

2 **What makes the 1891 bicycle a safety bicycle?**

B High-wheeler bicycle, about 1887

C Victor Spring safety bicycle, about 1891

Activity

Write a Paragraph Write a paragraph that tells how bicycles have become safer since the 1820s.

Research

Visit The Learning Site at **www.harcourtschool.com/ primarysources** to research other primary sources.

Main Idea
All businesses, large and small, work in much the same way.

Vocabulary

specialize

overhead

wage

profit

marketing

competition

How a Business Works

Today there are millions of businesses in the United States offering all kinds of products. Some businesses, such as automobile companies, are very large. These are usually run by a group of business people who make up a board of directors. The board members hold meetings to make business decisions. Other businesses may be run by one person or by partners. A family might own a small business. All businesses, whether large or small, work in much the same way.

Running a Business

Roberto Barrio owns a small bicycle shop in El Paso, Texas. He specializes in selling and repairing bicycles. To **specialize** is to do just one kind of work or to sell just one kind of product.

Roberto Barrio is proud of his bicycle shop.

Barrio and a worker make sure these young customers get the help they need.

Locate It

El Paso, Texas

"I'm proud of the way we run our business," Roberto Barrio says. "I think I have the best employees in El Paso." He explains that the shop did not always have so many bicycles to sell. "We started small," he says. "At first we had only a few bicycles. Now we have more than 100. We grew as I shared my interest in bicycle riding with the community."

The amount of money it takes to run a business is called its **overhead**. The overhead includes the costs of renting space, electricity, heating, and other things needed to run a business. It also includes paying the workers' wages. A **wage** is the money a worker is paid for the work he or she does.

A bicycle computer records miles or kilometers during a ride.

Roberto Barrio makes some money on each bicycle he sells. Store owners sell things for a little more money than they paid to buy them from the factory. They use the additional money they make to pay their overhead. If business is good, they make a profit. A **profit** is the amount of money that is left over after all the costs of running a business have been paid.

Review How does a business make a profit?

Barrio takes an order over the phone.

Selling a Product

The job of getting customers to want a product is called **marketing**. To market his bicycles, Roberto Barrio praises them in his newspaper advertisements for the shop.

Barrio also advertises his business in other ways. For example, he buys tickets to the local hockey team's games and gives them away. At the games, an announcer tells the crowd that some of the tickets came from Barrio's bicycle shop. The cost of the hockey tickets is part of overhead.

Barrio sets up his shop so customers can find what they need.

Roberto Barrio's bicycle shop is not the only one in El Paso. All the bicycle shops try to offer the best price or service so customers will come to them. The effort to get more customers is called **competition**. One shop competes with another for business.

Barrio has taught his employees to stop whatever they are doing when a customer comes into the shop. He wants them to greet customers in a friendly way and start to help them right away. "Customers come first in our shop," he says.

(Review) **What can businesses do to get more customers?**

Good service makes customers more likely to buy products and to visit the shop.

Barrio leads rides in his community to raise interest in biking and in his shop.

Lance Armstrong 1971–

Character Trait: Courage

When Lance Armstrong was 13, he won the Iron Kids Triathlon, a contest that included swimming, running, and cycling. He enjoyed cycling most, so he worked hard on that and started winning world championships. In 1996 Armstrong learned he had cancer. He was determined to beat it, and he succeeded. Soon he was racing again, and he has won the Tour de France, the world's most famous bike race, a number of times.

GO ONLINE

MULTIMEDIA BIOGRAPHIES
Visit The Learning Site at **www.harcourtschool.com/biographies** to learn about other famous people.

LESSON 3
Review

1 **Main Idea**   Explain how a business works.

2 **Vocabulary**   Use three of the vocabulary words in a sentence about Roberto Barrio's bicycle shop.

3 **Reading Skill—Compare and Contrast**   Compare a very large business like the Ford Motor Company with a small business like Barrio's bicycle shop. Describe the differences in how they are operated.

4 **Your Community**   Think about a business that you would like to have when you are older. Write a paragraph telling how you would get customers for your services or products.

   Performance—Write an Advertisement   Choose a product that makes your life more fun. Write an advertisement for it that you think will make your classmates want to buy it.

Tell Fact from Opinion

Vocabulary

opinion

▶ Why It Matters

You get information from many sources. You watch television, you read the newspaper, and you listen to what people tell you. To make good decisions, you need to be able to tell facts from opinions.

▶ What You Need to Know

Some of the information you get includes both facts and opinions. A fact is something that is true. It can be proved. An **opinion** is something that a person believes. Opinions may be supported by facts, but they cannot be proved.

▶ Practice the Skill

Many advertisements contain both fact and opinion. Look at the advertisement on the next page. Then use the information in the advertisement to answer these questions.

1 Look at the statement "All of Your Friends Will Want One!" Is this a fact or an opinion? How can you tell?

2 Make a list of the statements on the advertisement that are facts and those that are opinions.

3 Sometimes people think their opinions are facts. Why is it important for people to learn to tell fact from opinion?

▶ Apply What You Learned

Create an advertisement, and share it with your class. Practice finding the facts and the opinions in each person's advertisement.

Free Enterprise

In the United States, people have the freedom to start businesses and run them to make a profit. They can make or sell any product or service that is allowed by law. This is called **free enterprise**.

Main Idea
Free enterprise allows people to decide what goods or services they will make or sell.

Vocabulary

free enterprise

consumer

demand

supply

scarcity

Supply and Demand

In free enterprise, the government does not tell businesses what to produce and sell. The business owners decide, based on what they believe the consumers want. A **consumer** is a person who buys a product or service. The wants and needs of the consumers create the **demand** for the goods and services.

People can buy fresh fruit and other foods at this market in Seattle, Washington.

How Supply and Demand Works

SUPPLY		DEMAND		PRICE
High Supply	+	Great Demand	=	Low Price
High Supply	+	Low Demand	=	Very Low Price
Low Supply	+	Great Demand	=	Very High Price
Low Supply	+	Low Demand	=	High Price

Analyze Tables This table shows how supply, demand, and price can change.

◆ What do high supply and low demand equal?

The goods and services offered by businesses are the **supply**. The quantity of products or services supplied usually rises when demand is great. Businesses will produce or offer for sale more of a product or service if many consumers want it. If the demand for a product or service falls, businesses may produce or offer less of it. Both supply and demand determine the selling price of a product.

Review How can consumers cause an increase in supply?

Because not many of these old stamps are left, collectors will pay a lot for them.

The Price We Pay

Something else that affects the price we pay is **scarcity**. Scarcity means there is very little supply. If a hurricane strikes Guatemala and other banana-growing countries and destroys the banana crop, this fruit will suddenly be scarce.

People will still want to buy bananas, however. Scarcity will drive the price of bananas up. Producers will look to new places in the world to find enough bananas to supply the demand.

Sometimes there can be a scarcity of demand for goods and services. Perhaps people decide to save their money rather than spend it on goods and services.

Freeze damage to oranges can make them scarce.

Bananas are grown in Guatemala to help meet the demand for this fruit.

Then the price of goods and services goes down. If the prices drop far enough, some people may decide it is time to spend their money.

Review When do some people decide to spend their money?

LESSON 4
Review

1 **Main Idea** How does free enterprise help business owners?

2 **Vocabulary** Write sentences to explain **free enterprise** and **scarcity**.

3 **Reading Skill—Compare and Contrast** What is the difference between supply and demand?

4 **Your Community** Keep your newspaper every Sunday for a month. Look at the grocery store advertisements. Compare prices for the same items.

 Performance—Make a Chart Make a chart that compares prices of the food items in the above activity. Do they go up or down? Explain to a family member what this means about the supply and demand for these foods.

5

Main Idea
Products are traded among countries around the world.

Vocabulary

trade

barter

international trade

communication link

import

export

interdependence

The World Marketplace

Many of the products you buy, and the resources used to make them, come from places outside your community. They may come from other parts of the state or from other countries around the world.

Thanks to **trade**, or the exchange of one thing for another, consumers can buy or barter for things that their own communities do not grow or produce. To **barter** means to trade goods and services for something other than money.

In this painting from the 1300s, Marco Polo is leaving Venice, Italy, to go to Asia.

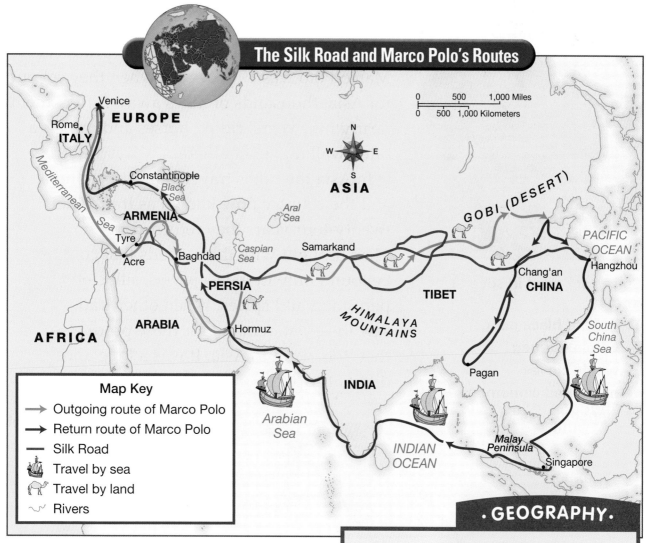

The Silk Road and Marco Polo's Routes

Map Key
→ Outgoing route of Marco Polo
→ Return route of Marco Polo
— Silk Road
 Travel by sea
🐪 Travel by land
〰 Rivers

International Trade

Long ago, traders traveled the world, trading products of their countries for products of other lands. Trade between countries is called **international trade**.

In 1271 a young man named Marco Polo left his home in Italy with his father and uncle. They were traders who knew about the silks and spices to be found in Asia. These products were not available in Italy.

• GEOGRAPHY •

The Silk Road

Understanding Human Systems

The Silk Road was an ancient trade route that linked countries in Europe, Asia, and Southeast Asia. European merchants and travelers carried ideas as well as goods to and from China. Marco Polo followed the general path of the Silk Road in his travels. When Polo returned and told others about China's riches, many more merchants began traveling the Silk Road.

Spices are used in several forms.
1. ground black pepper
2. whole nutmeg
3. whole cloves
4. powdered cinnamon
5. cinnamon sticks

The Polos were sure people in Europe would want to buy these interesting new products. Marco Polo was 17 years old when they set out for Asia, thousands of miles away. It took them nearly four years, riding horses and camels and often walking, to get there.

In Asia the Polos traveled to China, India, and the country now known as Iran. After twenty-four years they returned to Europe. They brought with them goods that could be found only in Asia—jewels, silk cloth, perfumes, and spices. When other traders saw the great demand for these products, they, too, went to Asia. It was a long and difficult trip.

Present-day cargo ships travel much faster and carry much more than the Polos did.

Today's ships, trains, and airplanes make moving goods around the world much faster than in Marco Polo's time. Modern communication links make ordering and paying for goods faster, too. A **communication link** is a kind of technology that lets people who are far apart share information instantly.

People can now use telephones, fax machines, and computers to buy and sell goods and services. Consumers can use home computers to shop for things on the Internet. The products arrive by modern transportation in days or weeks instead of in months or years.

Review How do communication links help international trade?

These workers, called telemarketers, take orders over the phone and put the information into computers.

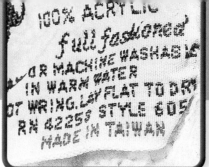

Clothing labels show that products are made throughout the world.

Countries Depend on One Another

Countries **import**, or bring in to sell, products and resources from other countries. Find out about things you use every day that were made in other parts of the world. The United States **exports**, or sends to other countries to sell, many products and resources.

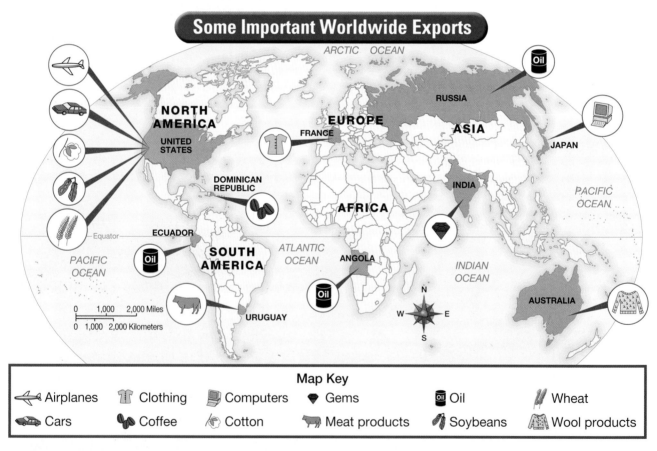

Some Important Worldwide Exports

Map Key

Airplanes	Clothing	Computers	Gems	Oil	Wheat
Cars	Coffee	Cotton	Meat products	Soybeans	Wool products

Movement This map shows some of the products exported by different countries.

Which country exports vehicles used for transportation?

In the world marketplace, scarcity of supply in one part of the world can increase the supply in another part of the world. For example, oil is scarce in Europe, so European countries buy oil from the nations in Southeast Asia where it is plentiful. In turn, these nations need and want telephones and computers. They buy these from businesses in Europe.

The world is a huge marketplace that can supply things that people want and need. In this marketplace, countries depend on one another for products for their citizens. Their dependence on one another for products and resources is called **interdependence** (in•ter•dih•PEN•duhns).

Review **Why is interdependence among countries important today?**

Workers on a Brownsville, Texas, dock load these rolls of sheet metal onto a ship that will take them to China to be sold.

LESSON 5
Review

1 **Main Idea** What is international trade, and why is it important?

2 **Vocabulary** Use the vocabulary words **import** and **export** in a paragraph about **trade**.

3 **Reading Skill—Compare and Contrast** How is importing a product different from exporting a product?

4 **Your Community** Some things you use every day were made in the United States, and some came from other countries.

On a sheet of paper, write the headings *United States* and *Other Countries*. List five things you use in each column.

 Performance—Create a Museum Exhibit Bring to school one object that was made in another country. Label it with the name of the country in which it was made. Also draw a small map that shows the country's location. Add your object and map to a class display.

Use Latitude and Longitude

Vocabulary
latitude   longitude

▶ Why It Matters

Mapmakers draw lines of latitude and longitude on maps and globes to form a grid system. You can give the exact location of any place by naming the lines of latitude and longitude closest to it.

▶ What You Need to Know

Lines of **latitude** run east and west around the globe. They measure distances in degrees (°) north and south of the equator.

Lines of latitude go from 0° at the equator to 90° at the poles. They are labeled N for *north* and S for *south*.

Lines of **longitude**, also called meridians, run north and south from pole to pole. They measure distances east and west of the prime meridian near London, England. They go from 0° at the prime meridian to 180° halfway around the globe. They are labeled E for *east* and W for *west*.

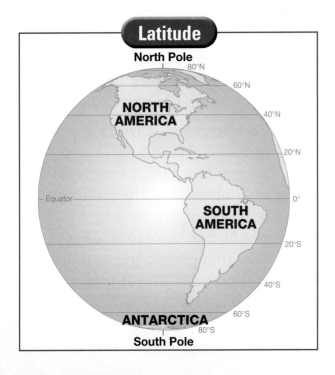

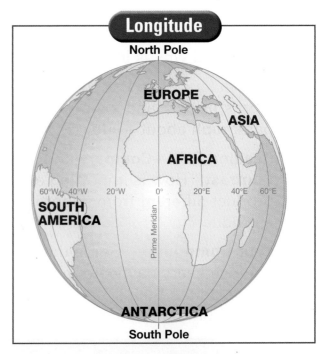

▶ Practice the Skill

Answer these questions using the map of Europe.

1 Near which line of latitude is Madrid, Spain?

2 Near which lines of latitude and longitude is Paris, France?

3 Near which line of longitude is Moscow, Russia?

4 Find Dublin, Ireland. Near which lines of latitude and longitude is this city?

▶ Apply What You Learned

Use an atlas or another map reference to find out the latitude and longitude of your town. Find three cities or towns in the world with the same latitude. Then find three with the same longitude. Share your list of world cities with a classmate.

Practice your map and globe skills with the **GeoSkills CD-ROM**.

Europe: Latitude and Longitude

11 Review and Test Preparation

Use Your Reading Skills

Complete this graphic organizer to show the items you compared and contrasted as you read. A copy of this graphic organizer appears on page 90 of the Activity Book.

Compare and Contrast Inventions

Assembly Line	Daguerreotype
The assembly line was a faster and cheaper way to make automobiles.	Before the daguerreotype introduced photography, all pictures were drawn or painted by artists.

What These Inventions Have in Common

_____

_____

_____

_____

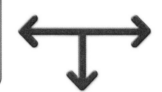

THINK & WRITE

Write a Newspaper Story
Imagine the questions people must have had when they heard that the government had begun granting patents to inventors. How does a patent protect a citizen's ideas? How do patents affect supply and demand? Write a newspaper story that answers these questions and explains to readers why patents are important.

Write a Business Plan Think of a product you could produce or a service you could provide to your neighbors. Write a business plan that lists your overhead costs, including advertising. What price would you have to charge to make a profit? Predict whether your business will succeed, and explain your prediction.

Use Vocabulary

Write the word or words that correctly match each definition.

> human resources (p. 382)
> technology (p. 386)
> profit (p. 396)
> international trade (p. 407)
> interdependence (p. 411)

1 the use of inventions in everyday life

2 the workers that are needed to make and sell a product

3 the exchange of goods and services between people in different countries

4 the amount of money left over after all the expenses of running a business have been paid

5 the dependence of countries on one another for goods and services

Recall Facts

Answer these questions.

6 How is an import different from an export? Give examples of both a United States import and a United States export.

7 How did the invention of the reaper change the lives of farmers?

8 What was Henry Ford's new way of making a product? Explain.

Write the letter of the best choice.

9 **Test Prep** Who changed the way pictures were made?
   A Jeanie Low
   B Granville T. Woods
   C Louis Daguerre
   D Hans Christiansen Lee

10 **Test Prep** What does *not* affect the price of a computer?
   F supply
   G scarcity of materials
   H fair market price
   J agriculture

Think Critically

11 You have invented a wooden toy you would like to make and sell. What do you need to find out?

12 How might a scarcity of wood affect the price of your toy?

13 What are some ways you could advertise your product?

Apply Skills

14 Look at the product map on page 385. What agricultural products are grown in the northeastern part of the state?

15 Read the advertisement on page 401. Choose one of the facts listed. How do you know it is a fact?

16 Look at the map on page 413. What is the latitude and longitude of Prague?

Mall of America

More than 270 million people from all over the world have visited the Mall of America since it opened in 1992. Located in Bloomington, Minnesota, it is the nation's largest mall. It has more than 500 stores, employs about 11,000 people, and makes more than one and a half billion dollars a year.

Locate It

MINNESOTA

Mississippi River

Mall of America

Being a Thoughtful Consumer

66 Never spend your money before you have it. **99**

—Thomas Jefferson, in a letter to Thomas Jefferson Smith, 1825

CHAPTER READING SKILL

Tell Fact from Opinion

A statement that can be proved is called a **fact**. An **opinion** is what someone thinks. Unlike a fact, an opinion cannot be proved.

As you read this chapter, identify facts about each topic. Then write your opinion about the topic.

TOPIC	FACT	OPINION

Main Idea
People are both producers and consumers.

Vocabulary

income

savings

How People Earn and Use Money

People work to earn money that they can use to buy goods and services. The money they are paid is their **income**. People earn their income in many ways. The clerk at a mall's clothing store earns an income by selling shirts and jeans. Some people in the same community work in factories that make the products sold at the mall. Others earn an income by delivering the products from the factories to the stores.

A busy shopping mall in Philadelphia, Pennsylvania

Bianca Schaut works on a car engine.

Earning Money

Bianca Schaut (SHAUT) is an automobile mechanic in San Diego, California. A mechanic repairs cars. Schaut earns her income by providing this service to car owners. Today one of every three workers in the United States earns an income by providing services to consumers.

"I like my work," Schaut says. She enjoys being useful in her community. This gives her a good feeling in addition to the money she earns.

When Bianca Schaut is working at the garage, she is a producer. She is paid for providing her service, just as a factory worker is paid for making a product.

Review How does Bianca Schaut earn an income?

Schaut looks for products that are on sale so she can get more for her money.

SALE PRICE
$29.99
$19.99

Spending Money

Bianca Schaut spends much of her income on her basic needs. She needs to eat, so she buys food. For clothing, she buys dark-colored pants and shirts for work and other clothes for home. She uses a big part of her income to pay the monthly rent for her apartment.

Once Schaut's basic needs are met, she can buy other items. She sometimes buys new furniture for her apartment. She also likes to see movies. When she spends money, she is a consumer. She is buying a product or service instead of making or providing one.

Review On what does Schaut spend her money?

Saving and Sharing

Bianca Schaut saves the money she has not spent. The money people do not spend is their **savings**. People save money so they will have it to spend in the future. They may need it in an emergency. Some people use their savings to take a vacation or buy a home. Many young people save for a college education. Many older people save for retirement. When they no longer work, they will earn no income.

Bianca Schaut shares with others some of the money she earns. She gives money to groups that help people in her community and around the world.

Schaut uses an automatic teller machine (ATM) to put her savings into the bank.

Review **What are savings?**

LESSON I
Review

① **Main Idea** What is the difference between a producer and a consumer?

② **Vocabulary** Write a short paragraph using the vocabulary words **income** and **savings**.

③ **Reading Skill—Tell Fact from Opinion** Make a chart with two columns labeled *Fact* and *Opinion*. Find two statements in the lesson that tell facts and two that give opinions. Write them in your chart.

④ **Your Community** Think about the workers and jobs in your community. List ways these workers are producers. Then list ways they are consumers.

Performance—Conduct an Interview Talk with an adult about what he or she does to earn a living. Report back to the class, telling whether the person performs a service or makes a product.

Skills
CHART AND GRAPH

Read a Flow Chart

Vocabulary

flow chart   economy

▶ Why It Matters

You can use a flow chart to learn how to do something or show how something works. A **flow chart** is a drawing that shows the steps it takes to do something. It also shows the order in which the steps must be followed.

A flow chart uses pictures, words, and arrows. The arrows on a flow chart help you read the steps in the correct order.

▶ What You Need to Know

The flow charts on these pages show how the economy of our country works. A country's **economy** is the way it produces and uses goods and services.

Flow Chart A below shows how money flows from people to industry and back.

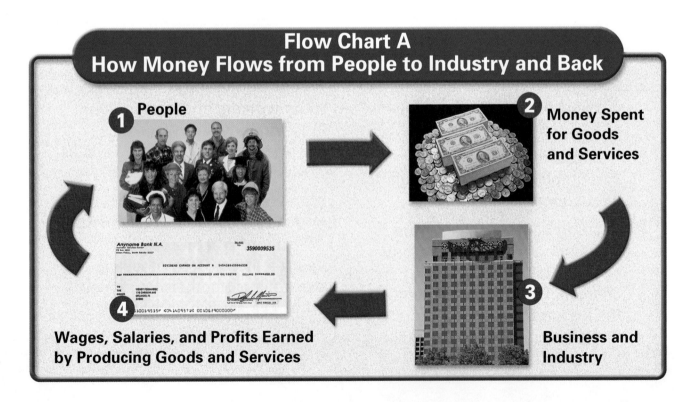

Flow Chart A
How Money Flows from People to Industry and Back

1 People

2 Money Spent for Goods and Services

3 Business and Industry

4 Wages, Salaries, and Profits Earned by Producing Goods and Services

▶ Practice the Skill

Look at Flow Chart B below. It shows how people use their skills to produce goods and services. Read the labels and follow the arrows to help you answer these questions.

1 What do people provide to business and industry?

2 The finished or purchased goods and products move from industry to where?

▶ Apply What You Learned

Work with a partner to make a flow chart that will explain to younger students how something works. Write each step on a strip of paper. Then paste the strips in order onto a sheet of poster board. Connect the steps with arrows, and give your chart a title. Use the chart with a group of younger students.

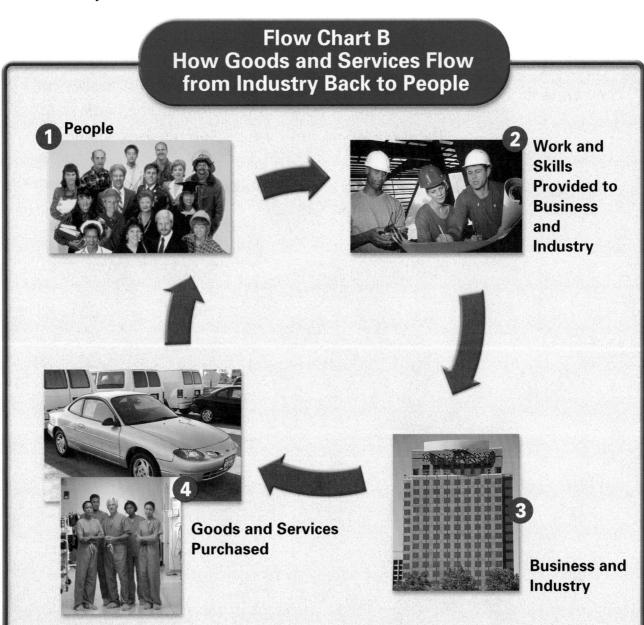

**Flow Chart B
How Goods and Services Flow
from Industry Back to People**

1 People

2 Work and Skills Provided to Business and Industry

3 Business and Industry

4 Goods and Services Purchased

Saving Money

Main Idea
People save money to handle emergencies and to meet future goals.

Vocabulary

bank

deposit

interest

investment

Saving money is important because things can happen that people do not expect. For example, a person's car might break down. Getting it repaired would cost money. If you save some money, you are ready for an emergency. People also save money to meet future goals.

Banks

Many people keep their money in a bank. A **bank** is a business that looks after people's money. When they can, people make **deposits**, or put money into their savings or checking accounts. The bank keeps the money safe until the person needs to spend it.

People who have checking accounts do not have to carry a lot of money with them. They can pay for things they buy with a check or a bank card. This way their money cannot be lost or stolen.

Money that is left in a savings account earns interest. **Interest** is the money a bank pays people to use their money while it is in the bank. For example, a bank might pay 10 percent interest if you keep money in the bank for one year. If you had $100 in your savings account, after one year your savings would grow to $110.

Review **What is interest?**

A bank keeps its customers' money in a vault, a room-sized safe with thick steel walls.

Analyze Tables

◈ After the second year, how much interest has been earned?

How Interest Can Grow at 10% a Year

YEAR	INTEREST INCOME	MONEY IN BANK
0	$0.00	$100.00
1	$100.00	$110.00
2	$110.00	$121.00
3	$121.00	$133.10
4	$133.10	$146.41
5	$146.41	$161.05

Investments

Many people make money with investments. To make an **investment** means to buy something that people believe will grow in value.

In one kind of investment, a person buys a small part of another person's business. Many large businesses sell shares in their companies on the stock market. People who buy them hope that the shares will grow in value over time. Then they can sell them for more than they paid and make a profit.

In another kind of investment, a person buys property, such as land or buildings. People who own property can rent it out to others to earn income. If the property grows in value, they can sell it and make a profit.

Review How do investments help people make more money?

The people who buy this building can rent its rooms to businesses.

This family has just bought their own piece of property.

Analyze Primary Sources

This 1906 stock certificate is from the Morning Hour Mining Company.

① This is the stock certificate number.

② This shows the number of shares purchased.

③ Here is the seal of the company.

④ This is the amount per share the purchaser paid.

◈ What does this document certify?

LESSON 2
Review

① **Main Idea** Why do people decide to save money?

② **Vocabulary** Use the vocabulary words **deposit**, **interest**, and **investment** in a sentence that tells some ways people use money.

③ **Reading Skill—Tell Fact from Opinion** Find an ad in the newspaper. Underline one statement of fact and circle one statement of opinion. Cut out the ad and bring it to class.

④ **Your Community** Is there a bank in your community where people can keep their money safe? Interview an adult family member. Find out whether he or she uses a bank and, if so, why.

Performance—Write a Description Do research about the services a local bank offers. Then write a short description about the services. Include information about the bank's investment opportunities. Share your description with the class.

Use a Line Graph

Vocabulary

line graph

▶ Why It Matters

Using a **line graph** can help you see patterns in information over time. Imagine that you have made an investment in the Tip-Top Toy Company. You bought the stock for $20 a share in January. Once a month, you check the stock's progress in the newspaper and record the results.

▶ What You Need to Know

To make a line graph, you mark points on a grid. Then you connect the points with lines. The diagram below shows the basic parts of a line graph.

A horizontal direction (across)

B vertical direction (up and down)

C dots which mark the points for the information

D lines which show the change from one dot to the next

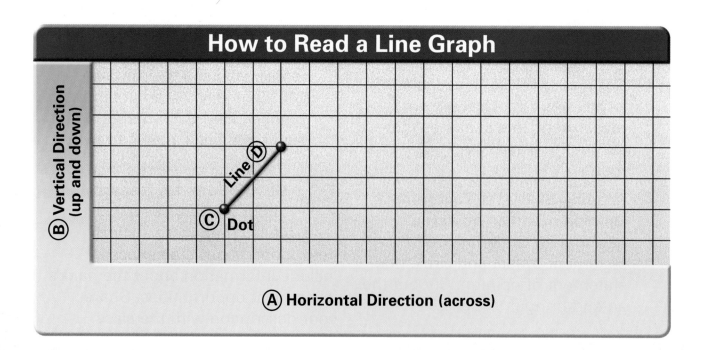

How to Read a Line Graph

Ⓑ **Vertical Direction (up and down)**

Line Ⓓ

Ⓒ **Dot**

Ⓐ **Horizontal Direction (across)**

▶ Practice the Skill

Use the line graph below to answer these questions.

1 What does the vertical direction show?

2 What does the horizontal direction show?

3 In which month was the stock's price highest? What was the price?

▶ Apply What You Learned

Work in a small group to create a line graph that will explain some data to classmates. You can work with baseball scores, movie ticket prices, or any other subject that interests you.

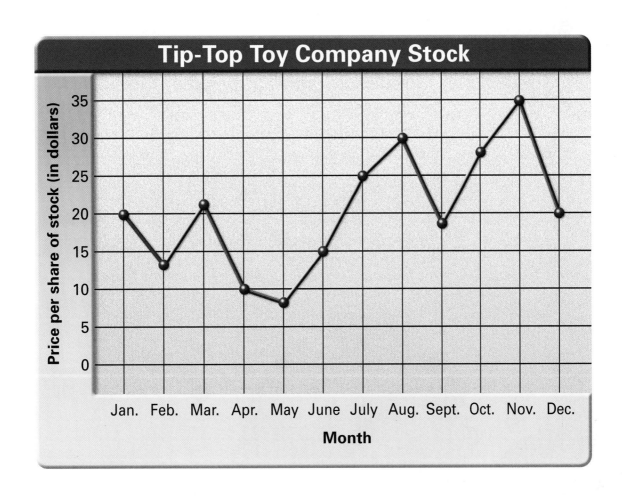

Tip-Top Toy Company Stock

Main Idea
Keeping a budget helps people decide how to spend their money.

Vocabulary

budget

Making a Budget

People use their incomes to meet their basic needs. They spend money to buy things they want. Since people cannot have everything, they have to plan how to use their money. A person's plan for spending and saving money is called a **budget**. Budgets help people manage their money well.

Gather Information

People of all ages can make and follow simple budgets. Kali, the girl shown here, has decided to make a budget. She will use a small notebook to record the ways she earns and spends her money.

These are some of the ways Kali can earn money.

In her notebook, Kali will record how much money she earns for helping do the yardwork.

Kali writes down the amount of money she earns from doing extra work around the house. She also writes down money that she receives as a gift or allowance. Then she writes down the items she buys and how much they cost.

After a few weeks, Kali will check her notebook. Then she can divide the information in it into two categories, *Incoming Money* and *Outgoing Money*. Writing down how she earns and spends money will help her plan a budget.

Review **What kind of information is included in a budget?**

Organize Information

Kali divides *Incoming Money* into several smaller categories. These include *Money Earned*, *Allowance*, and *Gifts*.

Kali then makes categories for *Outgoing Money* as well. She starts with *Food*, for snacks she buys herself. Her list also includes *Clothes* and *Toys*. She will need to add a category for *Entertainment* for the movies she sees.

Review **What categories of incoming money can be included in a budget?**

Once Kali knows where her money is going, she can decide what to spend less on.

Set Up a Plan

Kali thinks about the goals she wants to reach. Then she uses her budget to help her work toward them. Suppose she wants to buy a bicycle. Her budget will tell her whether she can buy it now. If not, she will need to save more money.

To buy something that costs as much as a bicycle, Kali may have to save for quite a while. When she reaches her goal, though, she will know it was worth the wait.

Review **What can a budget help people do?**

Kali pays for the bicycle with money she earned. Her budget helped her reach this goal.

LESSON 3
Review

1 **Main Idea** How do budgets help people decide how to spend their money?

2 **Vocabulary** Think of something you would like to buy. Use the vocabulary word **budget** in a sentence telling how you will reach your goal.

3 **Reading Skill—Categorize** Keep a list for a week of all the things you buy. Divide the list into two categories, *Important* and *Not Important*. How can doing this help you with your budget?

4 **Your Community** A community provides many services to its citizens, such as library services or parks and recreation. Choose one of these service providers. Then work with your classmates, and make up a budget for this service provider. What categories will you include?

Performance—Write a Letter Write a letter to a friend and explain the parts of a simple budget. In your letter, explain why people keep budgets. Then give your friend the letter.

Make an Economic Choice

Vocabulary

trade-off
opportunity cost

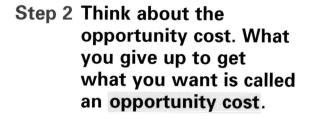

▶ Why It Matters

When you buy something at a store, you are making a choice about how to spend your money. You cannot buy everything you want, so you must spend your money wisely.

▶ What You Need to Know

Here are some steps that can help you make a wise choice.

Step 1 **Think about the trade-off. To buy or do one thing, you have to give up the chance to buy or do something else. This is called a trade-off.**

Step 2 **Think about the opportunity cost. What you give up to get what you want is called an opportunity cost.**

▶ Practice the Skill

Imagine that you need to buy a bicycle helmet. You have $25.00. You will have to make a choice about how to spend it.

Helmet A is at the bicycle store. It is the latest style, and it comes in bright designs. It costs $25.00. Helmet B is at a discount store, where it costs $15.00. It comes in solid colors only, but it is just as safe as Helmet A.

Helmet A

Helmet B

1. If you buy Helmet A, what is the trade-off? If you buy Helmet B, what is the trade-off?

2. What is the opportunity cost if you buy Helmet A? What is the opportunity cost if you buy Helmet B?

3. What choice will you make? Why?

▶ Apply What You Learned

Think about a recent choice you made when you bought something. What was the trade-off? What was the opportunity cost? Do you think your decision was a wise one? Explain your answer.

People Who Share

Main Idea
People share their money, skills, and time to make life better for others.

Vocabulary

donate

historic site

Some people enjoy sharing their money, skills, and time with others. They might choose to do this in their communities or in other countries. Their goal is to make life easier and better for others.

Sharing Money

Many people who have what they need **donate**, or give, some of their money to help those who have less. Some families and businesses make gifts of money to projects that help people.

Darla Moore, a banker, gave money to the University of South Carolina. The Moore School of Business there is named for her.

Gifts of money may be used to build hospitals, churches, art museums, and science centers. They may also pay for public television and radio stations, parks, and even sports stadiums. These gifts help all the citizens of the community.

Review How may gifts of money help a community's citizens?

CARNEGIE LIBRARY OF PITTSBURGH

· BIOGRAPHY ·

Andrew Carnegie
1835–1919

Character Trait: Responsibility

When Andrew Carnegie sold his steel company in 1901, he became the richest man in the world. Carnegie spent his fortune, about $350 million, on things that would help people help themselves. Carnegie built more than 2,800 public libraries around the world.

GO ONLINE

MULTIMEDIA BIOGRAPHIES
Visit The Learning Site at
www.harcourtschool.com/biographies
to learn about other famous people.

Sharing Skills

Anyone can help others. The doctors and nurses who work with Doctors Without Borders are volunteers, or people who work without pay. This organization was started by a group of doctors in France. These doctors believed that all people have the right to medical care no matter where they live.

Today more than 2,000 doctors donate their skills in 90 countries around the world. They care for people who are suffering in places where there are wars or hunger problems. They work to make sure that people in all countries have the medicines they need.

Dr. Marie-Eve Raguenau (rahg·NOH) from Doctors Without Borders holds the medal and certificate of the Nobel Peace Prize.

A doctor helps people after an earthquake in Turkey.

Another organization that helps people is the Red Cross. The Red Cross was started in 1863 in Europe to help care for those hurt in war. Today Red Cross workers continue to help, not only in times of war or disaster, but also in times of peace. For example, the Red Cross offers classes in first aid and water safety. In some countries the Red Cross is known as the Red Crescent.

The Red Cross gives people the supplies they need after disasters.

Review **How do the Red Cross and Doctors Without Borders help people?**

Clara Barton National Historic Site

The American Red Cross was started in 1881. Its first president, Clara Barton, lived just outside Washington, D.C. Barton directed the organization from her three-story home, which became the Red Cross headquarters in 1897. Soon its 30 rooms were filled with boxes of supplies. Today Clara Barton's home is a National Historic Site that people from all over the world visit. A **historic site** is a place that the United States government has recognized as culturally important.

Sharing Time

When some young people graduate from college, they decide to spend time helping others. They may donate two years of their lives by working in the Peace Corps (KAWR). Peace Corps volunteers work in communities around the world, showing people new ways to do things.

The Peace Corps volunteer shown here worked in a village where crops were grown on hillsides. The farmers were losing soil when rain washed it down the steep hills. He helped them plant trees and grasses to hold the soil in place.

Locate It

Ecuador

A Peace Corps volunteer works with citizens of Ecuador on a tree-planting project.

Thousands of Americans have volunteered in the Peace Corps since it began in 1961. Some people join after they finish college. Others volunteer after they retire from their jobs.

Their work spreads peace and understanding between citizens of the United States and people around the world.

Review **What do Peace Corps volunteers do to help others?**

Peace Corps worker in South Africa

Democratic Values
Common Good

In many parts of the world, people make a difference by volunteering for organizations. They volunteer their time and skills to help communities during disasters and in peacetime. Volunteers in these civic and nonprofit organizations serve the common good by helping to improve living conditions for many thousands of people.

Analyze the Value

1 How do volunteers in organizations serve the common good?

2 **Make It Relevant** Work with a classmate to think of a volunteer activity that you could do for your school. Write a letter to the principal stating why you think your activity would be helpful. Share your letters with the class.

LESSON 4
Review

1 **Main Idea** What are some ways citizens can help their communities?

2 **Vocabulary** Use the vocabulary word **donate** in a sentence.

3 **Reading Skill—Tell Fact from Opinion** Create an advertisement for a bicycle. In your ad, write two statements of fact and two statements of opinion. Share your ad with the class.

4 **Your Community** Think of someone who has made a difference in your community. Write a few sentences telling how this person has shared his or her money, skills, or time with your community.

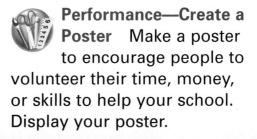
Performance—Create a Poster Make a poster to encourage people to volunteer their time, money, or skills to help your school. Display your poster.

Use Your Reading Skills

Complete this graphic organizer to show the facts and opinions about each topic. A copy of this graphic organizer appears on page 99 of the Activity Book.

Tell Fact from Opinion About Earning and Saving Money

TOPIC	FACT	OPINION
Earning Money	Today one of every three workers in the United States earns an income from a service job.	_____
Saving Money	_____	_____

THINK & WRITE

Write a Letter to the Editor Write a letter to the editor of your local newspaper, explaining some of the reasons school-age producers and consumers are important. In your letter give examples to support your opinion.

Write a Folktale Write a folktale that shows the importance of saving money. Think about the characters and events in folktales that you know. Remember that many folktales have one character who is successful and one who is not.

Use Vocabulary

Write the word that completes the sentence.

income (p. 418) investment (p. 426)
savings (p. 421) budget (p. 430)
interest (p. 425) donate (p. 436)

1 The money a bank pays to a person for keeping his or her money in the bank is called ___.

2 The money that people set aside for emergencies and goals is their ___.

3 The money people are paid for working is their ___.

4 A plan for spending and saving money is called a ___.

5 When people buy something that they think will grow in value, they are making an ___.

6 Some people ___ their services to help others.

Recall Facts

Answer the questions.

7 Can a person be both a producer and a consumer? Explain.

8 What can a budget help you do?

9 What are three ways a community might use a gift of money?

Write the letter of the best choice.

10 **Test Prep** Clara Barton is a famous American who—

A donated money for libraries.
B founded the American Red Cross.
C worked with Doctors Without Borders.
D volunteered for the Peace Corps.

11 **Test Prep** Which of the following is *not* an investment?

F shares in a company
G a house or another building
H land near a lake
J school supplies

Think Critically

12 If you received a gift of $25.00, how would you use that money?

13 What could you do to increase the amount of incoming money in your budget?

14 What are some budget categories you think your school should include under *Outgoing Money*?

Apply Skills

15 Look at Flow Chart A on page 422. From where does money flow?

16 Use the line graph on page 429. In which month was Tip-Top Toy stock the lowest?

17 Look at the bicycle helmets on page 434. What is the opportunity cost for choosing Helmet A?

AN AUCTION

Get Ready

An auction is an event at which people buy and sell goods. The person who sells the goods is called an auctioneer. Before the auction starts, people look at the goods and decide what they want to buy. Each buyer is given a number. When the auction begins, the buyer holds up the number to bid, or agree to pay the price being asked for an item. The person who agrees to pay the highest price gets the item.

Locate It
United States

Charlotte, North Carolina

What to See

A woman wants the auctioneer to sell her banjo.

A family decides to bid on the banjo.

START

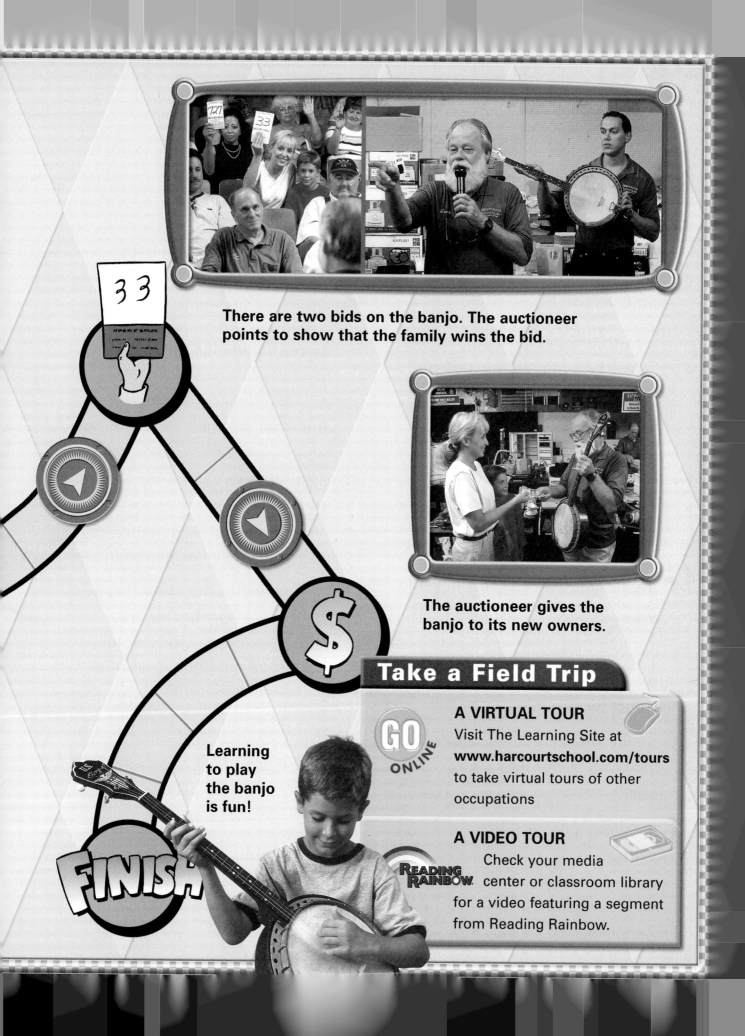

There are two bids on the banjo. The auctioneer points to show that the family wins the bid.

The auctioneer gives the banjo to its new owners.

Learning to play the banjo is fun!

FINISH

Take a Field Trip

A VIRTUAL TOUR
Visit The Learning Site at **www.harcourtschool.com/tours** to take virtual tours of other occupations

GO ONLINE

A VIDEO TOUR
Check your media center or classroom library for a video featuring a segment from Reading Rainbow.

READING RAINBOW

6 Review and Test Preparation

Use Vocabulary

Write the word or words that correctly match the definition.

1 money used to start a new company

capital (p. 381)   **overhead** (p. 395)

2 the workers that are needed to make a product

raw materials (p. 382)
human resources (p. 382)

3 person who buys a product or service

consumer (p. 402)
producer (p. 378)

4 something that can grow in value

import (p. 410)   **investment** (p. 426)

5 a plan for spending and saving money

budget (p. 430)   **patent** (p. 389)

6 money set aside for emergencies and goals

profit (p. 396)   **savings** (p. 421)

7 what you give up to get what you want

scarcity (p. 404)
opportunity cost (p. 434)

Recall Facts

Answer the questions.

8 What changed after the first assembly line was built?

9 What was the name of the organization that used Clara Barton's home as their headquarters in 1897?

10 Where did Marco Polo travel to, and what products did he bring back to Europe?

11 What are two categories a budget must have?

12 What are two things people can do with money besides spend it?

Write the letter of the best choice.

13 **Test Prep**   In 1901 Andrew Carnegie used his fortune to—
   A start an automobile company.
   B help build libraries.
   C import bananas.
   D export bicycles.

14 **Test Prep**   Lack of supply is known as—
   F technology.
   G scarcity.
   H investment.
   J profit.

Product Map of Texas

ARIZONA

NEW MEXICO

OKLAHOMA

ARKANSAS

MISSISSIPPI

LOUISIANA

Red R.

•Amarillo

Fort Worth• •Dallas

TEXAS

El Paso•

Rio Grande

Austin ★

San Antonio•

Houston•

MEXICO

•Corpus Christi

Gulf of Mexico

0   100   200 Miles
0   100   200 Kilometers

Symbol	Product	Symbol	Product
🐂	Beef cattle	💧	Natural gas
	Coal		Petroleum
	Cotton		Poultry
	Fruits and vegetables		Shrimp

15 Doctors Without Borders is—
   A a large bookstore.
   B a business that makes a profit.
   C an organization of volunteers.
   D a hospital on the Mexican border.

Think Critically

16 What are some expenses you might list in your budget?

17 What are some ways you might earn money? In which category would you list your earnings?

18 Why do you think people volunteer their time or skills?

19 Why do countries depend on one another for certain products?

Apply Skills

Use the product map of Texas above to answer these questions.

MAP AND GLOBE SKILLS

20 What fuel resources are found near Amarillo?

21 What food item is harvested from the Gulf of Mexico?

22 What agricultural product is raised near El Paso?

23 What is the symbol for beef cattle? Are more beef cattle raised in the eastern or western part of the state?

24 Where is poultry raised?

Unit Activities

 Visit The Learning Site at
**www.harcourtschool.com/
socialstudies/activities**
for additional activities.

Make a Map of Products from Around the World

First, make a list of products from other countries that you and your family use. Next, draw a map of the world and label the continents. Draw a symbol for each product on your list on the continent where it is made or grown. Then draw an arrow from that continent to where you live. Give your map a title, and make a map key that explains your symbols. Finally, share your map with a classmate.

Complete the Unit Project

Product Development—Bulletin Board
Create a bulletin board display that shows how a product is made or grown. Decide what product you want to show. Then research all the steps involved, from getting the raw materials to finishing the product. Draw pictures and write captions to explain what you are showing. Take turns presenting the product development steps to the other groups.

Visit Your Library

- *Prairie Town* by Bonnie and Arthur Geisert. Houghton Mifflin.

- *My Father's Boat* by Sherry Garland. Scholastic.

- *Supermarket* by Kathleen Krull. Holiday.

For Your Reference

Biographical Dictionary
R2

Gazetteer
R7

Glossary
R12

Index
R19

Biographical Dictionary

The Biographical Dictionary lists many of the people introduced in this book. The page number tells where the main discussion of the person starts. See the Index for other page references.

A

Addams, Jane *(1860–1935)* The founder of Hull-House in Chicago, which provided care and education to the poor. Addams won the Nobel Peace Prize in 1931. p. 68

Albright, Madeleine K. *(1937–)* A Czech American appointed as Secretary of State by President Clinton in 1996. p. 246

Armstrong, Lance *(1971–)* A world-champion American bicyclist. He survived cancer and later won the Tour de France, the world's most famous bicycle race. p. 399

Athena The Greek goddess of wisdom. The Romans had a similar goddess named Minerva. p. 211

Austin, Stephen F. *(1793-1836)* An important Texas leader. The city of Waterloo, Texas, was renamed Austin in 1839 to honor him. p. 36

B

Banneker, Benjamin *(1731–1806)* An American mathematician, farmer, and astronomer. He worked with Andrew Ellicott to survey the land for Washington, D.C. p. 347

Barrio, Roberto *(1960–)* The owner of a bicycle shop in El Paso, Texas. p. 394

Barton, Clara *(1821–1912)* The founder and first president of the American Red Cross, which began in 1881. During the Civil War, she gathered and handed out supplies for the wounded. p. 439

Belpré, Pura An author and the first Hispanic librarian at the New York Public Library. p. 247

Benz, Karl *(1844–1929)* A German automobile maker. He built the first gasoline-powered automobile in 1885. p. 378

Blackwell, Elizabeth *(1821–1910)* The first American woman to become a doctor. She founded a hospital for women and children in New York City. p. 247

Boone, Daniel *(1734–1820)* An American pioneer leader who helped settle the state of Kentucky. p. 216

Borglum, Gutzon *(1871–1914)* An American sculptor who carved the heads of four U.S. Presidents on Mount Rushmore. p. 232

Breyer, Stephen Gerald *(1938–)* An American appointed as the 108th Supreme Court Justice by President Clinton in 1994. p. 106

Bunyan, Paul A giant lumberjack in American folktales who, with his ox, Babe, performs superhuman deeds. p. 212

Bush, George *(1924–)* The 41st President of the United States from 1989 to 1993. p. 105

Bush, George W. *(1947–)* The 43rd President of the United States. Son of former President George Bush. p. 91

C

Carnegie, Andrew *(1835–1919)* A wealthy American who spent millions of dollars to build public libraries, improve public education, and promote international peace. p. 437

Cassatt, Mary *(1844–1926)* An American artist. Mothers and children were the subjects of many of her works. p. 267

Chavez, Cesar *(1927–1993)* A farmworker and American leader who worked for fair treatment of all farmworkers. p. 225

Clark, William *(1770–1838)* An American explorer who joined Meriwether Lewis as co-leader of The Corps of Discovery expedition to the Pacific Coast and back. p. 284

Clinton, William Jefferson "Bill" *(1946–)* The 42nd President of the United States. p. 105

Columbus, Christopher *(1451–1506)* An Italian explorer working for Spain who sailed to the Americas while trying to reach Asia from Europe. p. 332

Crockett, David "Davy" *(1786–1836)* An American pioneer who served as a U.S. representative from Tennessee. Crockett fought in Texas against Mexico and died at the Alamo. p. 219

Crusoe, Robinson The main character of Daniel Defoe's novel *Robinson Crusoe* of 1719. He is an English sailor who is shipwrecked on a small tropical island, where he survives for years. p. 140

Curry, Joseph A retired New York fire chief who led rescue teams at the site of the World Trade Center after the attack of September 11, 2001. p. 121

D

Daguerre, Louis *(1789–1851)* A French artist and early inventor in the field of photography. p. 386

Davis, Jefferson *(1808–1889)* An American soldier who served as president of the Confederate states during the Civil War (1861–1865). p. 353

Defoe, Daniel *(1660–1731)* The British writer of the famous novel *Robinson Crusoe*. p. 140

Demeter (dih•MEE•ter) The Greek goddess of the harvest. Her Roman name is Ceres. p. 211

Dice, Harvey A cattle rancher who was one of the first pioneers to arrive in Eagle, Colorado. Later he and his brother Tom built many of Eagle's important buildings. p. 49

Disney, Walt *(1901–1966)* An American animator and film producer known for the creation of EPCOT and cartoon characters. p. 15

Doolittle, William *(1947–)* A geography professor at the University of Texas in Austin, Texas. He studies both the physical and the human features of geography. p. 173

Douglass, Frederick *(1817–1895)* A leader and writer who was born in slavery in Maryland. He escaped in 1838 and helped in the fight against slavery. p. 220

E

Easley, Michael F. *(1950–)* The governor of North Carolina elected in 2001. p. 94

Edwards, William *(1828–1880)* The founder of a settlement he named Castle on the Eagle River in Colorado. p. 50

Einstein, Albert *(1879–1955)* A scientist who won the 1921 Nobel Prize for physics. His scientific theories changed the way people thought about space and time. p. 246

Ellicott, Andrew *(1754–1820)* An American surveyor. He worked with Benjamin Banneker to measure the land for Washington, D.C., and helped lay out the city. p. 347

F

Ford, Henry *(1863–1947)* An American automobile engineer and manufacturer. He invented the assembly line. p. 372

Franklin, Benjamin *(1706–1790)* A U.S. leader, writer, and scientist. He was one of the signers of the Declaration of Independence. p. 339

G

Ginsburg, Ruth Bader *(1933–)* An American appointed as a justice of the U.S. Supreme Court in 1993. p. 107

H

Hale, Sarah Josepha *(1788–1879)* An American writer who worked to make Thanksgiving a national holiday. p. 233

Hatshepsut (hat•SHEP•soot) *(1503 B.C.–1482 B.C.)* A female Egyptian pharaoh who expanded Egyptian trade routes. p. 316

Henry, John An African American railroad worker who became a folk hero. p. 204

Henson, Matthew *(1866–1955)* One of the first explorers to reach the North Pole in 1909. p. 39

Hera The wife of Zeus in Greek mythology. Her Roman name is Juno. p. 211

Houston, Sam *(1793–1863)* The first president of the Republic of Texas. After Texas was brought into the Union (1845), Houston served as a U.S. senator and later as governor of Texas. p. 229

Hutchison, Kay Bailey *(1944–)* The first woman senator from Texas. Her great-great-grandfather was one of the state's earliest settlers. p. 103

James I *(1566–1625)* The king of England who sponsored the Virginia Company. p. 307

Jefferson, Thomas *(1743–1826)* The third President of the U.S. (1801–1809). He wrote the first draft of the Declaration of Independence and presented it to Congress on July 2, 1776. p. 117

Jones, John Luther "Casey" *(1864– 1900)* An engineer for the Illinois Central Railroad. He gave his life to save others in a train crash. His story has become a legend. p. 214

K

Keller, Helen *(1880–1968)* An American writer who had lost her sight and her hearing at 19 months of age. She was taught by Anne Sullivan. p. 119

Kennedy, Anthony M. *(1936–)* An American appointed as a justice of the U.S. Supreme Court in 1988. p. 106

Key, Francis Scott *(1779–1843)* A lawyer and poet who wrote the words for "The Star-Spangled Banner." Congress adopted the song as the national anthem in 1931. p. 126

Khufu *(2500s B.C.)* An Egyptian king. He ordered the building of the Great Pyramid at Giza, the most famous of Egypt's pyramids. p. 316

King, Dr. Martin Luther, Jr. *(1929–1968)* An American minister and civil rights leader who worked to change unfair laws. He received the Kennedy Peace Prize and the Nobel Peace Prize in 1964. p. 120

L

Lawrence, Jacob *(1917–2000)* An American artist who was famous for his paintings of important historic events. p. 267

Lee, Hans Christiansen *(1984–)* At the age of 17, Lee invented DTCS (Differential Torque Control System), a device that helps control spin when cars skid. p. 391

L'Enfant, Pierre Charles *(1754–1825)* A French-born American builder and city planner. He planned and designed Washington, D.C., the nation's capital. p. 346

Lewis, Meriwether *(1774–1809)* An American explorer. In 1803, he and co-leader William Clark and The Corps of Discovery explored the land west of the Mississippi River. They journeyed overland across North America to the Pacific Coast and back. p. 284

Lincoln, Abraham *(1809–1865)* The 16th President of the U.S. (1861–1865). He was President during the Civil War. In 1863, he issued the Emancipation Proclamation, which made slavery against the law in the Confederate states. p. 253

Low, Jeanie The youngest inventor to be granted a United States patent, which she received at the age of eleven. p. 390

M

Musa, Mansa *(–A.D. 1332)* The Muslim emperor of Mali in 1324 who improved trade opportunities for the country. p. 321

Marshall, John *(1755–1835)* The fourth Chief Justice of the U.S. Supreme Court. p. 106

McAleese, Mary *(1951–)* The eighth president of Ireland. p. 250

McCormick, Cyrus *(1809–1884)* An inventor and manufacturer who developed a mechanical harvester in 1831. p. 388

McCoy, Elijah *(1844–1929)* An inventor of equipment that allowed machines to be oiled while they were being operated. p. 247

McDonald, Alex *(1856–1899)* A pioneer for whom the settlement of Castle, Colorado, was renamed. Later McDonald, Colorado, became Eagle, Colorado. p. 51

N

Ney, Elisabet *(1833–1907)* An American sculptor who settled in Texas and sculpted statues of Sam Houston and Stephen F. Austin. p. 229

Nogal, C. F. *(1865–1948)* The first business person to open a store, a hotel, and a post office in what is now Eagle, Colorado. p. 50

O

O'Connor, Sandra Day *(1930–)* The first woman justice on the Supreme Court. She was appointed by President Reagan in 1981. p. 106

Olmsted, Frederick Law *(1822–1903)* A landscape architect who was the chief designer of Central Park in New York City. p. 86

Ouray, Chief *(1833–1880)* A leader of the Southern Ute tribe in the mid-1800s. p. 48

P

Parks, Rosa *(1913–)* An African American civil rights leader. She refused to give up her seat on a bus to a white man. p. 224

Pasteur, Louis *(1822–1895)* A French chemist known for inventing the process of pasteurization, which made milk safer to drink. p. 297

Pecos Bill A tall-tale hero of the Southwestern frontier. His superhuman deeds showed the courage, strength, and humor needed to survive frontier life. p. 213

Pei, I. M. *(1917–)* The architect who designed Government Center in Boston. p. 246

Plenty Coups, Chief *(1848–1932)* A leader of the Crow nation of Native Americans in Montana. He helped the Crows keep some of their lands. p. 222

Pocahontas (poh•kuh•HAHN•tuhs) *(1595–1617)* Indian chief Powhatan's daughter. p. 311

Polo, Marco *(1254–1324)* An Italian explorer and trader who traveled all over Asia. He brought back information about the Far East to Europeans. p. 407

Poseidon The Greek god of the sea and the brother of Zeus. His Roman name is Neptune. p. 211

Powhatan (pow•uh•TAN) *(1550?–1618)* The chief of the Indian tribes who lived in the area that is now Virginia where settlers from England started Jamestown. Pocahontas was his daughter. p. 307

Q

Quinn, Jane Bryant *(1939–)* An economist who advises people on how to spend and invest their money. p. 405

R

Raguenau (rahg•noh), **Marie-Eve, Dr.** A physician with Doctors Without Borders who accepted the Nobel Peace Prize for the organization. p. 438

Ramirez, Virginia *(1938–)* A citizen in San Antonio, Texas, who works with C.O.P.S. (Communities Organized for Public Service) to create positive change in her community. p. 75

Reagan, Ronald *(1911–)* The 40th President of the United States (1981–1989). p. 105

Rehnquist, William *(1924–)* Chief Justice of the U.S. Supreme Court. He served as a justice from 1972–1986. p. 106

Riggle, JoAnn A historian and genealogist from Eagle, Colorado. p. 56

Roosevelt, Eleanor *(1884–1962)* First Lady who worked for human rights. Wife of President Franklin D. Roosevelt. p. 226

Roosevelt, Franklin D. *(1882–1945)* The 32nd President of the U.S. (1933–1945). He was reelected three times and died in office. p. 226

Roosevelt, Theodore *(1858–1919)* The 26th President of the U.S. (1901–1909). p. 232

S

Sacagawea (sak•uh•juh•WEE•uh) *(1786–1812)* The Shoshone woman who acted as an interpreter for Lewis and Clark's Corps of Discovery. p. 285

Salk, Jonas *(1914–1995)* An American scientist who developed a vaccine against polio. p. 223

Sanchez, Oscar Arias *(1941–)* The president of Costa Rica from 1986–1990. He was awarded the Nobel Peace Prize in 1987 for his work to improve the lives of all Central Americans. p. 76

BIOGRAPHICAL DICTIONARY

Scalia, Antonin *(1936–)* An American appointed as a justice of the U.S. Supreme Court in 1986. p. 106

Schaut, Bianca *(1966–)* An automobile mechanic in San Diego, California. p. 419

Smith, John *(1580–1631)* An English explorer who helped settle Virginia in 1607. He was elected leader of the Jamestown colony. p. 307

Souter, David Hackett *(1939–)* An American appointed as a justice of the U.S. Supreme Court in 1990. p. 106

Starley, J. K. *(1830–1881)* An English bicycle-maker known for his contributions to the bicycle industry, including introducing the safety bicycle. p. 392

Stevens, John Paul *(1920–)* An American appointed as a justice of the U.S. Supreme Court in 1975. p. 106

Thomas, Clarence *(1948–)* An American appointed as a justice of the U.S. Supreme Court in 1991. p. 106

Tubman, Harriet *(1820–1913)* An escaped slave who used the Underground Railroad to lead more than 300 slaves to freedom. p. 118

W

Washington, George *(1732–1799)* The first President of the U.S. (1789–1797). He is known as "The Father of Our Country." p. 44

Woods, Granville T. *(1856–1910)* An engineer who invented important tools for the railroads in the 1880s. p. 389

Z

Zeus In Greek mythology, the ruler of the heavens and the father of other gods. His Roman name is Jupiter. p. 211

Gazetteer

This Gazetteer is a geographical dictionary that will help you locate places discussed in this book. The page number tells where each place appears on a map.

A

Africa The second-largest continent. p. 40

Alabama A state in the southeastern United States. p. 45

Alaska A state of the United States, in the northwestern corner of North America. p. 41

Albany The capital of New York State. p. 97

Amarillo A city in northwestern Texas. p. 447

Amazon River A river in South America; it is the second longest in the world. p. A4

Angola A country in southwestern Africa. p. 410

Annapolis The capital of Maryland. p. 97

Antarctica The continent located at the South Pole, covered by an ice cap. p. 40

Appalachian Mountains (a•puh•LAY•chuhn) A mountain range in the eastern United States. p. 153

Arabia The great peninsula of southwest Asia. p. 407

Arabian Sea The part of the Indian Ocean that lies between India and Arabia. p. 407

Arctic Ocean The body of water north of the Arctic Circle. p. 40

Arizona A state in the southwestern United States. p. 45

Arkansas A state in the south central United States. p. 45

Arkansas River A river that begins in Oklahoma, runs through central Arkansas, and flows into the Mississippi River. p. 351

Armenia An ancient country in Asia. Today the country is part of Armenia, Turkey, and Iran. p. 407

Asia The largest continent. p. 40

Atlanta The capital of Georgia. p. 97

Atlantic Ocean The body of water that separates North and South America from Europe and Africa. p. 40

Augusta The capital of Maine. p. 97

Austin The capital of Texas. p. 97

Australia The smallest continent. p. 40

B

Baltimore A city on the Chesapeake Bay in Maryland. p. 170

Baton Rouge (bat•uhn•ROOZH) The capital of Louisiana. p. 97

Bismarck The capital of North Dakota. p. 97

Black Sea The sea between Europe and Asia. p. 407

Boise The capital of Idaho. p. 96

Boston The capital of Massachusetts. p. 97

Brasília (bruh•ZIL•yuh) The capital of Brazil, designed by Lúcio Costa. p. 156

Brazil A country in South America; covers about half of the continent. p. 156

C

California A state in the western United States. p. 45

Canada A country in North America. p. 41

Caribbean Sea (kar•uh•BEE•uhn) A part of the Atlantic Ocean. The West Indies and Central and South America form its boundaries on three sides. p. 156

Carson City The capital of Nevada. p. 96

Central America Countries connecting North and South America, between Mexico and Colombia. p. 243

Charleston The capital of West Virginia. p. 97

Chesapeake Bay An inlet of the Atlantic Ocean between Virginia and Maryland. p. 308

Cheyenne (shy•AN) The capital of Wyoming. p. 97

Chicago A city in northeastern Illinois. p. 255

China A country in eastern Asia. p. 154

Coastal Plain One of the two major plains along the Gulf Coast and the Atlantic Coast of the United States. p. 176

Colorado A state in the western United States. p. 45

Colorado River A river in the southwestern United States. p. 351

Columbia The capital of South Carolina. p. 97

Columbia River A river in southwestern Canada and the northwestern United States. p. 351

Columbus The capital of Ohio. p. 97

Concord The capital of New Hampshire. p. 97

Connecticut A state in the northeastern United States. p. 45

Constantinople A city in Turkey on the border of Europe and Asia. Known today as Istanbul. p. 407

Corpus Christi A city in southern Texas. p. 179

Cumberland Gap A pass through the Cumberland Mountains, connecting Tennessee and Kentucky. p. 217

Cumberland Mountains The southern section of the Appalachian Mountain range. p. 217

D

Dallas A city in northeastern Texas. p. 153

Dearborn A city located just outside of Detroit, Michigan. Home of the Henry Ford Museum. p. 376

Delaware A state in the eastern United States. p. 45

Denver The capital of Colorado. p. 97

Des Moines (dih MOYN) The capital of Iowa and the largest city in the state. p. 97

Dominican Republic A country that occupies two-thirds of the island of Hispaniola in the West Indies. p. 410

Dover The capital of Delaware. p. 97

E

Eagle A town near central Colorado. p. 12

Eastern Hemisphere (HEM•uh•sfeer) The eastern half of Earth. p. 39

Ecuador (EH•kwuh•dawr) A country in northwestern South America. p. 440

Egypt A country in northeastern Africa. p. 316

El Paso A city in western Texas. p. 395

equator An imaginary line around Earth, halfway between the poles. p. 38

Europe The second-smallest continent. p. 40

F

Fiji An island country in the southern Pacific Ocean. p. 161

Florida A state in the southeastern United States. p. 45

Fort Massac State Park Historical park located in southern Illinois. p. 324

Fort Worth A city in northeastern Texas. p. 72

Frankfort The capital of Kentucky. p. 97

G

Galapagos Islands Islands off the coast of Ecuador. p. 189

Georgia A state in the southeastern United States. p. 45

Gobi A desert in Asia that covers nearly 500,000 square miles. p. 407

Grand Canyon A gorge cut by the Colorado River, where the river crosses the northwest corner of Arizona. p. 183

Great Lakes A chain of five large lakes between the United States and Canada. p. 153

Greece A country in southern Europe. p. 210

Greenland An island off the coast of northeastern North America. p. 41

Guatemala A country in Central America. p. 260

Gulf of Mexico A body of water on the southeastern coast of North America. p. 41

H

Harrisburg The capital of Pennsylvania. p. 97

Hartford The capital of Connecticut. p. 97

Hawaii A state made up of a string of volcanic islands in the north central Pacific Ocean. p. 96

Helena The capital of Montana. p. 96

Himalaya Mountains A mountain range in south Asia. Mount Everest in the Himalayas is the tallest peak in the world. p. 37

Honolulu The capital of Hawaii. p. 96

I

Idaho A state in the northwestern United States. p. 45

Illinois A state in the central United States. p. 45

India A country in Asia. p. 407

Indiana A state in the north central United States. p. 45

Indianapolis The capital of Indiana. p. 97

Indian Ocean The body of water that separates Africa, Asia, Australia, and Antarctica. p. 40

Iowa A state in the north central United States. p. 45

Ireland The country that takes up most of the island of Ireland, off the coast of Great Britain. p. 248

GAZETTEER

Italy The country that is a boot-shaped peninsula in southern Europe. p. 407

J

Jackson The capital of Mississippi. p. 97
Jamestown The first lasting settlement in Virginia, at the mouth of the James River. p. 308
Japan A country in the western Pacific Ocean, off the east coast of Asia. p. 410
Jefferson City The capital of Missouri. p. 97
Juneau (JOO•noh) The capital of Alaska. p. 96

K

Kansas A state in the central United States. p. 45
Kentucky A state in the east central United States. p. 45
Kenya A country in Eastern Africa; borders the Indian Ocean. p. 37

L

Lansing The capital of Michigan. p. 97
Lincoln The capital of Nebraska. p. 97
Little Rock The capital of Arkansas. p. 97
Los Angeles A city on the coast of California. p. 252
Louisiana A state in the southeastern United States. p. 45

M

Mackenzie River A river in northwestern Canada. p. 351
Madison The capital of Wisconsin. p. 97
Maine A state in the northeastern United States. p. 45
Malay Peninsula The area of land in southeastern Asia that includes West Malaysia and Thailand. p. 407
Mali A country in western Africa. p. 320
Maryland A state in the eastern United States. p. 45
Massachusetts A state in the northeastern United States. p. 45
Mediterranean Sea A body of water that connects with the Atlantic Ocean. Europe, Asia, and Africa form its boundaries on three sides. p. 407

Mesopotamia One of the world's earliest civilizations; located in southwestern Asia. p. 315
Mexico A country in southern North America that borders on the Pacific Ocean and the Gulf of Mexico. p. 40
Mexico City The capital of Mexico. p. 259
Miami A city in southeastern Florida, on Biscayne Bay. p. 245
Michigan A state in the north central United States. p. 45
Minnesota A state in the north central United States. p. 45
Mississippi A state in the southeastern United States. p. 45
Mississippi River The longest river in the United States. p. 351
Missouri A state in the central United States. p. 45
Missouri River A river in the western United States that joins the Mississippi River. p. 351
Montana A state in the northwestern United States. p. 45
Montgomery The capital of Alabama. p. 97
Montpelier (mahnt•PEEL•yer) The capital of Vermont. p. 97

N

Nashville The capital of Tennessee. p. 97
Nebraska A state in the central United States. p. 45
Nevada A state in the western United States. p. 45
New Hampshire A state in the northeastern United States. p. 45
New Jersey A state in the northeastern United States. p. 45
New Mexico A state in the southwestern United States. p. 45
New York City A city in New York State. p. 10
North America The continent that includes the United States, Canada, Mexico, and some countries of Central America. p. 40
North Carolina A state in the southeastern United States. p. 45
North Dakota A state in the northwestern United States. p. 45
Northern Hemisphere The northern half of Earth. p. 38
North Pole The northernmost place on Earth, located in the Arctic Ocean. p. 38

GAZETTEER

Ohio   **Trenton**

GAZETTEER

O

Ohio A state in the north central United States. p. 45

Ohio River A river in the north central United States. p. 351

Oklahoma A state in the south central United States. p. 45

Oklahoma City The capital of Oklahoma. p. 97

Olympia The capital of Washington State. p. 96

Oregon A state in the northwestern United States. p. 45

Orlando A large city located in central Florida. p. 208

P

Pacific Ocean The body of water that separates North and South America from Australia and Asia. p. 40

Palm Springs A community in the southern California desert. p. 188

Panama Canal A human-made waterway that crosses Central America to connect the Atlantic and the Pacific Oceans. p. 165

Pan-American Highway An international highway system that stretches from the U.S.-Canadian border to Santiago, Chile, in South America. p. 156

Paterson A city in New Jersey. p. 257

Pennsylvania A state in the northeastern United States. p. 45

Persia A country in southern Asia, known today as Iran. p. 407

Philadelphia A city in southern Pennsylvania. p. 155

Phoenix The capital of Arizona. p. 96

Pierre (PIR) The capital of South Dakota. p. 97

Pineville Small city located on the Cumberland River in Kentucky. p. 34

Portland A large port city in Maine. p. 162

Portland A large city located in northeastern Oregon. p. 144

Providence The capital of Rhode Island. p. 97

R

Raleigh (RAHL•ee) The capital of North Carolina. p. 94

Rhode Island A state in the northeastern United States. p. 45

Richmond The capital of Virginia. p. 97

Rio Grande A river in the southwestern United States. p. 351

Rocky Mountains A mountain range in western North America. p. 153

Rome The capital of Italy. p. 210

Russia A country that for some years was a state of the U.S.S.R. (Union of Soviet Socialist Republics), or Soviet Union. Known today as the Russian Federation. p. 262

S

Sacramento The capital of California. p. 96

Salem The capital of Oregon. p. 96

Salt Lake City The capital of Utah. p. 96

San Antonio A city in south central Texas. p. 2

San Francisco A large port city in California. p. 243

Santa Fe The capital of New Mexico. p. 97

South America A continent in the Western Hemisphere that includes most of the countries of Central America. p. 40

South Carolina A state in the southeastern United States. p. 45

South China Sea The southern part of the China Sea, which lies between Japan and the Malay Peninsula. p. 407

South Dakota A state in the north central United States. p. 45

Southern Hemisphere The southern half of Earth. p. 38

South Pole The southernmost place on Earth, located in west central Antarctica. p. 38

Springfield The capital of Illinois. p. 97

St. Lawrence River A river in Canada. It forms a border between Canada and New York State. p. 351

St. Paul The capital of Minnesota. p. 97

T

Tallahassee The capital of Florida. p. 97

Tennessee A state in the southeast central United States. p. 45

Texas A state in the southern United States. p. 45

Tibet A region covering most of southwestern China. p. 407

Topeka The capital of Kansas. p. 97

Trenton The capital of New Jersey. p. 97

U

United States A country on the North American continent. p. 41

Uruguay A country that lies between Brazil and Argentina in South America. p. 410

Utah A state in the western United States. p. 45

V

Venice A city in Italy. p. 407

Vermont A state in the northeastern United States. p. 45

Vietnam A country in southeastern Asia. p. 261

Virginia A state in the eastern United States. p. 45

W

Washington A state in the northwestern United States. p. 45

Washington, D.C. The capital of the United States. pp. 97, 345

Western Hemisphere The western half of Earth. p. 39

West Virginia A state in the eastern United States. p. 45

Wisconsin A state in the north central United States. p. 45

Wyoming A state in the northwestern United States. p. 45

Y

Yukon River A river in Alaska and in the Yukon Territory in Canada. p. 351

GAZETTEER

Glossary

This glossary contains important social studies words and their definitions. Each word is respelled as it would be in a dictionary. When you see the ´ mark after a syllable, pronounce that syllable with more force than the other syllables. The page number at the end of the definition tells you where to find the word in your book. The boldfaced letters in the examples that follow show how these letters are pronounced in the respellings after each glossary word.

add, āce, câre, pälm; end, ēqual; it, īce; odd, ōpen, ôrder; tŏŏk, pōōl; up, bûrn; yōō as u in *fuse*; oil; pout; ə as a in *above*, e in *sicken*, i in *possible*, o in *melon*, u in *circus*; check; ring; thin; this; zh as in *vision*

A

adapt (ə•dapt´) To change for a purpose, such as usefulness or survival. (p. 161)

advertisement (ad•vər•tīz´mənt) Information that a business provides about its goods and services. (p. 388)

agriculture (ag´rə•kul•chər) The raising of crops and farm animals for sale. (p. 384)

amendment (ə•mend´mənt) A change made to something that is already written. (p. 353)

ancestor (an´ses•tər) Someone in a person's family, such as a great-great-grandparent, who lived a long time ago. (p. 49)

ancient (ān´shənt) From a time very long ago. (p. 314)

anthem (an´thəm) A patriotic song. (p. 126)

appoint (ə•point´) To choose for a government job without voting. (p. 77)

artifact (är´tə•fakt) An object that was used by people in the past. (p. 302)

assembly line (ə•sem´blē līn) A factory setup in which workers each add one part to a product as it passes them on a moving belt. (p. 380)

authority (ô•thär•ə•tē) The right of a leader to give orders, make decisions, or take action. (p. 77)

B

ballot (bal´ət) A list of the choices in an election. (p. 112)

bank (bangk) A business that looks after people's money. (p. 424)

bar graph (bär graf) A graph that uses bars of different lengths to stand for amounts or numbers of things. (p. 20)

barter (bär´tər) To trade one product or service for another. (p. 406)

Bill of Rights (bil uv rīts) An addition to the Constitution that names the rights and freedoms of all Americans. (p. 111)

biography (bī•ä´grə•fē) The story of a person's life. (p. 15)

border (bôr´dər) A line on a map that shows where a state or a nation ends. (p. 41)

boundary (boun´drē) Another word for a border. (p. 96)

budget (bu´jət) A plan for saving and spending money. (p. 430)

business (biz´nəs) An activity in which workers make or sell goods or do work for others. (p. 13)

C

canal (kə•nal´) A waterway built by people. (p. 164)

candidate (kan´də•dāt) A person who hopes to be elected. (p. 114)

capital (kap´ə•təl) Money used to start or add to a business. (p. 381)

capital city (kap´ə•təl sit´ē) A city in which government leaders meet and work. (p. 45)

capital resources (kap´ə•təl rē´sôr•səz) Money to run a business. (p. 382)

capitol (kap´ə•təl) The building in a capital city in which lawmakers meet. (p. 94)

cardinal directions (kär´də•nəl di•rek´shənz) The main directions *north, south, east,* and *west.* (p. 42)

cause (côz) An action or event that makes something happen. (p. 298)

century (sen´chə•rē) A period of time lasting 100 years. (p. 292)

character trait (kar´ik•tər trāt) A quality a person shows, such as strength, courage, or humor. (p. 213)

citizen (sit´ə•zən) A person who lives in and belongs to a community. (p. 12)

GLOSSARY

civil rights (si´vəl rīts) Rights of personal freedom. (p. 120)

civil war (si´vəl wôr) A war in which two parts of one country fight each other. (p. 352)

civilization (si•və•lə•zā´shən) A large group of people living in a well-organized way. (p. 314)

claim (klām) To say that something belongs to you. (p. 334)

climate (klī´mət) The kind of weather a place has over a long period of time. (p. 150)

coastal plain (kōs´təl plān) Flat land along a sea or ocean. (p. 148)

colonist (kä´lə•nist) A person who lives in a colony. (p. 338)

colony (kä´lə•nē) A settlement that is ruled by another country. (p. 306)

common good (kä´mən good) Something that is good for everyone in a community. (p. 75)

communicate (kə•myoo´nə•kāt) To share information. (p. 119)

communication link (kə•myoo•nə•kā´shən lingk) A kind of technology that lets people who are far apart share information instantly. (p. 409)

community (kə•myoo´nə•tē) A group of people who live and work in the same place. (p. 12)

compass rose (kum´pəs rōz) A drawing on a map that shows the cardinal directions to help people use the map. (p. 42)

competition (kom•pə•tish´ən) The efforts of two businesses with the same products or services to get customers to buy from them. (p. 398)

compromise (kom´prə•mīz) A way to settle a conflict in which each person gives up some of what he or she wants. (p. 82)

conflict (kän´flikt) A disagreement. (p. 80)

Congress (kong´grəs) The legislative branch of the national government. (p. 103)

consequence (kän´sə•kwens) Something that happens because of what a person does. (p. 27)

conservation (kon•sər•vā´shən) The act of saving resources and making them last longer. (p. 189)

constitution (kän•stə•too´shən) A written set of laws that describe how a government is to work. (p. 102)

consumer (kən•soo´mər) A person who buys a product or service. (p. 402)

continents (kän´tən•ənts) The seven largest land areas on Earth. (p. 37)

continuity (kän•tən•oo´ə•tē) Continuing, or staying the same. (p. 293)

cooperate (kō•ä´pə•rāt) To work helpfully together. (p. 26)

council (koun´səl) A group of citizens chosen to make decisions for a community. (p. 89)

county (koun´tē) Part of a state. (p. 93)

county seat (koun´tē sēt) The city or town in which the county's leaders meet. (p. 93)

court (kôrt) A place where a judge decides whether a person has broken the law, and if so, what the consequences will be. (p. 80)

crossroads (krôs´rōdz) A place where two roads cross. (p. 156)

culture (kul´chər) A way of life shared by members of a group. (p. 22)

custom (kus´təm) A way of doing something. (p. 22)

cutaway diagram (ku´tə•wā dī´ə•gram) A diagram that shows the outside and inside of an object at the same time. (p. 236)

D

decade (de´kād) A period of time lasting 10 years. (p. 292)

decision (di•si´zhən) A choice. (p. 251)

demand (di•mand´) The desire or need for a product or service. (p. 402)

democracy (di•mä´krə•sē) The form of government the United States has, in which each adult citizen has the right to vote. (p. 114)

depend (di•pend´) To rely on for help. (p. 18)

deposit (di•pä´zit) To put money into a bank account. (p. 424)

desert (dez´ərt) A place with a very dry climate. (p. 150)

disaster (di•zas´tər) A happening, such as an earthquake or flood, that causes great harm or damage. (p. 184)

disease (di•zēz´) An illness or other condition that harms a living thing. (p. 223)

distance scale (dis´təns skāl) A map feature used to measure the distance between two places; it tells what the distance on the map equals on the real Earth. (p. 42)

District of Columbia The location of the nation's capital city. (p. 345)

donate (dō´nāt) To give money or goods to those who need help. (p. 436)

E

economy (i•kä´nə•mē) The way a country produces and uses goods and services. (p. 422)

ecosystem (ē´kō•sis•təm) A system in which plants, animals, and the environment depend on one another. (p. 180)

effect (i•fekt´) The result of something that has happened. (p. 298)

elect (i•lekt´) To vote for, or choose, a leader. (p. 77)

election (i•lek´shən) A time when citizens vote. (p. 112)

empire (em´pīr) A collection of lands and people ruled by one country. (p. 320)

environment (in•vī´rən•mənt) All the physical and human features and conditions that make up a place. (p. 160)

equator (i•kwā´tər) A line that appears on a map or globe halfway between the North Pole and the South Pole. (p. 38)

erosion (i•rō´zhən) The wearing away of Earth's surface. (p. 182)

ethnic group (eth´nik grōōp) A group of people who share the same language and culture. (p. 23)

exact location (ig•zakt´ lō•kā´shən) The point where two lines meet, or cross, on a map. (p. 178)

executive (ig•ze´kyə•tiv) The branch of government, led by a mayor, governor, or President, that sees that the laws are obeyed. (p. 91)

expansion (ik•span´shən) An increase in size, as of the growth of a nation. (p. 350)

explorer (ik•splôr´ər) A person who goes to find out about a place. (p. 332)

export (eks´pôrt) To send a product or resource from one country to another to be sold. (p. 410)

F

fact (fakt) A statement of information that can be proved. (p. 218)

factory (fak´tə•rē) A building in which people use machines to make goods. (p. 310)

fair (fâr) The same for everyone. (p. 28)

famine (fa´mən) A time when crops fail and there is little or no food. (p. 248)

federal (fe´də•rəl) National; the federal government is the government of the whole nation. (p. 102)

festival (fes´tə•vəl) A joyful gathering of people to celebrate something. (p. 270)

fiction (fik´shən) A story that is made up. (p. 218)

flow chart (flō´ chärt) A drawing that shows the steps it takes to do something. (p. 422)

founder (foun´dər) A person who starts something, such as a business or a settlement. (p. 50)

free enterprise (frē en´tər•prīz) The freedom to start a business and to make and sell for profit any product or service allowed by law. (p. 402)

fuel (fyōōl) A natural resource, such as oil, coal, or wood, that is burned to release energy. The energy may be used to provide heat or to do work, such as producing electricity. (p. 161)

G

geographer (jē•ä´grə•fər) A person who studies Earth and its people. (p. 172)

geography (jē•ä´grə•fē) The study of Earth's features. (p. 146)

ghost town (gōst toun) An empty town with buildings but no people. (p. 294)

globe (glōb) A model of Earth. (p. 38)

goods (gōōdz) Products, or things that can be bought or sold. (p. 13)

government (guv´ərn•mənt) A group of elected citizens who solve problems and make laws for a community. (p. 27)

government service (guv´ərn•mənt sûr´vəs) Work that is done for a city or town by departments run by the government. (p. 84)

governor (guv´ər•nər) The elected leader of a state's government. (p. 94)

grid system (grid sis´təm) A set of lines the same distance apart that cross one another to form boxes. (p. 178)

growing season (grō´ing sē´zən) The months in which plants can grow. (p. 151)

H

harbor (här´bər) A protected place with deep water where ships can come close to shore. (p. 162)

GLOSSARY

hemisphere (hem´ə•sfir) Half of the globe when it is divided into either northern and southern halves or eastern and western halves. (p. 38)

heritage (her´ə•tij) A set of values and traditions handed down to a group from those who have lived before them. (p. 25)

hero (hir´ō) A brave or clever person who serves as an example. (p. 120)

historic site (hi•stôr´ic sīt) A building or place that was important in history. (p. 439)

historical society (hi•stôr´ə•kəl sə•sī´ə•tē) A group of people who have a special interest in the history of a community. (p. 302)

history (his´tə•rē) The story of what has happened in a place. (p. 48)

history map (his´tə•rē map) A map that shows how a place looked in an earlier time. (p. 356)

holiday (hä´lə•dā) A special day for remembering a person or an event that is important to the people of a community. (p. 24)

human feature (hyo͞o´mən fē´chər) Something people have built, such as a building, bridge, road, farm, or mine. (p. 154)

human resources (hyo͞o´mən rē´sôr•səz) The workers needed to make and sell a product or service. (p. 382)

immigrant (im´ə•grənt) A person who comes to live in a country from somewhere else in the world. (p. 242)

import (im´pôrt) To bring in products and resources from another country to sell. (p. 410)

income (in´kəm) Money earned by working. (p. 418)

independence (in•də•pen´dəns) Freedom from the control of another country. (p. 339)

industry (in´dəs•trē) A type of business, such as the automobile industry. (p. 381)

innovation (i•nə•vā´shən) A new product. (p. 390)

interdependence (in•tər•də•pen´dəns) The way countries depend on one another for products and resources. (p. 411)

interest (in´trəst) The money a bank pays a person for keeping money in the bank. (p. 425)

intermediate directions (in•tər•mē´dē•ət di•rek´shənz) The directions between the cardinal directions, for example, *northeast, southeast, northwest,* and *southwest.* (p. 166)

international trade (in•tər•nash´ən•al trād) Trade between countries. (p. 407)

invention (in•ven´shən) Something that has been made for the first time. (p. 315)

investment (in•vest´mənt) Something you buy that you hope will grow in value. (p. 426)

judge (juj) A person from the community who is chosen to work as a leader in the courts. (p. 28)

judicial (jo͞o•di´shəl) The branch of government that decides whether laws are fair and whether they have been fairly carried out. (p. 91)

jury (jo͝or´ē) A group of usually six to twelve citizens who sit in a courtroom and listen to the facts of a case. (p. 80)

justice (jus´təs) Fairness. (p. 116)

landform (land´fôrm) A physical feature such as a mountain range, valley, plateau, or plain. (p. 147)

landform map (land´fôrm map) A map that shows the physical features of the land such as mountains, plains, plateaus, lakes, rivers, and oceans. (p. 152)

landmark (land´märk) A natural or human feature that helps people find their way. (p. 351)

language (lang´gwij) The words and signs people use to communicate. (p. 252)

latitude (la´tə•to͞od) How far north or south a place is, measured by using lines that run east and west around a globe. (p. 412)

law (lô) A rule a community makes. (p. 26)

legend (le´jənd) A tale that may have started as a true story but has had details added that did not really happen. (p. 214)

legislative (le´jəs•lā•tiv) The branch of government that makes new laws. (p. 91)

line graph (līn´graf) A graph that uses a line to show changes over time. (p. 428)

GLOSSARY

literature (li´tə•rə•chər) Stories or poems that people write to share their ideas. (p. 210)

location (lō•kā´shən) The place where something is found. (p. 36)

longitude (lon´jə•tōōd) How far east or west a place is, measured by using lines that run north and south on a globe from pole to pole. (p. 412)

M

majority rule (mə•jôr´ə•tē rōōl) A system in which, when more than half of the people vote the same way, they get what they want. (p. 112)

manufacture (man•yə•fak´chər) To make products with machines. (p. 257)

map (map) A picture that shows the location of things. (p. 40)

map key (map kē) A box on a map in which map symbols are explained; also called a map legend. (p. 42)

map symbol (map sim´bəl) A symbol that stands for something real on Earth. (p. 42)

map title (map tī´təl) A title that tells what a map is about. (p. 42)

marketing (mär´kət•ing) The job of getting customers to want a product. (p. 397)

mayor (mā´ər) A leader of a community government. (p. 27)

mediator (mē´dē•ā•tər) A person who helps both sides settle a disagreement. (p. 82)

memorial (mə•môr´ē•əl) Something that keeps a memory alive. (p. 230)

millennium (mə•le´nē•əm) A period of time lasting 1,000 years. (p. 312)

mineral (min´ər•əl) A natural resource such as iron or gold. (p. 157)

minority rights (mə•nôr´ə•tē rīts) The idea that citizens who did not vote for the winner still keep their rights. (p. 113)

modern (mä´dərn) Present-day; up-to-date. (p. 314)

monument (män´yə•mənt) Something built to honor and remember a person or an event. (p. 228)

mountain range (moun´tən rānj) A large group of mountains. (p. 37)

museum (myōō•zē´əm) A place where objects from other times and places can be seen. (p. 14)

music (myōō´zik) Sounds made with voices or instruments. (p. 263)

myth (mith) A story that uses the actions of gods to explain why something in nature is the way it is. (p. 210)

N

nation (nā´shən) An area of land with its own people and laws; a country. (p. 40)

natural hazard (na´chər•əl ha´zərd) An event in nature, such as an earthquake, tornado, volcanic eruption, or flood, that can cause great harm. (p. 190)

natural resources (na´chə•rəl rē´sôr•səz) Materials from nature, such as wood and stone, that people can use. (p. 17)

needs (nēdz) Things we all must have, such as food, clothing, and a place to live. (p. 16)

nomad (nō´mad) A member of a group of people who have no settled home. (p. 328)

O

opinion (ə•pin´yən) Something that a person believes but that cannot be proven. (p. 400)

opportunity (ä•pər•tōō´nə•tē) The chance to find a job, get an education, or have a better way of life. (p. 242)

opportunity cost (ä•pər•tōō´nə•tē kôst) What you give up in order to get what you want. (p. 434)

oral history (ôr´əl his´tə•rē) A story of the past that is spoken rather than written. (p. 301)

overhead (ō´vər•hed) The amount of money it takes to run a business. (p. 395)

P

parish (par´ish) The name given to local governments in the state of Louisiana by the Roman Catholic Church while the region was under Spanish rule. (p. 93)

patent (pa´tənt) A government paper saying that only the inventor has the right to make or sell his or her invention. (p. 389)

patriotic symbol (pā•trē•ä•´tik sim´bəl) A symbol, such as a flag, that stands for the ideas the people of a country believe in. (p. 122)

patriotism (pā´trē•ə•ti•zəm) A feeling of pride citizens have for their country. (p. 122)

peace (pēs) A time of quiet and calm. (p. 29)

pharaoh (fer´ō) A king in Ancient Egypt. (p. 316)

physical feature (fi´zi•kəl fē´chər) Something found in nature such as weather, plant life, water, and land. (p. 146)

picture graph (pik´chər graf) A graph that uses pictures or symbols to stand for the numbers of things. (p. 20)

pioneer (pī•ə•nir´) A person who helps settle a new land. (p. 49)

plateau (pla•tō´) A landform that has steep sides and a flat top. (p. 148)

Pledge of Allegiance (plej uv ə•lē´jəns) A promise citizens of the United States make to be true to their flag and all that it stands for. (p. 125)

point of view (point uv vyoo) The way a person feels about something. (p. 266)

pollution (pə•loo´shən) Anything that makes a natural resource, such as air, soil, or water, dirty and unsafe to use. (p. 189)

population (pop•yə•lā´shən) The number of people living in a place. (p. 45)

population density (pop•yə•lā´shən den´sə•tē) The number of people living in an area of a certain size. (p. 258)

port (pôrt) A place where ships dock to take on goods or passengers. (p. 165)

predict (pri•dikt´) To say what you believe will happen in the future. (p. 159)

President (pre´zə•dənt) The title given to the leader of the United States of America. (p. 44)

primary source (prī´mer•ē sôrs) A record made by someone who saw or took part in an event. (p. 56)

private property (prī´vət prä´pər•tē) Property, such as a home, business, or farm, that belongs to one person or a group of people. (p. 81)

problem (prä´bləm) Something that makes life difficult. (p. 30)

producer (prə•doo´sər) Someone who makes a product. (p. 378)

product map (prä´dukt map) A map that uses symbols to show where products come from. (p. 384)

profit (prä´fət) The amount of money that is left over after all the costs of running a business have been paid. (p. 396)

property tax (prä´pər•tē taks) A tax that is paid by people who own land and buildings in the community. (p. 88)

public property (pub´lik prä´pər•tē) Property, such as a park or swimming pool, that belongs to everyone in the community. (p. 81)

public service (pub´lik sûr´vəs) Work done to help the community. (p. 74)

public works (pub´lik wərks) A department that provides services such as garbage collection for a community. (p. 87)

pyramid (pir´ə•mid) A tomb, or burial place, for dead kings and queens in ancient Egypt. (p. 316)

R

raw material (rô mə•tir´ē•əl) A resource used to make a product. (p. 382)

recreation (rek•rē•ā´shən) Any activity, hobby, or sport done for enjoyment. (p. 86)

region (rē´jən) An area with at least one feature that makes it different from other areas. (p. 174)

relative location (re´lə•tiv lō•kā´shən) The location of a place in relation to another place. (p. 172)

religion (ri•li´jən) A set of ideas a person has about a god or a group of gods. (p. 111)

representative (re•pri•zen´tə•tiv) A person chosen to act or speak for others. (p. 103)

republic (ri•pu´blik) A form of government in which citizens vote for the leaders who will make the decisions in the government. (p. 319)

responsibility (ri•spän•sə•bil´ə•tē) Something a person should do because it is necessary and important. (p. 29)

revolution (re•və•loo´shən) A fight for a change in government. (p. 338)

rights (rīts) Freedoms that all citizens of the United States have. (p. 110)

route (root) A path between one place and another that makes movement of people and goods possible. (p. 155)

rural (rûr´əl) Away from cities and large towns. (p. 47)

GLOSSARY

S

sales tax (sālz taks) Extra money that people must pay to support government services each time they buy something. (p. 88)

satellite (sa´təl•īt) A spacecraft, without a crew, that orbits Earth. (p. 177)

savings (sā´vingz) The money that people save. (p. 421)

scarcity (skâr´sə•tē) A shortage, or lack of supply, of a product. (p. 404)

sculpture (skulp´chər) A piece of art, such as a statue, that can be viewed from all sides. (p. 228)

secondary source (se´kən•dâr•ē sôrs) A record made by someone who was not present at an event. (p. 57)

sequence (sē´kwəns) The order in which events take place. (p. 54)

service (sûr´vəs) Work that someone does for someone else. (p. 18)

settlement (se´təl•mənt) A small village built by the first people to live in a new place. (p. 50)

settler (set´lər) One of the first people to live in a new place. (p. 307)

slave (slāv) A person who is owned by another person and forced to work without pay. (p. 118)

solution (sə•loo´shən) A way to solve a problem. (p. 30)

specialize (spesh´əl•īz) To do just one kind of work or sell just one kind of product. (p. 394)

suburb (sub´ərb) A small community that is close to a city. (p. 46)

supply (sə•plī´) The amount of goods offered for sale by a business. (p. 403)

Supreme Court (sə•prēm´ kôrt) The judicial branch of the national government and the most important court in the United States. (p. 106)

T

table (tā´bəl) A chart used to organize information. (p. 108)

tall tale (tôl tāl) A story that uses humorous exaggeration to explain how something came to be. (p. 212)

tax (taks) The money the government collects from citizens to pay for the services they need. (p. 88)

technology (tek•näl´ə•jē) The new inventions people use in everyday life. (p. 386)

time line (tīm līn) A drawing that shows when and in what order events took place. (p. 54)

trade (trād) The exchange of one kind of product or service for another. (p. 406)

trade-off (trād´ôf) The thing you give up the chance to buy or do in order to buy or do something else. (p. 434)

tradition (trə•di´shən) A custom, or way of doing something, that is passed on in a family. (p. 245)

transcontinental (trans•kän•tə•nen´təl) Crossing a continent from one side to the other. (p. 359)

transportation (trans•pər•tā´shən) The moving of people or things from one place to another. (p. 46)

V

vaccine (vak•sēn´) A medicine that prevents an illness. (p. 223)

valley (val´ē) A low area that lies between mountains or hills. (p. 148)

volunteer (väl•ən•tir´) A person who chooses to work without being paid. (p. 76)

vote (vōt) A choice that gets counted. (p. 111)

voyage (voi´ij) An ocean journey. (p. 249)

W

wage (wāj) The money a worker is paid. (p. 395)

Index

Page references for illustrations are set in italic type. An italic *m* indicates a map. Page references set in boldface type indicate the pages on which vocabulary terms are defined.

A

Acropolis (Greece), *318*
A.D. ("in the year of the Lord"), 313
Adams, John, *338, 339*
Adapt, 160, 161, *161*
Addams, Jane, 68-71, *68, 69, 70, 71, 74, 75*
Adler, David A., 136
Adobe bricks, 329, *329*
Advertisement, 322, **388,** 399, 400-401, *401,* 415
Africa, 37, *m37, m263*
    kente cloth from, *273*
    music of, 263, *263*
    Peace Corps in, *441*
    plains in, *37*
    slaves brought from, 243, 310, 334
African Americans
    in Chicago, 255, *255*
    civil rights of, 120
    culture of, 263, *263,* 270, *270*
    education of, 220, 221
    heroic, 118, *118,* 120, *120,* 220-221, *220, 221,* 224, *224*
    holiday customs and traditions of, 270, *270*
    as leaders, 118, *118,* 120, *120,* 220–221, *220, 221,* 224, *224*
    newspapers of, 221, *221*
    See also Slaves and slavery
Agriculture (farming), 157, *157,* **384**
    growing season in, 151
    jobs in, 17, *17*
    Native American, 329, 330
    plantations, 243, 352

    potato famine, 248–251
    product maps and, 384, *m385,* 447, *m447*
    slavery and, 243, 310, 334, 352
    tools used in, 388, *388*
    See also Crops
Ahearn, Dan, 71
Air brake, 389
Airport, 52
Alabama, African Americans in, 224, *224*
Alamo, Battle of, 219
Alaska, 160, *160, m160,* 326, 354, *m354*
Albright, Madeleine K., 246, *246*
Aldrin, Edwin, 361
Alexandria, Virginia, *46, m193*
Alloy, 373
Aluminum, *m385*
Amazon River, *156,* 169
Amendments, 353
American Indians. *See* Native Americans
American Red Cross, 439, *439*
American Revolution, *283,* 338–341, *341*
Americas, exploration of, 332, *332,* 333–334, *333, 334, m337*
"Amish, The" (Cipriano), 207
Ancestors, 49
    of Native Americans, 326–331, *326, 327, 329*
"Ancient Egypt" (Cipriano), 207
Ancient times, 282, *314,* 314–321
    China in, 317, *317, m317*

    Egypt in, 316, *316, m316*
    Greece in, 210–211, *210, m210,* 318, *318, m318*
    Mali in, 320, *320, m320,* 321
    Mesopotamia in, 315, *315, m315*
    Rome in, 319, *319, m319*
Andes Mountains, 147
Angelou, Maya, 201
Animals
    birds, *1,* 24, *24, 128, 181,* 225
    hunting of, 48, 326, *326,* 327–328, *327, 328,* 329
Antarctica, 37
Anthem, 126, 127
Appalachian Mountains, 147, 216, *216, m217,* 351, *m351*
Appoint, 77, *77,* 107
Architect, 190, *190*
Architecture
    in ancient Greece, 210, *318*
    in ancient Rome, *319*
    Gateway Arch, 231, *231*
    immigrants and, 246, *246*
Arctic, 39
Arctic Ocean, 37
Arias Sanchez, Oscar, 76, *76*
Arizona, county courthouse in, *93*
Armstrong, Lance, 399, *399*
Armstrong, Neil, 361
Art
    activities in, 15, 25, 47, 107, 127, 311, 391, 441

    in ancient Greece, 318, *318*
    culture and, 262, *262*
    determining point of view in, 241, 266–267, *267*
    of immigrants, 256
    murals, 240–241, *255, 256,* 297
    paintings, *102, 106, 117, 126,* 216, *233, 262, 262, 267, 272, 311, 330, 333, 341, 344*
    pottery, *273, 318,* 329
    sculpture, 228–229, *228, 229, 232, 232, 236–237, 236, 237, 242, 319*
Art fair, 265
Artifacts, 301, 302, *330*
Asheville, North Carolina, *m63*
Asia, 37, *m261*
    European trade with, *406,* 407–408, *m407*
    immigration from, 245, *m245, 254, 254,* 261
    recreation in, *14*
Assembly line, 374, *374, 379,* **380,** 414
Astronauts, 360, *361*
Athena, goddess of wisdom, 211, *211,* 318
Athens, Greece, 318, *318*
Atlanta, Georgia, *292–293*
Atlantic Ocean, 37
Auction, 444–445, *444, m444, 445*
Austin, Stephen F., 36, 229
Austin, Texas, *36,* 60–61, *60, 61*
Australia, 37
Authority, 77

Automatic teller machine (ATM), *421*
Automobiles
  inventions for, 391, *391*
  mass production of, 372–383, *373, 374, 376–377, 378, 381, 383*
  mechanics for, 419, *419*
  trade in, *m410,* 411
Avalon Park (Chicago, Illinois), 255, *255*

B

Babe, the Blue Ox, 212, *212*
Bald eagle (national bird), *1, 24, 24, 128, 181,* 225
"Ballad of Davy Crockett, The," 218
Ballot, 112, *113, 114, 115, 115. See also* Votes and voting
Baltimore, Maryland, *126, 126, 127, 170*
Bananas, 404
Banjo, *444, 445*
Banks and banking, 424, 425
  interest earned in, 425
  saving money in, 421, 424, *424, 425,* 446
Banneker, Benjamin, 347, *347*
Bar graphs, 20, *21, 33, 104, 186, 187, 195*
Bark painting, *272*
Barrio, Roberto, 394–398, *395, 397, 398*
Barter, 406
Bartholdi, Frédéric-Auguste, 236
Barton, Clara, 439, *439*
B.C. ("before Christ"), 313
Beliefs. *See* Religion
Bell, Alexander Graham, 359, *359*
Belpré, Pura, 247, *247*

Benson, Laura Lee, 136
Benz, Karl, 378
Bicycles
  as business, 394–398, *394, 395, 396–397, 398*
  helmets and, *79, 401,* 443
  racing, *398, 399, 399*
  racks for, *30, 31*
  repairs by volunteers, 133, *133*
  safety, 392–393, *392, 393*
Bill of Rights, 111, *342*
Bingham, Caleb, *216*
Biographies, 15
  Lance Armstrong, 399, *399*
  Benjamin Banneker, 347, *347*
  Andrew Carnegie, 437, *437*
  David "Davy" Crockett, 219, *219*
  Walt Disney, 15, *15*
  William Doolittle, 173, *173*
  Benjamin Franklin, 339, *339*
  Ruth Bader Ginsburg, *106, 107, 107*
  Sarah Josepha Hale, 233, *233*
  Matthew Henson, 39, *39*
  Thomas Jefferson, 117, *117*
  Helen Keller, 119, *119*
  Dr. Martin Luther King, Jr., 120, *120*
  Mansa Musa, 321
  Julia Morgan, 190, *190*
  Elisabet Ney, 229, *229*
  Jane Bryant Quinn, 405, *405*
  Oscar Arias Sanchez, 76, *76*
  Harriet Tubman, 118, *118*
Birds
  in forest, *181*
  national, *1, 24, 24, 128*
  oil pollution and, 189

Blackwell, Elizabeth, 247, *247*
Bloomington, Minnesota, *416–417, m416*
Board of commissioners, 93
Boats and ships
  canoes, 287, *287, 331,* 351
  of early settlers, *306,* 307
  of explorers, 332, *332*
  in Florida theme park, *208–209*
  in harbors, 162–163, *162–163, 332*
  immigrants on, *242,* 250, *250*
  Native American, *331*
Boise State University, 95
Bones, tools made from, 328
Boone, Daniel, 216, *216,* 217
Borders, 41, *m41*
  of states, 96–97, *m96–97,* 99, 135, *m135*
  of United States, 41, *m41*
Borglum, Gutzon, 232, *232*
Borglum, Lincoln, 232, *232*
Boston, Massachusetts, *133,* 240–241, *m240,* 249
Boundaries, 96, *m96–97,* 97
Brazil, *14,* 334
Breyer, Stephen Gerald, *106*
Britain. *See* England
Brownscombe, Jennie Augusta, *233*
Budgets, 430, *431–433*
Buffalo, 327–328, *328,* 329
Bunting, Eve, 280
Bunyan, Paul, 212, *212*
Bush, George, *1, 105*
Bush, George W., *91, 103, 105*

Business, 13, *394–399*
  automobiles and, *372–375, 378–383*
  capital in, **381**
  capital resources in, **382**
  competition in, **398**
  in early Colorado, 50
  human resources in, **382,** *382*
  investments in. *See* Investments
  overhead in, **395,** 397
  prices in, 404–405
  profits in, **396**
  running, 394–396
  sales in, 397–398, 418, *418–419*
  specializing in, **394**
  supply and demand in, 402, 403, *403,* 404
  See also Free enterprise
Business center, 13, *13*
Business plan, writing a, 414
Buttons
  campaign, 112, *112*
  designing, 29

C

Cabins, *50*
Cactus, *151*
Caesar Augustus, *319*
Cahokia, 330–331, *330, 331*
Cahokia Mounds State Historic Site, *330*
California, *m188*
  earthquakes in, 190, *190,* 191
  immigrants in, *252–253, m252, 253*–254, *254*
  police in, *18*
Cameras, 386–387, *386*
Campaign buttons, 112, *112*
Canada, claimed by French, 334
Canal, 164, *164,* 165, *165, m165*
Candidate, 114

Canoes, 287, *287, 331, 351*
Capital (business), 381
Capital city, *44,* **45,**
    344–349
    building, 346–347, *346*
    choosing location of,
        344–346, *346*
    of states, 96–97,
        m96–97, 99, 135,
        m135
Capital resources, 382
**Capitol Building
    (Washington, D.C.),**
    91, 103, 104, *104,* 347,
    348, *348, 349, 387*
Car(s). *See* Automobiles
Caravans, 320
Cardinal directions, 42
Carnegie, Andrew, 437,
    437
**Casey Jones Home and
    Railroad Museum
    (Jackson, Tennessee),**
    215
Cassatt, Mary, *267*
Categorizing, 73, 77, 81,
    89, 95, 98, 421, 427,
    433, 441
Catholicism, 93, 268
Cattle, *m385*
Cause, 298
Cause and effect,
    298–299, *298, 299, 323,*
    325, 331, 335, 343, 349,
    361, 362
Celebrations
    in communities,
        24–25, *24, 25, 51,* 55
    of our heritage,
        231–235, *231, 232,*
        233, 234, 235
    See also Holiday(s)
Central Pacific Railroad,
    358, 359
**Central Park (New York
    City),** 86, *86–87, m86*
**Central Square (Boston,
    Massachusetts),**
    240–241
Century, 292
Ceremony, citizenship,
    116

Ceres (Roman goddess),
    211
Chambers, 104
Changes
    in communities,
        51–53, *51, 52,*
        292–297, *292, 293,*
        294, 295, 296
    disasters and,
        184–185, *185,*
        190–191, *190, 191*
    in physical features,
        164–165, *164, 165*
    physical processes
        and, 182, *182,* 183
    rapid, 184–185, *184,*
        185
    slow, 182, *182, 183*
    unplanned, 295–296,
        295, 296
    unseen, 297, *297*
Character traits, 213
    civic virtue, 76, 107,
        121
    cooperation, 26, 39,
        173, 321, 339
    courage, 118, 399
    creativity, 347
    fairness, 28, 120
    inventiveness, 15
    perseverance, 119, 233
    responsibility, 190,
        405, 437
    self–discipline, 229
**Charbonneau, Toussaint
    (Corps of Discovery),**
    285
Charity. *See* Sharing
Chart(s)
    flow charts, 422, *423,*
        443
    making, 405
    weather, 151
Chart and graph skills
    comparing bar
        graphs, *104,* 186,
        187, 195
    reading flow charts,
        422, *423,* 443
    reading graphs, 20–21,
        21, 33
    reading tables,
        108–109, *108, 109,*
        131

    reading time lines,
        54–55, *54–55,* 59,
        297, 312–313, *312,*
        313, 323
    using line graphs,
        428–429, *428, 429,*
        443
Chassis, 373
Chattanooga, Tennessee,
    234
Chavez, Cesar, 225, *225*
Checking account, 425
Chemicals, *m385*
Chesapeake Bay, *m308,*
    310, *m310*
Chicago, Illinois, *13,*
    m255
    African Americans in,
        255
    business district in, *13*
    Hull–House in, 69–71,
        69, 71, 74
    immigrants in,
        255–256, *255, 256*
Chief justice, 106, *106*
Children
    car seats for, *79*
    education of, 85, *85,*
        95, *95,* 220
    parks and, 86
    Pledge of Allegiance
        and, 125, *125*
China, *m261*
    ancient, 317, *317,*
        m317
    Great Wall in, *154,*
        m154
**Chinatown (Chicago,
    Illinois),** 256
Chinese writing, 261,
    261, 317, *317*
Chipeta (Ute Indian), *48*
Christianity, *264,* 265
    See also Catholicism
**Christy, Howard
    Chandler,** *102*
Church, *264*
Cinco de Mayo, 269, *269*
Cipriano, Jeri, 207
Cities
    capital, *44,* 45. *See also*
        Capital city

    diversity in, 252–257,
        252–253, 254, 255,
        256, 257
    history of. *See*
        Community history;
        History
    immigrants in, 244,
        244, 249, *249,*
        252–257, *252–253,*
        254, 255, 256, 257
    Native American, 330,
        330
    population of, 45
    See also Communities;
        individual cities
**"Cities: Yesterday,
    Today, and
    Tomorrow" (Ring),** 9
Citizens, 2, **12**
    as leaders, 116–121
    responsibilities of, 29,
        29, 111–113, *112, 113*
    rights of, 110–113,
        110–111, 112, 113. See
        also Votes and voting
    as volunteers,
        132–133, *132, 133*
Citizenship
    common good and,
        75, 441
    justice and, 80, *80*
    models of, 116–121
Citizenship ceremony,
    116
Citizenship skills
    conflict resolution,
        82–83, *82, 83,* 99
    decision making, 251,
        251, 275
    economic choices,
        434–435, *434, 435*
    jury duty, 80, *80*
    problem solving,
        30–31, *30, 31, 33*
    voting, 114–115, *114,*
        115, 131
City council, 89, 103
City hall, *305*
City manager, 93
Civic virtue, 76, 107, 121
Civil rights, 120
Civil War, 352, *m352,*
    353, *353*
Civilization, 314

Claim, 334
Clark, William, 284–289, *284,* 350, 351, *m367*
Class magazine, 9, 64
Class picnic, planning, 235
Climate, 138, *138,* **150,** *150,* 151, *151.* See *also* Weather
Clinton, William Jefferson "Bill," *105*
Closer Look
   flag manners, 124
   Ford's assembly line, 379, *379*
   Washington, D.C., *348–349, 349*
Clothing, Native American, 222, 277, *329*
Coal, 158, 161, *m385*
Coastal plain, 148, *m176*
Coblentz, Catherine Cate, 325
Collage, 47
Colleges and universities, 95, *95*
Colonies, 282, *282,* **306,** *m335*
   Declaration of Independence by, 25, 338–340, *338, 340*
   laws of, 335, 338, 342
   See *also* Settlements
Colonists, 338
Colorado
   business in, 50
   mining in, 49, *49,* 55
   Native Americans in, 48, *48*
   pioneers in, 49, 50, *50*
   railroads in, 50, 51, *51,* 54
   See *also* Eagle, Colorado
Columbia River, 351
Columbus, Christopher, 332, *332, 333, 333, m337*
Columbus Day, 333, *333*
Common good, 75, 441
Communication, 119
   by telegraph, 359, *359, 389, 389*

by telephone, *55,* 359, *359,* 389
Communication link, 409, *409*
Communities, 12
   ancient, 314–321
   changes in, 51–53, *51, 52,* 292–297, *292, 293, 294, 295, 296*
   common good in, 75, 441
   depending on one another in, 18–19, *18, 19*
   diversity in, 22–25, *22, 23, 24*
   farming, 329, *329*
   government of. *See* Community government; Government services
   holidays and celebrations in, 24–25, *24, 25, 51, 55*
   hunting, 327–328, *327, 328*
   jobs in, 16–19, *17, 18, 19*
   laws of, 26–27, *26, 27, 29,* 78–79, *78, 79*
   leaders in, 64, 74–77, *75, 76, 77*
   location of, 36–41
   maps of, *m43,* 89
   reasons for living in, 12–15
   sizes of, 44–47
   See *also individual communities*
Communities Organized for Public Service (C.O.P.S.), 75, 75
Community government
   as local government, 93
   members of, 27–28, *28*
   responsibilities of, 84–89, 95
   role of, 78–81
   town meetings of, 90, *90*

Community heroes, 121, *121*
Community history, 48–53, 300–311
   ancient, 314–321, *315, 316, 317, 318, 319, 320*
   beginnings of, 48, 50, *50*
   changes over time, 51–53, *51, 52*
   learning from people, 300–301, *300, 301*
   places to learn from, 302, *302, 303, 303*
   research on, 300–303, *300, 301, 302, 303*
   time capsule containing, 304–305, *304, 305*
   tracing, 306–311, *307, 308, 309, m310, 311*
Community projects, 60–61, *60, m60, 61*
Comparing and contrasting, 377, 383, 391, 399, 405, 411, 414
Compass rose, 42
Competition, 398
Compromise, 82
Computers, 409, *409*
   in libraries, *19*
   researching history on, 302
   trade in, *m410*
Conclusions, 35, 41, 47, 53, 58
Confederate States of America (Confederacy), 353, *m352*
Conflict, 80
   American Revolution, *283,* 338–343, *341*
   Civil War, 352–353, *m352, 353*
   Korean War, 365, *365*
   resolving, 82–83, *82, 83,* 99
   Vietnam War, 364, *364*
Congress, 103, *103,* 104, *104*
Consequence, 27
Conservation, 189

Constitution, 101, **102,** *110,* 342–343, *342*
   Amendments to, 353
   approval by states, 343
   Bill of Rights in, **111,** *342*
   on branches of government, 102, *102,* 110
   signing of, *102,* 339
   writing of, 342
Consumers, 370, *370,* **402,** *402,* 416–417, *417,* 420, *420,* 422
Continents, 37
Continuity, 293
Contrasting. *See* Comparing and contrasting
Conveyor belt, 374, *374*
Cooney, Barbara, 280
Cooperate, 26, 39, 173, 321, 339
C.O.P.S. (Communities Organized for Public Service), 75, *75*
Corn, 329, *m385*
Corps of Discovery, 284–289, *285,* 351
Corpus Christi, Texas, *m179,* 332
Council, 89, 103
County, 93
County board of commissioners, 93
County government, 92, 93, *93*
County seat, 93, *93*
Courage, 118, 399
Court(s), 28, *28,* **80,** *80,* 91, *91.* See *also* Judicial branch of government; Supreme Court
Courthouses, 28, 72–73, *m72,* 93
Crafts. *See* Handicrafts
Creativity, 347
Critical thinking, 33, 59, 63, 99, 131, 135, 169, 195, 199, 239, 275, 279, 323, 363, 367, 415, 443, 447

Crockett, David "Davy," 218, *218,* 219, *219*

Crops

bananas, 404

corn, 329, *m385*

product maps of, 384, *m385,* 447, *m447*

soy, *m385*

tobacco, 310

wheat, *m385, m410*

See also Agriculture (farming)

Crossroads, 156

Crow Indians, 222, *222*

Crusoe, Robinson, 146

Cruzatte (Corps of Discovery), *285*

Culture(s), 22, *22,* 209, 260–265

African American, 263, *263,* 270, *270*

architecture, 231, *231,* 247, *318,* 319

art and, 262, *262. See also* Art

dance, *255, 269*

diversity of. *See* Diversity; Immigrants

holiday customs and traditions, 268–271, *268, 269, 270, 271*

immigrant, 245, *245, 246, 246*

language, 245, 252, 253, 254, *254,* 256, 261, *261*

literature. *See* Literature

in Mali, 320

Mexican, 60–61, *60, m60, 61,* 256, *256*

music. *See* Music

Native American, 276–277, *276, m276, 277,* 329

Cumberland Gap, 216, 217, *m217*

Cuneiform writing, *315*

Curry, Joseph, 121, *121*

Customs, 3, **22,** *22. See also* Holiday customs and traditions

Cutaway diagrams, 236, *237, 239*

Czech Republic, *14*

D

Daguerre, Louis, 386–387, *386*

Daguerreotypes, 387, *387,* 414. *See also* Photography

Dams, 191

Dance, *255, 269*

Davis, Jefferson, 353

Dear Juno **(Pak),** 280

Decade, 292

Decision, 251

Decision making, 251, *251*

Declaration of Independence, 25, 338–340, *338, 340*

Defoe, Daniel, 146

Delaware, *m308, m335*

Demand, 402, *403,* 404

Demeter (Greek goddess), *211*

Democracy, 114, 318

Democratic values

common good, 75, 441

justice, 80, *80,* 116

Dependence, 18

in communities, 18–19, *18, 19*

interdependence in trade, 411

Deposit, 421, *421,* **424,** *424, 425*

Descriptions, writing, 168, 427

Deserts, 150, 151, *151,* 161

DeSpain, Pleasant, 140–143

Details, supporting, 11, 15, 19, 25, 29, 32

Diagrams

cutaway, **236,** *237,* 239

of ecosystem, 185

Diary entries, 58, 136

Dias, Bartholomeu, *m337*

Dice, Harvey, 49

Differential Torque Control System (DTCS), 391, *391*

Dioramas, 311

Directions

cardinal, **42**

intermediate, **166,** *166,* 167, *m167*

Disaster(s), 184, 185, *185,* 190–191, *190, 191*

Diseases, 223

early settlers and, 308

malaria, 308

Native Americans and, 331

pasteurization and, 297, *297*

polio, 223, *223*

around Washington, D.C., 346

Dish, *330*

Disney, Walt, 15, *15*

Distance, 42

Distance scale, 42, 43, 199

District of Columbia (D.C.), 345, 348. *See also* Washington, D.C.

Diversity

in cities, *240–241, 252–257, 252–253, 254, 255, 256, 257*

in communities, 22–25, *22, 23, 24*

See also Immigrants

Division of labor, *379*

Dr. Martin Luther King, Jr. **(Adler),** 136

Doctors Without Borders, 438, *438*

Donate, 436, *436,* 437, *437. See also* Sharing

Doolittle, William, 173, *173*

Douglass, Frederick, 220–221, *220, 221*

Drawings

of inventions, 391

learning from, *91*

making, 25

Drums, 263, *263,* 341

E

E Pluribus Unum **(national motto),** 128

Dioramas, 311

Eagle (national bird), *1,* 24, *24, 128, 181*

Eagle, Colorado, 4–9, *12, m43*

celebrations in, *51, 55*

courthouse in, *28*

families in, 52–53, *53*

government in, 27, *28*

growth of, 50, 51–53, *51, 52*

history of, 48–55, *48, 49, 50, 51, 52, 54–55*

holidays in, 24–25, *24, 55*

judge from, *28*

locating, *m12*

mining in, 49, *49,* 55

"Eagle, Colorado" (Hoyt-Goldsmith), 4–9

Earthquakes, 184, *187, 190, 190, 191*

Easley, Michael F., 94, *94*

Eastern Hemisphere, 39, *39*

Economic choices, 434–435, *434, 435*

Economics. *See* Free enterprise

Economist, 405, *405*

Economy, 422

Ecosystem, 180, *180,* 181, *181,* 185

Ecuador, *440, m440*

Education

of African Americans, 220, 221

public, 85, *85,* 95, *95,* 220, 221

See also School(s)

Edwards, William, 50, *50*

Effect, 298. *See also* Cause and effect

Egypt, ancient, *282,* 316, *316, m316*

Einstein, Albert, 246, *246*

El Paso, Texas, *m395*

Eleanor **(Cooney),** 280

Elections, 77, 112, *112, 113, 113,* 130. *See also* Votes and voting

Electrical equipment, 389

Ellicott, Andrew, 347
Ellis Island (New York City), 244, *244*
Emancipation Proclamation, 353, *353*
Empire, 320
England
  in American Revolution, 338–341, *341*
  colonies of, 306–311, *307, 308, m309, m310, 311,* 322, 334, 335, *m335,* 338
  land claimed by, 334
Entrepreneurs
  Roberto Barrio, 394–398, *395, 397, 398*
  Andrew Carnegie, 437, *437*
  Walt Disney, 15, *15*
  Henry Ford, 372–383, *372*
  Cyrus McCormick, 388, *388*
  C. F. Nogal, 50
  Granville T. Woods, 389, *389*
Environment(s), 160, 161–165
  adapting to, *160,* 161, *161*
  changing physical features of, 164–165, *164, 165*
  conservation and, 189
  human processes and, 188–191
  physical processes and, 180–185
  pollution of, 189, *189*
  using resources, 162–163
EPCOT, 15
Equator, 38, *38*
Erosion, 182, *182, 183*
Eskimos (Inuit), *39,* 160
Ethnic groups, 23, *23.* *See also* Culture(s); Diversity; Immigrants
Europe, 37, *m262*
  Asian trade with, *406,* 407–408, *m407*

early settlers from, 306–311, *307, 308,* 334
immigrants from, 243, 248–250, 255, *255,* 256, *256*
Everglades (George), 200
Exact locations, 178
Executive branch of government, 91, *91, 92, 105, 105. See also* President
Expansion, 350
Explanatory writing, 168
Exploration, *m337*
  of Americas, 332, *332, 333–334, 333, 334, m337*
  of North Pole, 39, *39*
  of space, 360–361, *360–361*
  of West, 284–289, *m284,* 350, 351
Explorers, 332
  William Clark, 284–289, *284,* 350, 351, *m367*
  Christopher Columbus, 332, *332, 333, 333, m337*
  Bartholomeu Dias, *m337*
  Vasco da Gama, *m337*
  Matthew Henson, 39, *39*
  Meriwether Lewis, 284–289, *284,* 350, 351, *m367*
  Ferdinand Magellan, *m337*
  Native Americans and, *285, 286, 286*
  Robert Peary, 39
  Marco Polo, *406,* 407–408, *m407*
  ships of, 332, *332*
  Amerigo Vespucci, *m337*
Exports, 410, *m410*

F

Fact(s), 400
  opinion and, 400–401, *401,* 417, 442

telling fiction from, 218–219, *218, 219,* 239
Factories, 310, *310. See also* Manufacturing
Fairness, 28, 120
Families
  in Eagle, Colorado, 52–53, *53*
  history of, 300, *300,* 301
Famine, 248, 249–251
Farms, 157, *157. See also* Agriculture (farming)
Federal government, 102. *See also* National government
Festivals, 270, 271
Fiction, 218, *218,* 219, *219,* 239
Field trips
  auction, 444–445, *444, m444,* 445
  community project, 60–61, *60, m60,* 61
  monuments and memorials in Washington, D.C., 364–365, *364, m364,* 365
  Niagara Falls, 196–197, *196, m196,* 197
  powwow, 276–277, *276, m276,* 277
  young active citizens, 132–133, *132, 133*
Fighting for the Forest (Rand), 200
Fillmore, Parker, 137
Fire(s), 184, *185,* 190, 191
Firefighters, 18, *18,* 81, 121, *121*
Fireworks, 235, 317
First Ladies, *119,* 226–227, *226, 227*
Fish, *182*
Flag(s)
  creating, 127, 349
  displaying, *124*
  saluting, *124*
  of United States, *65,* 122–124, *122, 123, 124,* 234
Fleming, Candace, 368

"Flight Days" holiday, 24, *24,* 55
Floods, 184, 191
Florida, 208–209, *m208,* 334, *334*
Flow charts, 422, *423,* 443
Folktales, *260*
  Paul Bunyan, 212, *212*
  John Henry, 204–207, *205, 206, 207*
  Pecos Bill, 213, *213*
  writing, 442
Food(s)
  ethnic, 23
  fresh, *402*
  German American, 23
  growing. *See* Agriculture (farming); Crops
  Hispanic American, 256
  Korean American, 254
  Native American, 329, 330
  storage of, 329
Food banks, 133, *133*
Ford, Henry, 372–382, *372*
Ford Motor Company, 372–375, *373, 374,* 378–383, *382*
Forest(s), *180,* 181, *181,* 189
Forest fires, 184, *185,* 191
Fort Castillo de San Marcos (St. Augustine, Florida), 334, *334*
Fort Mandan (Missouri), 286, *286*
Fort Massac (Illinois), 324–325, *m324*
Fort McHenry (Baltimore, Maryland), 126, *126,* 127
Fort Worth, Texas, 72, *m72*
Forum (Rome), 319, *319*
Fossil, *182*
Founder, 50
Fourth of July, 25, *25,* 234–235, *234, 235*

France
Franklin as
ambassador to, 339
land claimed by, 334
Louisiana and, 93
Franklin, Benjamin, *338,*
339, *339*
Free enterprise, 371, *371,*
402, 403–405
agricultural. *See*
Agriculture
(farming)
agricultural
equipment, 388
automobile
manufacturing,
372–383, *373, 374,*
376–377, 378, 379,
380–381, 382, 383
bicycle sales and
repairs, 394–398,
394, 395, 396–397,
398
capital in, 381
capital resources in,
382
in colonial Virginia,
309, *m309*
consumers in, 370,
370, 402, *402,* 420,
420, 422
electrical equipment,
389
human resources in,
382, *382*
international trade
and, 406–411
prices in, 404–405
producers in, 370, *370,*
378, 418, 419, *419,*
422
supply and demand
in, 402, 403, *403,* 404
See also Trade
Freedom
African Americans
and, 220–221, 353
Bill of Rights and, 111,
342
immigrants and,
242–243
of press, *111,* 117
of religion, 111, 117,
243, 265

of speech, 111, 117
See also Votes and
voting
Fuels, 161. *See also* Coal;
Oil
Furnace, steam-boiler,
389, *389*

G

Gagarin, Yuri, 361
Galápagos Islands,
m189
Galveston, Texas,
295–296, *295, 296,* 298
Gama, Vasco da, *m337*
Garland, Sherry, 448
Gateway Arch (St. Louis,
Missouri), 231, *231*
Gaylord, Frank, 365, *365*
Geisert, Arthur, 448
Geisert, Bonnie, 448
Generalizing, 101, 107,
113, 121, 127, 130
Geographer, 172, 194
Geography, 137, **138,**
138, 145–151, **146**
bodies of water, 149,
149
Central Park (New
York City), 86,
86–87, m86
climate and, 150–151,
150
Cumberland Gap, 216,
217, *m217*
Grand Canyon, 183,
183, m183
landforms, 147–148,
147, 148
plant life and, 151, *151*
rivers and mountains,
351, *m351*
Silk Road, 407, *m407*
See also Map(s); Map
and globe skills
"Geography Tools"
(Ruben), 143
George, Jean Craighead,
200
George Washington: A
Picture Book
Biography **(Giblin),**
136

Georgia, *292–293,* 335,
m335
German Americans, *23,*
256
Ghost town, 294, *294*
Giblin, James Cross, 136
Ginsburg, Ruth Bader,
106, 107, *107*
Girls' Leadership
Workshop (Val-Kill,
NY), 230, *230*
"Glaciers Change the
Earth" (Ruben), 143
Glass factory, 310, *310*
Globe, 38, *38,* 40, 173
Gold
discovery of, 333
mining of, 294, *294*
Goods, 13
Gorbachev, Mikhail, 281
Government, 27
branches of, 90–92, *91,*
92, 103–107, *103,*
104, 105, 106, 107
community. *See*
Community
government
county, 92, 93, *93*
federal, **102.** *See also*
National
government
immigrants and, 246,
246
leaders in, 77, *77,*
103–105, *103, 105*
levels of, 92
local, 92, 93
national. *See* National
government
protection of people
and property by, 81
responsibilities of, 81,
84–89, 95, *95*
state, 92, 94, *94,* 95, *95*
Government services,
84, *88*
cost of, 88–89, 95
education, 85, *85,* 95,
95
parks and recreation,
86, *86–87*
protection of people
and property, 81
public works, 87, *87*

safety and health, 81,
84, *84,* 85, 95
Governor, 67, *67,* **94,** *94*
Grand Canyon, 183, *183,*
m183
Graph(s)
bar, **20,** 21, 33, *104,*
186, *187,* 195
line, **428,** *428,* 429, *429,*
443
picture, **20,** *21,* 33
reading, 20–21, *21,* 33
Graphic organizers, 32,
58, 98, 130, 168, 194,
238, 274, 322, 362, 414,
442
Great Britain. *See*
England
Great Plains, hunting
on, 327
Great Pyramid (Egypt),
316, *316*
Great Seal, 128, *128, 129*
Great Wall of China,
154, m154
Greece
ancient, 210–211, *210,*
m210, 318, *318, m318*
myths of, 210–211, *211*
Greektown (Chicago,
Illinois), 256
Grid system, 178, *178,*
179, *m179, m193,* 195
Growing season, 151
Growth
of Eagle, Colorado, 50,
51–53, *51, 52*
of United States,
350–355, 356, *m357,*
358
Guatemala, *m260,* 404

H

Hale, Sarah Josepha,
233, *233*
Hall, Donald, 368
Hall of Fame, creating,
19, 247
Handicrafts
African kente cloth,
273
Mexican bark
painting, *272*

Native American, *273*, 276–277, *276, 277,* 329
pottery, *273, 318,* 329
Russian nesting dolls, *272*
weaving, *17*
Harbor, 162, *162–163, m162, 163, 332*
Hatmaker's Sign, The (Franklin), *368*
Hatshepsut (Egyptian queen), *316*
Hawaii, 123, *m354*
Health
checking immigrants for, 244
government and, 84, *84, 85,* 95
polio and, 223, *223*
Health care, 18, 297, *297,* 438, *438*
Helmets, bicycle, *79, 401, 443*
Hemisphere, 38, *38, 39, 39*
Henry Ford Museum, *376–377, m376*
"Henry Ford's Dream," 372–375
Henry, John, 204–207
Henson, Matthew, *39, 39*
Hera (Greek goddess), *211*
Heritage, 25, 228–235
Clara Barton National Historic Site, *439, 439*
Columbus Day, 333, *333*
Dr. Martin Luther King, Jr., Day, 120
Fourth of July, 25, *25*
Liberty Bell, 127, *127*
Louisiana parishes, 93, *m93*
monuments and memorials, *100–101, m100,* 228–232, *228, 229, 230, 231, 232,* 302
New Year's Day celebration, 271, *271*
Olvera Street (Los Angeles, California), 253, *253*

places of worship, 264, *264*
places that celebrate, 231–232, *231, 232*
Hero, 120, 211
Heroic individuals, 220–227
African American, 118, *118,* 120, *120,* 220–221, *220, 221,* 224, *224*
Lance Armstrong, 399, *399*
astronauts, *360, 361*
Cesar Chavez, 225, *225*
David "Davy," Crockett, 218, *218,* 219, *219*
Frederick Douglass, 220–221, *220, 221*
Hispanic American, 225, *225*
Thomas Jefferson, 100, 117, *117,* 232, *232,* 284, *338, 339, 351,* 417
John Luther "Casey" Jones, 214–215, *214, 215*
Helen Keller, 119, *119*
Dr. Martin Luther King, Jr., 120, *120*
Abraham Lincoln, 232, *232, 233,* 353, *353,* 358
Native American, 222, *222, 285, 286*
Rosa Parks, 224, *224*
Chief Plenty Coups, 222, *222*
rescue workers, 121, *121*
Eleanor Roosevelt, *119,* 226–227, *226, 227,* 230
Sacagawea, *285, 286*
Jonas Salk, 223, *223*
Harriet Tubman, 118, *118*
George Washington, 44, *45, 192,* 232, *232, 343, 343, 344*
Highlands, *37, 37*
Highways, 155, 156, *m156, 375, 375*

Himalayan mountain ranges, *37, m37*
Hispanic Americans
in Chicago, 256
heroic, 225, *225*
holidays of, 269, *269*
leaders, 225, *225*
in Los Angeles, 253, *253*
Historic marker, *302*
Historic site, 439, *439*
Historical society, 302
History, 3, 48
of community. *See* Community history
of Eagle, Colorado, 48–55, *48, 49, 50, 51, 52, 54–55*
of family, 300, *300,* 301
oral, **301,** *301*
research on, 300–303, *300, 301, 302, 303*
History maps, 356, 357, *m357, 363*
History museum, 56–57, *56, 57*
Hogs, *m385*
Holiday(s), 24
celebrating our heritage, 233, *233*
Cinco de Mayo, 269, *269*
Columbus Day, 333, *333*
in communities, 24–25, *24, 25*
Dr. Martin Luther King, Jr., Day, 120
"Flight Days," 24, *24, 55*
Fourth of July, 25, *25,* 234–235, *234, 235*
Kwanzaa, 270, *270*
Memorial Day, 234, *234*
New Year's Day, 271, *271*
St. Patrick's Day, 268, *268*
Thanksgiving Day, 233, *233*
Holiday customs and traditions, 268–271
African American, 270, *270*
Irish, 268, *268*

Mexican, 269, *269*
Horse Mountain (Colorado), *49*
Horseshoe Falls, 196, *196*
House(s). *See* Shelters
House of Representatives, 103–104, *104,* 109
Houston, Sam, 229, *229*
Houston, Texas, 296
How We Crossed the West: The Adventures of Lewis and Clark (Schanzer), 284–289
Hoyt-Goldsmith, Diane, 4–9
Hull, Charles, 69
Hull-House (Chicago, Illinois), 69–71, *69, 71, 74*
Human features, 139, *139,* **154,** *154*
Human processes, 188–191
Human resources, 382, *382*
Hunting, 326, *326, 327–328, 327, 328,* 329
Hurricanes, 295–296, *295, 296,* 298
Hutchison, Kay Bailey, 103
Hydroelectric power, *197*

I

Idaho, 175, *m174*
changes in towns in, 294, *294*
mining in, 294, *294*
representatives from, *104*
Idea, main, 11, 15, 19, 25, 29
Illinois, *13,* 324–325, *m324. See also* Chicago, Illinois
Immigrants, 242, *242,* 243–273, *m243*
arrival at Ellis Island, 244, *244*
Asian, 245, *m245,* 254, *254,* 261

in cities, 244, *244*, 249, *249*, 252–257, *252–253*, *254*, *255*, *256*, *257*
contributions of, 246, *246*, 247, *247*
creating Hall of Fame for, 247
European, 243, 248–250, 255, *255*, 256, *256*
Irish, 248–251, *248–249*, *m248*
languages of, 245, 252, 253, 254, *254*, 256, 261, *261*
Mexican, 245, *m245*, 253, *253*, 256, *256*
music and, 263, *263*
Muslim, 264, *264*
present–day, 245, *m245*
reasons for moving, 242–243, 248–251
Imports, 410
Income, 371, 418
earning, *371*, 418–419, *418*, *419*, *431*, 446
recording sources of, 430–431, *430*, *431*
Independence, 339
Independence Day (Fourth of July), 25, *25*, 234–235, *234*, *235*
Independence Hall (Philadelphia, Pennsylvania), *338*
Independence Square (Philadelphia, Pennsylvania), 127
Indian(s). *See* Native Americans
Indian Ocean, 37
Indiana
firefighters in, *18*
population of, *m279*
product map of, *m385*
representatives from, *104*
Indianapolis, Indiana, *18*
Industrial robots, 383, *383*
Industry, 381

Inferences, 145, 151, 158, 165, 168, 177, 191
Information
gathering, 430–431, *430*, *431*
organizing, 432, *432*
Ink stand, *339*
Innovations, 390. *See also* Inventions
Interdependence, 18–19, **411**
Interest, 425
Intermediate directions, 166, *166*, *167*, *m167*
International Space Station, *360*, *361*, *361*
"International Space Station" (Ring), 9
International trade, 406–411, *406*, **407,** *m407*, 408–409, *410*, *m410*, *411*
Internet, 302, 409
Interviews, conducting, 53, 321, 421
Inuit, 39, *160*
Inventions, 315, 359, 386–393
air brake, 389
automobiles, 372–383, *373*, *374*, *375*, *376–377*, *378*, *381*, *383*
comparing and contrasting, 414
Differential Torque Control System (DTCS), 391, *391*
drawing, 391
fireworks, *235*, 317
industrial robots, 383, *383*
kiddie stool, 390, *390*
paper, 317, *317*
pasteurization, 297, *297*
patents on, 389, *389*, 390, *390*
photography, 386–387, *386*, *387*, 414
polio vaccine, 223, *223*
printing, *302*, 317, *317*
reaper, 388, *388*

safer bicycles, 392–393, *392*, *393*
space station, *360*, 361, *361*
steam-boiler furnace, 389, *389*
telegraph, 359, *359*, *389*, *389*
telephone, *55*, 359, *359*, 389
transcontinental railroad, *358*, **359**
wheeled cart, 315
writing, 315
Inventiveness, 15
Inventors
Alexander Graham Bell, 359, *359*
Louis Daguerre, 386–387, *386*
Hans Christiansen Lee, 391, *391*
Jeanie Low, 390, *390*
Cyrus McCormick, 388, *388*
Elijah McCoy, 248, *248*
Samuel Morse, 359, *359*
Louis Pasteur, 297, *297*
Jonas Salk, 223, *223*
Granville T. Woods, 389, *389*
"Inventors and Their Inventions" (Martin), 375
Investments, 420–421, **426,** *426*, *427*, 428–429, *428*, *429*
Invitation, writing an, 238
Ireland
customs of, 268, *268*
immigrants from, 248–251, *248–249*, *m248*
potato famine in, 248–251
Iron, mining of, *49*
Islam. *See* Muslims
Italy, ancient Rome in, 319, *319*, *m319*, 406

J

Jackson, Ellen, 368
Jackson, Tennessee, *214*
James I, king of England, 308
James River, 307, 308
Jamestown, Virginia, 306–311, *307*, *308*, *m308*, *m309*, *m310*, *311*, 322, 334
Japan, recreation in, *14*
Jay, John, *106*
Jeanie Johnston **(immigrant sailing ship),** 250
Jefferson, Thomas, 100, 117, *117*, 232, *232*, 284, *338*, *339*, 351, 417
Jefferson Memorial (Washington, D.C.), *100–101*, *m100*, 348, *349*
Job(s), 16–19, *17*, *18*, *19*
See also Work
Job skills, 16–17, *17*
"John Henry" (Keats), 204–207, *205*, *206*, *207*
Jones, John Luther "Casey," 214–215, *214*, *215*
Judaism, 264, *264*, 265
Judge, 28, *28*
Judicial branch of government, 91, *91*, 106–107, *106*, *107*
Juno (Roman goddess), *211*
Jupiter (Roman god), 211, *211*
Jury, 80, *80*
Justice, 80, *80*, **116**
Justices, of Supreme Court, 106–107, *106*, *107*, 109

K

Kalman, Bobbie, 64
Kansas, *m174*, *175*
Karenga, Maulana, 270
Keats, Ezra Jack, 204–207

Keller, Helen, 119, *119*
Kennedy, Anthony M., *106*
Kennedy, John F., 65
Kentucky, *34–35, m34,* 216, *m217*
Key, Francis Scott, 126–127, *126*
Kiddie stool, 390, *390*
"Kids Making Money" (Martin), 375
Kimchi (Korean food), 254
King, Dr. Martin Luther, Jr., 120, *120*
Kipling, Rudyard, 369
Korean Americans, 254, *254*
Korean War Veterans Memorial (Washington, D.C.), 365, *365*
Koreatown (Los Angeles, California), 254, *254*
Krull, Kathleen, 448
Kwanzaa, 270, *270*

L

Labor
    division of, *379*
    human resources, 382, *382*
Lakes, *36, 37*
Land, types of, 36, 37, *37*
Land bridge, 326
Land grants, 309, *m309*
Land use papers, *50*
Landform(s), 139, *139,* **147,** *147,* 148, *148,* 169
Landform map, **152,** 153, *m153,* 169, 199, *m199*
Landmarks, **283,** *283,* **351**
Language(s), **203,** 245, **252,** 253, 254, *254,* 256, 261, *261*
Latinos. *See* Hispanic Americans
Latitude, **412,** *m412,* 413, *m413,* 415
Law(s), **26**
    colonial, 335, 338, 342

community, 26–27, *26, 27,* 29, 78–79, *78, 79*
    national, 104
    seat belt, 79, *79*
    state, 94
    traffic, 26–27, *26, 27, 78*
Lawmakers
    community, 26–27
    Congress, 103–104, *103, 104*
    state, 94
    See also Government
Lawrence, Jacob, *267*
Leaders
    African American, 118, *118,* 120, *120,* 220–221, *220, 221,* 224, *224*
    in community, 64, 74–77, *75, 76, 77*
    good citizens as, 116–121
    in government, 77, *77,* 103–105, *103, 105*
    Hispanic American, 225, *225*
    honoring, 64
    national, 103–105, *103, 105*
    Native American, 48, 222, *222, 308*
    Roman, 319, *319*
    Eleanor Roosevelt, *119,* 226–227, *226, 227,* 230
"Leaders for Peace" (Ahearn), 71
Lee, Hans Christiansen, 391, *391*
Lee, Richard Henry, 340, *340*
Legends, **214,** 214–219
    Daniel Boone, 216, *216,* 217
    Davy Crockett, 218, *218,* 219, *219*
    Casey Jones, 214–215, *214, 215*
Legislative branch of government, **91,** *91,* 92, 103–104, *103, 104*
L'Enfant, Pierre Charles, 346–347, *346*

Leopold, Aldo, 35
Letter writing, 81, 98, 274, 322, 433, 442
Lewis, Meriwether, 284–289, *284,* 350, 351, *m367*
"Lewis and Clark" (Ring), 289
Liberty. *See* Freedom
Liberty Bell, 127, *127, m355*
Libraries
    exploring history in, 302
    need for, 19, *19*
Library of Congress, 192
Lin, Maya, 364, *364*
Lincoln, Abraham, 232, *232,* 233, *348,* 353, 358
Lincoln Memorial (Washington, D.C.), *348,* 364, *364*
Line graphs, **428,** *428,* 429, *429,* 443
List, writing, 58, 194, 274
Literature, **210,** 260, *260*
    "The Amish" (Cipriano), 207
    "Ancient Egypt" (Cipriano), 207
    ancient Greek, 210–211, *211,* 318
    "Cities: Yesterday, Today, and Tomorrow" (Ring), 9
    Dear Juno (Pak), 280
    Dr. Martin Luther King, Jr. (Adler), 136
    "Eagle, Colorado" (Hoyt-Goldsmith), 4–9
    Eleanor (Cooney), 280
    Everglades (George), 200
    Fighting for the Forest (Rand), 200
    folktales, 204–207, *205, 206, 207,* 212–213, *212, 213,* 260, 442
    "Geography Tools" (Ruben), 143

George Washington: A Picture Book Biography (Giblin), 136
    "Glaciers Change the Earth" (Ruben), 143
    The Hatmaker's Sign (Franklin), 368
    "Henry Ford's Dream," 372–375
    How We Crossed the West: The Adventures of Lewis and Clark (Schanzer), 284–289
    "International Space Station" (Ring), 9
    "Inventors and Their Inventions" (Martin), 375
    "John Henry" (Keats), 204–207
    "Kids Making Money" (Martin), 375
    "Leaders for Peace" (Ahearn), 71
    legends, 214–219, *214, 215, 216, 218, 219*
    "Lewis and Clark" (Ring), 289
    "Living in the Antarctic" (Ruben), 143
    My Father's Boat (Garland), 448
    myths, 210–211, *211*
    "New England Town Meeting" (Ahearn), 71
    Nothing Ever Happens on 90th Street (Schotter), 64
    Old Home Day (Hall), 368
    Peace and Bread: The Story of Jane Addams (McPherson), 68–71
    A Picnic in October (Bunting), 280
    "Pioneer Living" (Ring), 9
    Prairie Town (Geisert and Geisert), 448

INDEX

Robinson Crusoe, 140–143

"Sights, Sounds, Celebrations" (Cipriano), 207

Supermarket (Krull), 448

telling fact from fiction, 218–219, *218, 219,* 239

"Transportation: Yesterday and Today" (Ring), 289

Turn of the Century (Jackson), 368

Two Days in May (Peck), 64

"Wall Street" (Martin), 375

Washington D.C.: A Scrapbook (Benson), 136

Water Dance (Locker), 200

What Is a Community? (Kalman), 64

"Where Water Comes From" (Ahearn), 71

"World Monuments" (Ring), 289

Little Italy (Chicago, Illinois), *255, 256*

"Living in the Antarctic" (Ruben), 143

Local government, *92, 93. See also* Community government

Location, 2, 36
of community, 36–41
exact, **178**
relative, **172,** *172, 173*

Locker, Thomas, 200

Locomotives, *215*

London Company, 309, *m309*

Longitude, 412, *m412,* 413, *m413,* 415

Los Angeles, California, *18, m252*
immigrants in, 253–254, *m252, 252–253, 254*
Koreatown in, 254, *254*

Olvera Street, 253, *253*

Louisiana, parishes in, 93, *m93*

Louisiana Purchase, 350

Low, Jeanie, 390, *390*

Lowlands, 37, *37*

M

Magellan, Ferdinand, *m337*

Main idea, 11, 15, 19, 25, 29, 32

Maine, 162–163, *162–163, m162,* 335, *m335*

Majority rule, 112

Mali, 320, *320, m320,* 321

Mall (Washington, D.C.), *348–349*

Mall of America (Minnesota), *416–417, m416*

Mansa Musa, 321

Manufacturing, 257
assembly line in, 374, *374, 379,* **380,** 414
of automobiles, 372–383, *373, 374, 376–377, 378, 379, 380–381, 382, 383*
of glass, 310, *310*
production efficiency in, 374, *374*
of reapers, 388

Map(s), 40
borders on, 41, *m41*
of communities, *m43,* 89
distance scale on, **42,** *43, 199*
finding locations with, 173
following routes on, 336–337, *m337,* 363, 367
history, **356,** *m357,* 363
kinds of, 192–193, *m192, m193*
landform, **152,** 153, *m153,* 169, 199, *m199*
making, 89, 192–193, *192, m192, 193,* 355
of moon, 177
of North America, *m41*

population, 258–259, *m259,* 275, *m279*
product, **384,** *m385,* 415, 447, *m447,* 448
reading, 42–43, *m43,* 59, 63, *m63,* 415
state capitals and borders on, 96–97, *m96–97,* 99, 135, *m135*
of world, *m40*

Map and globe skills
comparing history maps, 356–357, *m357,* 363
finding intermediate directions, 166–167, *166, m167*
following routes on a map, 336–337, *m337,* 363, 367
landform maps, 152–153, *m153,* 169, 199, *m199*
reading maps, 42–43, *m43,* 59, 63, *m63,* 415
reading product maps, **384,** *m385,* 415, 447, *m447,* 448
state capitals and borders, 96–97, *m96–97,* 99, 135, *m135*
using a map grid, 178–179, *m179, m193,* 195
using latitude and longitude, 412–413, *m412, m413,* 415
using population maps, 258–259, *m259,* 275, *m279*
See also Map(s)

Map grid, 178–179, *m179, m193,* 195

Map key, 42, *m43, m63*

Map symbols, 42, *m43,* 96, *m96–97,* 356, *m357*

Map title, 42, *m43*

Marketing, 397

Marshall, John, 106

Martin, Eleana, 375

Martin Luther King, Jr., Day, 120

Maryland, 126, *126,* 127, *170, m308, m335,* 345

Masjid, 264, *264*

Massachusetts, *175, m175,* 240–241, *m240,* 249, *249, m335*

Mayor, 27, 93

McAleese, Mary, 250, *250*

McCormick, Cyrus, 388, *388*

McCoy, Elijah, 247, *247*

McDonald, Alex, 51

McPherson, Stephanie Sammartino, 68–71

Medals, 71, 136

Mediator, 82

Medicine
polio vaccine, 223, *223*
See also Diseases

Memorial(s), 100–101, *m100,* **230,** *230,* 232, *232,* 303, 348, *348–349,* 364–365, *364, m364,* 365

Memorial Day, 234, *234*

Meridian, 412, *m412, m413*

Mesopotamia, 315, *315, m315*

Metro (Washington, D.C.), 46, *46*

Mexican Fine Arts Museum (Chicago, Illinois), 256

Mexico
Cinco de Mayo holiday in, 269, *269*
claimed by Spanish, 334
culture of, 60–61, *60, m60,* 61, 256, *256,* 269, *269*
immigrants from, 245, *m245,* 253, *253,* 256, *256*
population density in, 258, *m259*

Michigan, *m376*

Middle East, immigrants from, 257

Millennium, 312

Mills, Robert, 365, *365*

Minerals, 157

Mining, 157–158, *158*
in Colorado, 49, *49*

of gold, 294, *294*
in Idaho, 294, *294*
of iron, *49*
of silver, *49*, 294, *294*
working conditions
of, *226*
Minnesota, *416–417*,
m416
Minority rights, 113
Mississippi River, *331*,
351
Missouri
explorers in, 285, 286
Gateway Arch in, 231,
231
Missouri River, 285, *285*,
351
Modern times, 314
Money, 418–421
budgeting, 430–433
depositing, 421, *421*,
424, *424*, 425
earning, 418, *418*, 419,
419, *431*, 446
interest earned on, 425
investments of,
420–421, 426, *426*,
427, 428–429, *428*,
429
saving, **421**, *421*,
424–427, *424*, *425*,
426, *427*, 446
sharing, 421, 432,
436–437, *436*, *437*
spending, 420, *420*
Montgomery, Alabama,
224, *224*
Monticello
(Charlottesville,
Virginia), *117*
Monuments, 203, *203*,
228, *228*, 229, *229*, 231,
231, *302*, 348, *348–349*,
364–365, *m364*, *365*
Moon map, studying,
177
Moore, Darla, *436*
Morgan, Julia, 190, *190*
Morse, Samuel, 359, *359*
Mosque, *320*
Motto, national, 128
Mound Builders
(Cahokia), 330–331,
330
Mount Hood, *144*

Mount Rushmore, 232,
232, *m354*
Mount Saint Helens
(Washington) *184*
Mount Vernon, *m192*
Mountains and
mountain ranges, 37,
37, *138*, 147, *147*, 351,
m351. See also
individual mountains
Murals, 240–241, *255*,
256, 297
Museum(s), 14
Casey Jones, *214*
creating exhibits for,
411
exploring history in,
290–291, 301, 302,
302
Henry Ford, 376–377,
m376
history, 56–57, *56*
making, 289, 368
Mexican, 256
time capsules in,
304–305, *304*, *305*
Music, 263, *263*
immigrants and, 263,
263
mariachi, 253
national anthem,
126–127
patriotic, 126–127
See also Songs
Musical instruments,
263, *263*, *341*, *444*, *445*
Muslims, 265
in ancient Mali, 321
as immigrants, 257
masjid of, 264, *264*
mosque of, *320*
My Father's Boat
(Garland), 448
Myths, 210, 211, *211. See*
also Folktales;
Legends

N

Nation, 40
National anthem,
126–127
National Farm Workers
Association (NFWA),
225, *225*

National government,
102–109
branches of, *44*, 45, 91,
91, 92, 103–107, *103*,
104, *105*, *106*, *107*
Constitution and, **102,**
102, 342–343, *342*,
343
establishing, 342–343,
343
executive branch of,
91, *91*, 92, 105, *105*
judicial branch of, **91,**
91, 106–107, *106*, *107*
legislative branch of,
91, *91*, 92, 103–104,
103, *104*
location of, *44*, 45. *See*
also Washington,
D.C.
offices in, 108–109, *109*
responsibilities of, 95
National Guard, 76
National Statuary Hall
(Washington, D.C.),
228, *228*
National symbols. *See*
Patriotic symbols
Native Americans
agriculture of, 329,
330
ancestors of, 326–331,
326–327, *329*
boats and ships of,
331
cities of, 330–331, *330*
clothing of, *222*, 277,
329
in Colorado, 48, *48*
conflict with
Europeans, 334
crafts of, *273*, 276–277,
276, *277*, 329
culture of, 276–277,
276, *m276*, *277*, 329
explorers and, *285*,
286, *286*
first Thanksgiving
and, 233, *233*
foods of, 329, 330
heroic, 222, *222*, *285*,
286
hunting by, 326, *326*,
327–328, *327*, *328*,
329

leaders, *48*, 222, *222*,
307, *307*, 308
naming of, 333
powwows of, 276–277,
276, *m276*, 277
religion of, 328, 330,
330
shelters of, 328, *328*,
329, *329*
tools of, 328, *328*
trade of, 329
Virginia settlers and,
306, 307, *307*
See also individual
groups
Natural disasters,
184–185, *185*, 190–191,
190, *191*
Natural hazards,
190–191, *190*, *191*
Natural resources, 3, *3*,
17, 382
fuels, **161**
mining of. *See* Mining
Needs, 16, *16*, 420, 430
Nelson, Louis, 365, *365*
Nelson, Rich, 140–143
Neptune (Roman god),
211
Nesting dolls, *272*
"New England Town
Meeting" (Ahearn),
71
New Hampshire, 90,
m335
New Jersey, *m335*
immigrants in, 257,
257, *m257*
manufacturing in, **257**
New Year's Day, 271, *271*
New York (state), 230,
230, 304–305, *m335*
New York City
Central Park in, 86,
86–87, *m86*
Ellis Island in, 244,
244
immigrants in, 244,
244, 249, *249*
locating, *m10*
St. Patrick's Day in,
268
Statue of Liberty in,
236–237, *236*, *237*,
242, *m355*

transportation in, 10–11
Newspapers
African American, 221, *221*
Korean language, 254
in museum, *305*
reading, *111*
research and, 95, *301*
writing articles for, 227, 343, 362, 414
Ney, Elisabet, 229, *229*
Niagara Falls, 196–197, *196, m196, 197*
Niagara River, 196, *196*
Nigeria, 263, *m263*
Nogal, C. F., 50
Nomads, 328
North, in Civil War, *m352,* 353, *353*
North America, 37, *m41*
North Carolina, *m63, m335*
governor of, **94,** *94*
libraries in, *21*
representatives from, *104*
State Capitol Building in, *m94*
North Pole, 38, *38,* 39, *39*
North Star **(newspaper),** 221, *221*
Northern Hemisphere, *38*
Northwest Side (Chicago, Illinois), 255
Nothing Ever Happens on 90th Street **(Schotter),** 64

O

Ocean, 37
Ocean voyage, planning, 250
O'Connor, Sandra Day, *106*
Oil, 161, *175, m176,* 189
Old Home Day **(Hall),** 368
Olmsted, Frederick Law, 86
Olvera, Agustin, 253

Olvera Street (Los Angeles, California), 253, *253*
Open pit mines, 158
Opinion, 400, 401, *401,* 417, 442
Opportunity, 202, 242
Opportunity cost, 370, *370,* **434,** 435, 443
Oral history, 301, *301*
Oregon, *144–145, m144*
O'Reilly, Edward, 213
Orlando, Florida, *208–209, m208*
Ouray, Chief (Ute) 48
Outcomes, predicting, 159, 171, 194
Overhead, 395, 397

P

Pacific Ocean, 37, 288, *288,* 350
Paintings, *102, 106, 117, 126,* 216, *233,* 262, *262, 267, 311, 330, 333, 341, 344*
Pak, Soyung, 280
Palm Springs, California, *m188*
Pan American Highway, 156, *m156*
Panama Canal, 164–165, *m165*
Paper, invention of, 317, *317*
Paragraphs, writing, 32, 98, 168, 194, 393
Parish, 93, *m93*
Parks, *34–35,* 86, *86–87, m86, 185, 301, 324–325, m324*
Parks, Rosa, 224, *224*
Parthenon (Greece), *210, 318*
Pasteur, Louis, 297, *297*
Patent, 389, *389, 390, 390*
Paterson, New Jersey, 257, *257, m257*
Patriotic symbols, 122, 123–129
capital. *See* Washington, D.C.
flag, *65,* 122–124, *122, 123, 124, 127, 234*

Great Seal, 128, *128, 129*
Liberty Bell, 127, *127, m355*
medal, 71, 136
monuments and memorials, *100–101, m100,* **203,** *203,* **228–232,** *228, 229, 230, 231, 232, 348, 348–349, 364–365, 364, m364, 365*
national anthem, 126–127
national bird (bald eagle), *1, 24, 128, 181,* 225
Pledge of Allegiance, **125,** *125*
Statue of Liberty, 236–237, *236, 237, 242, m355*
Treaty Seal, *129*
Patriotism, 67, *67,* **122,** 123–127
holidays celebrating, 25, *25,* 234–235, *234, 235*
Peace, 29
Peace and Bread: The Story of Jane Addams **(McPherson),** 68–71
Peace Corps, 440–441, *440, 441*
Peale, Charles Willson, *117*
Peale, Rembrandt, *344*
Peary, Robert, 39
Pecos Bill, 213, *213*
Pei, I. M., 246, *246*
Pennsylvania, 127, *127, 133, m155, m335*
Performance
conducting interviews, 53, 421
creating dioramas, 311
creating flags, 127, 349
creating Hall of Fame, 19, 247
creating museum exhibits, 411
creating radio interviews, 321
creating travel brochures, 257
designing buttons, 29

diagramming an ecosystem, 185
drawing inventions, 391
holding an art fair, 265
making charts, 405
making collages, 47
making displays of cultures, 331
making drawings, 25
making maps, 89, 355
making postcards, 15
making posters, 107, 441
making a time line mural, 297
making weather charts, 151
planning a class picnic, 235
planning a festival, 271
planning an ocean voyage, 250
recycling research, 191
researching, 95, 191, 361
researching transportation systems, 361
simulation, 217, 383
studying a moon map, 177
writing advertisements, 399
writing descriptions, 427
writing letters, 81, 433
writing newspaper articles, 227, 343
writing poetry, 41, 121
Perseverance, 119, 233
Persuasive writing, 32, 98
Pharaoh, 316, *316*
Philadelphia, Pennsylvania, 127, *127, m155,* 338
Photo story, *4–9, 12, m12*
Photographs
analyzing, *292–293*
as primary sources, 392–393, *392, 393*
Photography, 386–387, *386, 387,* 414

Physical features, 146, 164–165, *164, 165*
Physical features model, 143, 200
Physical processes, 180–185
Physicians, women, 247, *247*
Picnic, class, 235
Picnic in October, A **(Bunting),** 280
Picture graph, 20, *21, 33*
Pilgrims, first **Thanksgiving of,** 233, *233*
Pineville, Kentucky, *34–35, m34*
Pioneer(s), 49, 50, *50*
"Pioneer Living" (Ring), 9
Pitt, William, 340, *340*
Plains, 37, *37*
Plant(s)
climate and, *138,* 151, *151*
in forest, 181, *181*
trees, 189. *See also* Forest(s)
Plantations, 243, 352
Plateaus, 148, *148*
Play
presenting, 368
writing, 238
Playground, 70, *70*
Plaza, 60–61, *60, m60, 61*
Plaza Saltillo, *60*
Pledge of Allegiance, **125,** *125*
Plenty Coups, Chief, 222, *222*
Plymouth (Plimoth) **Plantation,** *290–291, m290*
Pocahontas, *311*
Poetry
performing, 158, 165
writing, 41, 121, 130
Point of view, 266, 340, *340*
determining, 241, 247, 250, 257, 265, 266–267, 271
drawing conclusions about, 274
in letters, 274

in pictures, 266–267, 267
Poles, 38, *38, 39, 39*
Police officers, 18, *18, 79, 81, 121*
Polio, 223, *223*
Polish Americans, 255, *256*
Political rallies, *110–111*
Politics, *246,* 250, *250*
candidates in, **114**
Pollution, 189, *189*
Polo, Marco, *406, 407–408, m407*
Population, 45
of cities, 45
of District of Columbia (D.C.), 348
of Eagle, Colorado, 50, 51
of Indiana, *m279*
representatives and, **103,** *104*
Population density, 258, *m259*
Population maps, 258–259, *m259,* 275, *m279*
Port(s), 165
Portland, Maine, *162–163, 162–163, m162*
Portland, Oregon, *144–145, m144*
Portugal, land claimed **by,** 334
Poseidon (Greek god), *211*
Postcards, making, 15
Posters, making, 107, 441
Potato famine (Ireland), 248–250
Potomac River, 345, *m345*
Pottery
Greek, *318*
Native American, 273, 329
Poultry, *m385*
Powhatan (Indian **leader),** 307, *308*
Powhatan Indians, 307, *307*

Powwow, 276–277, *276, m276, 277*
Prairie Town **(Geisert** **and Geisert),** 448
Predict, 159, 171, 194
President, 44, 91, *91*
first, 44, *45,* 232, *232, 343, 343*
laws and, 104
as leader, 105, *105*
qualifications of, 109
role of, 105
term of office of, 109
See also Executive branch of government
Press, freedom of, *111,* 117
Price, 404–405
Primary sources, 56
analyzing, 57, 112, 129, 193, 273, 305, 309, 393, 427
campaign buttons, 112, *112*
cultural objects, 272–273, *272, 273*
history museum, 56–57, *56*
land grants, 309
landforms and bodies of water, 148
maps, 192–193, *m192, m193*
patriotic symbols, 128–129, *128, 129*
safer bicycles, 392–393, *392, 393*
stock certificates, *427*
time capsules, 304–305, *304, 305*
Prime meridian, 412
Printing, *302,* 317, *317*
Private property, 81, *81*
Problem, 30
Problem solving, 30–31, *30, 31, 33*
Producer, 370, *370,* **378,** 418, 419, *419,* 422
Product development **bulletin board,** 375, 448
Product maps, 384, *m385,* 415, 447, *m447,* 448

Production efficiency, **374,** *374*
Profit, 396
Projects. *See* Community projects; Unit projects
Property
private, **81,** *81*
public, **81**
Property tax, 88
Public education, 85, *85, 95, 95,* 220, 221
Public property, 81
Public service, 74, *75,* 119, 226–227, *226, 227, 439, 439*
Hull–House (Chicago, Illinois), 69–71, *69, 71,* 74
Public transportation, 46, *46*
Public works, 87, *87*
Pueblo (village), 329
Pueblo Indians, 329, *329*
Pyramids, 316, *316*

Q

Questions, writing list **of,** 274
Quinn, Jane Bryant, 405, *405*

R

Radio, creating **interview for,** 321
Raguenau, Marie-Eve, **Dr.,** 438
Railroads
in Colorado, 50, 51, *51*
in folktales and legends, 204–207, 214–215, *215*
inventions used by, 389, *389*
locomotives and, *214*
in museums, 215
transcontinental, *358,* **359**
in Washington, D.C., 46, *46*
Raleigh, North **Carolina,** *m94*

Ramirez, Virginia, 73, 74–75, *75*
Rand, Gloria, 200
Raw materials, 382
Read a Book, 9, 71, 143, 207, 289, 375
Reading skills
  categorizing, 73, 77, 81, 89, 95, 98, 421, 427, 433, 441
  cause and effect, 298–299, *298, 299,* 323, 325, 331, 335, 343, 349, 361, 362
  comparing and contrasting, 377, 383, 391, 399, 405, 411, 414
  determining point of view, 241, 247, 250, 257, 265, 266–267, 271, 274
  drawing conclusions, 35, 41, 47, 53, 58
  generalizing, 101, 107, 113, 121, 127, 130
  graphic organizers for, 32, 58, 98, 130, 168, 194, 238, 274, 322, 362, 414, 442
  main idea and supporting details, 11, 15, 19, 25, 29, 32
  making inferences, 145, 151, 158, 165, 168, 177, 191
  predicting a likely outcome, 159, 171, 194
  reading cutaway diagrams, **236–237,** *237,* 239
  sequence, **54, 291,** 297, 303, 311, 321, 322
  summarizing, **209,** 217, 227, 235, 238
  telling fact from fiction, **218–219,** *218, 219,* 239
  telling fact from opinion, **400**–401, *401,* **417,** 442
  using, 32, 58
Reagan, Ronald, *105*
Reaper, 388, *388*

Recreation, 14, *14,* 15, **86,** *86–87*
Recycling, 191
Red Cross, 439, *439*
Reference works, 302
Regions, 139, 174
  identifying, 174–176
  of United States, 174–176, *m174, m176*
Rehnquist, William, *106*
Relative location, 172, *172,* 173
Religion, 111, *264,* 265, *265*
  in ancient civilizations, 211, *211,* 318
  in early settlements, 309
  freedom of, 111, 117, 243, 265
  of Native Americans, 328, 330, *330*
  places of worship and, 264, *264,* 320, 330, *330*
  See also individual religions
Representative, 103, 104, *104*
Republic, 319
Rescue workers, 121, *121*
Research
  on community history, 300–303, *300, 301, 302, 303*
  medical, 223, *223*
  newspaper articles and, 95, *301*
  on recycling, 191
  on transportation systems, 361
Resources
  capital, **382**
  human, **382,** *382*
  natural. *See* Natural resources
Responsibility, 29
  as character trait, 190, 405, 437
  of citizens, 29, *29,* 111–113, *112, 113,* 437
  of government, 81, 84–89, 95, *95*

Restaurants, *23,* 50, *254,* 255, *256*
Revolution, 283, *283,* **338**
  American, *283,* 338–341, *341*
Rhode Island, 335, *m335*
Riggle, JoAnn, 56
Rights, 110
  Bill of, **111**
  of citizens, 110–113, *110–111, 112, 113*
  civil, **120,** 353
  minority, **113**
  Universal Declaration of Human Rights, 227, *227*
  voting. *See* Votes and voting
Ring, Susan, 9, 289
Río Áquila railroad station, 51, *51*
River(s), *331,* 351, *m351. See also individual rivers*
Riverbank, 148
Roads
  cleaning and repairing, 87, *87*
  crossroads, **156**
  highway system of, 155, 156, *m156,* 375, *375*
  Oregon Trail, 303, *303*
  Roman, 319
  Silk Road, 407, *m407*
  Wilderness Road, 216, *216*
Robinson Crusoe (Defoe), 140–143
Robots, industrial, 383, *383*
Rochester (New York) City Hall, *305*
Rochester (New York) Museum and Science Center, 304–305, *304, 305*
Rocky Mountains, 52, 53, 147, 351, *m351*
Rodeo, 9, *9*
Roman myths, 210–211, *211*
Rome, ancient, *m210,* 319, *319, m319*

Roosevelt, Eleanor, *119,* 226–227, *226, 227,* 230
Roosevelt, Franklin Delano, 74, 226, *226*
Roosevelt, Theodore, 232
Routes, 155, 156, *m156*
  of explorers, *m337, m367*
  following on maps, 336–337, *m336, m337,* 363, 367
  See also Roads
Ruben, Alan M., 143
Rules. *See* Law(s)
Rural areas, 47, *47*
Rushmore, Mount, 232, *232, m354*
Russia, 262, *m262,* 326

S

Saarinen, Eero, 231, *231*
Sacagawea (Corps of Discovery), *285,* 286
Safety
  bicycle, 392–393, *392, 393*
  of drinking water, *76,* 87, *87,* 189
  government and, 81, 84, *84, 85,* 95
  seat belt laws and, 79, *79*
St. Augustine, Florida, 334, *334*
St. Louis, Missouri, 231, *231*
St. Patrick's Day, 268, *268*
Sales, 397–398, 418, *418*
Sales tax, 88, *88*
Salk, Dr. Jonas, 223, *223*
Saltillo, Mexico, 60
San Antonio, Texas, *m2,* 219
Satellites, 177, *177*
Saunders, Wallace, 215
Savings, 421, *421,* 424–427, *424, 425, 426, 427,* 446
Savings account, 425
Scalia, Antonin, *106*
Scarcity, 404

Schanzer, Rosalyn, 284–289

Schaut, Bianca, 419–421, *419,* 420, *421*

School(s)
  in Chicago, 71, *71*
  in Colorado, 6, 51, *51*
  need for, 19
  oldest, *334*
  See also Education

School board, 85

Schotter, Roni, 64

Science and technology
  immigrant contributions to, 246, *246, 247*
  industrial robots, 383, *383*
  satellites, 177, *177*
  Washington, D.C.'s Metro, 46, *46*
  See also Technology

Sculpture, 228, *228,* 229, *229,* 232, *232,* 236–237, *236, 237, 242, 319*

Scythe, 388

Seals
  creating, 129
  Great, 128, *128, 129*
  of Texas, *67*
  Treaty, *129*

Seaman (Corps of Discovery), *285*

Seat belts, 79, *79*

Secondary sources, 57, *57*

Self-discipline, 229

Senate, 103, 104

Senator, *103,* 109

Sequence, 54, 291, 297, 303, 311, 321, 322

Service, 18. *See also* Government services; Public service

Settlements, 50
  in Colorado, 50–51, *50, 51*
  European, 306–311, *307, 308, m309, 334*
  in Florida, 334, *334*
  in Kentucky, 216
  in Virginia, 306–311, *307, 308, m309, m310, 311, 334*

Settlers, 307, 308–311

Shannon (Corps of Discovery), *285*

Sharing, 436–441
  money, 421, 432, 436–437, *436, 437*
  skills, 438–439, *438, 439*
  time, 440–441, *440, 441*

Shelters
  cabins, *50*
  Native American, 328, *328, 329, 329*
  tepees, 328, *328*

Shenandoah Valley (Virginia), 47

Shields (Corps of Discovery), *285*

Ships. *See* Boats and ships

Shopping, 16, 416–417, *m416*

Short play, writing, 238

Shoshoni Indians, 286, *286*

Sierra Nevada, 351, *m351*

"Sights, Sounds, Celebrations" (Cipriano), 207

Sign language, *203*

Silk Road, 407, *m407*

Silver, mining of, *49, 55,* 294, *294*

Silver City, Idaho, 294, *294*

Simulations, 217, 383

Sioux Indians, 328

Skills, sharing, 438–439, *438, 439. See also* Chart and graph skills; Citizenship skills; Map and globe skills; Reading skills; Writing activities

Slaves and slavery, 118
  Africans brought to colonies as, 243, 310, 334
  in ancient Greece, 318
  Civil War and, 352–353
  end of, 353
  escape from, 118, *m118*

opposition to, 118, *118,* 221

Smith, Goldie Capers, 171

Smith, John, 307, *307,* 309, 310

Snake River, 351

Solution, 30

Songs
  "Ballad of Davy Crockett," 218
  about Casey Jones, 215
  national anthem, 126–127
  patriotic, 126–127
  "The Star–Spangled Banner," 126–127

Sources
  primary, **56,** *56. See also* Primary sources
  secondary, **57,** *57*

Souter, David Hackett, *106*

South, 174, *m176*
  in Civil War, 352, *m352*

South America, 37, 156, *156, m156, m189*

South Carolina, *m335*

South Pole, 38, *38, 39, 39*

Southern Hemisphere, 38

Southern region of United States, *m176*

Soy, *m385*

Space exploration, 360–361, *360–361*

Space station, 360, 361, *361*

Spain, land claimed by, 334

Specialize, 394

Speech(es)
  freedom of, 111, 117
  writing, 32, 130, 362

Speed limits, 79, *79*

Spices, 408, *408*

Sputnik, 360

Starley, J. K., 392, *392*

Starr, Ellen, 69

"Star–Spangled Banner, The," 126–127

Start with a Story. *See* Literature

States
  approval of Constitution by, 343
  borders of, 96–97, *m96–97, 99, 135, m135*
  capitals of, 96–97, *m96–97, 99, 135, m135*
  in Civil War, *m352*
  government of, 92, 94, *94, 95, 95*
  number of, on flag, 123, *123*
  representatives from, 103–104, *104*

Statewide Operations Center (Baltimore, Maryland), *170*

Statue(s), 228–229, *228, 229, 236–237, 236, 237, 242, 319*

Statue of Liberty, 236–237, *236, 237, 242, m355*

Steam-boiler furnace, 389, *389*

Steam drill, 204–207

Steel, 373, *m385*

Stevens, John Paul, *106*

Stocks, 426, *427, 428–429, 428, 429*

Stories, 210–219
  folktales, 204–207, *205, 206, 207, 212–213, 212, 213, 260, 442*
  legends, 204–207, 214–219, *214, 215, 216, 218, 219*
  myths, 210–211, *211*
  as oral history, **301,** *301*
  photo, 4–9, *12, m12*
  writing, 200

Story scrapbook, 207, 280

Suburbs, 46, *46*

Subways, 46, *46*

Sullivan, Anne, 119

Sumer, 315, *315, m315*

Summarizing, 209, 217, 227, 235, 238

Supermarket **(Krull),** 448

Supply, 403, *403,* 404

Supporting details, 11, 15, 19, 25, 29, 32

Supreme Court, 106, *106,* 107, *107,* 109

Supreme Court Building (Washington, D.C.), *91*

Surveying, 347, *347*

Symbols
arrows, *129*
map, **42,** *m43,* 96, *m96–97,* 356, *m357*
olive branch, *129*
patriotic. *See* Patriotic symbols

Synagogue, 264, *264*

T

Tables, 108, *108,* 109, *109,* 131, *315*

"Talking drum," 263, *263*

Tax(es), 88, 89
lowering, *91*
property, **88,** *88*
as responsibility of citizens, 111
sales, **88,** *88*

Tax assessor, 89

Taylor, Harriet Peck, 64

Teachers, *85*

Technology, 386
air brake, 389
assembly line, 374, *374, 379,* **380,** 414
automobiles, 372–383, *373, 374, 375, 376–377, 378, 381, 383*
cameras, 386–387, *386*
communication link, **409,** *409*
computers, *19,* 302, 409, *409, m410*
immigrant contributions to, 246, *246, 247*
industrial robots, 383, *383*
International Space Station, *360,* 361, *361*

locomotives, *215*
satellites, 177, *177*
steam-boiler furnace, 389, *389*
steam drill, 204–207
telegraph, 359, *359,* 389, *389*
telephones, *55,* 359, *359,* 389
using, 9, 71, 143, 207, 289, 375
Washington's Metro, 46, *46*

Telegraph, 359, *359,* 389, *389*

Telemarketers, *409*

Telephones, *55,* 359, *359,* 389

Temples, 330, *330*

Tennessee, *215,* 234

Tepees, 328, *328*

Texas
Battle of the Alamo in, 219
business in, 394–398, *m395*
capital of, *36,* 60–61, *60, 61*
community leaders in, 75
courthouse in, *72–73, m72*
governor of, *67*
harbor in, *332*
hurricanes in, 295–296, *295, 296,* 298
libraries in, *21*
location of San Antonio in, *m2*
map grid of Corpus Christi, *m179*
oil in, *175, m175, m176*
product map of, 447, *m447*
representatives from, *104*
state seal of, *67*
water in, *36*

Thanksgiving Day, 233, *233*

Think About It, 9, 71, 143, 207, 289, 375

Think and Write, 32, 58, 98, 130, 168, 194, 238, 274, 322, 362, 414, 442

Thirteenth Amendment, 353

Thomas, Clarence, *106*

Tiber River, 319

Timbuktu (Mali), *320,* 321

Time, sharing, 440–441, *440, 441*

Time capsule, 304–305, *304, 305*

Time lines, 54, *54–55,* 55, 59, 297, 312–313, *312, 313,* 323

Time periods, 292, 312–313, 323

Titles, map, 42, *m43*

Tobacco, 310

Tombstone, Arizona, *93*

Tools
agricultural, 388, *388*
bone, 328
map-making, *192*
Native Americans, 328, *328*
surveying, *347*

Tornadoes, 191, 299, *299*

Town. *See* Cities; Communities

Town Lake (Texas), *36*

Town meeting, 90, *90*

Trade, 406
in ancient Mali, 320, *320,* 321
between Europe and Asia, *406,* 407–408, *m407*
exports in, **410,** *m410*
imports in, **410**
interdependence in, **411**
international, 406–411, *406,* **407,** *m407, 408–409,* 410, *m410,* 411
of Native Americans, 329
See also Free Enterprise

Trade-off, 434, 435

Traders, 407, 408

Traditions, 203, *203,* **245,** *245. See also* Holiday customs and traditions

Traffic laws, 26–27, *26, 27, 78*

Transcontinental railroad, *358,* **359**

Transportation, 46
by automobile, 372–375, *373, 374, 375,* 378–383, *378, 381, 383*
by caravan, 320
in New York City, *10–11*
public, 46, *46*
by railroad. *See* Railroads
researching systems of, 361
by road. *See* Roads
into space, 360–361, *360–361*
by travois, 328, *328*
by wagon, 303, *303*
by wheeled cart, 315

"Transportation: Yesterday and Today" (Ring), 289

Travel brochures, creating, 257

Travois, 328, *328*

Treaty of Paris (1783), 339

Trees, planting, *189*

Tubman, Harriet, 118, *118*

***Turn of the Century* (Jackson),** 368

***Two Days in May* (Peck),** 64

U

Underground Railroad, *m118*

Union (North), *m352,* 353, *353*

Union League of America Medal, *305*

Union Pacific Railroad, *358,* 359

Unit projects
class magazine, 9, 64
making a museum,
289, 368
patriotic medal, 71,
136
physical features
model, 143, 200
product development
bulletin board, 375,
448
story scrapbook, 207,
280
**United Nations, Human
Rights Commission
of,** 227, *227*
United States, *m354–355*
borders of, **41,** *m41*
capital of. *See*
Washington, D.C.
Constitution of. *See*
Constitution
customs in, **22,** *22. See
also* Holiday
customs and
traditions
exploration of West,
284–289, *m284, 350,
351*
exports of, **410,** *m410*
flag of, *65,* 122–124,
122, 123, 124, 234
Great Seal of, 128, *128,*
129
growth of, 350–355,
354–355, 356, m357,
358
heritage of, **25,**
228–235
location of towns
named Washington
in, *m45*
national bird of (bald
eagle), *1, 24, 24,* 128,
181, 225
national motto of, 128
patriotic symbols of.
See Patriotic
symbols
Pledge of Allegiance
to, **125,** *125*
recreation in, *14*

regions of, **174–176,**
m174, m176
**Universal Declaration
of Human Rights,**
227, *227*
Universities, 95, *95*
Use Technology. *See*
Technology, using
Utah, railroads in, *358*
Ute Indians, 48, *48*

V

Vaccine, 223, *223*
Val-Kill, New York, 230,
230
Valleys, 148, *148*
Vanadium, 373
Venice, Italy, *406*
Vespucci, Amerigo,
m337
Vietnam, *m261*
**Vietnam Veterans
Memorial
(Washington, D.C.),**
364, *364*
Viewpoint. *See* Point of
view
Virginia, *m135, m308,
m335*
colonial, *m192,*
306–311, *307,* 308,
m309, m310, 311,
322, 334
donating land for
capital, 345
libraries in, *21*
representatives from,
104
rural areas in, *47*
suburbs in, *46*
Virginia Company, 309,
m309, 310
Volcanoes, 184, *184, 190*
Volunteers, 66, *66,* **76,**
132–133, *132, 133,*
438–441, *438, 439, 441*
Votes and voting, 67, *67,*
111, 112–115, *112, 113,
114, 115,* 131
in ancient Greece, 318
in ancient Rome, 319

Voyage, 249, 250

W

Wages, 395
Wagons, 303, *303*
"Wall Street" (Martin),
375
Wars
American Revolution,
283, 338–341, *341*
Civil War, **352,** *m352,*
353, *353*
Korean, 365, *365*
Vietnam, 364, *364*
Washington (state), *180,
184*
Washington, D.C., 44,
344–349, *m345*
building, 346–347, *346*
Capitol Building in,
91, **94,** *94, 103,* 104,
104, 347, 348,
348–349, 387
government buildings
in, *91, 103, 104*
monuments and
memorials in,
100–101, m100, 348,
348–349, 364–365,
364, m364, 365
National Statuary
Hall, 228–229, *228*
present-day, 348–349,
348–349
size of, 45
suburb of, *46*
transportation in, **46,**
46
youth mayor of, 132,
132
Washington, George
in American
Revolution, 341, *344*
as first President, 44,
45, 232, *232,* 343, *343*
maps drawn by, *192,
m192, m193*
in selection and
building of capital,
345, 346, 347

*Washington D.C.: A
Scrapbook* (Benson),
136
**Washington
Metropolitan Area
Transit Authority
(WMATA),** 46
**Washington Monument
(Washington, D.C.),**
235, 348, 348, 365, 365
Wastewater, 87
Water
safety of, *76, 87, 87,*
189
types of, 36–37, *36,
149, 149*
Water Dance (Locker),
200
Water treatment plants,
87, *87*
Waterfalls, *149,* 196–197,
196, m196, 197
Weather
hurricanes, 295–296,
295, 296, 298
tornadoes, 191, 299,
299
See also Climate
Weather charts, 151
Weaving, *17*
Webb, Mary, 291
West, exploration of,
284–289, *m284, 350,*
351
West Virginia, *104*
Western Hemisphere,
39, 39
What Is a Community?
(Kalman), 64
Wheat, *m385, m410*
**"Where Water Comes
From" (Ahearn),** 71
**White House
(Washington, D.C.),**
91, 347, 348
Whitman, Walt, 145
Wiegent, Ralph, *304*
Wilderness Road, 216,
216
Williams, Paul R., 241
Wood, *3, 161, 189*

Woods, Granville T., 389, *389*

Work
in business centers, 13, *13*
jobs in communities, 16–19, *17, 18, 19, 369*
skills in, 16–17, *17*
See also Job(s)

Workers. *See* Labor

World, *m40*

"World Monuments" (Ring), 289

World Trade Towers, attack on, 121, *121*

Worship, places of, 264, *264, 320,* 330, *330*

Writing
Chinese, 261, *261,* 317, *317*
cuneiform, *315*

Writing activities
advertisements, 322, 399
business plans, 414
descriptions, 168, 427
diary entries, 58
explanations, 168
folktales, 442
invitations, 238

letters, 81, 98, 274, 322, 433, 442
lists, 58, 194, 274
newspaper articles, 227, 343, 362, 414
paragraphs, 32, 98, 168, 194, 393
persuasion, 32, 98
poetry, 41, 121, 130
questions, 274
short play, 238
speeches, 32, 130, 362
stories, 200

Yellowstone National Park, *185*

York (Corps of Discovery), *285*

Zeus (Greek god), 211, *211*

For permission to reprint copyrighted material, grateful acknowledgment is made to the following sources:

Carolrhoda Books, Inc., a division of the Lerner Publishing Company: From *Peace and Bread: The Story of Jane Addams* by Stephanie Sammartino McPherson. Text copyright © 1993 by Stephanie Sammartino McPherson.

Charlesbridge Publishing: Cover illustration by Iris Van Rynbach from *Washington, D.C.: A Scrapbook* by Laura Lee Benson. Illustration copyright © 1999 by Iris Van Rynbach. Cover illustration by Jan Davey Ellis from *Turn of the Century* by Ellen Jackson. Illustration copyright © 1998 by Jan Davey Ellis.

Children's Better Health Institute, Benjamin Franklin Literary and Medical Society, Inc., Indianapolis, IN: "Our History" by Catherine Cate Coblentz from *Child Life* Magazine, October 1945. Text copyright © 1945 by Child Life, Inc.

Crabtree Publishing Company: Cover illustration from *What is a Community? From A to Z* by Bobbie Kalman. Copyright © 2000 by Crabtree Publishing Company.

Farrar, Straus and Giroux, LLC: Cover illustration by Leyla Torres from *Two Days in May* by Harriet Peck Taylor. Illustration copyright © 1999 by Leyla Torres.

Harcourt, Inc.: Cover illustration by Nancy Carpenter from *A Picnic in October* by Eve Bunting. Illustration copyright © 1999 by Nancy Carpenter. Cover illustration by Emily Arnold McCully from *Old Home Day* by Donald Hall. Illustration copyright © 1996 by Emily Arnold McCully. Cover illustration from *Water Dance* by Thomas Locker. Copyright © 1997 by Thomas Locker.

HarperCollins Publishers: Cover illustration by Wendell Minor from *Everglades* by Jean Craighead George. Illustration copyright © 1995 by Wendell Minor.

Holiday House, Inc.: Cover illustration by Colin Bootman from *Dr. Martin Luther King, Jr.* by David A. Adler. Illustration copyright © 2001 by Colin Bootman. Cover illustration by Melanie Hope Greenberg from *Supermarket* by Kathleen Krull. Illustration copyright © 2001 by Melanie Hope Greenberg.

Henry Holt and Company, LLC: Cover illustration by Ted Rand from *Fighting for the Forest* by Gloria Rand. Illustration copyright © 1999 by Ted Rand.

Houghton Mifflin Company: Cover illustration by Arthur Geisert from *Prairie Town* by Bonnie Geisert. Illustration copyright © 1998 by Arthur Geisert.

Alfred A. Knopf Children's Books, a division of Random House, Inc.: From *John Henry: An American Legend* by Ezra Jack Keats. Copyright © 1965 by Ezra Jack Keats; copyright renewed 1993 by Martin Pope, executor of the estate of the author.

National Geographic Society Books: From *How We Crossed the West: The Adventures of Lewis and Clark* by Rosalyn Schanzer. Copyright © 1997 by Rosalyn Schanzer.

Scholastic Inc.: Cover illustration by Robert Andrew Parker from *The Hatmaker's Sign: A Story by Benjamin Franklin,* retold by Candace Fleming. Illustration copyright © 1998 by Robert Andrew Parker. Published by Orchard Books, an imprint of Scholastic Inc. Cover illustration by Ted Rand from *My Father's Boat* by Sherry Garland.

Illustration copyright © 1998 by Ted Rand. Published by Scholastic Press, a division of Scholastic Inc. Cover illustration by Michael Dooling from *George Washington: A Picture Book Biography* by James Cross Giblin. Illustration copyright © 1992 by Michael Dooling. Cover illustration by Kyrsten Brooker from *Nothing Ever Happens on 90th Street* by Roni Schotter. Illustration copyright © 1997 by Kyrsten Brooker. From "Maps" by Goldie Capers Smith in *Instructor.* Text copyright © 1964 by F. A. Owen Publishing Company.

Smithsonian Institution Press: "Henry Ford's Dream" from *A Kid's Guide to the Smithsonian* by Ann Philips Bay. Text © 1996 by The Smithsonian Institution.

Viking Penguin, an imprint of Penguin Putnam Books for Young Readers, a division of Penguin Putnam Inc.: Cover illustration from *Eleanor* by Barbara Cooney. Copyright © 1996 by Barbara Cooney. Cover illustration by Susan Hartung from *Dear Juno* by Soyung Pak. Illustration copyright © 1999 by Susan Hartung.

ILLUSTRATION CREDITS

Page A14, Studio Liddell, 91, Bernadette Lau; 92, 401, Jun Park; 140-143, Rich Nelson; 148-149, Stephen Durke; 211, 212, 213, 218, Scott Cameron; 237, Don Foley; 284-289, Frank Riccio; 326-327, Luigi Galante; 348-349, Chuck Carter; 354-355, 379, Jon Edwards; 364-365, Dale Gustafson; 444-445, Havana Street Design.

All maps by MAPQUEST.COM.

PHOTO CREDITS

Cover: FPG International (statue); Thomas E. Franklin, The Record (Bergen Co., NJ)/Corbis Saba (flag raising); Adam Woolfitt/Woodfin Camp & Associates (train); Pictor (flag); Meridian Graphics (map).

PAGE PLACEMENT KEY: (t)-top (c)-center (b)-bottom (l)-left (r)-right (fg)-foreground (bg)-background

TITLE PAGE AND TABLE OF CONTENTS

Insert (bg) Don Mason/Corbis Stock Market; (fg) Minden Pictures; Title page (bg) Don Mason/Corbis Stock Market; (fg) From the City of Orlando Public Art Collection; ii, iv From the City of Orlando Public Art Collection; v Tony Heffernan; vi Eric Lessing Culture and Fine Arts Archives/Art Resource; vii National Center for Korean Traditional Arts; viii The Granger Collection, New York; ix IFA/Stock Photography/PictureQuest.

UNIT 1

Opener: (fg) From the City of Orlando Public Art Collection; (bg) Lawrence Migdale; (spread) Lawrence Migdale; 1 (t) From the City of Orlando Public Art Collection; 2 (t) Mark Lewis/Stone; 2 (b) Superstock; 3 (tl) Indiana State Archives; 3 (tr) Philip Gould/Corbis; 3 (b) Lawrence Migdale/Stock, Boston; 4-8 Lawrence Migdale; 9 Courtesy of Carl & Joetta Gray; 10-11 Phil Degginger/Color-Pic; 12 Lawrence Migdale; 13 Mark Segal/Stone; 14 (tl) Charles Gupton/Stock, Boston; 14 (tr) Joe Viesti/The Viesti Collection; 14 (bl) James P. Blair/Corbis; 14 (br) Herb

Zulpier/Masterfile; 15 © Disney Enterprises; 17 (t) David Cavagnaro/Peter Arnold, Inc.; 17 (bl) Stephen Frisch; 17 (br) Raymond Gehman/Corbis; 18 (t) David Madison; 18 (b) John Starkey/Black Star/Harcourt; 22 Telegraph Colour Library/FPG International; 22 (inset) Keith Wood/International Stock; 24 (t) Daniel J. Cox/Stone; 24 Lawrence Migdale; 25 John McGrail; 27 (t) Bob Daemmrich/Stock, Boston/PictureQuest; 28 Lawrence Migdale; 34-35 Jeff Bergdoll/Earth Scenes; 36 Gerald French/Corbis; 37 (inset) Charles O'Rear/Corbis; 37 Galen Rowell/Corbis; 39 Bettmann/Corbis; 44 Mark Downey/Lucid Images; 45 Corbis; 46 (t) Tisara; 46 (b) Photri-Microstock; 47 Richard A. Cooke/Corbis; 48 Montrose County Historical Society; 49 (t) George Eastman House/William Henry Jackson/Hulton/Archive; (b) Hulton/Archive; 50 Eagle County Historical Society; 51 (t) Jackson C. Thode, *George L. Beam and the Denver & Rio Grande,* Denver, CO, Sundance Publications, 1986-1989, 231-233; 51 (b) Fanny Gamble Collection, Eagle, CO; 52 (t) Eagle County Historical Society; 52 (inset), 53 Lawrence Migdale; 54 (l) Albert Rose/Hulton/Archive; 55 (r) Eagle Historical Museum; 55 (l) Harcourt Library; 56 Toni Axelrod; 60-61 Bob Daemmrich Photography

UNIT 2

Opener: (fg) Tony Heffernan; 65 Tony Heffernan; 66 (t) Elaine Thompson/AP/Wide World; 66 (c), (b) Bob Daemmrich Photography; 67 (c) Spencer Grant/PhotoEdit; 67 (b) AP Photos/Paul Sakuma/AP/Wide World Photos; 67 (tl) Texas Highway Department; 67 (tr) Courtesy of the Office of the Governor of Texas; 68 (b) Swarthmore College Peace Collection; 69-71 Wallace Kirkland Papers (JAM neg. 261, 1425) The University Library, University of Chicago at Illinois; Jane Addams Memorial Collection; (JAMC neg. 437,146, 528,21) University Library, University of Illinois at Chicago; 72-73 Annette Coolidge; 74 Phil Martin/PhotoEdit; 75 (t) Brian Diggs; 75 (b) Elizabeth Garza-Williams; 76 (t) Cindy Karp/TimePix; 76 (b) Todd Buchanan/Black Star; 77 Bob Daemmrich Photography; 78 Norbert Von Der Groeben/The Image Works; 79 (tl) D. Young-Wolff/PhotoEdit; 79 (tr) Angela Peterson/The Orlando Sentinel; 79 (b) Jim Roshan; 80 John Neubauer/PhotoEdit; 81 Jeff Greenberg/PhotoEdit; 84-85 Courtesy of Florida Department of Health, Orange County Government Florida; 85 (t) Levine-Roberts; 85 (inset) Courtesy of Florida Department of Health, Orange County Government Florida; 86-87 (b) Panoramic Images; 87 (t) William Tauic/Corbis Stock Market; 87 (c) Transparencies; 88 (t) Mark E. Gibson; 90 Paula Lerner/Woodfin Camp & Associates; 90 (inset) Owen Franken/Stock, Boston; 91 (tc) Joseph Sohm/Visions of America/PictureQuest; 91 (tl) G. Petrov/Washington Stock Photo; 91 (tr) Adam Woolfitt/Corbis; 91 (b) Ron Edmonds/AP/Wide World Photos; 93 (t) John Elk III/Stock, Boston; 93 (b) Michael Maslan Historic Photographs/Corbis; 94 (t) Courtesy of the Office of the Governor of North Carolina; 94 (b) Gene Ahrens/Bruce Coleman, Inc.; 95 Courtesy of Boise State University; 100-101 Vic Bider/PhotoEdit; 102 The Granger Collection, New York; 103 (t) Sandy Schaeffer/Time Life Syndication; 103 (b) Courtesy of the Office of Senator Kay Bailey Hutchison; 104 David R. Frazier; 105 (c) The White House; 105 (tl) David Wells/The Image Works; 105 (tr) Corbis; 105 (bl)

US Department of Defense/Hulton/Archive; 105 (br) Michael Geissinger/The Image Works; 106 (t) National Portrait Gallery; 106 (b) Richard Strauss/Collection of the Supreme Court of the United States; 106 (inset) The Supreme Court; 107 Rob Crandall/The Image Works; 110-112 Phil Sandlin/AP/Wide World; 110 (inset) Joseph Sohm/Chromosohm/Corbis; 111 Gary Conner/PictureQuest; 112 (tl), (tr) Museum of American Political Life; 113 Bob Daemmrich/Stock, Boston; 116 Beth A. Keiser/AP/Wide World Photos; 117 (t) The Granger Collection, New York; 117 (b) Andre Jenny/International Stock; 118 (t) Library of Congress; 118 (b) National Geographic Society; 119 (b) AP/Wide World Photos; 119 (t) Bettmann/Corbis; 120 AP/Wide World Photos; 121 TimePix; 122 (l) The Granger Collection, New York; 122 (r) Harcourt Library; 123 (b) The Granger Collection, New York; 123 (bg) Rob Crandall/Stock, Boston; 124 (bl) Bob Daemmrich Photography; 124 (br) Bettmann/Corbis; 125 (t) Ed Bock/Corbis; 126 (t) The Granger Collection, New York; 126 (b) Corbis; 127 Rudi Von Briel/PhotoEdit; 128 (t) Stephen G. Maka/The Viesti Collection; 128 (b), 129 The National Archives; 132 Ray Amati/NBA Photos; 132 (bg) David R. Frazier; 133 (t) Pete G. Wilcox/The Times Leader; 133 (b) The Greater Boston Food Bank.

UNIT 3

Opener: (fg) Eric Lessing Culture and Fine Arts Archives/Art Resource; (bg) Joseph Sohm/Chromosohm/Corbis; (spread) Joseph Sohm/Chromosohm/Corbis; 137 Eric Lessing Culture and Fine Arts Archives; 138 (c) Pictor International/Pictor International, Ltd./PictureQuest; 138 (tl) H. Armstrong Roberts, Inc.; 138 (tr) G. Hampfler/H. Armstrong Roberts, Inc.; 138 (b) J. Lotter Gurling/Tom Stack & Associates; 139 (t) Peter Aaron/Esto; 139 (c) Larry Brownstein/Rainbow/PictureQuest; 139 (b) J. Faircloth/Transparencies; 144-145 Steve Terrill/Corbis Stock Market; 146-47 (r) Gisela Damm/Estock Photo/Leo De Wys, Inc.; 147 (t) Jim McDonald/Corbis; 148 Brian Miller/Bruce Coleman, Inc.; 149 Mark E. Gibson Photography; 150 (t) Jeff Schultz/Alaska Stock Images; 150 (b) Tom Bean; 151 (l) Superstock; 151 (r) Papilio/Corbis; 154 Steve Vidler/Estock; 155 J. Blank/H. Armstrong Roberts, Inc.; 156 Mario Emmanuel Gentinetta, © Bike It Solo; 157 (t) David Simson/Stock, Boston; 157 (b) Mark E. Gibson; 158 Chris Jones Photo/Corbis Stock Market; 158 (inset) Dr. E.R. Degginger/Color-Pic; 160 (l) Calvin W. Hall/Alaska Stock; 160 (r) Chris Arend/Alaska Stock; 161 (l) Bill Gleasner/The Viesti Collection; 161 (r) Superstock; 162 (t) G.H. Harrison/Bruce Coleman, Inc.; 162-163 (b) Claudia Dhimitri/The Viesti Collection; 163 (t) Jeff Greenberg/International Stock; 164 (t) Bettmann/Corbis; 164 (inset) J.B. Grant/Estock; 170-171 Greg Pease/Stone; 172 Joseph Sohm/ChromoSohm/Corbis; 173 (t) George Diebold/Corbis Stock Market; 173 (b) Courtesy of Dr. William Doolittle, University of Texas, Austin; 175 (tl) R. Hamilton Smith/AGStock USA; 175 (tr) Joseph Sohm/Stock, Boston; 175 (bl) John Alves/Mystic Wanderer Images; 175 (br) Bob Daemmrich Photography; 177 Earth Imaging/Stone; 180-181 Jack S. Grove/PhotoEdit/PictureQuest; 181 (tr) B. von Hoffmann/H. Armstrong Roberts, Inc.; 181 (br) Mike Zens/Corbis; 181 (cr) Stan Osolinski/Index Stock Imagery/PictureQuest; 182 (t) Scott Camazine/Photo Researchers; 182-183 (b) Ray

Juno/Corbis Stock Market; 184 Gary Braasch/Corbis; 185 J.B. Diederich/Contact Press Images/PictureQuest; 188 S.J. Krasemann/Peter Arnold, Inc.; 189 (t) Ricardo Mazalan/AP/Wide World; 189 (b) Jose L. Pelaez/Corbis Stock Market; 190 (t) Special Collections; University Archives; Cal Poly; 190 (b) Corbis; 191 Roger Ressmeyer/Corbis; 192 (t) Philadelphia Museum of Art/Corbis; 192 (b) Library of Congress; 192 (l), 193 (inset) Museum of the History of Science, Oxford; 193 (t) Library of Congress; 196 Bill Bachmann/Transparencies; 197 (b) Michael S. Yamashita/Corbis; 197 (b) (inset) Mike Yamashita/Woodfin Camp & Associates; 197 (t) (inset) Scott Wm. Hanrahan/International Stock.

UNIT 4

Opener: (fg) National Center for Korean Tradition Arts; (bg) Gary Conner/PhotoEdit; (spread) Gary Conner/PhotoEdit; 201 National Center for Korean Tradition Arts; 202 (b) Bettman/Corbis; 203 (b) Max & Bea Hunn/The Image Finders; 203 (tl) Mug Shots/Corbis Stock Market; 203 (tr) Don Stevenson/Index Stock Imagery/PictureQuest; 208-209 Superstock; 210 James Davis/Corbis; 214 (t) The Bruce Gurner Collection, Water Valley Casey Jones Railroad Museum; 214 (b) Bettmann Archive/Corbis; 215 (t) C Squared Studios/PhotoDisc; 215 (b) Raymond Gehman/Corbis; 216 (t) Kentucky Historical Society; 216 (b) Washington University Gallery of Art, St. Louis, MO; 219 Burstein Collection/Corbis; 220 University of North Carolina Special Collections; 221 (t) Library of Congress; 221 (b) National Archives; 222 Plenty Coups State Park Historical Photos; 223 (t) Bettmann/Corbis; 223 (b) Wener Wolff/Black Star/TimePix; 224 (t) Ruth Fremson/AP/Wide World; 224 (b) Don Cravens/TimePix; 225 (t) Kim D. Johnson/ AP/Wide World Photos; 225 (b) Victor Aleman/Black Star Publishing/PictureQuest; 226 Bettmann/Corbis; 227 Topham/The Image Works; 228 Michael Freeman/Corbis; 229 (t) Elizabet Ney Museum; 229 (b) Bob Daemmrich Photography; 230 Girls Leadership Workshop, The Eleanor Roosevelt Center at Val-Kill; 231 (t) Jefferson National Expansion Memorial/National Park Service; 231 (b) Richard Pasley/Stock, Boston; 232 (t) Underwood & Underwood/Corbis; 232 (b) Superstock; 233 (t) Burnstein Collection/Corbis; 233 (c) (inset) Library of Congress; 233 (b) (inset) Hulton/Archive; 234 (b) Robin Rudd/Unicorn Stock Photos; 235 (l) Jean Higgins/Unicorn Stock Photos; 235 (r) William S. Helsel/Stone; 236 Bill Ross/Corbis; 240-241 Jeff Dunn/Stock, Boston; 242 Brown Brothers; 243 The Granger Collection, New York; 244 (t) Library of Congress; 244 (b) Hulton/Archive; 245 Lawrence Migdale; 246 (b) Marty Lederhandler/AP/Wide World Photos; 246 (tl) Bettmann/Corbis; 246 (tr) AFP/Corbis; 247 (t) Brown Brothers; 247 (c) Moorland-Spingarn Collection #2012, Founders Library, Howard University, Washington, D.C.; 247 (b) The Pura Belpre Papers, Centro de Estudios Puertorriqueños/Hunter College, CUNY; 248-249 Derek Croucher/Corbis Stock Market; 249 (t) Museum of the City of New York, The Byron Collection, 93.1.1.17307; 250 (t) The Jeanie Johnston Project; 250 (b) AP/Wide World Photos; 252-253 Lawrence Migdale; 254 (t) Joseph Sohm/ChromoSohm/Corbis; 254 (b) Peter Stone/Black Star/Harcourt; 254 (c) Brian Hagiwara/Foodpix; 255, 256 (all) Todd Buchanan/Black Star/Harcourt; 257 James M. Mejuto; 260-263 (b) Lawrence Migdale; 264 (t) Bill Bachmann/PhotoEdit; 264 (br) Michael

Newman/PhotoEdit; 264 (bl) Jack Alter; 267 (l) Collection of the National Academy of Design; 267 (r) Geoffrey Clements/Corbis; 268 Martha Cooper/The Viesti Collection; 269 (t) Lawrence Migdale; 270 Merritt Vincent/PhotoEdit; 271 Priscilla Alexander Eastman/Scenic & Nature Photography; 272 (t) Bruce Forster/Stone; 272 (c) Danny Lehman/Corbis; 273 (b) University of New Mexico Maxwell Museum of Anthropology; 273 (t) The Newark Museum/Art Resource, NY; 273 (c) Kea Publishing Services Ltd./Corbis; 276-277 Annette Coolidge.

UNIT 5

Opener: (fg) The Granger Collection, New York; (bg) John Elk III/Stock, Boston; (spread) John Elk III/Stock, Boston; 281 The Granger Collection, New York; 282 (t) Hilary Wilkes/International Stock; 282 (b) Brownie Harris/Corbis Stock Market; 283 (t) A detail, John Trumbull, "The Surrender of Lord Cornwallis at Yorktown, 19 October, 1781", Yale University Art Gallery, Trumbull Collection; 283 (c) Superstock; 283 (b) Bettmann/Corbis; 290-291 Plimoth Plantation; 292 Ron Sherman; 293 Courtesy of the Atlanta History Center; 294 (t) George Rocklin/Bruce Coleman, Inc.; 294 (b) Idaho Historical Museum; 295 (t) (inset) The Granger Collection, New York; 295 (b) Rosenberg Library, Galveston and Texas History Center; 296 (t) Jeffrey Boan/AP/Wide World Photos; 296 (b) Rosenberg Library, Galveston and Texas History Center; 297 The Granger Collection, New York; 303 Steve Bly/Dave G. Houser Photography; 304-305 Rochester Museum and Science Center; 306 Susan Van Edder/PhotoEdit; 307 (t) Chapin Library, Williams College, Williamstown, Massachusetts; 307 (b) BAL10692 Town of Pomeiooc, Virginia (w/c) by White, John (fl.c) British Museum, London/Bridgeman Art Library, London; 308 A. H. Robins photo by Don Eiler; 309 Hulton/Archive ; 310 (b) The Granger Collection, New York; 311 (t) National Portrait Gallery, Smithsonian Institution, Washington D.C., transfer from National Gallery of Art, Gift of Andrew W. Mellon; 311 (b) Richard Nowitz; 314 Werner Forman Archive, British Museum, London/Art Resource; 315 C M Dixon; 316 (t) Erich Lessing Culture and Fine Arts Archives; 316 (b) David Ball/Corbis Stock Market; 317 (t) Erich Lessing/Art Resource; 317 (b) Mark Downey; 318 (t) The British Museum of London; 319 (t) Soprintendenza alle Antichita, Rome, Italy/Scala/Art Resource, NY; 319 (b) Robert Emmett Bright/Photo Researchers; 320 Werner Forman/Art Resource, NY; 321 The Granger Collection, New York; 324-325 Richard Day/Earth Scenes; 328 (t) William Manning/Corbis Stock Market; 328 (b) Edward Curtis, 1904/Library of Congress; 328 (b) (inset) Founders Society Purchase with funds from Richard A. Manoogian, The Detroit Institute of Arts; 328 (t)(inset) Kit Howard Breen; 328 (c) (inset) Marilyn "Angel" Wynn/Nativestock; 329 (br) Adam Woolfitt/Corbis; 329 (bl) Superstock; 330 Cahokia Mounds Historic Site; 331 Alex S. MacLean/Landslides; 331 (inset) Courtesy of the Adirondack Museum, Photo by James Swedberg; 332 Bob Daemmrich Photography; 333 (b) Hideo Haga/HAGA/The Image Works; 334 (t) Silver Image; 334 (b) Jessica A. Ehlers/Bruce Coleman, Inc.; 338 George Widman/AP/Wide World Photos; 339 (t) The Granger Collection, New York; 339 (b) Independence National Historical Park; 340 (t) The Bridgeman Art Library International; 340 (b) The Granger Collection, New York; 340 (c) Independence National

Historical Park; 341 (t) Guilford Courthouse National Military Park; 341 (b) Historical Society of Pennsylvania; 342 (b) John Neubauer/PhotoEdit; 343 The Granger Collection, New York; 344 The Corcoran Gallery of Art/Corbis; 345 Smithsonian Institution, Division of Political History, Neg.#81-5397; 346 (t) Brown Brothers; 346 (b) 347 (t) Schomburg Center for Research in Black Culture/The New York Public Library; 347 (b) Jeff Greenberg/Unicorn Stock Photos; 348 P. Kresan/H. Armstrong Roberts, Inc.; 350 (insets) Independence National Historical Park; 350 (bg) David Muench Photography; 353 (t) Library of Congress; 353 (b) Louis A. Warren Lincoln Library and Museum, Fort Wayne, Indiana; 358 Utah State Historical Society; 359 Brown Brothers; 359 (insets) Bettmann/Corbis; 360 (t) Karl Ronstrom/Reuters/Time; 360-361 NASA; 364 (b) Adam Woolfitt/Woodfin Camp & Associates; 364 (t) J. Blank/H. Armstrong Roberts, Inc.; 365 (t) Kunio Owaki/Corbis Stock Market; 365 (b) Gayna Hoffman/Stock, Boston/PictureQuest.

UNIT 6

Opener: (fg) IFA/Stock Photography/PictureQuest; (bg) Bob Rowan/Progressive Image/Corbis; (spread) 369 Bob Rowan/Progressive Image/Corbis; 370 (t) Brownie Harris/Corbis Stock Market; 370 (c) David Young Wolff/PhotoEdit/PictureQuest; 370 (b) Jose Luis Pelaez/Corbis Stock Market; 371 (t) Lawrence Migdale; 371 (b) Bob Daemmrich Photography ; 372, 373 (t) Henry Ford Museum & Greenfield Village; 373(b) Bettmann/Corbis; 374 (t) Henry Ford Museum/Research Center; 374 (b) Gendreau Collection/Corbis; 375 Lester Lefkowitz/Corbis; 376-377 Photri-Microstock; 378 Henry Ford Museum & Greenfield Village; 380 (t) Archive Photos/PictureQuest; 380 (inset), 380-381 (b) Hulton/Archive; 381 (tr) Hulton-Deutsch Collection/Corbis; 382 Corbis; 383 David R. Frazier; 386 (l) George Eastman House/Archive Photos; 386 (r) Museum of Photography at George Eastman House - Dobbs Ferry, NY; 387 (t) John Plumbe Jr./Corbis; 387 (b) Hulton/Archive; 388 Brown Brothers; 389 (tr) United States Patent Office; 389 (bl) Neal McEwen; 389 (br) Harcourt Library; 391 (b) Courtesy of Linda Lee; 391 (t) Scott Campbell; 392 (t) Science Museum/Science & Society Picture Museum; 392 (b), 393 Bicycle Museum of America; 394-398 Don Couch; 399 Doug Pensinger/Allsport; 401 Kevin Dodge/Masterfile; 402 (b) Lee Foster/ PictureQuest; 402 (inset) Bob Daemmrich/Stock, Boston/PictureQuest; 403 W.S. Nawrocki/Nawrocki Stock Photo; 404 (t) (c) Reueters NewMedia Inc./Corbis; 404 (b) Mireille Vaultier/Woodfin Camp/PictureQuest; 405 The Washington Post Writers Group. Reprinted with permission; 406 Hulton/Archive; 408-409 Ian Clark/International Stock; 409 (tr) Jeff Greenberg/PhotoEdit/PictureQuest; 410 (l) Tony Freeman/PhotoEdit; 410 (r) (c) Myrleen Ferguson/PhotoEdit; 411 Bob Daemmrich/Stock, Boston/PictureQuest; 416-417 M. Siluk/The Image Works; 418 Joseph Nettis/Stock, Boston; 419-421 Lawrence Migdale; 422 (tl) Jim Pickerell/Stock Connection/PictureQuest; 422 (tr) Richard Laird/Estock Photo; 422 (br) Jeff Greenberg/PhotoEdit; 423 (tl) Jim Pickerell/Stock Connection/PictureQuest; 423 (tr) Jon Riley/Stone; 423 (bl) Michael Newman/PhotoEdit; 423 (br) Jeff Greenberg/PhotoEdit; 423 (cl) Pictor International, Ltd./PictureQuest; 424-425 T.J. Florian/Rainbow/PictureQuest; 426 (t) Bob Daemmrich/The Image Works; 426 (b) Shelley Gazin/Corbis; 427 (t) Bettmann/Corbis; 436 Moore School of Business, University of South Carolina; 437 (t) Andre Jenny/Focus Group/PictureQuest; (b) The Granger Collection, New York; 438 (t) AFP/Corbis; 438 (b) Reuters/HO/Archive Photos; 439 (t) Lisa Quinones/Black Star; 439 (b) Clara National Historic Site/National Park Service; 439 (inset) Bettmann/Corbis; 440 Steve Maines/Stock, Boston/PictureQuest; Per-Anders Petterson/Black Star/Time Life Syndication.

All other photographs by Harcourt photographers listed below, © Harcourt:

Ken Kinzie, Weronica Ankororn, Tom Barlett/Quebecor.